S0-ARM-072

9/2/05
ss Barnes

Ezra Taft
Benson

Ezra Taft Benson

A Biography

by Sheri L. Dew

Deseret Book Company
Salt Lake City, Utah

© 1987 Deseret Book Company

All rights reserved. No part of this book may be reproduced in any form or by any means without permission in writing from the publisher, Deseret Book Company, P.O. Box 30178, Salt Lake City, Utah 84130. This work is not an official publication of The Church of Jesus Christ of Latter-day Saints. The views expressed herein are the responsibility of the author and do not necessarily represent the position of the Church or of Deseret Book Company.

Deseret Book is a registered trademark of Deseret Book Company.

First printing in hardbound edition, November 1987
First printing in paperbound edition, March 1989

Library of Congress Cataloging-in-Publication Data
Dew, Sheri L.
    Ezra Taft Benson.

    Bibliography: p.
    Includes index.
    1. Benson, Ezra Taft.   2. Mormon Church—Presidents—
Biography.   3. Church of Jesus Christ of Latter-day
Saints—Presidents—Biography.   4. United States. Dept.
of Agriculture—Officials and employees—Biography.
I. Title.
BX8695.B38D48   1987   289.3'32'0924   [B]   87-22247
Hardcover edition: ISBN 0-87579-110-7
Paperbound edition: ISBN 0-87579-217-0

Printed in the United States of America
10   9   8   7

Contents

Preface

In honor of President David O. McKay's ninety-fourth birthday, Elder Ezra Taft Benson was invited to deliver a tribute to the prophet. On that occasion, he began his remarks by stating, "It's a wonderful thing to focus attention on a great life."

Indeed it is. An inscription on one wall in the Library of Congress puts such musings in lofty perspective: "The history of the world is the biography of great men."

I believe that you will find in this biography the story of a truly great man. Not a perfect man, nor a man who hasn't faced and even struggled with mortality's challenges. But a man of conviction and courage. A man who has remained true to the principles in which he deeply believes—despite criticism, at times. A man who has responded to assignments within the gospel kingdom that have demanded total commitment and faith in the Lord. This is a man who has faced hardships, has worked to overcome personal shortcomings, has had triumphs, and through it all has turned his life completely over to the Lord.

In the mid-fifties a young man working in Washington, D.C., became acquainted with Ezra Taft Benson, then Secretary of Agriculture. After observing the Secretary function in his demanding, often controversial, post while trying to retain the dignity and deportment of an apostle, the man asked Elder Benson how he managed to handle everything. Elder Benson replied, in words to this effect, "I work as hard as I can and do everything within my power. And I try to keep the commandments. Then I let the Lord make up the difference." There, in a nutshell, lies the formula to President Benson's life and to his success.

But while Ezra Taft Benson's life has all the makings of a remarkable story, telling it is challenging. Biography itself is an intimidating art form—one made all the more demanding when written about a living subject. And that becomes even more difficult when the man belongs, by virtue of his spiritual calling, to a very elect group—one of only thirteen in this dispensation to culminate his life with service as president of The Church of Jesus Christ of Latter-day Saints. A living prophet.

President Benson himself once set forth the parameters within which LDS biography should be written: "No writer can accurately portray a prophet of God if he or she does not believe in prophecy."

May I say from the outset that I believe in prophecy. And I have a deep conviction that Ezra Taft Benson is a prophet of God. This book is written from that perspective, and it is this orientation that has governed decisions regarding which materials to include and which to lay aside.

For that reason, this biography does not tell everything. Certainly, it would require a multivolume work to thoroughly analyze Ezra Taft Benson's involvement and contributions in government and other areas of activity. For example, one 600-page autobiographical account covers his eight cabinet years alone. The amount of materials extant on his life is enormous.

Further, there are episodes and elements of President Benson's life that have been left out of this biography. It is no secret that his unequivocal and vocal support of freedom and the U.S. Constitution, and his condemnation of communism, socialism, and, in fact, anything that he has perceived as a threat to man's freedom, has aroused controversy and prompted certain critics to oppose him over the years. By and large, these episodes have not been detailed in this biography. While some may wonder if these omissions point to the fact that President Benson feels uncomfortable about his past or has reversed his stand on some of these issues, nothing could be further from the truth.

It would be presumptuous of me to assert that I have reviewed everything documenting the life of Ezra Taft Benson, but little has escaped my attention. I have read every page of his personal journal, dating back to 1939; literally thousands of pieces of correspondence written to, by, and about him; a large portion of the 9,000 pages of religious speeches he has given through the years (as well as hundreds of pages of secular addresses); and thousands of newspaper clippings, magazine articles, and books written about and by him. I have viewed newsreels, television programs, and speeches preserved and housed in the National Archives and the Library of Congress, as well as interviewed dozens of individuals who have had intimate association with President Benson in various capacities. Through it all I have not found anything that seems inconsistent with his calling as prophet, seer, and revelator. In fact, even during times when he was most vocally criticized for his patriotic activities or philosophies, he repeatedly responded to his critics with kindness and tolerance. President Benson has requested that those who have opposed him over the years not be treated critically in his biography. Yet, a full and accurate telling of some incidents involving his critics would likely reflect negatively on those individuals, so the episodes have not been included. As Nephi explained in his writings, I have not told everything, but what I have told is true.

Space limitations make it difficult to mention everyone who has assisted in some way with the preparation of this biography. But I must single out a few individuals, hoping that the many others who made substantive contributions will know of my sincere appreciation for their efforts.

President Benson himself was most cooperative, consenting to numerous interviews and providing encouragement throughout. I am grateful for his kindness to me. Other members of the Benson family responded to frequent requests for interviews and access to documents and correspondence held by the family. Each of President Benson's children—Reed Benson, Mark Benson, Barbara Walker, Beverly Parker, Bonnie Madsen, and

Beth Burton—submitted to lengthy interviews and assisted in other ways. Their contributions were invaluable. Special mention must be made of Flora Parker, a granddaughter of President and Sister Benson, who played a crucial role. I do not overstate the facts to say that, had it not been for her thousands of hours of painstaking research, as well as for her assistance in so many other ways, this book would very simply not have seen the light of day.

Both of President Benson's counselors in the First Presidency, many members of the Twelve, and a number of other General Authorities granted personal interviews in which they reflected on their association with President Benson. I am grateful for their time, reflections, and interest in this project.

I received assistance from researchers and librarians at the Library of Congress and National Archives in Washington, D.C., the Eisenhower Library in Abilene, Kansas, and the Church Historical Department and Archives in Salt Lake City. I also recognize the cooperation of the Department of Religious Instruction at Brigham Young University. In addition, several readers reviewed this manuscript at various stages and offered timely suggestions, criticisms, and comments. Their responses were most helpful. I am most grateful to Ronald A. Millett and Eleanor Knowles of Deseret Book Company for their encouragement and patience.

I deeply appreciate friends who, in numerous ways, relieved me of responsibilities in other areas of my life so that I could devote more time to what became an all-consuming endeavor. This includes professional associates, those with whom I serve in Church capacities, and close friends who seemed to know when and how to offer encouragement. I am most deeply grateful for the support of my family, in particular that of my mother and father, Charles and JoAnn Dew, who seem to have unending confidence in me. Their support transcends anything else earthly.

Though others have been involved in various ways in the preparation of this biography, I am the author. I alone produced the text and therefore take responsibility for this interpretation of the life of Ezra Taft Benson.

This project has taught me many things. First, that Ezra Taft Benson, like his predecessors, is indeed a prophet of God. I have learned that, truly, man's ways are not God's ways, and that at times we must be willing to listen to and be directed by a higher voice than our own. I have learned that in times of sincere need and inquiry the Lord will respond to His children, that He will strengthen and guide them and make them equal to the righteous tasks before them. And I have come to understand, perhaps in a way unique to a biographer of a prophet, that it is under the Lord's direction that a man is schooled and prepared to assume the mantle of the prophet.

Through it all I have reached the conclusion that, at times, in the interest of honesty, we mortals do injustice in the way we evaluate history. We try very hard to demonstrate that great men and women are fallible; or, in the Church context, that a leader or a prophet, as in this case, is just a mortal man, complete with personal weaknesses. While I enthusiastically favor an honest depiction of any individual, I would hope that such a focus not sidetrack us from or obscure something that is perhaps more significant.

Certainly, a prophet is but a mortal man. It doesn't take scholarly analysis to arrive at that conclusion. I wonder, however, if this conclusion isn't shortsighted. The purpose of evaluating the life of a prophet, in my view, is not to focus in the main on his mortality, but to demonstrate how a mortal man can live his life in such a way that the Lord would see fit to call him as His mouthpiece. It is this very process that should give all of us comfort and encouragement.

It is a humbling experience to carefully examine, to even probe, a prophet's life. A biographer sees so much—the good and the bad; the trials and the triumphs; the joys and the pains. To the biographer goes the fragile responsibility of analysis, of putting into perspective a person's life, of drawing conclusions about a man's contributions, his dreams and aspirations, his motives, and so forth. From the outset I respected President Benson as a man with a divine calling. But the more I researched and read and reflected, the more I came to realize how truly remarkable Ezra Taft Benson is.

This biography is simply my attempt to share what I have learned about this man. My intention is not that, after reading this book, you will agree with everything Ezra Taft Benson has said or done, but that you will understand him; that you will have a sense for what has driven him, and why; that you will respect him for the life he has lived.

Elder Neal A. Maxwell has written, "Since we are here to be thus proved, how can that occur except we are tested? If we are to learn to choose wisely, how can that occur except there be alternatives? If our soul is to be stretched, how can that happen without growing pains? . . . When anciently we shouted for joy in anticipation of this mortal experience, we did not then think it would be an ordinary, pedestrian thing at all. We sensed the impending high adventure."

For Ezra Taft Benson, life has indeed been high adventure. From eleven lonely, dangerous, but rewarding months in post–World War II Europe, to eight demanding years in the U.S. cabinet, to over four decades as a General Authority, his life has been adventurous. It has been a life of preparation, a life destined to culminate in the most ennobling service mortal man can render. Elder Orson F. Whitney explained, "Each succeeding president of the Church ought to vary in some respects from all other incumbents of that high and holy position. For this reason: The work of the Lord is always progressing, and consequently always changing—not its principles, nor its aims; but its plans, its instruments, and its methods of procedure. . . . Hence a variety of leaders is essential. Today is not yesterday, nor will tomorrow be today. The Lord provides the men and the means whereby He can best work, at any given time, for the carrying out of His wise and sublime purposes. The Man of the Hour will be ready whenever the Hour strikes."

President Heber J. Grant was once asked how a man becomes president of the Church. He replied, "He is called to the Council of the Twelve Apostles and then outlives his associates." While that may seem a very simple formula, President Gordon B. Hinckley explained the wisdom of such a precedure: "Once a man is called to the Council of the Twelve, a new regimen comes into his life. . . . His is a world mission. Over the years that follow he is likely to travel far and wide in the pursuit of that ministry. He develops a depth of vision and understanding that comes in no other way. He sees the Church in operation in a great variety of environments. As the years pass, in the very process of this work he is disciplined and refined, polished and softened, strengthened and humbled. Only after many years of such seasoning does he become senior Apostle."

It is this journey, the life journey of Ezra Taft Benson, that I have endeavored to tell.

Pedigrees of
Ezra Taft and Flora Amussen Benson

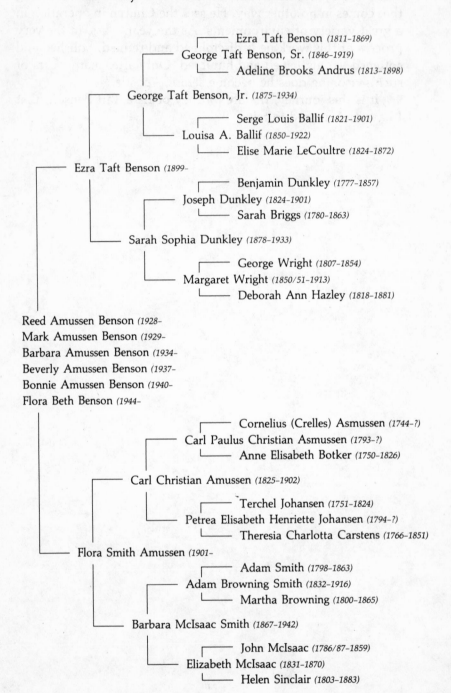

Ezra Taft Benson *(1811-1869)*
George Taft Benson, Sr. *(1846-1919)*
Adeline Brooks Andrus *(1813-1898)*
George Taft Benson, Jr. *(1875-1934)*
Serge Louis Ballif *(1821-1901)*
Louisa A. Ballif *(1850-1922)*
Elise Marie LeCoultre *(1824-1872)*
Ezra Taft Benson *(1899-*
Benjamin Dunkley *(1777-1857)*
Joseph Dunkley *(1824-1901)*
Sarah Briggs *(1780-1863)*
Sarah Sophia Dunkley *(1878-1933)*
George Wright *(1807-1854)*
Margaret Wright *(1850/51-1913)*
Deborah Ann Hazley *(1818-1881)*

Reed Amussen Benson *(1928-*
Mark Amussen Benson *(1929-*
Barbara Amussen Benson *(1934-*
Beverly Amussen Benson *(1937-*
Bonnie Amussen Benson *(1940-*
Flora Beth Benson *(1944-*

Cornelius (Crelles) Asmussen *(1744-?)*
Carl Paulus Christian Asmussen *(1793-?)*
Anne Elisabeth Botker *(1750-1826)*
Carl Christian Amussen *(1825-1902)*
Terchel Johansen *(1751-1824)*
Petrea Elisabeth Henriette Johansen *(1794-?)*
Theresia Charlotta Carstens *(1766-1851)*
Flora Smith Amussen *(1901-*
Adam Smith *(1798-1863)*
Adam Browning Smith *(1832-1916)*
Martha Browning *(1800-1865)*
Barbara McIsaac Smith *(1867-1942)*
John McIsaac *(1786/87-1859)*
Elizabeth McIsaac *(1831-1870)*
Helen Sinclair *(1803-1883)*

Ezra Taft Benson

*"I thank the Lord for my heritage, for my parents,
my grandparents, and my great-grandparents who have
seen fit to give their all to help in the establishment
of this the kingdom of God upon the earth."*

Chapter 1

A Rich Heritage

I n the year 1638, England was ruled by the unpredictable, tyrannical Charles I, and political and religious fugitives were leaving in great numbers. Among them were John Benson and his family, who fled Caversham, Oxfordshire, England, aboard the *Confidence* that year to search for peace and prosperity in the New World. Some 341 years later one of John Benson's most celebrated descendants, Ezra Taft Benson, would proclaim, "Since I was a small boy I have had a keen awareness that . . . a noble heritage is one of life's greatest treasures."[1]

Indeed, the family line and legacy John Benson carried to the New World would spawn offspring of international repute and influence. His descendants would prove resilient, devoted to principle, intensely loyal to country, and receptive to truth.

In America, John Benson received a land grant in the Massachusetts Bay Colony. The subsequent five generations of Bensons, mostly farmers and laborers—Joseph, Benoni, Benoni, Jr. (a shoemaker-turned-lieutenant who marched as a Minute Man following Paul Revere's ride through Lexington), John (also an officer in the Revolutionary War) and John, Jr.—lived primarily in and around Mendon, Massachusetts. The Bensons were God-fearing people who praised the Almighty for guiding

1

them to America and spoke fiercely in defense of their new republic.

It was in Mendon, on February 22, 1811, that John, Jr., and Chloe Taft Benson became the parents of their fourth child and first son—Ezra T. (for Taft). The young Ezra, of necessity, was an industrious boy who labored with his father on the family farm where apples were grown and hogs were raised. Ezra remembered his parents as religiously inclined, though they never joined any religious group. Firm believers in the Bible, they taught their children to observe the Sabbath.

In 1832 Ezra married Pamelia Andrus, and during their first years of married life they enjoyed a healthy income from Ezra's investments in a hotel and, later, cotton mill. But they also buried their first two children. And when unexpected reverses stripped them of their funds, Ezra found work where he could. But he was restless, with a deep desire to go west.

Eventually his yearnings prevailed, and by 1838 Ezra had worked his way to Quincy, Illinois, where he first met the "Mormons," as members of The Church of Jesus Christ of Latter-day Saints were known. They were a small band of religious patriots recently driven from Missouri by mobs and Governor Lilburn W. Boggs, who demanded they be "expelled or exterminated."

Ezra T. Benson was a tall, stocky man with deep, penetrating eyes. Though virtually unschooled, he had a discriminating mind and a knack for eliciting trust in others, even strangers. In Quincy he boarded with an amiable Mormon family, the Thomas Gordons. Initially Ezra found the Mormons "very peculiar," but over time, as he became better acquainted with the Saints and as the Gordons introduced him to the gospel message, Ezra decided the Saints were a "very agreeable" lot of people whose "spirits amalgamated with mine." Nevertheless, he kept them at arm's length. He was very disturbed when two of them, George D. Grant and Edmond Bosley, predicted he would join the Church.[2]

In July 1840 Ezra's curiosity was aroused when he observed Joseph Smith, prophet and president of the Church, as the Prophet attended a religious debate. Ezra determined that Joseph seemed too pleasant a man to be the rogue his detractors made him out to be.

Some time later Ezra and his wife attended a gathering in which Orson Hyde, a member of the Church's Quorum of the Twelve Apostles, delivered a moving discourse on the gathering of the Jews. Elder Hyde called upon John E. Page, another apostle, to pray, and Ezra recorded that he had never "heard the like before. They took up a collection to assist them on their mission to Palestine, and I threw in a half-dollar, being all I had. This was the first time I had ever helped any missionary." (Ironically, Elder Page was later excommunicated from the Church, and Brigham Young would select the young convert, Ezra T. Benson, to fill his place in the Quorum of the Twelve.[3]) At the close of the meeting Pamelia asked her husband if he had made a donation; when he replied affirmatively, she responded, "That is right. If I had money I would have helped them, too, for they are deserving of it."

Late one night, after learning much more about the Church, Ezra retired to a snow-covered grove to seek spiritual guidance. Shortly after beginning to pray, he heard a sound as though someone were walking toward him on the frozen snow; instinctively he jumped up, but he could see nothing. The noise recurred three times. After the last encounter he became convinced it was an opposing power trying to discourage him from prayer. At that point he shouted out, "Mr. Devil, you may break snow crust, but I will pray!" Ezra did pray, and the sounds did not return.

Pamelia received a confirmation of the gospel message before her husband. As she and Ezra returned from a meeting, she picked up a Bible, turned to Paul's discourse on prophets and apostles in the twelfth chapter of First Corinthians, and said she couldn't imagine why the same organization shouldn't exist today. "She said she firmly believed Joseph Smith was a prophet of God," said Ezra T. years later. "The remark produced in me a peculiar sensation, as I perceived that she was convinced of the truth of the doctrines." Nevertheless, he asked her to wait to be baptized, hoping he would be ready to join her soon.[4]

Non-Mormon neighbors tried to divert the Bensons' attention from Mormonism. When Ezra asked a Unitarian minister if he baptized by immersion for the remission of sins, the min-

ister answered that that was an option but not really necessary—whatever Ezra wished. Ezra said he "thought this was
getting salvation a little too easily."[5]

Things began to move quickly, and Ezra soon gained a witness of the truth. On Sunday, July 19, 1840, he and Pamelia
attended a meeting during which a dispute arose between two
individuals administering the sacrament, and harsh words were
spoken. Concerned that the unruly display would dissuade her
husband, Pamelia asked Ezra what he thought of it all. He
replied that he couldn't imagine the actions of its members alter-
ing the truth of Mormonism. Afterwards, Daniel Stanton baptized them both in the Mississippi River in the presence of some
three hundred curious onlookers. When the ordinances were
completed a shout went up, "The Mormons have got them!"

The Bensons readily embraced their new religion, and soon
their lives revolved around it. Shortly after Ezra was ordained
an elder, his wife became very ill. "I reflected upon my calling
and perceived it was my prerogative to administer to her," he
said. "I laid my hands upon her head and rebuked the disease
and it left her instantaneously."[6]

Upstream from Quincy, the Saints had already begun their
colonization of Commerce, later named Nauvoo, and in April
1841 the Bensons moved there. By the fall of 1843 Ezra had
completed a red brick home, near Heber C. Kimball's, complete with two stories and a cellar. On April 27, 1844, Ezra
entered plural marriage, taking a second wife, Pamelia's younger
sister, Adeline Brooks Andrus. Adeline was a slight woman
who stood but a fraction over five feet tall.

Pamelia and Adeline saw their husband very little, for soon
thereafter Ezra left on the first of two missions in the East. On
the first of these he returned to Mendon and was disheartened
to find that his "most intimate acquaintances would not come
to hear" him. He was even mobbed and spat upon with tobacco
juice. En route he became schooled in matters of the Spirit. At
a meeting in Chambersburgh, Illinois, he preached eloquently
and, he said, "felt as though my feet were about six inches
from the floor, for when I stepped I could not feel it. Many
said . . . they had never heard such a discourse in their lives

Ezra T. Benson (1811–69), who was called to the Council of the Twelve July 16, 1846. Ninety-seven years later, in July 1943, his great-grandson and namesake was also called to the apostleship

and I really began to think I was a preacher." The next day he preached again. "But not having put my trust in the Lord as much as I should it proved the driest discourse I ever heard; and had there been a back door, I think I should have been missing."[7]

During his second mission he learned of the martyrdom of Joseph Smith, and he quickly returned to Nauvoo. In the fall of 1844 he was called to serve on the high council in Nauvoo, and in December of that year he went East again to preside over the Boston Conference. In May 1845 he returned to Nauvoo to work on the temple by day and stand guard at night. The political climate was tense, with the Saints uncertain about their safety. By February 1846 many of them were leaving Nauvoo.

Just prior to the expulsion of the Saints from Nauvoo, Brigham Young, who had succeeded Joseph Smith as head of the Church, advised Ezra to join the first company heading west. Ezra replied that he had no provisions and few resources to obtain them. Brigham answered, "Go down the street and ask every man you meet to give you some help until you get a conveyance."

The first man Ezra stopped, Jared Porter, loaned him a horse. A second provided another horse and a double harness. A Brother Chidester sold him a wagon, while Stephen Farnsworth gave him cloth for a wagon cover. Ezra traded his wives' beautiful woven shawls for two hundred pounds of flour, a few bushels of Indian cornmeal, twelve pounds of sugar, and a little bedding.

Though both Pamelia and Adeline were soon to bear children, they packed a few clothes and, on February 9, 1846, crossed the frozen Mississippi, leaving behind a home filled with belongings. Ezra later remarked about his wives, "Never at any time did I hear a murmur from their lips."

A month after crossing the Mississippi, Pamelia delivered a child. A crudely draped canvas protected her and the child from the bitter elements, with only a bed raised on brush to insulate her from torrential rains. The baby soon died. On May 1, 1846, Adeline delivered her first child, George T. Benson, in a wagon box at Garden Grove, Iowa. Midwife Patty Sessions charged Ezra T. $1.50 for her services. Years later Adeline's eldest great-grandson, Ezra Taft Benson, would explain, "These were not people who were used to living in poverty. . . . These were refined, well-educated people for the day. They were not used to roughing it . . . but they joined an unpopular faith and . . . were true [and] faithful, so they met the test."[8]

At Sugar Creek, Iowa, the rains had been so heavy that the loaded wagons sank at times to the hub. Ezra's team was weak, and he finally told Brigham Young he would not be able to proceed further. Brigham asked what could be unloaded, and in short order Ezra T. had been relieved of six hundred pounds of wheat and other foodstuffs, which were distributed among the Saints. Heading into the wilderness, he had only fifty pounds of flour and a half bushel of meal with which to support his family. After that, when others complained about their wagons sinking in mud to their axles, he would respond, "Go to Brother Brigham, and he will lighten your load."[9]

It was on the trail that Ezra T. was called to the Quorum of the Twelve by Brigham Young—the first such appointment since the death of Joseph Smith. The journey ahead would require a unique breed of leader, one anxious and able to serve under grave conditions. President Young instructed Ezra, in part, "If you accept this office, I want you to come immediately to Council Bluffs, to prepare to go to the Rocky Mountains."[10] Ezra Benson, at age thirty-five, was ordained an apostle on July 16, 1846, by President Young and promised that he should yet have "the strength of Samson." Nearly a year later, he was in the first company of pioneers that entered the Salt Lake Valley on July 24, 1847. He spoke in the first sacrament meeting held there, and then headed back across the trail to inform other companies en route that a place of settlement had been located.

During subsequent years Ezra would serve a number of missions, Europe and Hawaii among them, travel in and out of Salt Lake City, and play a key role in colonizing the Great Basin, particularly Tooele, Utah, where he milled lumber, and, later, Cache Valley.

Prior to leaving for a mission to England, Ezra was promised in a blessing at the hands of Jedediah M. Grant that he would lift his voice "like a trumpet and cause the hearts of the Saints to rejoice and the wicked to quake," and would ultimately possess "power to overcome all your enemies."[11] Such qualities would resurface three generations later in his namesake and great-grandson.

Ezra was called to preside over the Saints' settlement of Cache Valley. Many years later Heber J. Grant, who was then president of the Church, would jokingly tell Elder Ezra Taft Benson the story of Ezra T. Benson's settlement in northern Utah. "Did I ever tell you about the mean trick Brigham Young played on your great-grandfather?" he asked Elder Benson. "No, President, I didn't know Brigham Young ever played a mean trick on anyone," Elder Benson replied.

"Oh, yes, he did. I'll tell you about it," President Grant said. "Your great-grandfather built the finest home in Salt Lake City, with the exception of Brigham Young's home. It was a beautiful, two-story home with a porch at both levels, a white picket fence, and a yard filled with fruit and ornamental trees and even a small stream. He was just ready to move his families in from their log cabins when President Young called him

7

into the office and asked him to move to Cache Valley and pioneer that area. 'We suggest you sell your home to Daniel H. Wells,' President Young said. Now, Daniel H. Wells was Brigham Young's counselor," President Grant concluded. "Wasn't that a mean trick?"

Mean trick or not, Ezra T.'s leadership proved most effective. During the nine years under his direction, the settlements in Cache Valley prospered. He organized the building of homes, mills, schools, canals, and churches; fostered the development of cooperative institutions, patterned after those he'd seen prospering in Great Britain; occupied a seat in the territorial legislature; acted as brigadier general of the Cache Valley militia; and served as spiritual leader to the Saints in that area.

On September 3, 1869, at age fifty-eight, Ezra T. Benson died suddenly and unexpectedly. Some four thousand attended his funeral, including three hundred Indian braves who paid their respects to the man who had befriended them. He once explained, "I want most to have a testimony of Jesus Christ that will pierce like a cannonball."

George T. Benson was deeply affected by his father's passing. He had grown close to him—traveled with him, worked at his side, observed his gospel service. It was a rich heritage that Ezra T. passed on to his eldest son, and George in turn inherited his father's capacity for leadership.

George spent his boyhood in Logan, Utah, where he eventually met and married Louisa Alexandrine Ballif, a woman of French descent. Her father, Serge Louis Ballif, had first heard of the Church in 1852 in Lausanne, Switzerland, while serving as a clergyman in the Cathedral of Lausanne. Two young men knocked at his door and told him, in halting French, that the gospel had been restored. Serge had earlier participated in publishing *The Gospel of the Holy Ghost*, a series of books disputing the Protestant Reformation's claim to the authority lost by the Catholics. This gave him a respectable background in religious issues, and he accepted the gospel message almost immediately. Before leaving for America, he filled a mission for the Church in Switzerland, published gospel tracts, and provided financial assistance to missionaries.

The family of George Taft Benson Sr. and Louisa Ballif Benson. George T. Benson Jr., father of Ezra Taft Benson, is fourth from left in back row

Serge's daughter Louisa and George T. Benson became the parents of thirteen children. George served on the first high council in Cache Valley, and later he and his wife were called to further the settlement of Preston, Idaho, in the northern part of the valley. Subsequently he served as bishop of the Whitney (Idaho) Ward in the Oneida Stake for over twenty years. On one occasion Joseph F. Smith, who later became sixth president of the Church, visited Whitney and took a meal at the Benson farm. The table was laden with food, and the large family had gathered around. Before blessing the food, Elder Smith turned to George, stretched out his long arms, and said, "Bishop Benson, all this, and the gospel, too."

Louisa Ballif Benson, a woman of great faith, served for many years as president of the Oneida Stake Relief Society, a stake that extended as far north as Baker, Oregon, and south to the Utah line. Her calling demanded that she make frequent visits—by horse and buggy to neighbors and via train for longer trips.

On one occasion as she was returning from Oregon by train and walking down the aisle, she heard a voice say, "Sister Benson, sit down and take hold of the seat." She glanced over her shoulder but saw no one. After walking a few steps further, she heard the voice again. Quickly she sat down and took hold of the seat arms. Almost immediately the train jumped the tracks and wrecked. Many were injured but she was unharmed. She removed her white petticoat, made bandages, and administered relief to the injured. The Union Pacific Railroad awarded her a citation for bravery and compassionate service.

Louisa and George's fourth child and second son, born June 24, 1875, carried the name of his father—George T. Benson Jr.

The spirit of country and the soil surged through George Jr.'s veins. He loved horses and rode a spirited mount named Kit. Schoolwork didn't come naturally to him, and he preferred farming to studying.

Even as a boy, George Jr. was methodical. His brother Serge wrote, "George was always dependable and father had great confidence in him. He always took good care of his things. He was slower and more deliberate than I . . . and would still be smoothing and folding his pants when I was in bed and asleep, if we had come home at the same time." Often when George and his brothers arrived home in the evening, the brothers would start to dash inside, only to have George call back, "We must groom and feed the animals before we can expect to feed ourselves." Not only was George his father's namesake, but he was a replica when it came to the gospel. As Serge said, "George was intensely religious, and father and mother never had to drive him to church. He was always ready to go."[12]

George's prompt, methodical nature extended even into courtship. He insisted on having the horse and buggy every Wednesday evening and again on Friday if there was a dance in Franklin, Preston, or Whitney. He would always see his girlfriend home on Sunday night. Neighbors could tell when George had had a nice evening out, because he'd whistle or sing all the way home.

Who was this girlfriend? George had eyes for only one—Sarah Dunkley. Sarah was born in Franklin, Idaho, in 1878, the sixth of thirteen children of Joseph and Margaret Dunkley. Joseph had been taught the gospel on the streets of his native England. Though not aligned with any religious group, he was a serious student of the Bible and had investigated the doctrines of many denominations. When he heard the message taught by the Latter-day Saint missionaries, he studied the scriptures even more avidly. In time he gained a testimony of the restored gospel. Though his family was opposed to the Mormons, Joseph was relentless in his search for truth, even paying for the elders' lodging at times. He married Margaret Leach, and they studied the gospel together, finally joining the Church against the will of his parents. When Joseph and Margaret announced that they were immigrating to Utah, their families tried to thwart the couple's ambitions. But on April 1, 1854, Joseph and Margaret set sail for America.

The couple were not, however, blessed with children; and with Margaret's consent, Joseph took a second wife, Mary Ann Hobbs, who subsequently died in childbirth. Later he took a third wife, Margaret Wright, and to them were born thirteen children, eight sons and five daughters.

In the late 1850s Brigham Young called Joseph as one of eight men to settle Franklin, Idaho, in northern Cache Valley. Not the least of the pioneer group's troubles were caused by Indians, and night after night Joseph sat watch atop nearby Little Mountain. Men and women alike faced the possibility of confrontation with the natives. One morning as Margaret Wright was alone in her kitchen, she was startled to see a large Indian with his nose pressed against the windowpane. He walked around to the open door and Margaret asked what he wanted. "Me want flour," he answered. Margaret gave him flour. The Indian then said, "Me want sugar," and Margaret supplied sugar. Not satisfied, the Indian demanded, "Me want more flour," to which Margaret said, "No." She had just enough flour left to make biscuits for lunch. Later, when she reported the incident to Joseph, he said, "Margaret, I'm sorry you didn't give him more flour." "But you would have had to go without bread for lunch," she countered. "That would have been better," her husband insisted. "Remember the counsel of President Brigham Young that it is better to feed the Indians than fight them?" That night one of Joseph's finest horses was stolen from the barn.

The Dunkleys homesteaded a parcel of land with a high white alkali content, not the best soil for crops. The rural existence did, however, provide an excellent setting for the development of industry, cooperation, perseverance, and loyalty— all qualities that Sarah Sophia, their sixth child and second daughter, inherited.

Sarah's childhood was typical of pioneer life in Cache Valley—harsh winters, but summers of horseback riding, swimming, and outings in the canyon. She was a young beauty—flashing dark eyes, abundant black hair, and a radiant personality. Around the community she was characterized as "little mother" because of her pleasant and stabilizing influence on other youths. She and her sister Kate became close friends with Addie and Florence Benson, daughters of George T. Benson Sr., and the four were inseparable—playing and singing together and working out on a homemade tumbling mat.

George Benson Jr. was three years older than Sarah, and for a time he thought of her as his younger sisters' friend. But as Sarah matured, George became enthralled with the girl. They took buggy rides, went on picnics in Cub River Canyon, and attended stake conferences in Preston and weekly dances in Franklin. The young couple waltzed beautifully together as old-timers nodded approvingly from the sidelines.

After a wedding date was set, George worked long hours with the railroad to earn extra money (one foreman called him one of the hardest workers he had ever seen) to build a home for his bride. He hauled timber from the nearby Wasatch Range to build a two-room home with a small shanty in back of the house for washing. The home sat on a forty-acre farm a mile and a half northeast of Whitney. Sarah and her mother carded wool and sewed pieces of material together to make patchwork quilts, curtains, bedspreads, and other accessories. At seventeen Sarah completed an advanced sewing course in Logan, and throughout her life she was a superb seamstress. Her talents would prove invaluable in clothing her seven sons and four daughters.

On October 19, 1898, Sarah and George were married in the Logan Temple. The small home they had built and furnished themselves was ready for occupancy. While not elaborate, it was adequate for a young couple in love. One day as George anxiously left the house to go to his work, Sarah called after him, "You forgot something." As he came back, she said, "Oh, never mind," and splashed soapsuds on him. After he had driven off, she explained to her sister-in-law, who was visiting the couple, "We have decided that neither of us leave the other without a good-bye kiss. He sure has a time remembering it."

"I've never forgotten the picture of the house, meager furniture, Sarah washing on the board, the newly planted trees, the beginning of a home, and the wholesomeness of it all," the sister-in-law recalled.[13]

George was a leading farmer in the valley. He later acquired fifteen Holsteins and sold milk to the local milk-condensing plant. He drove a fine team and took excellent care of his livestock. Early one April morning his younger brother Frank burst in on the sleeping George and shouted, "Your young Jersey is stuck in the manger. It's suffocating!" George was in the barn in seconds. Just as he found the calf okay, he heard Frank call from outside, "April Fool's!" For his prank, Frank ate a few meals standing up.

George thrived on working in the soil and living by the law of the harvest—that you can only reap what you sow. Though not terribly patient (he was sometimes criticized for expecting too much of others and being impatient with their faults), he was a man of sterling character who felt that no one owed him a living and whose ambition was to help his children help themselves. His wife had qualities to match, particularly when it came to rearing children.

When Sarah learned they were to be blessed with their first child, she and George were ecstatic. They prayed and planned together about their family, and eagerly awaited the baby's arrival.

On August 4, 1899, as Sarah's labor began, George administered to her. Dr. Allan Cutler attended her in the bedroom of their farm home, with both grandmothers, Louisa Benson and Margaret Dunkley, there. The delivery was protracted. As the baby, a large boy, was delivered, the doctor couldn't get him to breathe and quickly laid him on the bed and pronounced, "There's no hope for the child, but I believe we can save the mother." While Dr. Cutler feverishly attended to Sarah, the grandmothers rushed to the kitchen, praying silently as they worked, and returned shortly with two pans of water—one cold, the other warm. Alternately, they dipped the baby first in cold and then in warm water, until finally they heard a cry. The

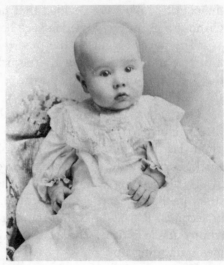

*Ezra Taft Benson
at three months*

11¾ pound boy was alive! Later both grandmothers bore testimony that the Lord had spared the child. George and Sarah named him Ezra Taft Benson.

From the time he could walk, "T.", as young Ezra was nicknamed, was his father's shadow—riding horses, working in the fields, hitching up the horse and buggy for meetings, playing ball and swimming in the creek. He had a rich sense of heritage, stemming from his birthright as Ezra T. Benson's eldest great-grandson, but also because he idolized his father and, as a young boy, felt an unusual sense of security and deep pride in who he was. Years later, after George Benson died, his eldest son overheard one of the few non-Mormons in Whitney say, "Today we buried the greatest influence for good in Cache Valley." Without question, George Benson was a powerful influence in the life of his eldest son.

*"I was reared in an ideal home. Though
poor in material things, my parents were
loving, industrious, and had a love
of God in their hearts."*

Chapter 2

A Boy from Whitney

I n many ways, Ezra Taft Benson was born, as Charles
Dickens put it, in the best of times, yet the worst of times.
The early 1890s were unsettling years for Americans. It
seemed that the moorings of society were being swept
away. Agrarian unrest, industrial violence, a sluggish economy,
class conflict, and even a march of the poor on Washington
indicated just some of the country's problems. The United States
had rebounded from a devastating civil war, but American
morale was soon to reach low tide with the assassination of
President William McKinley.

On the other hand, the early twentieth century was an exciting, invigorating era. The Wright brothers inaugurated a new
age with their twelve-second flight at Kitty Hawk, and by the
end of the century's second decade, automobiles were quite commonplace. The world became much smaller as man, with his
new technology, learned to span the continents.

Closer to home, the Manifesto had announced the end of
polygamy for the Church, and Utah had subsequently gained
statehood. Accordingly, the Saints achieved some measure of
national acknowledgment, if not respect. Heber J. Grant would
soon open the Japanese Mission. Just over a quarter of a million Saints lived in forty-three stakes and nineteen missions.

The Church was poised for a period of growth destined to inter-nationalize the religious movement that had heretofore been largely confined to the Intermountain West.

It was a time of bridging the gap between old and new. But oblivious to all this, young Ezra Benson's world didn't extend much beyond the small LDS farming community of Whitney, Idaho.

Whitney was, in many ways, an ideal community for a boy born in the dawn of the twentieth century. The northern end of Cache Valley was beautiful, with access to lakes and forests; and, though winters were severe, spring and summer brought the sweet smell of cowslips, wild roses that lined ditchbanks and red hay flowers in the pasture, clear streams that flowed down through the Cub River Canyon, and long, warm days. People were friendly; most of the neighbors were related one way or another; families visited each other without warning and stayed for supper; Ezra's grandpa was also the bishop, had been since anyone could remember; and all but one of the three hundred townspeople were members of the Church (and that one man finally joined). It was a place where a boy worked a man's hours, but also reveled in the freedom of farm life.

Despite Ezra's precarious birth, he was anything but frail and grew into a robust, husky boy. The out-of-doors was in his blood, and he took readily to farming and rural life.

Ezra wasn't an only child for long. Fifteen months after his birth he was joined by a brother, Joseph; fifteen months later, a sister, Margaret—and so on. He eventually had six brothers and four sisters, five of whom were born before Ezra turned eight.

Sarah Benson was adept at handling her brood and intended to raise them properly. She was determined to teach her eldest son some manners. He was, for example, to greet people with a polite "How do you do?" One afternoon the family was seated at the dinner table, with assorted uncles and aunts present, when Ezra looked down from his high chair, noticed the big bowl of boiled eggs, and said, courteously, "How do you do, eggs?" Those at the table erupted in laughter, and it was a fam-ily joke that was retold for years.

The Bensons were a happy, unified group. Laughter and singing were heard coming from the little house throughout the day. Ezra would often say that he grew up in an "ideal family," the son of "ideal parents"; his sister Margaret would add, "Those were wonderful days. I could live every one of them over again and love every minute." Sarah had a way of making life fun for her family and a dry sense of humor that caused her husband to teasingly protest that many times he couldn't tell if she was joking or not. But Sarah and George adored each other, and from the outset they created a warm, fun atmosphere in their home.

Nevertheless, farm life was not easy. At an age when most children are scarcely allowed out of their mother's sight, Ezra was an apprentice field hand. As the eldest son, he grew up fast. George Benson relied on his boy to shoulder, in many cases, a man's responsibility.

At age four, Ezra climbed onto the seat of a harrow and, mustering his most grown-up voice, commanded two horses to "giddy-up." By the time he turned five he could drive a team; at seven he was thinning beets, herding cattle, tending chickens, "hunting" eggs ("in the machine shed, in a straw stack, and in any other unlikely place we would find them, ofttimes beneath a defiant hen who had her own ideas about the hatchery business"), cultivating potatoes, and milking cows. As the Benson family expanded, so did their stucco, two-room family home, their acreage, and the chores.

George Benson was an exceptional farmer, the best in Cache Valley, some said. He not only had agricultural savvy, but he was also efficient and generally regarded as a perfectionist. When the rains fell and it was too muddy to get in the fields, he already had chores in the tool shed set aside so time wouldn't be wasted. For a time he worked as a field man for the local sugar factory, teaching farmers how to get maximum tonnage out of their sugar beets. One day as he and Sarah drove to Preston, passing field after field of sugar beets, George repeatedly commented on the straight rows, "My, the man who drilled those must have surely known his business." Finally Sarah asked, "Yes, and who drilled them?" George laughed, pleased at his joke as he replied, "I had the honor."

George took pains to teach his eldest son the finer points of agriculture. From the time Ezra learned to drive a team, he and his father worked together in the fields, in the sheds, and during haying and thrashing seasons. To George's delight, Ezra caught on quickly, liked farm work, and was responsible. He was also intrigued about the scientific aspects of farming—how to increase efficiency, improve varieties of seed, and the like. George let him subscribe to farm magazines to keep abreast of new developments, and Ezra often stayed up late to read the latest information under the glow of a coal oil lamp.

In the dark early-morning hours and numbing cold, Ezra milked a string of dairy cows (using what he humorously referred to as the "arm strong" method) and fed lambs and steers; later he managed his own herd of thirty milk cows. When it came time to build corral fences and cut wood for winter fuel, he drove a wagon team into the nearby forests to chop pine poles. He rode the range, but he also "rode the stick" behind six horses on an old header—a big cutter bar that cut the stalks of grain and left them lying on the ground. In the fall he herded cattle up on the range in the Cache National Forest, living on blue grouse and white potatoes. In the early winter George and the boys felled a few Lombardy poplar trees, a row of which lined the south and east sides of the farm. After the horses had been allowed to eat the bark from the trees, the boys sawed the wood first into blocks and then into smaller pieces. It was their job to keep the large woodbox near the kitchen full, and during the winter it seemed to Ezra that he had to stuff the box continually as the wood burned in the stove so rapidly.

All of Ezra's daily chores had to be done before he left for school in the morning or did homework in the evening. At age eight he enrolled in the little Whitney grade school, but his attendance was sporadic. As was typical of the times, if he was needed on the farm, particularly during planting season or harvest, George didn't hesitate to keep him home.

During haying season, everyone helped. The older children pitched hay as it was pitched onto the wagons, while the younger ones drove wagons, tromped hay down, rode derrick horses, carried water, and ran errands. Grain harvest was also a major event. Sarah and the girls baked bread and pies days in advance.

For the better part of a week a crew of twenty or so pulled in with a huge threshing machine and harvested the crop. Afterwards, the children had their bed ticks stuffed with clean, fresh straw. Harvesting the sugar beets was another time when a call for help went out. Even the girls harvested beets—no easy task after hooking, pulling, and cutting the tops off each one.

Tilling the soil was, however, a matter of survival, for the Bensons relied upon their garden of carrots, turnips, and all manner of vegetables and fruits to feed the growing family. Potatoes and apples were placed in pits covered with straw and soil to last the winter; carrots and turnips left in the ground and covered with straw could be dug up all winter long.

Farming is no occupation for a tenderfoot. Only a rare breed of man will work his knuckles to the bone while putting his livelihood at the mercy of the elements, and do it year after year. In any era, it is a tough way to make a living; but at the turn of the century, when farmers homesteaded without milking machines, diesel tractors, and hybrid seed, the challenge of survival was stark. Despite its inherent hardships, farming is something that can get in a man's—and a boy's—blood. It is a reverence for, a love affair with, the land. So it was with young Ezra.

In 1909, when a U. S. Presidential Commission insisted that there had never been a time "when the American farmer was as well off," the Bensons might well have disagreed. Making ends meet to feed the constantly growing family was not easy. But scratching out a living taught Ezra and his brothers and sisters that they couldn't expect to reap what they didn't sow—and cultivate. They also learned how to work and persist at something without immediate reward. Often the crops were damaged by weather and insects. Years later his sister Margaret would say, "We had our hard times, our difficulties. There was nothing easy about raising eleven children in those days." As Ezra recalled, "I presume by some standards we were poor, but no government official ever told us we were, so we never knew it."

For one thing, though there were few extras, there was always plenty to eat. George saw to it that they had a year's supply of staples. Coal was ordered by the carload. Flour, sugar, and other basic commodities were stored in a cellar. Usually a calf or hog was killed in winter and hung under the porch where it stayed frozen until it was eaten.

Then again, it was Sarah's homemaking wizardry that kept her large brood from feeling deprived. A meticulous housekeeper and exceptional cook, she made do. Ezra was often enticed into the kitchen by the aroma of hot bread. He and his brothers loved to cut the top off a loaf, put butter on it, and down it in short order. It took a great deal of persuasion to get her to agree to this, but she usually succumbed to their pressure. Occasionally she purchased bakery bread, at which George always complained, "Where did you get this stuff? It tastes like cotton!" Rather than resort to store-bought bread when she ran short, Sarah made "Lumpy Dick," a porridge created by stirring whole wheat flour into hot milk. Ezra didn't care for the concoction except when his mother laced it with cinnamon and a little sugar.

At least once a year the family hitched the horses to the white-topped buckboard and made their pilgrimage to Brigham City, Utah, some thirty-five miles south, for a load of peaches, cantaloupes, tomatoes, watermelons, and other orchard fruits. They raised apples, pears, plums, and raspberries. Sarah put up hundreds of bottles of fruit, plus jams and jellies, every year.

Ezra's responsibilities weren't confined to farming. Every Wednesday night George and Sarah went to choir practice, leaving him to tend younger brothers and sisters. Sometimes he wondered if his parents didn't expect a little much of him. "But they had full confidence in my ability to meet almost any situation," he admitted. "That helped me have confidence."

When the family was young, they got along, for the most part, without modern conveniences—no running water, electricity, telephone, or even gloves for their hands because gloves were too expensive. On Saturday one of the boys, usually Ezra, pumped water until his arms ached so Sarah could do the washing. That evening an old tub was dragged into the center of the kitchen and filled with water that had been heated on the stove. The girls bathed first; then the boys carried the tub outside, dumped the water, and poured in fresh water for their baths.

Every family member went through the ritual. Ezra never forgot the day his mother first turned on running water from the tap. She cried.

The home was enlarged as the family grew, but the only heat in the upstairs bedrooms came through a grill over the kitchen stove that funneled heat into the girls' rooms. As more bedrooms were needed, Ezra and one of the other boys slept on the screened porch off the kitchen. More than once he awoke in the winter covered by a light dusting of snow.

Any kind of serious discouragement was not part of young Ezra's experience. "Very seldom, if ever, did I find mother depressed," he remembered, "and never can I remember her raising her voice, except when she called father in from the field when something urgent had occurred."

George Benson was by nature a happy man. First thing in the morning he shouted, "Let a little sunshine in. Clear the darkened windows, open wide the door, let a little sunshine in." If the season was warm, he would open the front door, then call his children—"Ezra, Joe, Margaret, time to get chores done"—and shake the stove vigorously. The boys' room was directly upstairs, and that was the sign they had better get up.

Though they worked hard to carve out an existence, the Bensons had recreation too. Ezra remembered, "Father and mother seemed to enjoy each other to the fullest. Never were they so happy as when they were together and the children were with them." George loved to do things with his family, for he understood that the rigors of farm labor needed to be spiced up. After the beets were hoed, thinned, or topped, or all the hay was hauled, he would take the family on a trip—to Bear Lake to fish and swim for a day or so, or to the canyon to camp out. Some of the work was, to a boy, half work and half play—trapping muskrats and rounding up cattle in the canyons.

George always provided good horses for the family to ride. In the winter he kept one team sharp-shod so they could be driven along the road to shine with the bobsleighs down near the church. In winter, as many of the Bensons as were old enough got into the action of breaking colts, a task made easier in deep snow. Even the girls joined in.

Most Saturdays were half-holidays. Around one in the afternoon, the work stopped, and the family joined in everything
from horse and foot races to baseball games and small rodeos,
where the boys tried to ride calves. Swimming, hiking, and pic-
nicking were favorite activities. It was said that Sarah could
pack the finest picnic basket in the valley. The Bensons had the
first phonograph in the area, and the boys had a basketball
court with backboards at both ends and a dirt playing surface
that George rolled until it was smooth and packed solid. The
Benson farm was a gathering place for young people.

The family loved to sing—Ezra in particular. As soon as
someone else was old enough to babysit, he joined his parents
at choir practice. Sarah sang as she sewed at the treadle machine,
hymns such as "Have I Done Any Good in the World Today?"
and popular tunes such as "Annie Laurie" and "In the Evening
by the Moonlight." At nighttime the family gathered around
the old piano for singing.

There was even fun during Idaho's cold, harsh winters. When
the snow drifted over the fences, Ezra put on skis, tied a long
rope to a saddle horn, and skiied behind his horse. When the
road became snowpacked, the boys skated holding onto a horse's
tail or dragging behind a rope tied to a bobsleigh.

George's brother Serge ran the local store, and when he
came to visit at Christmas, he would bring a washtub full of
presents, one for each child. Once he taught his nephew Ezra in
three classes a week—priesthood, Sunday School, and MIA. A
series of lessons on courage, particularly moral courage, had a
great impact on young Ezra's character. Serge was popular with
youth, had a great influence with boys, and could teach without preaching. Serge may also have preserved Ezra's life. While
on a fishing expedition with his uncle, Ezra reached to climb
over a ledge. Just then a blast from his uncle's gun fired over
his head, and he looked up in time to see a coiled rattlesnake
blown into the canyon several hundred feet below.

Marbles was a favorite game, and Ezra became proficient.
One season he started with ten and won well over a thousand.
Serge provided a place in front of his store where the boys
could play marbles on their way home from school. Sometimes
he gathered them inside for wrestling matches. Ezra thought

Serge was one of the greatest "boys' men" he ever met. George never seemed to worry when his son was with Serge.

Serge seemed to have a special feeling for his nephew. Once when a neighbor remarked how straight and proudly Ezra T. carried himself, Serge replied, "Why shouldn't he? He's the only boy I know who has never done anything of which he should be ashamed." Serge often told his own children that Ezra was not an ordinary young man, but one chosen for a special mission.

There was mutual respect between Serge and George. Uncle Serge told Ezra about the time George was helping build a home near the Whitney store. One of the workmen continually told vulgar stories. When the man announced that he had an especially good story and, in a mock tone, asked, "Are there any women present?" George immediately replied, "No, but there are gentlemen present and if you can't say something decent, keep your mouth shut." The foul language stopped.

Patriotic holidays were big events for the Bensons, who never missed a celebration—July 4th in Preston, July 24th in Whitney, and June 15th, Idaho Day, in Franklin. The boys shined the white-top buckboard, curried the horses, and put flags in the horses' bridles. There was always a big parade early in the morning, followed by a stirring patriotic gathering. Years later Margaret still remembered the impact of those events. "There would be wonderful talks about our country, and we'd all stand and sing 'Oh Say, Can You See!' It would thrill us, it was so stirring. Even today, when I sing the national anthem, I can feel the thrill I had when I sang that song as a child." Sarah took plenty of fried chicken and salads, and after the assembly the family would spread quilts on the lawn for a picnic. Each child got a few pennies to spend on whatever he or she wanted— ice cream, hot dogs, popcorn, the Ferris wheel.

Christmas and Thanksgiving were exciting holidays spent alternately with the Benson or the Dunkley grandparents. The family traveled by bobsleigh with bells on the horse. Both families were music enthusiasts, and singing and dancing filled the grandparents' homes. Grandma Dunkley could sometimes be persuaded to dance the Highland fling and tell Indian stories.

Like all children, Ezra and his brothers and sisters looked forward to Christmas for months. On Christmas Eve they listened for the sound of sleighbells, which their father rang during the night. If the children weren't in bed, Santa wouldn't stop. On Christmas morning there would be Santa taking toys off the tree and presenting them to the children. Then he'd be off with a "Ho, ho, ho!"

It didn't dawn on the children that their father was always out doing chores alone on Christmas morning, until one summer day they stumbled across a Santa Claus costume at the bottom of a big trunk. So that's why Father always arrived *after* Santa left! After that, whenever Father and Mother made their visits to Santa, the older children hunted to find toys they'd brought back. One year the boys discovered a sleigh in the top of the granary.

Uncle Serge often brought books for the children to read. Between chores and church work, there wasn't a lot of time for reading, but George and Sarah were careful about the literature that came into their home. Two statements influenced young Ezra: "Be as careful of the books you read as of the company you keep" and "Except a living man, there is nothing so wonderful as good books." On stormy days when he couldn't work outside, on Sundays, and some evenings, Ezra holed up with a book.

As a boy, Ezra read the scriptures, particularly the Book of Mormon, and volumes of success stories by Horatio Alger and the biographies of George Washington and Abraham Lincoln. Upon graduation from the eighth grade, at which time he felt "he'd learned about everything there was to learn," his grandparents gave him a two-volume set, *Little Visits with Great Americans*, by Orison Marden, which he thumbed until it was dog-eared. During high school, Tolstoy's *What Men Live By* and Bunyan's *Pilgrim's Progress* stirred him.

To Ezra, his dad was his hero. Such admiration of his father was in many ways a tradition with the Bensons. The family was unified and loyal, though occasional domestic flare-ups occurred. "We children had our differences and arguments," Margaret said. "Father was very strict about not letting us quarrel when he was in the house. How mother ever put up with eleven of us with our water fights, pranks, and teasing is more than I can comprehend."

George Taft Benson Jr.   *Sarah Dunkley Benson*

But underneath the everyday tangles was a foundation of harmony and love. On April 27, 1915, the *Deseret News* carried an article reporting that President Joseph F. Smith had announced the home evening program. He promised that to those who obeyed, "great blessings will result. Love at home and obedience to parents will increase. . . . The youth of Israel . . . will gain power to combat the vile influences and temptations which beset them." That evening George Benson told his family, "The Presidency has spoken, and this is the word of the Lord to us." From that time forward, not a week passed without home evening. Each child had an assignment— to pray, to conduct, to give the lesson, to plan the program, to prepare refreshments ("which we loved because then we could have what we wanted," Margaret said). They sang songs, read from the scriptures, told pioneer stories, wrote letters to relatives and missionaries, played games, and shared talents.

George Benson was a man who took Church leaders at their word. Morning and evening prayers, with everyone kneeling around the table, were never missed. "The spirit of gratitude and thanksgiving was always emphasized in our family prayers," Ezra says. Because his parents relied heavily upon the Lord, Ezra, while still a boy, patterned after them. His father often counseled, "Remember that whatever you do or wherever you are, you are never alone. Our Heavenly Father is always near. You can reach out and receive His aid through prayer." In 1954 Ezra would write in a *Reader's Digest* article, "All through my life the counsel to depend on prayer has been prized above any other advice I have ever received. It has become an integral part of me, an anchor, a constant source of strength."[1]

Attending church was accepted as a matter of fact. Work on the farm ceased on the Sabbath day, and the whole family made preparations the night before. Margaret baked a cake every Saturday for many years. Usually at least one of the eleven had a talk to prepare. All laid their clothes out so there would be no scrambling for shoes and socks the next morning. George Benson was fastidious and punctual. He felt that the Spirit of the Lord was present when the meeting began, and if family members weren't there on time, they missed out. Every Sunday morning he announced, like a local stationmaster, "The buggy will leave at twenty minutes to ten. Those who aren't ready will have to walk." The buggy often pulled out of the yard as a child or two, sometimes with boots or coat in hand, ran to catch up. Only once did George Benson arrive late. That Sunday he had a sick horse, and by the time he and the veterinarian had attended to it, the family was behind schedule. Even so, they still walked in during the opening hymn. One of George's sisters lived across the street from the church, and she set her watch by George. When she saw the Benson buggy approaching, she knew it was time to leave for church. However, that Sunday morning, as she walked out of her home, she could hear music. She immediately confronted George, a confused look on her face. "They're singing. Are we late?" she asked.

The little rock meetinghouse in Whitney had one big room heated by a pot-bellied stove on the main floor and a large room in the basement that was often used for dances and parties. On Sunday, both rooms were partitioned off by curtains for classrooms. The ward was close-knit, and parties were for everyone, with babies sleeping on benches and daughters dancing with fathers. In the summer the ward met at the ball diamond for baseball and picnics, often featuring Grandma Benson's fried chicken, corn on the cob, and watermelon.

George and Sarah were sticklers for proper behavior. "Where gospel principles were concerned Father was very strict," Margaret remembers. "When he said no the first time, we knew that meant no." Though the children could always "expect Father and Mother's support when we were in the right, it was a bit perilous to ask for their support when we were in error," says Ezra Taft. And when the children were in the wrong, they faced the music.

One day Ezra T. and his brother Joe, who was small for his age, were walking home from school when a group of older boys, cousin George B. Parkinson among them, started to heckle Joe. In defense of his younger brother, Ezra T. intervened, and soon sharp words turned into a fisticuffs. George B. went home with a bloodied nose, Ezra T. with his hands skinned and covered with blood. Sarah didn't chastise her son for defending Joe, but she promptly asked him to run over to the home of Aunt Lulu (George B.'s mother) to fetch a start of yeast. "Mother, please don't ask me to do that," Ezra pleaded. But Sarah would not relent, and mother's requests were the same as a demand for the children. George had taught them that. When Ezra arrived, Aunt Lulu pulled both boys into a bedroom and gave them a "good lecturing about cousins living together in peace. I would have been happy to leave the yeast and run," Ezra said. When he finally escaped Aunt Lulu's clutches, he hurried home "feeling somewhat repentant but that I had done my duty to protect my young brother."

On the whole, stern discipline wasn't an everyday occurrence in the Benson home. "We were too busy to get into a lot of trouble," Ezra recalled.

That does not mean that boys would not be boys. Ezra was a prankster and, along with his brothers and friends, had his moments. On Halloween they were known to press their luck to the limit. Using horses, they disengaged outhouses and relocated a few wagons. Late one holiday night, he and his friends slipped into the watermelon patch owned by the local sheriff (who was known to be somewhat timid). Hearing noise in the patch, the sheriff shot his revolver into the air. One of the boys, who was carrying a six-shooter, fired back into the air. Immediately the sheriff yelled, "Shoot in the air, boys. That's what I'm doing." "That's about the closest we ever came to any real friction," Ezra insisted.

William Poole, a cousin about Ezra's age, got his hair cut at Uncle George's, who had the only clippers in town. Ezra T. did the cutting. "He'd start at the back and come right over to the front," William remembered. "Then he'd go by one ear over to the other ear. Then he'd get the mirror and show us how we looked, and we had four patches of hair. He'd say, 'Is that the way you wanted it?' We'd tell him no, and then he'd always discover that the clippers wouldn't cut anymore. He'd tease us for a long while, and then finally the clippers would start working and he'd finish our hair."[2]

Ezra once convinced two friends to steal a platter of fudge from a cousin's house. But despite his periodic mischief, Grandma Benson always told other family members, "Don't ever say anything bad about Ezra. I have a lot of special grandchildren, but Ezra T. will make us all very proud someday."

Ezra got some of his fun-loving spirit from his father, who, though no-nonsense on the basics, was a tease. When one of the girls was anticipating the arrival of her date, George sat in his favorite chair, took his shoes off and put them on the table, or draped his socks over a chair—any silly thing to fluster them.

For most of Ezra's growing-up years, his grandfather, George Benson Sr., was bishop of the Whitney Ward, and he frequently emphasized the theme of missionary work. Year after year Ezra listened to returned missionaries relate their experiences—all of them mentioning the difficulties they had had. He wondered why the missionaries almost always said these were the happiest years of their lives. Nevertheless, Ezra wanted to serve a mission, and even as a boy he worried that he might not have the opportunity.

One Sunday when two missionaries reported their missions, seventeen-year-old Ezra sat on the front bench, thoroughly entranced. Afterwards he asked his father how old he had to be to receive his patriarchal blessing. His father replied there wasn't a standard age requirement, but that a person had to be worthy. "Am I worthy?" Ezra asked. His father thought for a moment, then answered, "As your father, I think you are. But it's for the bishop to say. Why don't you go ask the bishop?" Ezra located the bishop, his grandfather, and the two found an isolated corner of the chapel, where Bishop Benson asked Ezra some questions. Finally he wrote on a slip of paper authorization for the blessing. The stake patriarch was visiting that day, and Ezra handed the white-haired man, John Edward Dalley, the slip of paper. "My boy," Brother Dalley said, "if you'll come with me, we'll walk up the street to brother Bert Winward's, and I'll give you the blessing today."

That day Brother Dalley pronounced a blessing that answered the boy's prayers. Ezra was told that, if faithful, he would go on a mission to the nations of the earth, that his life would be preserved on land and sea, that he would raise his voice in testimony and would grow in favor with the Almighty, and that many would rise up and bless his name. Ezra went home walking on air.

The influence of the gospel permeated Ezra's upbringing. Often he found his mother bending over the ironing board, pressing long strips of white cloth. Newspapers lined the floor to keep the material from getting soiled. When Ezra asked what she was doing, she answered, "These are temple robes, son. Your father and I are going to the temple in Logan." Then she would place the flatiron on the stove and tell her son how important it was to be able to go to the temple. She also expressed how much she hoped her children would enjoy temple blessings.

For Sarah Benson, no sacrifice was too much, no assignment too demanding, when it came to the Church. Though rearing eleven children in the process, she occupied several challenging callings, ward Relief Society president among them. During that time, seven-year-old Ezra harnessed the horse and got the buggy ready for his mother to go to her midweek Relief Society meetings. He also gathered a half bushel of wheat from the granary and put it in the buggy. In a forerunner of the welfare program, Relief Society sisters stored and distributed wheat. (Following World War I, President Herbert Hoover called for that wheat to relieve suffering and hunger in central Europe.

And some three decades later it would be Sarah's eldest son who coordinated shipments of grain and other goods for needy Latter-day Saints in Europe following World War II.)

George, too, was called upon to serve in an unexpected but demanding way. In the spring of 1912 a chicken pox epidemic raged in the Whitney Ward. One Sunday morning Sarah and George went to sacrament meeting without their children, leaving them at home where they wouldn't be exposed to the contagious disease. At meeting's close, the owner of the Whitney store opened his store long enough for the farmers to pick up their mail.

As they drove toward home, Sarah sorted the mail and found a letter addressed to George T. Benson Jr. The return address on the envelope was Box B, Salt Lake City, Utah. Mission calls were issued from Box B. In those days, no one asked if you were ready, willing, or able to fill a mission; the bishop assessed worthiness and the call came. Sarah hurriedly opened the letter. The news was bittersweet: her husband had been called on a mission. He was to leave as soon as he could get his affairs in order. Sarah was carrying their eighth child.

As the couple drove into the yard, the children ran out of the house to find both of their parents crying. Ezra recalled, "We'd seen father in tears and mother offering comfort, and mother weeping and father offering consolation. But never both of them at once." All seven of the children crowded around the buggy, unsettled at their parents' lack of composure. Then their parents reassured them, "Everything is fine. Come into the living room. We want to talk to you."

The children quickly gathered inside on the worn sofa, and their father explained what had happened. Through her tears, Sarah told them: "We're so proud that Father's considered worthy to go on a mission. We're crying a little because it means two years of separation, and your father and I have never been separated more than two nights at a time since our marriage."

To finance the mission, George sold his eighty acres of dry land, and Sarah and the children doubled up and shared their home with James Chadwick and his new bride, who helped farm the row crops. Twelve-year-old Ezra was left to supervise a dairy herd and care for the pasture land and a few remaining acres of hay.

In addition to greatly missing his father, to whom Ezra had grown even closer in his early teenage years, the strapping boy was affected by George Benson's unexpected mission call in other ways. Hard as the work on the farm might have been heretofore, things would be entirely different. His father had been his best friend; Ezra had always had him to look up to. Now his younger brothers and sisters, even his mother, would be counting more on him, and he didn't want to let them down. "I always considered my father the ideal, and I hoped I could follow his example," Ezra said.

Measuring up to George Benson's example was a tall order— one that required integrity, industry, devotion. Ezra knew he no longer had the luxury of being a boy. In his father's absence, he would be the man of the house. The worry-free days of boyhood were gone.

"Those days on the farm when Father was away were a real test for the family. But there came into our home a spirit of missionary work that never left it."

Chapter 3

Man of the House

In a matter of weeks George Benson was fifteen hundred miles away, answering his call to the Northern States Mission. At home his expectant wife and their seven children were trying to adjust. Valdo, the youngest, walked for days through the barnyard calling, "Daddy, Daddy."

"We had some real tests on the farm," Ezra remembered, many of which affected him directly. He took on extra chores and worries, sandwiching them in before and after school—when he could get there. He dug vegetables from under the snow, comforted brothers and sisters who missed their father, helped discipline and encourage them, and resisted, at least part of the time, the urge to behave as a boy his age could be expected to behave.

He bore his duties well. George hadn't been gone long, however, when Ezra faced a challenge of larger proportions. A raging smallpox epidemic invaded the crowded farmhouse, and a red flag hanging out front cautioned visitors to stay away. Everyone became seriously ill—including Ezra and his mother. In her delicate condition, Sarah became critically ill, and the doctor decreed that she must call George home from the mission field. She protested, but the physician was adamant. He was concerned about the unborn baby, but even more so about this thirty-four-year-old woman who, in his judgment, couldn't possibly fight off smallpox while carrying a child—all with her husband half a country away.

When Sarah went into delivery, her condition became so precarious that the doctor insisted George be called home. But Sarah had the last word. "No," she insisted in her weakened condition. "Let him stay and finish his mission. The Lord will take care of me." Shortly thereafter she delivered a son, their fifth, and named him George Taft III. The infant appeared to have grown to full size while in the womb, but was born shriveled from lack of nourishment. In time, though, both Sarah and her baby recovered.

There were other kinds of challenges. One evening as Sarah and Margaret drove home in a one-horse buggy, a violent storm arose, buffeting the lightweight carriage. Sarah quickly pulled into a neighbor's yard about a half mile from home and huddled Margaret to her. But she feared the children at home were in danger, so she prayed and felt prompted to prod the horse back onto the road.

As the frightened horse struggled for footing, trees crashed around them and limbs flew like arrows. Suddenly a huge tree crashed behind them, blocking the road. Had Sarah hesitated even a few seconds, she and Margaret would have been blocked from home and might even have been injured. Instead, Sarah arrived at the homestead to find the living room window blown out and the children huddled in the kitchen around a flickering lamp.

As the children grew older, they reflected with wonder on that period and their mother's endurance and faith. More than one of them said, "Never did we hear a murmur from her lips."

Before he left on his mission, George arranged for monies from the sale of half his farm to go to the family during his absence; nevertheless, Sarah and the children, by and large, provided for themselves. They sold milk and traded eggs for groceries at the store in Whitney, tended their garden and orchard, and stored potatoes and apples for use all winter. Frugal by nature and experienced at making do, Sarah churned butter, patched and repatched clothing, and kept meals simple. Suppers of bread and milk with tender green onions were com-

Sarah Benson and seven of her children at time of her husband's call to mission. (The eighth child was born shortly thereafter.) Ezra is standing behind his mother

mon. Ezra arose early, milked the cows, and did other chores before leaving for school. In the evening he tended chores before doing homework. When he milked the cows, his younger brothers and sisters often came to the barn so he could squirt milk in their mouths. He was fairly accurate, though sometimes he misfired, not always accidentally. " 'T' did the work of a man, though he was only a boy," Margaret remembered. "He took the place of father for nearly two years."

Meanwhile, the family received frequent letters from George with such postmarks as Des Moines, Cedar Rapids, and Chicago—places that seemed halfway around the world. In the evening by the faint glow of a coal oil lamp, with the children hunched around the kitchen table, Sarah read the prized letters. "We had great spiritual moments in our home while Father was on his mission," Ezra said. "In our prayers at night Mother prayed that Father would be successful and that he wouldn't worry about home. She prayed that our work would go well in the fields, that we'd be kind to each other. She may have wept in the privacy of her bedroom, but she never doubted Father's call. When your mother prays with such fervor, night after night, you think twice before you do something to disappoint her."

With each week, as letters arrived and George related his experiences of perseverance and faith, a spirit of missionary work enveloped the farm house. Ezra, in particular, relished each letter. His father's stories and words excited him, even moved him. (In time, all eleven of George's children served missions, some more than one.)

In those days it was customary for missionaries to room in the homes of local Saints. In one city, however, as Elder Benson and his companion found lodging in a home where the elders had lived for years, they were astonished to learn that the homeowners weren't members of the Church. Finally George asked the head of the house, "How long have you known the missionaries?" "Ten years," was the reply. "Ten years!" George exclaimed. "You have an obligation. Have you prayed about it? Have you read the Book of Mormon?" "Yes, we have read the Book of Mormon," the man answered, "but only a little of it. And no, we have never prayed about it."

That night the family called on George Benson to offer a prayer, which turned into a kneeling sermon. He challenged them to read the Book of Mormon in its entirety, and he and his companion taught them the gospel. A child overheard the parents say that they must look into this religion, and in time all were baptized. (Four decades later George's son Ezra Taft Benson, by then an apostle, would perform the marriage of a daughter of that family.)

Ezra absorbed these stories coming from the father he idolized. They made the extra work at home worth it. Ezra seemed naturally inclined toward religion. As Margaret said, "The Church seemed to be his first priority. He loved to participate in anything he was asked to do." A friend commented, "He was just a little bit more spiritual than the rest of us."[1]

Ezra couldn't remember when he didn't have a testimony— not that his early life was marked by dramatic spiritual milestones, but he accepted the gospel and was willing to try to live its teachings. In this and other ways, he modeled after his father. His sister Sarah said, "Our father was very strong, physically

35

and spiritually. He was also very tender. Ezra inherited those qualities."

George read the scriptures, particularly the Book of Mormon, to his children, and Ezra always rejoiced on those occasions. Family prayer, held regularly, was a time to thank the Lord for their abundant blessings. Ezra couldn't remember his father ever going to the field without first having family prayer. If he forgot, Sarah always reminded him. And attending church on Sunday, choir practice on Wednesday evening, priesthood meeting on Monday night, and other meetings in between was routine. Ezra's first attempt to give a talk in a church meeting was at a meeting of the Young Men's Mutual Improvement Association, one of the Church's youth organizations. He made two key points: there is always room at the top, and America is another name for opportunity.

In this atmosphere, Ezra's spiritual inclinations flourished, but in such a natural way that it never occurred to him that his upbringing was different from any other. Religious activity was not contrived, never forced. Behavior was modeled. In particular, Ezra observed his father closely, and one of the first qualities he discerned was integrity. It was commonly accepted in the community that if George Benson thought something was all right, it was all right. It seemed to him that Edgar A. Guest must have been writing about his father when he wrote "A Real Man," which began,

> Men are of two kinds, and he
> Was of the kind I'd like to be.
> Some preach their virtues, and a few
> Express their lives by what they do.
> That sort was he.

When George Benson returned home after almost two years, he found a growing, changing, but happy family and a farm that had survived his absence (in fact, he was able to purchase additional acres, all tillable and some more fertile than those he had sold to finance his mission, which caused him to say his mission had been prosperous, in more ways than one). He also found that the twelve-year-old boy he had waved good-bye to had become a young man.

It's possible that George's mission did as much for his eldest son as it did for himself. The firsthand experience with faith, the shouldering of heavy responsibility—it all prodded Ezra to handle more than he might have otherwise done. And as George sat on a one-legged stool, milking cows and singing at full voice "Ye Elders of Israel," "Israel, Israel, God Is Calling," and "Come, All Ye Sons of God," Ezra could see that his father had also grown. The songs echoed through the barn and fields so often that Ezra learned every word of these and other missionary songs and could repeat them throughout his life.

In addition to emphasizing missionary work, the family's sacrifice reinforced their total commitment to the gospel—something of which Ezra saw repeated evidence.

As tithing settlement approached one December, Ezra overheard his parents discussing a fifty-dollar note due at the bank and the fifty dollars they owed in tithing. Yet they had only fifty dollars to their name. George had tried, without success, to earn money to cover the deficit by selling a hay derrick he had built. Their alternatives were clear: they could either pay the bank note and hope to pay their tithing soon, or they could pay the tithing and hope to meet the note when it came due. They decided to pay the tithing, and the next evening they handed the bishop their fifty dollars. As they drove home, a neighbor stopped them to inquire about the hay derrick. When he learned the asking price, he made out a check for fifty dollars on the spot. George paid back the bank.

Ezra learned from his father in other ways. Though George was a man of few words, his interests became Ezra's interests. One thing that caught George's attention was patriotism and, to some degree, politics. He believed that the Founding Fathers of the United States had been inspired, and on one occasion he openly supported a particular candidate and even made mention of the man in family prayers. When George's candidate lost the election, Ezra was anxious to hear what his father would say in his next prayer. George prayed for the man who had won. When Ezra asked how he could pray for the man who had defeated his candidate, he replied, "Son, I think he'll need our prayers even more than my candidate would have."

At age fourteen Ezra graduated from the small elementary school in Whitney. Though he had missed school often in the fall for sugar beet harvest and in the spring for planting, he had completed the required study in six years. The following year, 1914, he was off to the Oneida Stake Academy in Preston, a Church-sponsored school where morning devotional and prayer began each day's activities and the instructors opened new worlds to the farmboy. From Harrison R. Merrill, a large man who had a home up the Cub River, he acquired a love of literature—poetry in particular. Ezra also enjoyed carpentry, often staying late to work on projects. He crafted a cupboard and table, an oak desk with shelves on either side, and a hat rack, and was "quite proud" of himself.

It was at the academy that Ezra first met Harold B. Lee, who was a year ahead of him in school. They became good friends, and both sang in the school's first choir. Ezra also played trombone, though his major interests were agriculture and vocational training. He felt that "a man ought to be able to repair something," and he pursued manual training wholeheartedly. He played basketball with the same intensity and enthusiasm. George Benson enjoyed basketball and encouraged all seven of his sons in the game. Once he issued a challenge through the *Franklin County Citizen* that his family would take on any other family in basketball. "We were probably fortunate we didn't have any takers," Ezra said.

George had his younger sons milk the cows so Ezra could travel with his high school team. Ezra, who played forward and was the most accurate shooter, was captain of the team. They traveled up and down the Snake River Valley, taking on any organized team they could find—town teams, high school teams, even the teams from Ricks Normal College at Rexburg Idaho, and the Brigham Young College in Logan, Utah. In Shelley, Idaho, where there was no basketball court, they drained the swimming pool and attached temporary backboards on either end.

Participation in competitive athletics taught Ezra several things, including sportsmanship. "I learned to play fair. Father always stressed that. 'It is better to lose than lose your temper,' he'd always say." But even George got caught up in the competition. Sarah frequently put her hand on his arm and said, "Now, George, don't overdo it." Ezra remembers his father swearing only once. The Oneida Stake Academy was playing Brigham Young College in Logan, and late in the game Oneida trailed by a point after failing to convert on several attempts. Ezra suddenly got the ball and an exasperated George yelled, "Hell, 'T', put it in!" "It was shocking to the local citizens coming from George Benson, but apparently they understood his enthusiasm and anxiety," Ezra said. "When we finished with a one-point victory, Father was overjoyed."

During one game, Marion G. Romney, who would serve with Ezra as a General Authority many years later, suited up for the opposing team from Ricks. Though Oneida won by a point, the Rexburg team treated the Oneida squad to a bobsleigh ride to Sugar City for a contest there. Ezra drove the team most of the way. In later years he'd say he "always received a greater thrill driving a good team of horses than from the finest automobile."

Until his brothers were old enough to attend Oneida Academy with him, Ezra usually rode his pony to school. En route, he would stop at Worm Creek to check his string of muskrat traps. In the evening he would check them again and gather up the day's take. Before milking cows and cleaning the stable in the evening, he skinned and stretched the pelts over a cedar shingle, shaped them with his pocket knife to proper size, and hung them to dry. Then he shipped them to a Chicago furrier. The proceeds helped pay for books and clothing and added to the family coffer.

The Oneida Stake Academy was noted for its discipline. One day while taking an economics exam, Ezra's pencil lead broke. As he leaned across the aisle to borrow a penknife, the teacher walked up the aisle, took his papers, accused him of cheating, and announced, "You will not be allowed to play in the basketball game tonight." Ezra tried to explain what had happened, but the instructor would hear nothing of it.

Heartsick at the accusation and frustrated at failing to clear his name and being disqualified from competition, he went home to talk with his father. "Father asked me if I had cheated and

George T. and Sarah Benson with their family during sugar-beet harvest on the farm in Whitney, Idaho, about 1917

looked on the other person's paper," Ezra recalled. "I assured him that I had not cheated, and looked him squarely in the face as I told him so." George believed his son and replied, " 'T', it's all right. Things will work out. Don't worry. Now go do your milking." While Ezra was milking cows, the coach called and said that the principal wanted to see Ezra before the game. Ezra went reluctantly, still disappointed and discouraged. When the principal asked Ezra to confess his dishonesty, Ezra again insisted that he had not been dishonest. Minutes before the game he received permission to play. "But my spirits were so broken I was unable to put my heart fully into the game," he said. "We lost, which of course was a disappointment, but the greater disappointment to me was the fact that I had been misjudged and accused of violating a principle that had been an important part of my training. It's the only time I can remember having my honor questioned. I did learn from the incident how important it was to keep my name and my father's name above reproach." He also learned to avoid even the appearance of evil.

Ezra's father was undoubtedly proud of his eldest son. Ezra worked hard on the farm, progressively accepting more responsibility. He was strong, capable of doing a man's work. Area farmers traded chores to cut down on hiring of help, and Ezra was called upon frequently. At age sixteen, Ezra earned lasting local fame by thinning an acre of beets in one day. It was back-breaking work, using a wide-bladed, short-handled hoe, and the surprised farmer paid him two five-dollar gold pieces and two silver dollars. Ezra had never felt so rich.

William Poole, Ezra's cousin, explained the significance of the feat: "I would stake out three-fourths of an acre of beets and get up before sunrise and work until dark to finish. 'T' was the first person I remember who thinned an acre of beets in one day.

"Uncle George taught all the boys to work hard," William continued. "My father liked to hire 'T' to pitch hay because he worked hard. I liked to tromp hay for 'T' because he could pitch a fork of hay exactly where I needed it."

As a teenager, Ezra dug trenches for the pipes that brought water from a nearby spring through underground pipes into the Benson home, and postholes for the posts that supported wires that carried electricity into Whitney. He also drove teams into the nearby forests with his father to fell timber for derricks or fences. Sometimes he slept under a load of timber to escape the elements.

"I grew up believing that the willingness and ability to work is the basic ingredient of successful farming," Ezra said. "Hard, intelligent work is the key. Use it, and your chances for success are good."[2]

But there was time for fun, too. Sarah's brother, John Dunkley, purchased the first car in the community, a Ford. After church, children gathered around, hoping to see him crank it and start down the road, kicking up dust as he went. In 1915 George purchased his first car, a Dodge. The self-propelled buggy was a miracle in its time, though the ride wasn't much better than that of the hay wagon. Occasionally George let Ezra take the car out alone. One Saturday Ezra drove to Logan. The only stretch of pavement was a short distance between Smithfield and Logan, and heading down a slight grade on that stretch, Ezra pushed the speed to fifty-one miles an hour. When he reported his feat, George could scarcely believe him. His mother protested, "You could have been killed."

In the winter the family still opted for the bobsleigh over the car. En route to church they would pick up passersby, and the sleigh would be full, with people standing on the runners at the side of the carriage. When Ezra drove, he couldn't resist skidding around corners—especially if he and his friends were going to a social function. The corner by the Whitney store became especially slick from all the whirling, making the sport dangerous. But Ezra was skillful in handling the horses, and though he liked to have fun, he wasn't reckless. Even then Margaret wondered if her oldest brother was meant to serve a great mission, for he was always protected, whether it be riding horses, operating large machinery, or pursuing any other activity with an element of danger.

By this time Ezra had become a tall, handsome, strapping man, and the girls "all swooned over him," as Margaret put it. He was well liked and active in the local social group, but no one in particular had caught his eye.

Ezra got along well with others, though he was a tease. One friend explained, "He was quite a joker. . . . He could make friends with anybody. . . . He had that personality."[3] Margaret said that he "had a sense of humor and made fun for everyone." Being only two years younger, she caught the brunt of his antics. One December morning she was standing on the top rung of a stepladder, putting decorations on the Christmas tree, when Ezra entered. Seeing his sister perched precariously, he tromped across the floor to give the ladder a good shake. Margaret shrieked in protest and tossed a dustpan at him. The edge of the pan caught him on the lip and tore it open, leaving a permanent scar. "The cut lip didn't change his personality," Margaret said. "He still loved to tease and joke."

Ezra was secretary of the Young Men's Mutual Improvement Association in the ward while Margaret was secretary for the Young Women's MIA, and for two years they attended meetings together. A young lady who moved into the ward noticed that Ezra Benson always accompanied Margaret home. Finally she asked Margaret if she was going steady with Ezra. They got a chuckle out of that.

Despite his more human moments, Ezra had a desire to be "a leader of boys," and in 1918 he got his first formal opportunity when Bishop Benson called his grandson, Ezra, as assistant Scoutmaster to twenty-four lively, mischievous Scouts. (He later became Scoutmaster.) Ezra took to the assignment like a veteran. In those days the YMMIA sponsored choruses for the teenage boys, and the Scoutmaster was expected to get them to practice. The choirs sang not only for pleasure and entertainment but also in competitions. After weeks of practice and pushing and prodding on Ezra's part, his choir won first place in the Franklin Stake competition, which qualified them to compete in the Logan Tabernacle against six other winning groups. This was a big event for the boys, some of whom had never been as far from home as Logan.

To motivate his troop, Ezra promised them—"in a moment of anxiety or weakness," he wasn't sure which—that if they won the regional competition, he would lead them on a thirty-five-mile hike across the mountains to Bear Lake.

On the night of the competition each choir drew lots for placement. The Whitney chorus drew last place, which prolonged their anxiety. When they were finally announced, twenty-four boys marched up the aisle and onstage while the pianist played "Stars and Stripes Forever." Ezra crouched between two benches to direct their performance. "They sang as I'd never heard them sing, and of course I'd not tell the story had we not won first place in Logan," he said.

A promise made is a debt unpaid, and the Scouts had barely been declared the winners when they gathered around their Scoutmaster to remind him of the hike. At a subsequent prehike planning session, one twelve-year-old Scout excitedly suggested, "Mr. Scoutmaster, I'd like to make a motion. We should all clip our hair off so we will not be bothered with combs and brushes on the trip." The older Scouts squirmed (crewcuts, they thought, would not attract young women), but the motion carried—not, however, before one of the older Scouts said, "How about the Scoutmasters?" It was Ezra's turn to squirm.

The following Saturday Ezra took his place in the barber's chair, with twenty-four Scouts looking on. As the barber neared the end of Ezra's haircut, he said, "If you'll let me shave your head, I'll cut the hair of the rest of your boys for nothing." Two days later, twenty-four Scouts and one bald Scoutmaster, with his bald assistants, set out for Bear Lake. The ten-day hike was "glorious nevertheless," filled with fishing, camping, hiking, swimming, and camaraderie. "One of the joys of working with boys is that you get your pay as you go along," Ezra later explained. "You can observe the results of your leadership daily. . . . Such satisfaction cannot be purchased at any price; it must be earned."[4]

Ezra kept in touch with his Scouts. Years later, while visiting the Whitney Ward as a General Authority of the Church, he ran into seven of them. All were serving in leadership positions. They could account for the whereabouts, and faithfulness, of all their troop except two. Several years later, while in southern Arizona, Ezra ran into one of those two. The man had married out of the Church, but his wife had later joined. After corresponding with the couple for some time, Ezra performed their temple sealing. Later, while in Burley, Idaho, he saw the other Scout. Again, Ezra officiated at the temple sealing.

Despite ordinary squabbles, a deep unity developed as the Benson family matured. They worked together and counted on one another—physically, emotionally, and spiritually. Whatever else had happened during the day, the Bensons prayed together. One significant by-product of their pleadings was deep family loyalty, a quality that sank to the heart of Ezra's soul—loyalty to family and also to country.

During Ezra's teenage years at Oneida Academy, the United States became embroiled in World War I, and many young men left for war. "There was a great patriotic spirit in our little Whitney Ward, as well as throughout the country, and a large number of boys enlisted," Ezra recalled. Though he wasn't subject to the draft, he felt impelled to get involved. When one ward member returned, attired in his dress blues, after honorable duty, Ezra "desired to get in." Not long after that, he learned that a military program was being established at Utah Agricultural College (now Utah State University) in nearby Logan, and he pled with his parents for permission to enlist.

George Benson was a patriot. He didn't say much about the war, but his sons knew he looked favorably upon young men who served their country. After prolonged consideration, he and Sarah gave Ezra their consent to enlist in what was the equivalent of a Reserve Officers Training Camp (ROTC) program. Soon thereafter, Ezra left for Logan. The year was 1918.

By that fall, so many local boys had followed suit that farmers found themselves shorthanded for sugar-beet harvest. Military officials were approached about giving the recruits a two-week leave to assist with harvest. Permission was granted. The mass furlough was to begin on a Saturday. On Friday morning, Ezra felt a strong impression that he should leave for home immediately. When the feeling persisted a second and then a third time, he requested permission to leave early, caught a ride to Whitney, and arrived home around noon.

Almost immediately he was stricken with a severe fever. Delirious for three days, the only thing Ezra later remembered of that period was the doctor leaning over him and telling his parents, "Only the power of the priesthood of God can save him." George and Grandfather Benson administered to the young man, and Sarah watched over him day and night, mopping his forehead with cool towels to control the fever. Finally it broke and he began to recover. The flu epidemic, which killed thousands of persons worldwide, broke out in the barracks in Logan the same day Ezra became ill, and the young men who had cots on either side of him there both died. One of those youths was Ezra's cousin, George B. Parkinson. Ezra felt that the Lord had a hand in preserving his life. "Why should I get the impression to go home early on Friday?" he asked. "Had I waited, I would have suffered there with the rest of them, and probably passed away."

As it was, the war ended that fall, and Ezra didn't serve active duty. He returned home, and in the spring of 1919 he graduated from the Oneida Stake Academy. In the winter of 1921 he returned to Logan to start his first quarter at Utah Agricultural College. He attended college during winter quarters and took correspondence courses during the fall and spring, when he stayed home to help his father with harvest and planting. More than once, farm work cut directly into his education.

One fall Ezra, Margaret, and Joseph were all planning to leave for school, but unseasonal weather made it impossible for George to find help to get the beets in. The whole family had to pitch in—including the college students, who had planned to be

*Flora Amussen was
involved in many
activities at school—
but skiing wasn't
her best sport*

in Logan by then. The fields had turned into acres of oozy mud. George bought waterproof overalls for everyone; in the morning they each put on a clean pair and headed for the fields. At noon, caked with layers of mud, they tromped home and Sarah handed out clean overalls before sending them back to the fields. "We topped every beet," Margaret recalled. "Those were hard times, in that respect. But we also had good times together—even out in that muddy field."

In the early fall of 1920 Ezra spent a weekend in Logan preparatory to enrolling for winter quarter. He and a cousin were standing on a curb on Main Street when an attractive young woman drove by in a Ford convertible and waved to a friend. A few minutes later she drove by a second time and waved again. "Who is that?" Ezra asked. "Flora Amussen," his cousin replied. There was something about the girl that impressed Ezra, and he responded enthusiastically, "When I come down here this winter, I'm going to step her." "Like heck you will," the cousin answered, adding, "she's too popular for a farm boy like you." "That makes it all the more interesting," Ezra countered. He received the distinct impression that he would marry her.

A few weeks later Ezra was surprised when the same young woman walked into Sunday School in the Whitney Ward. Flora was a weekend guest of Ann Dunkley, Ezra's cousin. After the meeting Ann's father, Uncle Joseph, approached Ezra. "These girls are bothering me something fierce to take them on a drive to Lava Hot Springs this afternoon," he said. "I've got the old Ford gassed up, but I wonder who might be able to drive them for me."

"Why, if I can find someone to milk my cows for me," Ezra replied, not slow to sense opportunity, "I'll be happy to do you the favor, Uncle."

For the first time Ezra was in Flora's company, and he liked it. She was vivacious, happy, sensible, and appreciative of the slightest favor—something that impressed Ezra. He felt that she radiated goodness. When she returned to Logan at the end of the weekend, he resolved to get better acquainted with her. To Flora, Ezra was a curiosity. "I never knew of such a person," she said. "He was a plain, typical farm boy—homespun in his appearance and manner. But he had that wholesome, honest, God-fearing look that farm folks seem to have."

That winter Ezra and Margaret lived with Grandma Benson in Logan. They were part of the same crowd, went to the same parties, and often accompanied each other to dances and other activities. One evening "T" arrived home to find that Margaret had accepted a date to the dance that evening. Without a partner, perhaps this was his chance to call Flora Amussen. Soon he had her on the phone, but she explained that she had decided not to accept a date to the dance. As student body vice-president, she was to present letter sweaters to the football players at intermission. "I don't mind sitting out a dance or two while you take care of your responsibilities," Ezra insisted. A few hours later the farm boy from Whitney, wearing a blue serge suit that was shiny in the back, pulled up in front of Flora's large three-story home, took a deep breath, and wondered what he'd gotten himself into, calling on the most popular—and apparently one of the wealthiest—young women on campus.

Flora's was a home of obvious culture and refinement, but Barbara Amussen, her widowed mother, quickly put Ezra at ease. "Almost immediately this good woman was talking to me about farming and my family, both subjects on which I spoke with confidence," Ezra remembered. As he and Flora prepared to leave, she kissed her mother good-bye tenderly. That impressed him. He knew he was escorting an unusual girl, and he determined to make the most of it. Their courtship proceeded, and Ezra's impression that he had found the woman for him was confirmed.

But marriage, assuming Flora would have him, was down the road. In the summer of 1921 a letter postmarked Salt Lake City and signed by President Heber J. Grant arrived in Whitney, addressed to "Elder" Ezra Taft Benson. He was being called on a mission! He quickly replied to President Grant and pledged, simply, "I am very pleased and thankful that I have been counted worthy to fill a mission and will try to do my duty."[5]

Since those early days in the rock meetinghouse in Whitney, Ezra had waited for this day. Finally, at age twenty-one, he had been called on a mission—to Great Britain.

Chapter 4

A Mission to England

I t was quite an adventure. Prior to 1921, the most ambitious outings for the farm boy from Whitney, Idaho, had been a few thirty-five-mile trips to Logan, Utah, and an occasional 120-mile excursion to "the city"—Salt Lake City. Not only had Ezra Taft Benson never been far from home, but he'd not been exposed to divergent views or life-styles, had never faced religious opposition—let alone ridicule—and had never been without the support of family nearby. But with his call to the British Mission, that changed.

When George Benson learned of his son's call, he was elated. This was something he had looked forward to with great anticipation since his own mission eight years earlier. Ezra, too, was thrilled with the news. "I was pleased because I have English blood in my veins. And I knew I'd be close to Scotland, and I have Scottish blood in my veins. It seemed right somehow."

Flora Amussen also took the news with good spirits. Undaunted that her frequent companion would spend over two years an ocean away, she sensed how important the experience would prove to him, was pleased that he had chosen to serve a mission, and knew he would work hard. Working hard physically was no test for Ezra but in England the work would be grueling spiritually and mentally as well, developing new dimensions in his character and personality. It was in England that his testimony and his knowledge of gospel principles would flourish.

As the day for departure drew near, Ezra could hardly bear the anticipation. He was more keyed up than at Christmas time. Flora threw a party for him at her elegant home. Anticipating his week aboard ship crossing the Atlantic, she unveiled a roll of paper and had everyone write him a letter—each of which she dated for opening. At home George and Sarah held a special home evening honoring their eldest son. Because the old rock church was being rebuilt, his farewell was held on a nearby tennis court.

On July 13, 1921, George ordained Ezra an elder, and early the following morning George and Sarah went through the Logan Temple with him. Then, with Flora joining them, they were off to Salt Lake City. There, Elder Seymour B. Young of the First Council of the Seventy set Ezra apart to serve in the British Mission with headquarters in London. England—a place Ezra had only read about. Yet, in a couple of weeks he'd be there! It was still almost beyond comprehension.

The evening of July 16, Elder Benson shook his father's hand and embraced him, kissed his mother, and boarded the Continental Limited No. 20 in Salt Lake City. Flora rode with him as far as Ogden, where he bid her "a quick and snappy good-bye."

Six days later, on July 22, he and some missionary companions set sail on the *Victorian*, an English ship, from Montreal, Canada. Before boarding, he was thrilled to hear a concert in the park conducted by John Philip Sousa. On his first day at sea Ezra opened, as Flora had instructed, the letter marked "First Day on Board." The next day he read the second letter and opened a cake she had sent. "I had mail every day on the boat," he remembered, "and that was something! It was so nice to be able to open a letter out in the middle of the ocean, and Flora had masterminded it all. It made me think of her at least once a day."

By and large, the weather during the ten-day crossing was cold, foggy, and windy, resulting in rough seas. Elder Benson's companion was homesick, and both endured seasickness. Ezra

*Ezra Taft Benson,
missionary to
England*

read the scriptures, joked with the ship's stewards, and talked
with other passengers. At midnight on August 1, they docked
at Liverpool, and by eight o'clock the next morning they were
at mission headquarters. Without delay mission president Orson
F. Whitney, a member of the Council of the Twelve, assigned
Elder Benson to the Carlisle Branch of the Newcastle Conference, in the Lake District near the Scottish border.

Though many years later Ezra would say, "I've never had a
real test of my faith, because I've always felt that regardless of
the seriousness of conditions, the Lord was on our side," what
he found in England, as a young missionary unused to bitter
prejudice, presented as great a test of his mettle and endurance
as anything he would experience for many years to come.

Elder James T. Palmer met Elder Benson and another missionary at the train station in Carlisle and took them to his room in a boardinghouse. Elder Palmer described their accommodations: "There was a bed and a narrow cot. . . . Elder Benson and I slept on the bed. The springs at the best were stretched and old; with the weight of two men, we slept with sunken springs almost to the bare floor. . . . Elder Benson [and I] . . . called this situation home for better than the whole next year."[1]

Some of the Church's most fruitful proselyting had occurred in England in the late 1830s and 1840s, but by the time Elder Benson arrived, anti-Mormon sentiment was rampant. A plague of opposition to the Church, initiated in large measure by the clergy and festered by the English press, had infected much of the British Isles. Anti-Mormon movies, plays, and articles appeared regularly. Winifred Graham, among others, had popularized a series of vicious novels that depicted Mormons as immoral and deceitful. In 1922 a film titled *Trapped by the Mormons*, adapted from one of Graham's books, was representative of dramatic fare that characterized missionaries as villains who mesmerized young women and lured them to Salt Lake City. It's little wonder the missionaries had difficulty proselyting wherever the film was shown. In some areas they couldn't secure lodging, and some were even beaten on occasion. David O. McKay, after his arrival in England as mission president in late 1922, told the First Presidency, "Winifred Graham and her . . . associates have opened the flood gates of hell, and are deluging England with the vilest slander that impure minds can imagine."[2]

Initially none of this frightened the young elder, who was caught up in the spirit of missionary work. He bore his testimony twice during his first Sunday in England and soon thereafter got a taste of tracting, which he called "bonny stuff." On his second Sunday in Carlisle he took charge of Sunday School and sacrament meeting and preached a sermon on the Apostasy.

Elder Benson would be called on to preach many sermons, and, without the advantage of structured missionary discussions that were developed in later decades, embarked on his own study program. "We'd had a lot of reading of the scriptures in our home, and at least I'd been exposed to them enough to feel confident about reading and using them," he reflected. His mission log, in which he accounted for every shilling spent, frequently noted the purchase of secondhand books. He studied the writings and debates of Elder Orson Pratt, "eagerly devoured the Book of Mormon," read the complete *History of the Church* by Joseph Smith, and studied the life of the Prophet. Near the end of his mission he would write: "Each day I am learning to love books more."

Before Ezra left Utah, he and Flora had agreed to write each other once a month, and the letters were to be "newsy and inspirational, *no mush!*" In large part, they held to their monthly pact, though Ezra's log of letters written reveals he slipped in an extra missive once in a while. He was prodigious in writing to family and friends; his mother heard from him more than anyone else, his sister Margaret was a close second, and Flora a distant third.

From home he received a constant flow of encouragement and parental counsel. "Be prayerful, Ezra T.," his mother warned, "and do not fail to keep the commandments of the Lord and trust in him at all times and he cannot help blessing you to fill an honorable mission."[3]

How important were the letters, Christmas cards, and small packages that came from home? "Received mail which I read time and time again," he wrote in his journal. Years later he explained their significance: "Mother and father poured out their hearts to me in letters, and were a real strength to me as a young man. Flora's were full of spirit and encouragement, never any sentimental stuff. I think that increased my love and appreciation for her more than anything."

What prompted Ezra and Flora to keep their letters newsy and infrequent, one can only speculate. But in England, Elder Benson's conviction that missionaries were better off without girlfriends was confirmed. One of his companions was preoccupied with a girl he had left behind, writing her almost daily. Concerned, Elder Benson said, "She'll get sick of you. You can't possibly keep up this pace, and she won't have time to answer your letters." "Oh, Elder Benson, you don't know what love is," his companion replied. When Ezra explained his and Flora's agreement, his companion was astonished. "Your relationship won't possibly last," the elder warned. But in fact, it was the companion's friendship that fizzled. "I learned it isn't good to leave a girl behind and *expect* her to wait for you," Ezra reflected later. "It distracted my companion. It took him a while to get the spirit of missionary work."

Such a grace period was impractical in England in the 1920s, when missionaries were forced to season quickly. From the beginning Ezra's responsibilities were manyfold—teaching, speaking, fellowshipping branch members and recent converts, blessing the sick, presiding at weekly Relief Society meetings, and tracting, always tracting. After only five days in Carlisle, he had his first taste of door-to-door solicitation. A month passed before he sold his first Book of Mormon to an investigator.

The proud parents at home followed their son's progress as best they could via delayed mail. Ezra's mother wrote, "Papa in bearing his testimony was telling of you tracting twelve hours a day. We are glad you are working hard. Of course, we were not worried . . . for you always worked hard at home."[4]

In the little time left after tracting and attending to branch duties, Ezra studied voraciously, usually in preparation for speaking assignments. His range of topics was as diverse as it was demanding, on such subjects as the Atonement, the Restoration, faith, the Book of Mormon, sacrifice, premortal life, baptism, and prophecy. In church and during street meetings, he worked on perfecting his delivery and ability to communicate. He faithfully recorded his "Index to Antidotes [Anecdotes] & Happenings," a compilation of stories, quotations, and object lessons pertinent to gospel topics. On indifference: "An immigrant went to sleep in his bunk after the ship had been in collision. When aroused, not too gently, and told that the vessel was sinking, he said impatiently, 'Let her sink; it is not mine.' This is the attitude of many people with regard to the world in which we live and the conditions prevailing." On teaching the gospel: "Every little girl thinks her doll best. Don't tear it to pieces to show it's made of sawdust—give her a better one and she'll leave the old."

While he enjoyed speaking, Ezra didn't feel he was developing well along that line. At one meeting a woman fainted while he was speaking, and after another attempt he recorded that he was disgusted with his "frail attempt at speaking."

Despite such critical self-examination, one of Ezra's greatest mission experiences occurred when he and his companion, Elder James T. Palmer, were invited to speak at the South Shields Branch. "We have a number of friends who don't believe the lies being printed about the Church, and we feel certain we can fill our little chapel, if you'll come," branch leaders wrote.

The elders fasted and prayed about the meeting. As promised, the little chapel was filled to capacity. Elder Palmer recorded in his journal what happened: "Elder Benson was assigned to speak on the apostasy. . . . He mentioned that he was humble and nervous about speaking. But he was impressed by the spirit . . . and gave a strong and impressive discourse of the truthfulness of the Book of Mormon, never once remembering that his subject was to be of the apostasy."

Ezra later recalled, "I spoke with a freedom I had never experienced. Afterwards, I couldn't recall what I had said, but several nonmembers surrounded me and said, 'Tonight, we received a witness that Joseph Smith was a prophet of God, and we are ready for baptism.' It was the experience of a lifetime. The Lord sustained me. I couldn't have done it otherwise. It was the first experience of that kind I'd had, where I knew that the Lord was with me."[5] The inspiration to speak on the Book of Mormon would be a recurring theme throughout his life.

There were many spiritual moments in England. One day he told his companion he had the impression that his grandmother Louisa Benson had just passed away. Ten days later he learned that she had indeed died—at almost the exact hour he had received the impression. "The Spirit," he later preached, "is very real. Prayer is very real."

It could well have been providence that during Ezra's first month or so of tracting, he suffered no serious confrontation. While few people showed interest in his message, even fewer demonstrated opposition. But in mid-November 1921 his fortunes began to change. Tracting in an affluent area, he found the people "bitter and narrowminded." Two days later he ran into some "hot people and was told to go to hell."

The missionary harvest was painstakingly slow, though occasionally it bore fruit. On December 18 he spoke on the Resurrection at sacrament meeting, with "a new investigator present, [a] result of my tracting." The *Millennial Star* reported that on September 29, 1921, Elder Benson and Elder Gray baptized and confirmed three individuals. Every person counted. Every visitor, investigator, or new member bolstered the ranks of the branches appreciably. Ezra recorded many meetings where attendance was sparse, such as fast and testimony meeting on September 4, 1921: "19 present. Two Saints bore testimonies."

The missionaries were responsible for much more than proselyting. Often Ezra and his companion were required to exhort the Saints, even call them to repentance. At a time when the Church was being badgered with criticism, some of its members slackened their pace. One evening he visited a family and "exhorted them to be more dutiful." He straightened out "branch squabbles," hunted up "backsliders," warned a sister to "cease her drunkedness," and had a long talk with one man about the harmful effects of tobacco. "Tobacco is a weed / the devil sewed the seed / It drains your pockets, scents your clothes / and makes a chimney of your nose," he wrote. To those who had difficulty giving up their tea, he quoted Doctrine and Covenants 89:3, teaching that the Word of Wisdom was adapted to "the capacity of the weak and weakest of all Saints" in the hopes that none would want to be classified in that category.[6]

While his focus in England was missionary work, Ezra's interests evidenced breadth and depth. He seemed aware of current and world events, making frequent note in his journal of elections, athletic events, and other happenings. On Saturdays, when time permitted, he and his companion discarded their "iron horses," as they called their bicycles, and walked through the countryside, stopping to visit branch members. Their principal means of travel was by bicycle, and Ezra wore out several pairs of pants and had to have them "reseated." It wasn't fancy, but in those days men wore coats that were a little longer than current fashions.

On New Year's Day in 1922, a Sunday, Ezra headed his journal with an enthusiastic, "Make it a banner year!" With five months' experience, no longer a newcomer, he was poised for more responsibility.

Opposition to the Church heated up in early 1922, owing in some part to the influence of the movie *Trapped by the Mormons*. The uneventful days of tracting were a thing of the past. On January 10, Ezra mentioned in his journal, without elaboration, the movie's author: "Winnifred Graham on our track again." Also that day he noted, "Ran into one of those birds that knows more about the Mormons than I did." The next day he was kicked out of one house, and a week later there were still "more stories of the terrible Mormons." On Sunday, January 29, someone attempted to break up one of their meetings. A week later he noted, "Tracting in South Street, women rather excited, afraid they're going to be taken to Utah."

One morning Ezra and his companion knocked on a door, and a woman answered. As soon as the word *Mormon* was uttered, her husband jumped up and joined her at the door. "Oh, I know all about you Mormons," he challenged. "When I was in the British Navy we sailed right into Salt Lake City port, and those Mormons wouldn't let us land."

The only area where Ezra seemed to make any headway was a poor section of the city: "Tracting in Union Street, one of the lowest in the city, people the best."

As the opposition intensified, Ezra kept good spirits, though at times he had to work at it. One Sabbath he took a stroll through the countryside while reciting from the poem "America for Me":

'Tis fine to see the Old World, and travel up and down
Among the famous palaces and cities of renown,
To admire the crumbly castles and the statues of the kings,
But now I think I've had enough of antiquated things.

So it's home again, and home again, America for me!
My heart is turning home again, and there I long to be,
In the land of youth and freedom beyond the ocean bars,
Where the air is full of sunlight and the flag is full of stars.

A series of one-liners in his journal indicates the challenges: "Cussed by a little 18 yr. old maid . . . tracting among the rich—enjoyed it in spite of their bitterness"; "detectives on our trail at present"; "two ministers watching us tract. ha! Rain and snow." Maids in some wealthy homes usually answered the door, and some subsequently accused the missionaries of trying to lure them away. An anti-Mormon lecture, "Inside of Mormonism," was held one evening while the Saints were holding an MIA meeting. "Town in uproar about Mormons. All of vast assembly voted to have us put out of town," Ezra wrote on March 30, 1922. He penned a rebuttal for the *Cumberland News* denouncing lies published about Mormonism.

Despite the rejections, Ezra kept his sense of humor ("Went tracting, was kicked out twice is all") and perspective ("Kids yelling Mormons! as we go down to church, but thank the Lord I'm one"). But conditions continued to intensify to the point where the missionaries even called on the police for protection. In April 1922, while trying to rent a hall for a meeting, Ezra lamented, "Searched in vain for a hall but no success. The world seems to be against the work of the Lord."

Opposition notwithstanding, some good came of the anti-Mormon tirades. The *Millennial Star*, reporting on a meeting held in Grimsby on March 31, 1922, noted, "It was the unanimous opinion that more good than harm was resulting. All the meetings are better attended than they have been for years past and many new friends are being made."[7]

On May 8, 1922, Elder Benson was called to serve as conference clerk and set apart by President Whitney. Later that week he moved to Sunderland, near the North Sea. As clerk, he oversaw distribution of the *Millennial Star* to members and handled all mission reports, including membership records that were in poor shape. On his first Sunday in Sunderland, May 21, Ezra was also called as branch president. Wearing at least three hats—as missionary, conference clerk, and branch president—the young elder found his days were hectic, the demands insistent. The morning after he was called as branch president, he had to settle a squabble with a branch member. He spent much time compiling reports, attending to local members' needs, organizing reports of branches throughout the conference, and tracting and holding cottage meetings. He spent days "punching the typewriter" and sending off "Stars" and "Juveniles," referring to the Church's *Millennial Star* and *Juvenile Instructor*. Many Church records were handwritten in pencil, and the tedious work strained Ezra so that he had to be fitted for glasses.

With responsibility come rewards, and Elder Benson had many rewarding experiences. On June 25, 1922, he took the ferry across the Tyne River to North Shields to visit Brother and Sister Horrors, arriving to find her "gone into a fit . . . gasping for breath and holding her hands over her heart as tho in great pain." Elder Benson blessed her that her health would be "speedily restored." Less than ten minutes later she was working in the kitchen. The experience left its mark on the young elder who wrote: "Is not God's power with the Priesthood in the household of faith? The honor and the glory be to Him forever."

Dates of note didn't escape Elder Benson's attention. On June 27 he wrote, "78 yrs. ago today, Prophet Joseph killed." On July 4, he celebrated Independence Day from a distance: "Wouldn't I like to be home today just to give one good yell!" Just ten days later it was a landmark of a different nature. "One year since I left the dear home in the [mountains]. Has been the most beneficial year of my life, because it has been spent in the service of the Master."

Nevertheless, the fruits of tracting and ferreting out investigators provided a meager harvest. By and large, the people were indifferent and bitter. Ezra kept himself going by "devouring the Book of Mormon," particularly the missionary experiences of the sons of Mosiah.

His record-keeping obligations as conference clerk were complicated by the fact that many Saints fell away from the Church or had been "lost" from the records, and over the years the records had become an entangled mass of confusion. "Still hard at the records day in and day out," he wrote. "Many are shown to have apostatized and many lost. Almost without exception, those marrying out of the Church fall away." Occasionally there was success, such as the day he exulted, "To my joy, found some of the lost members."

Elder Benson (seated, far right), president of the Newcastle Conference, is pictured with his mission president, David O. McKay, and Sister McKay, 1923

In November 1922 Orson F. Whitney was released as mission president and was succeeded by David O. McKay, also a member of the Council of the Twelve Apostles. President McKay and his wife, Emma Ray, along with five of their six children, settled into the mission residence, Durham House, in Liverpool. In addition to serving as president of the British Mission, he supervised the presidents of eight other missions—Swiss-German, French, Swedish, Norwegian, Danish, Netherlands, Armenian, and South African. Thus, with enormous distances to travel, the mission president had only semifrequent contact with the missionaries. Even so, President McKay was to have a profound influence on Elder Benson.[8]

On January 8, 1923, Ezra met his new mission president and recorded his first impression: "He is . . . truly a man of God. . . . He gave some excellent advice. He said for us to hold our own and fear not man. Go with head up, we have nothing to be ashamed of. The world steps aside for the man that knows where he's going." The young elder pondered that advice, believing it to be in perfect harmony with everything he had been taught, and he felt that he knew where he was going. However, an unexpected call from the new mission president a few days later stunned him, for he received a letter from President McKay announcing that he, Ezra, was being appointed as president of the Newcastle Conference, taking in all of northern England. "Never did I feel so weak and humble," Ezra wrote. "I felt weak because I know my inability and yet I felt thankful to think the Lord has as much faith in me and that he would entrust to my care the supervising of 8 branches of the Church, preside over some 600 saints and eleven elders."

Now the welfare of both his fellow elders and the Saints was his concern. He found himself consoling offended elders, spurring on negligent members, continuing his search for "lost" members, visiting scattered Saints, and conducting conferences. One evening he visited a Sister Taylor, who had been ill. She offered Ezra supper but had no butter for the bread. "Just as I was sitting up to eat a knock came at the door. A little boy appeared with a slice of butter," he wrote.

Antagonism toward the Mormons continued to hamper the missionary effort. In March 1923 Ezra tried to secure a hall in South Shields for a conference, "but was treated as an undesirable." President McKay wrote that "the bigotry of the people here is quite in keeping with the dense fog that hangs like a pall over Liverpool."[9]

On May 9 President McKay sent out a circular for all missionaries to Great Britain, calling them to repentance: "We regret to say that the reports of the month of April on the number of hours tracting are anything but satisfactory. Kindly urge your Elders to renewed activity in this labor." And further, "Keep yourself above suspicion, by avoiding the very appearance of evil, by leaving the young ladies absolutely alone. We must request Conference Presidents to report hereafter any and all infringements of this rule." He concluded with a fitting analogy: "A very large ship is benefited very much by a very small helm in the time of a storm, but being kept workways with the wind and the waves."[10]

Elder Benson took his leader's counsel seriously, and he was to learn to follow counsel precisely. Word came from President McKay that, because opposition had become so intense, tracting in some areas and all street meetings were to be discontinued until further notice. Before discontinuing, however,

Ezra and his companion reasoned that it would be permissible to conduct a street meeting already announced for the following Sunday night in Sunderland.

On Sunday evening the elders, dressed in black suits and bowlers, began their open-air assembly near the railway station in Sunderland. As the meeting progressed, attendance increased steadily. Some persons became rowdy, and when the pubs closed, a large group of men, many inebriated, swelled the audience. In order to make themselves heard, the elders turned their backs to each other and shouted their message. Some persons on the periphery began to yell, "What's all the excitement?" Others shouted back, "It's those dreadful Mormons." With increasing pandemonium, the shout went out, "Let's get 'em and throw 'em in the river!"

The elders became separated, with the crowd pushing Ezra down one side of the railway station and his companion down the other. As he was pushed along in a man-made circle some ten feet in diameter, Ezra began to pray silently for help. "When it seemed that I could hold out no longer," he reported, "a big husky stranger pushed his way through to my side. He looked me straight in the eye and said in a strong, clear voice, 'Young man, I believe every word you said tonight.' As he spoke a little circle cleared around me. This to me was a direct answer to prayer. Then a British bobby appeared."

The policeman escorted Ezra home with strict instructions to stay put. But when his companion didn't return, Ezra disguised himself in an old English cap and jacket and set out to find him. An onlooker who quickly saw through the disguise told Ezra that the elder's head had been "mashed in." Ezra started off in a sprint to find him and ran into the same policeman, who confirmed that the elder had had a nasty blow, but that he, the policeman, had helped him safely home.

"I went back to the lodge and found my companion disguising himself in order to go out and look for me," Ezra wrote. "We threw our arms around each other and knelt together in prayer. To my knowledge it is the only time in my life that I did not immediately follow the counsel given me by my presiding officer. It almost cost us our lives. Resorting to prayer in such a time of crisis was not born of desperation. It was merely the outgrowth of the cherished custom of family prayer with which I had been surrounded since earliest childhood."[11]

Perhaps because England was shrouded in outspoken resentment toward the Mormons, and hence its missionaries, President McKay expected members to aid the proselyting effort. In late 1922 he explained, in a conference in London, "The aim of the British Mission for 1923 . . . is that each member of the Church . . . bring at least one soul to a knowledge of the gospel." Later he wrote to Rudger Clawson, president of the Council of the Twelve, "Our aim is to have every member a missionary, not in the sense of leaving their homes or work, but in the sense of opening the way for elders." Thus the phrase "Every member a missionary" was coined. In conferences throughout the mission President McKay gathered enthusiastic support for the program. "President McKay knew how to reach people," Ezra recorded. "He had the confidence of every missionary in England. He was a great leader and a hard worker, and we in turn worked for him." Four decades later, at a dinner honoring President McKay's ninety-fourth birthday, Ezra would pay tribute to his mission president: "I shall never forget how he lifted us, how he inspired us, how we loved him, how we hung on his every word. . . . His wisdom to the missionaries was the wisdom of Solomon."[12]

Such spiritual boosts were important to the young elder, who by this time had aged beyond his years in maturity and wisdom. He continued to tract, to teach, to conduct conferences, and to exhort the Saints. His preaching was evidently effective, for even many years later some British Saints were referring to him as "our Benson."

On November 2, 1923, Elder Benson received his release. "I am a bit reluctant about accepting it as I feel there is so much to do in the field and so few to do it," he recorded. To a friend in the United States he wrote, "I certainly do loath leaving these dear good Saints. . . . Really it is the hardest part of my mission." The *Millennial Star* reported a farewell party given in his honor: "President Benson received many gifts from the Saints and Elders. He thanked them for their support and exhorted them to live the Gospel they had embraced. . . . The hall was filled with Saints and friends." The outpouring of affection from those with whom he had labored was intense and gratifying. Ralph Gray, a companion, summed up Ezra's mission twenty years later when he wrote upon Ezra's call to the Twelve: "True to your pattern, as I knew you in England, you have continued on with the same energy and loyalty to self and church that characterized your Mission Field Activities."[13]

Ezra's mission had taught him much. His knowledge of the gospel had increased greatly and his conviction that it provided the only way for a happy life was solid. He had survived intense opposition, finding an inner calm in the Savior and sense of purpose the only sure antidote. And he had had his first exposure to the international scope of the Church.

Ezra bid good-bye to friends in Sunderland and arrived in Sheffield in time to participate in a semiannual conference. From there he traveled with President McKay to Liverpool. En route, President McKay was pulled over by a policeman for speeding in a small English town. "President McKay was always at his best when he met with a bobby," Ezra remembered. "He said, 'Now officer, I know you're out here for our protection. And if I've done *anything* wrong, I'm in a repentant mood.' The officer chuckled and waved us off."

After his release, Elder Benson made a short visit to the continent. The occasion called for his first airplane flight, from London to Paris. There were just two other passengers. "After ten minutes the can was called for. We were all three sick while the Frenchman chuckled," he reported. He toured France, Switzerland, Germany, and Belgium. In Lausanne, Switzerland, where his great-grandfather had lived and preached prior to joining the Church, he enjoyed a reunion with his uncle, Serge Ballif, president of the Swiss Mission.

On December 2, accompanied by another elder, Ezra set sail for home on the *Metita*. They resolved to have scripture study each morning, but rough seas cut short their plans. "We lacked the desire to do anything but heave and reheave," he said. "First we think we're going to die, and then we're afraid we're not."

On Christmas Eve, after nearly a month of travel, he arrived in Whitney. The reunion with his parents was sweet. They sat up all night, filling stockings for the other children and gather-

George T. Benson Jr. (right) and his sons: from left, Volco "Ben," Ross, George, Valdo, Orval, Joseph, and Ezra

ing presents that had been hidden around the farm. Ezra remembered, "It was a choice evening. My love for my parents had never been quite so great." When his ten brothers and sisters arose early the next morning, he couldn't hold back the tears as he once again was embraced by the unity that prevailed in their family circle.

En route to Whitney, Ezra had stopped long enough in Salt Lake City to receive a blessing at the hands of the Church Patriarch, Elder Hyrum G. Smith. With his mission over, and sensing that his life was different than he had pictured it thirty months earlier, he wished for additional guidance. The Patriarch promised Ezra that his name, like unto that of his predecessors, would be held in honorable remembrance throughout the generations of time. And, perhaps in prophetic vision, Elder Smith counseled, "Be true to thy righteous convictions; be humble in thy devotion; shrink not from duty when it's made known, but keep thy trust in the Lord and thou shalt live even unto a goodly age to fill up the full measure of thy mission and creation."

*"Ours was a glorious courtship
during which I discovered in Flora
a rare combination of virtues."*

Chapter 5

Her Name Was Flora

After the holiday reunion with his family, made even more festive by the season, Ezra looked forward to renewing other acquaintances—in particular, with the girl he'd left behind. And on the Sunday following his return he had his chance.

In sacrament meeting, while Ezra was reporting on his mission, Flora unexpectedly walked in and sat in the back of the chapel. Temporarily flustered, he managed to regain some composure and bring his remarks to a close. The bishop then invited Ezra to return that evening to an MIA meeting and continue his remarks. Ezra eyed the girl in the back, preoccupied with their reunion. But before the "last word of the closing prayer had quite left the mouth of the benedictorian," Ezra wrote in his journal, "Flora, with her characteristic indifference in not wanting me to think she was chasing me, left the meeting." The congregation crowded around Ezra afterward to welcome him home, and it was an hour or so before he again spotted Flora.

Then, finally, the nervous anticipation of seeing each other was past, and they were laughing and enjoying one another's company as before. As Ezra was planning a trip to Logan the next day, and Flora had missed her ride back to Logan that evening, he volunteered to drive her home.

When David O. McKay had released Ezra as Newcastle Conference president and as a missionary, he had challenged the young missionary to return home, find a wife, and settle down. Ezra was smitten by the vivacious Flora Amussen and more than willing to obey his mission president's counsel.

The young woman who caught Ezra Benson's fancy was, by almost anyone's standards, a catch. She was popular, attractive, spiritual, and intelligent. She was equally comfortable with the homeless and with those of aristocratic bearing. And she came from a distinguished and faithful lineage, as did her farm boy suitor.

Flora was born in Logan on July 1, 1901, to Carl Christian and Barbara McIsaac Smith Amussen. Carl Amussen was one of Utah's first jewelers and watchmakers, a highly respected, influential businessman of the pioneer era. The third of four sons of a sea captain named Carl Paulus Christian Asmussen, Carl Christian Amussen (who later dropped the first *s* in his surname) chose not to follow his father's occupation and apprenticed himself to a master watchmaker, O. F. K. Peterson, in his native Kjoge, Sjaelland, Denmark. Peterson would allow no student his credentials until he had mastered the intricate art of handcrafting a watch. Carl wore the watch he made during his apprenticeship for many years, winding it with a tiny gold key.

After Carl's apprenticeship, the lure of adventure took him to Copenhagen, Paris, Amsterdam, and London, where he was employed by the watchmaker for Queen Victoria and Prince Albert. At one point he crafted jewelry for Czar Nicholas of Russia. His love of the sea ultimately took him to Australia, and after a disastrous flirtation with gold prospecting, he settled down to build a prosperous jewelry business in Melbourne.

Melbourne was a frontier city in a country that originally served as a prison colony, and Carl slept with firearms under or near his pillow. Few months passed that he didn't fight off thieves, and the strain took a toll on his health. In time his condition became so grave that an assistant checked on him several times a night to see if he had passed on. Carl wrote his parents, "I am still living. I have no pain . . . but am wasting away. . . . My only desire is that I might yet have the pleasure of seeing you all again and put into your hands the money I have made here."

Eventually Carl sold his business and shipped his gold dust and gold nuggets to the Danish mint, where it was minted into coins. At twenty-nine—single, affluent, but in broken health—he returned to Europe, where he spent three years recuperating and traveling. With his health regained, he was poised for a new adventure. He again sailed to the South Pacific, settling in 1857 in Auckland, New Zealand, a busy seaport on the crossroads of the expanding British Empire. Again his jewelry business prospered—but in New Zealand, he found even greater riches.

Inquisitive about religion, Carl had examined various sects and denominations, but none had satisfied his longings. One day, while strolling in Christchurch, New Zealand, he noticed a pamphlet on the sidewalk—*A Voice of Warning* by Parley P. Pratt. He read and reread it, prayed about it, and felt certain that the doctrines it taught were correct. The name of a church, The Church of Jesus Christ of Latter-day Saints, and an address in Liverpool, England, were stamped on the back. Assuming that Liverpool was the headquarters of the unfamiliar church, he left his business in the hands of an employee and departed for England.

In England Carl contacted the missionaries and learned more about this new church, and on September 29, 1864, he was baptized by Elder E. A. Groves. Carl's parents received the news with bitterness, mortified at their son's behavior. But Carl knew that the gospel was true, and he felt compelled to join the Saints in Salt Lake City. He left for America in 1865 and crossed the plains to the Church's headquarters in Salt Lake City. Because of his wealth, he traveled in style, accompanied by a cook and a driver.

The following year Carl returned to New Zealand, this time as a missionary, and in due time he disposed of his business and baptized seven of his friends. In response to a letter regarding opposition he was experiencing in New Zealand, Brigham Young replied, "The devil hates this work, and if he can influence the people by whom you are surrounded, you may depend upon it he will stir them up to anger against you. Every faithful elder has had this to contend with."[1]

Tradition has it that while Carl was returning to Salt Lake City, again crossing the plains, he met a young Danish convert, Anna K. Nielson, who proposed to him. Upon arrival, he requested an audience with Brigham Young and asked if he should marry the woman. President Young's two-part reply stunned Carl. First, President Young said he could see no reason why Carl shouldn't. And second, the President explained that men who were able to support more than one family were encouraged to marry more than one wife.

Carl also requested permission to purchase a lot on Main Street to build a jewelry store. Permission was granted, and in 1869 he had wagons loaded in St. Louis with slate shingles, plate glass windows and mirrors, and a generous supply of jewelry, and transported to Salt Lake City. The establishment he subsequently constructed, a two-story sandstone structure, was hailed as the foremost addition to the business district. (The facade of that building was still intact over a hundred years later as the entrance to a Salt Lake City bank. The plate glass mirrors that lined his walls later adorned the walls of the Salt Lake Temple.) Carl also helped establish ZCMI (Zion's Cooperative Mercantile Institution), the Utah-Idaho Sugar Company, and other enterprises in the fledgling territory.

Following President Young's advice, Carl married Anna Nielson on August 2, 1869. He subsequently took Martha Smith, a young woman from Tooele, Utah, as his second wife on November 6, 1884. The following year, on October 3, 1885, Carl was married to his third (and final) wife—Barbara McIsaac Smith, Martha's sister. They were sealed in the Endowment House in Salt Lake City.

Barbara found in her marriage to the kind and gentle Carl Amussen the stable, peaceful home life she had never enjoyed. Both her parents had embraced the gospel in their native Scotland and subsequently immigrated to Utah, where they met each other. Barbara's mother, Elizabeth McIsaac Smith, died when Barbara was two, and an older sister, Elizabeth, filled in as best she could until their father, Adam Browning Smith, remarried. The stepmother created an oppressive environment,

Carl Christian Amussen   *Barbara Smith Amussen*

and eventually the marriage ended in divorce—but not, however, before the sensitive young girl had gone through much suffering.

Times were difficult for those living the law of plural marriage in the 1880s; to elude federal marshals, they were often relegated to life on the underground. Before Carl married the third time, he consulted Anna about Barbara. Later Barbara related: "Aunt Anna had a beautiful dream. . . . She saw me married to [Carl] and the posterity that was added to his glory and his kingdom. When my husband asked me to be one of his wives . . . I hesitated." The decision to enter plural marriage was not an easy one, and Barbara prayed about it for some time. "Our people were sorely persecuted for this kind of marriage," she said. "Nevertheless . . . I had reasons to believe it to be a most sacred and proper thing to do."

As persecution against polygamy intensified, Carl relocated Martha and her family and Barbara in California. They didn't find refuge there, and eventually they moved to Vancouver Island in British Columbia. After three years of relative tranquillity, Barbara, at her husband's insistence, returned to Utah, where she took up residence in Weber County under an alias. In 1887 her first child, Victor, was born. Three months later she returned

to Canada with her infant, this time lodging with the family of
Charles Ora Card, founder of the settlement that ultimately
bore his name, Cardston. There she served as a counselor to
Zina Card in Canada's first Young Woman's Mutual Improvement Association organization. Over the next few years Barbara
endured a transient life, living in Canada, returning to Utah,
relocating again in California, returning to Canada, and making intermittent visits to Utah. She was frequently separated
from her husband, though over time she bore seven children,
one of whom died at birth.

When her baby died, Barbara felt deeply the sacrifices inherent in the polygamous life-style. Carl was in California at the
time, attending to Anna, who was deathly ill. His words of
comfort by mail didn't begin to assuage the hurt. He wrote: "I
had a couple of hours cry . . . fearing I might lose you also. . . .
Dear Barbara, I wish I could say something kind to you to
comfort you. I am so sorry for what has happened and sorry
that I should be away."[2]

But though plural marriage was demanding of its partici-
pants, and, Barbara said, she was "cruelly driven and persecuted" by enemies of polygamy, she always referred to plural
marriage as "that glorious principle."

Carl Amussen was always a dignified, aristocratic gentleman. George Albert Smith, who later became an apostle and
then president of the Church, remembered him as "perhaps the
most particularly dressed merchant in Salt Lake City. He wore
a black suit . . . of Prince Albert pattern, a white shirt and a
necktie which he tied around his collar. He always appeared to
me to be dressed to meet company. . . . He was the personifi-
cation of dignity."

John A. Widtsoe, who also later became an apostle, once
called on Carl Amussen for assistance in raising funds for a
ward building. "In parting [Carl] took out his purse, took out a
five-dollar gold piece and gave it to me as a contribution to
take to the bishop. I had expected a contribution of a dollar or
two. . . . With considerable pride I delivered the five-dollar gold
piece to the bishop." Some years later Barbara summarized her
husband's virtues in a journal entry: "What a noble man he

was. He expected strict obedience, but was very liveable, unselfish and sympathetic. Treated all alike, never showed partiality to anyone."

An avid horseman, Carl Amussen rode in a luxurious surrey pulled by a team of white Arabian horses in black harness. He also had one of the finest libraries and collections of oil paintings in the territory.

Carl Amussen was generous with his third wife. According to Barbara's youngest daughter, Flora, "My father would give Mother a certain amount each month to manage her family. She often didn't need it all. The second wife told her not to tell their husband because he would decrease her allowance, but Mother said she certainly would tell him. When she [did] he was so happy that he gave her twice as much because she had managed so well."

In July 1896 Carl purchased a fourteen-room home in Logan to house Martha's and Barbara's families. Before he purchased the home, he took both women to inspect it. While Martha complained about living so far from Salt Lake City, Barbara responded, "What a nice place. I couldn't say one word against it. How many would be thankful for such a home."

Such an attitude was reflective of Barbara Amussen's three-point philosophy about life: first, live the gospel; second, be loyal to your husband and be satisfied with what he can provide; and third, teach children to obey their parents. It was a philosophy that she ingrained in her children. The youngest child, Carl Amussen's last child, was born in Logan on July 1, 1901. Though frail at birth, the infant survived. Her name: Flora Smith Amussen.

By this time Carl's health had begun to fail. Flora was only fifteen months old when her father died suddenly of cardiac asthma on October 29, 1902. He was survived by fourteen children, forty-one grandchildren, and three great-grandchildren. Barbara was thirty-four years old at the time. Though her life with him had been interrupted frequently, she felt his loss deeply. Thirteen years later she recorded in her journal, "Before my husband died he told me that if I wished to marry again to do so. . . . I am not married again yet, and I don't think I will." And she didn't. Carl's business success enabled him to provide well for his survivors, and Barbara was left, by prevailing standards, a wealthy woman.

Barbara Amussen was deeply devoted to the gospel, her testimony nourished through lonely years living a principle that perhaps tested her spiritual mettle. And she was adamant about teaching the gospel to her children. In a letter to her son George dated February 2, 1916, she wrote: "You haven't said a word in your letters to me of going to Church. . . . When you spend six days in the week for your temporal welfare you certainly should be willing to get spiritual food one day in the week. . . . Don't you know how I long for your development in spiritual things as well as temporal ones?"

Charles Ora Card, in a blessing pronounced upon Barbara's head, said, "Thou art one of the chosen and honored mothers, and as reward of thine integrity the Lord will honor and preserve thy children down to the latest generation, and I bless you that you may enjoy wisdom in the rearing and instruction of your family. . . . Your children shall . . . vindicate the cause of good."[3]

Barbara didn't allow her abundant means to separate her from those whose financial situations were less generous. A close friend who worked with her for many years in the Logan Temple, Luella Cowley, wife of apostle Mathias Cowley and mother of another apostle, Matthew Cowley, said, "She was easy to approach, seemed to put people at ease. Although she was better off financially than most of us, you would never know it from her manner. She was content to live as the humblest. Her interests were in spiritual not material possessions."

Barbara attended the temple frequently, and on March 14, 1916, William Budge, president of the Logan Temple, called her to officiate in that sacred edifice. For twenty years, until July 22, 1936, she faithfully went every day the temple was open. In order to traverse the slippery snow-covered streets in winter, she had a blacksmith fashion metal "ice creepers" that fastened onto her shoes. Her diary entries often began with phrases such as this: "Another happy day in the temple."

One day in February 1933 she recorded, "Today . . . there has been a real blinding snowstorm. . . . And in spite of this stormy weather the Saints are coming to the Temple by the

hundreds both day and night and we are having four companies in the day and two at night which often brings the number
of dead endowed to one thousand or more in one day." On one
occasion, a fellow temple worker, Jan Molen, told her, "I saw a
most beautiful light over your head and your face was the same.
At first I thought it was the sun, but no, it was a beautiful light
that was more than mortal."[4]

In 1936 Barbara broke her ankle, and even after recovery,
she had difficulty walking. Mildred Evans, a close friend,
recalled: "When her health was such that she could not carry
her full share of duties, . . . she said it never indicated a true
love for the Lord's work when we continue to hold on to a position after we become incapacitated and others are required to
carry part of our load. . . . So she asked to be released [as] an
ordinance worker." Barbara did, however, tend children so their
parents could attend the temple.

Barbara loved the scriptures, particularly the writings of
Paul, who preached many character traits that she strived to
develop. Mildred Evans said, "Sister Amussen could apply herself to the rich and poor—the old and young. She knew just the
right thing to say to the sad and lonely, the sick, the lame, the
halt, the blind, the odd. . . . The Christ spirit in her sought the
Christ spirit in you."

And she loved life. At age sixty she invited friends to her
home to join her in exercising. "We had a jolly good time,
laughed and exchanged girlhood experiences," remembered Luella
Cowley. "She is the kind of person who is loved and remembered for the things she did. Her voice wasn't heard much in
public. She was quiet and unassuming, a true and loyal friend.
To have been one of her friends is a blessing."[5]

Barbara Amussen and her daughter Flora were very close.
Fourteen years younger than her eldest brother, Victor, and
three years behind the sister closest in age, Eleonora, Flora often
had her mother's undivided attention. Flora suffered several bouts
of serious illness, including scarlet fever and appendicitis, and
Barbara nursed her back to health.

Flora adored her mother, and as a teenager she vowed to
never leave her. When Barbara explained to her daughter that

*Young Flora
with her dog "Dash"*

she could not attain the highest degree of glory without celestial marriage, Flora replied, perhaps naively but with some insight, "Then I want to marry a poor man materially, but rich spiritually, so we can get what we get together." After a pause she added, "I'd like to marry a farmer." (Years later when Flora repeated this story to her children, her husband would add, "You not only married a poor man materially, but a man in debt.")

Flora's childhood was spent in relative prosperity. She drove her own car and played tennis on the court in the backyard. She and her mother traveled—to Chicago, California, and elsewhere—and she saw more of the world than many of her peers. But there were lonely times. When she was in her teens she was the only child still at home. With her mother working every day in the temple, she frequently had lunch alone at the Bluebird, a popular restaurant on Logan's Main Street, and rode the streetcar to an empty house after school. Always fearful about who or what might be lurking in corners of their three-story mansion, she would shout when she arrived home "Who's there? Get out of here!" She disliked coming home to an empty house and vowed she would avoid such a situation in her own family.

While Flora was a child, the stake patriarch visited Barbara Amussen's home to pronounce blessings on the older children. As he prepared to leave he noticed Flora, sitting in a high chair, and said, "I feel impressed that I should give this child a blessing." In this blessing he made the unusual promise that no man would ever deceive her. Even as a child, Flora exhibited discernment and keen instincts and compassion for people. Through the years this gift would prove an immeasurable blessing to her husband.

Barbara Amussen's home was a haven for children. Boxes of toys, dolls, and costumes were available for Flora and her friends. They were allowed to play in the living room, which was furnished with exquisite imported rugs and furniture, and a large sandbox and swings were in the yard. Hundreds of books lined the library, and Barbara loaned them freely. She believed home should be the principal training ground for a child, and that such training should be as enjoyable as possible. It was a philosophy that her daughter would subscribe to with her own children.

Barbara and Flora sang together in the Logan Fifth Ward choir. They also enjoyed attending the German dances at the Ninth Ward meetinghouse, where they waltzed and did the two-step. Not only did mother and daughter sometimes dance together (they were champion waltzers), but it was there that Barbara set an example of compassion for Flora. They talked with the immigrants, often took foodstuffs to those in need, and sought out the friendless and others who needed attention. Sometimes they took suitcases full of food and supplies to Barbara's father in Tooele. Flora remembers visits with the aged man and whitewashing the walls in his cottage.

Flora acquired many of her mother's traits, including compassion and the desire to mingle with persons from all walks of life. The farm boy Ezra Benson would later assess that she was "not stuck up, though she lived somewhat above the rest." Her open and unpretentious ways were endearing, and as she matured, she was popular among her peers. Because she was petite and attractive, friends nicknamed her "Dolly." But her mother insisted that she not respond to the name. At Utah Agricultural College she was, according to her farm-boy suitor, "the most popular girl on campus." "Oh, go on," Flora would protest, "you're prejudiced." "I may be prejudiced, but I'm also right," he'd answer. Indeed, Flora had many suitors, one of her professors among them, which Ezra considered "pretty stiff competition."

At the college the slender, dark-haired coed's interests were varied. She was an independent spirit, but she was also well-rounded in her interests. She was elected to the Periwig Club, the national dramatic society, and as a junior took the lead role of Viola in Shakespeare's *Twelfth Night*. The campus newspaper wrote on April 16, 1924, "Flora Amussen is a delightful Viola," and the college yearbook noted that she "carried her part to perfection."

Flora was a member of Sorosis, a social club, chairman of the junior prom committee, and president of the Girls' Athletic Club. An excellent tennis player, she won the university's women's tennis singles one year. The campus paper reported, "Flora Amussen won by defeating Miss Mabel Spaude, 9–7, 6–4, in one of the best contests seen on the courts." She also was elected studentbody vice-president. In announcing her selection, the campus newspaper said she was "one of the most popular girls in the school. She . . . says that we are certainly going to have [a good time] the remainder of the summer."

Many who associated with Flora insisted that her popularity was in direct proportion to her kindness to and willing acceptance of everyone. She herself said that any credit, if due, was owed her mother, who set the tone and direction of her life. Many years later, in a tribute, Flora quoted from a brother's letter to their mother: "I am so grateful I have been raised in a home with a foundation in spirituality—where everything that ever occurred, the question was asked beforehand, is it right? There I learned to pray in family prayer. There I learned the power of faith. . . . You always showed me the better way. How can I help but succeed?"

When Ezra returned from his mission and renewed his friendship with Flora, he was confident she was "just right." To make

Flora Amussen at a California beach (this photo is one of Ezra Taft Benson's favorites of his wife)

certain, he decided to get a second opinion from an expert—his mother. He and his mother devised a plan. Flora wasn't the only young woman interested in the handsome returned missionary: throughout his mission another girl had showered him with letters. The plan was that a friend would invite Flora and Ezra would invite the other girl to visit the Bensons in Whitney. When the foursome arrived, the senior Bensons welcomed them in. During the visit Ezra's brother Volco tripped in the family room, hit the floor hard, and started to wail. Flora immediately jumped up and consoled the boy, teasing him out of his tears by asking, "Oh, did you make a hole in the floor?" The boy stopped crying and all started to laugh. Later that evening, as the couples were leaving, Ezra pulled his mother aside. "How about it?" he asked. "Oh," she replied, "there's no question. It's Flora."

Sarah knew that Flora was the woman for her son—and her son, Ezra, knew it. His ambition was to settle down on the Idaho farm with a wife and to rear a family. Even Flora seems to have been agreeable. And at twenty-three, she was certainly of marriageable age. But in her judgment the timing wasn't right. She saw in Ezra Benson more than a hard-working farm boy who would stay loyal to the faith and make a fine father and husband; she saw potential that might not surface if he returned to the farm immediately. She didn't discuss her apprehensions with him, but "prayed and fasted for the Lord to help me know how I could help him be of greatest service to his fellowmen. It came to me that if the Bishop thought I was worthy, [he would] call me on a mission. The Church came first with Ezra, so I knew he wouldn't say anything against it."[6]

With unusual resolution, Flora talked quietly with her bishop. Then, a few months after Ezra's return from England and before he had formally proposed, she made her own announcement: She had been called to serve a mission in the Hawaiian Islands.

The news shocked Ezra. "I was ready to settle down on the farm," he recalled, "and I didn't have too much briefing as to why she was leaving. It was really tough. She was the light of my life."

Flora knew she was taking a calculated risk. Though convinced her boyfriend needed to finish his education and that both of them would profit by maturing spiritually before tying themselves down, she also recognized the possibility he might not wait two years. Flora never admitted as much, but she seemed to have had some premonition of the scope of Ezra's future, and she feared that if they married immediately, he would return to the farm and forfeit other opportunities.

On August 26, 1924, Flora and Ezra boarded the westbound train in Salt Lake City, and he rode with her as far as Tooele, where he said good-bye. He recorded in his journal, "We were both happy because we felt the future held much for us and that this separation would be made up to us later. It is difficult, though, to see one's hopes shattered. But though we sometimes had a cry about it, we received assurance from Him who told us it would all be for the best."

*"There are few things in the world
which give a man such courage
as the faith of a noble companion.
Flora had more faith in me than I
had in myself."*

Chapter 6

A Wait—Then Marriage

Separated from Flora by the Pacific Ocean and her call from the Lord, Ezra thrust himself wholeheartedly into farming. In the fall of 1924 he and his brother Orval consummated an agreement to purchase their father's farm, including the family homestead, for $17,000. Civic duties (George Benson was county commissioner, a member of the school board, and an executive of the Franklin County Sugar Company) demanded most of George's time, and Ezra and Orval, who had ambitions to become full-fledged farmers, saw this as their opportunity to launch into professional agriculture.

The brothers moved ahead with enthusiasm. They were progressive in their approach to farming and imaginative in marketing their products such as selling bottles of fresh milk with the slogan, "You can whip our cream, but you can't beat our milk."

"Father let us experiment," Ezra remembered of the days working under his father's direction. "We'd come home with some new idea, and whether he believed in it or not he'd let us find out if it was good or bad. Father was generous that way, more generous than we sometimes were with him."

Orval and Ezra agreed that their business would have greater chances of being profitable if they both got an education. During the nine months since he returned from England, Ezra had enrolled in only one semester at UAC, where he sang in the male chorus, played basketball, and joined a fraternity. But one semester had just given him a taste of higher education, and he longed for more. Orval also wished to attend college and serve a mission. They agreed to alternate semesters at school, and Ezra enrolled at Brigham Young University in Provo, Utah. His first semester was all he had hoped for. "I was moving ahead to be a farmer," he said, "and things looked favorable. I was getting the best technical knowledge available. Everything I'd wanted was coming to fruition."

That summer Ezra spent six weeks at BYU's summer school, held at the "Alpine School" in Provo Canyon. The students lived in tents and held "laboratory in God's great out of doors." With instruction by Dr. Adam S. Bennion, and a firsthand experience with the mountains, streams, and birds, it was, Ezra said, "all so unusual, so good, so beautiful." At the time attorneys William Jennings Bryan and Clarence Darrow were arguing the case of evolution in the Scopes "monkey trial" in the South, and this prompted open debate on science versus religion, which Ezra absorbed with interest. He strongly opposed Darwin's theory of species development and took that stand in his debate. Required also to write an essay entitled "Why I Am What I Am," he analyzed his life and the influences that had affected him, saying he received "all of the advantages of the training found in a good LDS home."[1] An occasional letter from Hawaii also helped the time pass quickly.

The following fall Orval and Ezra both attended BYU and "batched it," purchasing a Ford roadster to drive home for sugar-beet harvest. But the realities closed in. Farm life is a difficult taskmaster, and both finally acknowledged that one of them had to remain on the farm at all times. They agreed that Ezra should finish school, then run the farm while Orval went to school and on a mission.

Ezra returned to BYU, where, in an effort to graduate by the summer of 1926, he averaged twenty hours a quarter. Though his heart may have been in Hawaii, he also took full advantage of campus activities. He was elected president of the Agricultural Club, a prestigious organization since agriculture was seen as the profession of the future. He was also president of a men's glee club, chairman of the senior entertainment committee, and a member of the Mask Club. He wrote of an ice and snow carnival, canyon parties and studentbody dances, dramatic productions, and lyceums. All the while he was becoming a mature young man respected by his peers. As a returned missionary, he held an edge over those who hadn't experienced the personal growth, spiritual insight, and self-control a mission can engender.

While visiting Whitney during semester break, Ezra was driving along a gravel road one night when another old vehicle, lit only by carbide lamps attached to the hood, approached. The lamps were faint, and Ezra didn't see the car until he was nearly on top of it. Quickly he steered his Dodge off the road and landed on a railroad right-of-way. Mark Hart, the driver of the other auto, remembered that Ezra came over to him and, with unusual restraint, asked, "Say, what on earth are you boys driving? What kind of light do you have on that contraption?" Said Hart, "He should have been furious with us, but he just advised us to get our relic off the road before we killed someone, and then he left. He showed tremendous self-restraint."

On one trip home from college Ezra undertook an assignment from his sociology professor, Dr. Lowrey Nelson, to make a survey of his community, including the standard of living, number of homes with electricity, and percent of the population who finished grade school. After he made a verbal report in class, Ezra was asked to remain afterwards. Dr. Nelson quizzed him further and finally concluded, "I have made several studies of Mormon communities, but based on your record this is the finest community I have heard of in the intermountain area."

Ezra was pleased with the remark and with the A grade he earned in the class. With a major in animal husbandry and a minor in agronomy, he pored over the books. Often the questions he raised in class were prompted by current problems he and Orval faced on the farm. When the Agriculture Club visited Whitney to get a firsthand look at agriculture, Ezra was like a proud parent, showing off his acreage.

Banyan, Brigham Young University

As a senior at Brigham Young University, Ezra was voted Most Popular Man. This page appeared in the BYU yearbook

He had not allowed the social whirl to overshadow his motives for attending school. "The girls were always tagging us," he admitted. But, he added, "we clipped our hair so the girls would let us alone. We wanted to study." That strategy was apparently only partially successful. Toward the end of the school year Ezra was named BYU's Most Popular Man, an honor that no doubt flattered him but which he insisted was "all rather embarrassing though interesting."

After this social triumph, close friends wrote to Flora in Hawaii and begged her to communicate with Ezra more frequently or else lose him to another girl. But she persisted in writing him just once a month. Her peace of mind and faith were well founded, and she refused to be distracted. For his part, Ezra wasn't interested in the abundant social opportunities that came his way.

At one session of general conference during Flora's absence, Ezra encountered Elder David O. McKay and took the occasion to introduce his former mission president to his parents. Elder McKay immediately inquired, "Well, Brother Benson, are you married yet?" "No," Ezra answered. "It's this darn church I belong to. They went and called my intended on a mission to the Islands." Elder McKay immediately broke into a smile and in mock sympathy replied, "Well, isn't that too bad."

Actually, even Ezra would admit that the separation wasn't all that bad. Not that he cared any less for Flora, but during the twenty-two months of her absence both of them enjoyed significant personal growth. Ezra graduated from college while experiencing the stretching, fulfilling relationships unique to college life. And Flora put her future in the Lord's hands in order to serve a mission. (Years later her son Mark would evaluate the impact of that decision: "Mother's missionary experience had great bearing on her. She put the kingdom first. I've always felt her mission was part of the plan, not only so Dad would be required to wait a while for marriage, but also so that Mother would gain another spiritual dimension she probably wouldn't have acquired otherwise.")

Flora arrived in Hawaii on September 6, 1924, aboard the *S. S. Calawaii*. A throng of well-wishers, including mission president Eugene J. Neff and other Saints, crowded the pier as the steamer docked, and thousands of colorful leis were quickly draped around disembarking passengers. The lush tropical growth and climate were unlike anything Flora had imagined, and she found the abundance of delicious fruit and the friendliness of the people so much to her liking that she later claimed no homesickness.

The new missionary was quickly put to work. In addition to teaching investigators, she served in the mission home, planning meals and supervising the staff. And Flora had a knack for dealing with children. She could go into a group of rowdy children and quiet them immediately. On October 21 she was granted a license to teach English in the territory of Hawaii, and President Neff put her to work supervising the local Primaries and teaching in the elementary school in Laie, where she had children from seven nationalities in her classroom.

In general, missionary work in Hawaii was progressing favorably (the mission reported 455 baptisms in 1926), and President Neff described Sister Amussen as "a very good, energetic missionary."[2] She also worked in the Hawaii Temple and wrote home often to request that more family names be sent so she

Among her missionary assignments, Flora Amussen taught schoolchildren

could perform the ordinance work. One evening as she prepared to leave the temple after a day of officiating, she found that her associates had already left and she was alone. In order to get to the mission home, she had to hop a fence and pass by an immigrant workers' camp. The night was dark, and she was suddenly fearful for her safety. She knelt and prayed that she would be protected. When she left the temple door a circle of light surrounded her and moved with her over the fence, past the village, and to the mission home door. She felt strongly that the Lord had heard her prayer, and considered the occurrence a benchmark in her spiritual growth.

Flora loved missionary work and all that it encompassed—teaching children, serving in the temple, even supervising housework at the mission home. She sang solos in meetings, participated in baptisms for the dead, learned to speak some Hawaiian, even directed a Church play. In her estimation, all of these activities were integral to serving the Lord. An aunt wrote, "Your dear father loved [you] so much. . . . His greatest desire was that his children should grow up to be true and faithful Latter-day Saints. And whenever I think of you, I think of . . . the great joy you are giving him in . . . doing God's will."[3]

*Flora enjoys a lighter moment
while on her mission in Hawaii*

Back on the mainland, family and friends missed Flora. A
nephew, Billy Preston, wrote, "We sure miss you. It seems you
have been gone a year. . . . We are just fine but don't get along
half as well as if you were here." Ezra no doubt agreed with
that appraisal, though he wrote only once a month, as agreed,
and occasionally sent candy or other presents.

Flora had been in Hawaii for thirteen months when her
mother, who had been called on a special short-term mission,
joined her there on October 31, 1925. President Neff assigned
them as companions, and they rented an apartment on Beretania
Street in the heart of Honolulu.

Flora didn't wait for things to happen. She realized her mother
would need a way to get around easily, so when Barbara arrived,
Flora asked if she wouldn't like to purchase a secondhand auto.
"I wouldn't think of doing anything like that until I talked with
President Neff," Barbara replied. But Flora had foreseen her
mother's reaction and had obtained the necessary permission.
"If we can get one at a reasonable price, we will do so," her
mother answered. Flora had already scouted the city for such a
car, and three days after her mother's arrival, a suitable roadster was delivered to the mission home.

Flora and Barbara relished their reunion and subsequent
service for seven months as missionary companions. On December 12, 1925, the Hawaiian Mission celebrated its Diamond Jubi-

lee—seventy-five years since the first missionaries arrived in the Islands. Flora narrated an ambitious pageant, performed for an audience of some eight hundred, to commemorate the anniversary.[4]

When the Sisters Amussen encountered Tomizo Katsunuma, a Japanese gardener whom Carl Amussen had converted in Logan (and one of the Church's first Japanese converts in the United States), and learned that he had slipped into inactivity, they fellowshipped him and he returned to the Church.

Shortly before the end of their missions, Barbara and Flora toured the mission with President Neff, who also would soon be released. Of the tour Barbara wrote: "Every place we went, the Saints met us in large numbers. Their homes, automobiles and churches were at our disposal. And oh! how they decorated us with leis or wreaths of sweet fragrant flowers. . . . Such great love and hospitality, I have never seen!"

When Flora and her mother, with the Neffs, set sail for California on June 9, 1926, aboard the *S. S. Maui*, Flora took with her tender feelings for the Saints in Hawaii and a deeper testimony of the gospel. En route home President Neff dictated some of his final correspondence as mission president. In a letter to the bishop of Flora's home ward, he reported, "We know of no missionary who has ever come into the field [who] has given [her] heart and soul, time, and talents to the work of the Lord as Sister Amussen has done. She has won the love of many people, and has been the means of inspiring them to a bigger and better life."[5]

There was one young man back in Utah who was certain he would be inspired just to be with Flora Amussen again, though he insisted he wasn't "waiting" but was simply "anxious" for her to return.

Ezra graduated with honors from BYU the spring of 1926 (he was also voted the man most likely to succeed). His marks earned him a research scholarship in agricultural economics at Iowa State College. He had written Flora of his intention to go to Iowa that fall and strongly hinted he would like her to accompany him. She answered that he ought to hold the invitation until he saw her first.

When Flora returned to Logan in June, Ezra found her sweeter than he remembered, though her clothes were less fashionable than before. She had written from Hawaii, "When I come back I'll be thin as you were [after your mission], your suit shining like a dollar, and you looking like you had no pep. I'll be just the same. Please have patience with me." As predicted, Ezra teased her, "Honey, you are just exactly what you said you'd be." But that soon changed. He later added that "the other girls were modeling after her as they used to do."

Ezra and Flora were soon inseparable. "There was so much to tell and we seemed to enjoy each other so very much," Ezra said. It had been a seven-year courtship with four and a half years of interruption. Nevertheless, Ezra reflected, "It was a perfect courtship during which I discovered in Flora a great character and a rare combination of virtues. The competition at times was strenuous, but I was determined." Some who sensed that marriage was inevitable for Ezra and Flora wondered what the young socialite saw in the rough-cut Idaho farm boy. "Why, she'll always outshine him. He's only a *farm* boy!" was the sentiment commonly expressed in hushed conversations.

The young couple talked for hours, exploring their feelings about a future together. Ezra made Flora promise that she would be willing to spend her life on the farm. She announced her intention to turn the allowance from her father's estate back to her mother so she and Ezra could "get what they got together." The more they talked, the more comfortable they felt with each other. "T. was practical, sensible and solid," Flora said. "I wasn't looking for handsome, but I knew he was. He was sweet to his parents, and I knew if he respected them, he'd respect me."

On July 12, 1926, they announced their engagement. There was nothing intimidating about asking for Flora's hand. Ezra liked Barbara Amussen so much that he was often accused of dating Flora so that he could spend time with her mother. Barbara in turn had unusual respect and admiration for her daughter's suitor, and frequently marked scriptural passages that posed questions she assumed the returned missionary would be able to answer. Many evenings the three of them discussed religion into the night. (Prior to her death Barbara Amussen confided in a fellow temple worker that her son-in-law would one day be an apostle.)

Others weren't so sure about Ezra Benson. "Everyone was amazed when they heard I was engaged to this farm boy," Flora admitted, "and thought it would never go through." When one acquaintance questioned her decision, Flora was overheard to say, "This man I am marrying is a diamond in the rough, and I am going to do all within my power to help him be known and felt for good, not only in this little community but for the entire world to know him."

Ezra's first mission president, Elder Orson F. Whitney, was enthusiastic when Ezra wrote to tell President Whitney he was marrying the "finest girl in the world." President Whitney replied, "Allow me to congratulate you on getting the 'finest girl in the world,' and to commend your good taste in shooting so high and your luck in hitting the mark."[6]

Ezra was scheduled to leave for Iowa in late September, so there was little time to prepare for wedding festivities. With her mother's help, Flora hurriedly gathered a trousseau. Ezra worked on the farm up until the final week before the marriage, hiring his cousin William Poole and another boy to help him herd sheep forty-four miles from Grace, Idaho, to Whitney. It took them three days, walking and tossing pebbles at the sheep to keep them moving. "T paid me two dollars a day plus fifteen cents each for three candy bars," William remembered. "He agreed to pay all expenses. T kept saying, 'Hurry up, boys, I've got to get to Logan to get married.' "

On September 8, 1926, Ezra loaded his old Model-T Ford pickup with a half-ton box on the back filled with trunks, camping gear, and all of their belongings. Two days later he and Flora were married in the Salt Lake Temple by Elder Whitney. Sarah and George Benson, Barbara Amussen, and Ezra's brother Joseph witnessed the 9:30 A.M. sealing. "The wedding ceremony was too beautiful for words," Ezra wrote. "Everything went off so quiet and peaceful. . . . It all made us so thankful for the Restored Gospel and all that it holds out to us. Surely we had never been happier."

The newlyweds were honored at a wedding breakfast in the President's Suite at the Hotel Utah. In addition to family, Pres-

*Flora Amussen Benson
in her wedding photo,
September 1926*

ident and Sister Neff, Ann Dunkley, and Elder and Sister Whitney
were present. Everything went perfectly. Then, after one aborted
attempt, the couple managed to steal away. They took a guest
elevator up one floor, ran to a rear service elevator, and made
their way down to the back alley. There they hailed a taxi and
hurried to a relative's home on Sixth Avenue, where they had
parked the truck, hoping to hide it from those who wanted to
decorate it. They changed clothes and by 3:30 P.M. were on the
road, headed east toward Wyoming, their "cares behind and
[their] joys ahead," as Ezra wrote.

Most of the roads between Salt Lake City and Ames, Iowa,
were rough and often unpaved, which made driving the unpre-

dictable old truck an adventure. Too poor to pay for overnight lodging, they spent eight nights en route in a leaky tent. But to the newlyweds, the finest hotel might have offered splendor but no more joy, for they were finally together. Flora knew that her husband "didn't have the wealth of the world, but he had the more valuable wealth of character, industry, health, honesty, and a love of righteousness."

With plenty of time to reach Ames, they drove as far each day as suited them. Ezra's journal of the trip is filled with notations of climate, crops, livestock, and soil conditions. And now and again they noticed signs marking the trail of the Mormon pioneers. At Council Bluffs Ezra noted that this was the place his great-grandfather had been called and ordained an apostle.

Ezra's passion for the land is evident in his comments as he discovered in Iowa the simple checkerboard beauty of cultivated acres that stretched, in some cases, as far as the eye could see. "Iowa in the heart of the famous corn belt is an inspiration. . . . It was a beautiful sight to ride along the smooth clay roads, kept in perfect condition . . . with corn on either side and cattle and hogs in the ever green pastures. . . . House and buildings painted white and surrounded by green made a beautiful sight," he wrote. Several times they turned down the lane of a farmstead and Ezra asked the farmer questions about his crop rotation, management, and livestock program. "I was especially impressed with the businesslike manner of the majority of these farmers. Never did I find one who in any way apologized for his station in life," he wrote.

In addition to the sticky humidity of the Midwest, the trip afforded other inconveniences. One afternoon, while climbing a steep hill on a detour, Ezra shifted into low and "one of the magnets from the fly wheel came loose and flew thru the casing and tore things up pretty badly." They got a tow to the nearest garage, where a mechanic worked all day to get the vehicle running, finishing just in time for Ezra and Flora to make camp in a wooded area overlooking a stream. That night it poured and by midnight they were sleeping between soggy quilts. Recalled Ezra later, "I was so embarrassed! I never felt so sorry for my wife. The rain kept coming through and I worried for fear she'd catch cold."

By morning the rains abated, and they found that the river near where they had camped had reached its highest level in thirty years. The Ford wouldn't start, so again they had to be towed. Late that day they reached Ames, and by nightfall they rented a one-room unit in the Lincoln Apartments on Boone Street just a block from campus.

Their accommodations were humble. The cockroach-infested apartment had a bed in one corner, a desk in another, and a kitchen area so small "you had to back out of it." Flora cleaned the rug and put an insecticide powder underneath, but still the roaches came. They shared a shower down the hall with three other couples.

But Ezra was ecstatic. "I suppose that more or less every person gets a thrill of satisfaction when they start their first housekeeping," he wrote. "With us it was more instead of less. It soon looked like the coziest little cottage one can ever imagine. Flora is so cute and womanly in her management of the house. I wouldn't be single again for one million gold." Despite their modest dwelling, they invited Dr. C. L. Holmes, dean of Iowa State's Department of Agricultural Economics, to dinner and served the meal on a rickety card table. "Mother told me that no matter who you entertain, give them the best you have but make no apologies," Flora said.

Things were arranged nicely enough that when Orval Benson visited, he sent glowing reports back to Whitney. Margaret, who had not been able to attend the wedding, wrote to Ezra, "Orval told us what a nice little apartment you have . . . and he hasn't stopped raving about Flora's good cooking yet." She concluded, "T., we all think you surely have a wonderful little wife. We use[d] to think you couldn't get anyone good enough for you, but I think you['re] pretty well matched. We're all proud of you both and your good taste."[7]

Ezra quickly got situated in school, enrolling in courses in advanced farm management, economic geography, marketing, and statistics. Flora joined the faculty women's club and enrolled in home economics classes. The nearest branches of the Church were in Des Moines (thirty-two miles away) and Boone (eighteen miles). Five other Latter-day Saint families lived in Ames, and every other week they held Sunday School in one of the homes there. On alternate Sundays, Ezra and Flora attended one of the organized branches out of town.

Finances were tight. As promised, Flora had returned to her mother, who had fallen on difficult financial times, the monthly allowance she had been receiving from her father's estate. Ezra's scholarship gave them just $70.00 a month for living expenses, of which $7.00 went to tithing, $22.50 to rent, and $20.00 to food. In addition, he and Orval were still making payments on the farm. Thus, he and Flora could afford to drive the truck only once a week—to get groceries.

Ezra noticed that other graduate students often carried empty quart jars with their sack lunches. One day he saw a spigot in the dairy building with a sign that read "Free buttermilk for graduate students." Ezra disliked buttermilk, but as money was tight, he started filling his own jar and eventually came to enjoy the thick, creamy beverage. Students could also visit the college's experimental farm and glean such vegetables as hickory squash and turnips, and pick walnuts from trees in nearby pastures (which they always did on Mondays so their stained hands would be clean by Sunday). "Flora was a good sport," her husband recalled. "I was pleased with how she met the situation."

Life was not limited strictly to school work and financial survival. A few months after they arrived in Ames, Ezra suggested to Flora that they enjoy a game of tennis. Flora was willing. It was the worst beating he ever took. Flora had never mentioned to him that she won the women's singles tournament at UAC.

They also attended lectures, lyceums, and other free entertainment that the college offered. They decked out in tuxedo and gown for the President's Reception and the Inaugural Ball, but took in few of the football games, which cost four dollars. They read many books together, discussing and debating their contents. On Saturdays they scoured Ames for bargains. Other newlyweds expressed surprise at how much time the Bensons spent together, but there was nothing they enjoyed more than being with each other.

The newlyweds wrote often to their families in Logan and Whitney, and their mothers kept them apprised of events at home. When Ezra's brother Valdo needed counsel and Ezra supplied it, his mother expressed her thanks: "I am thankful for the wonderful letter you wrote Valdo, you always give such good advice it will be such a help to him, he thinks his big brother is a wonder." Sarah obviously was proud of her eldest son. On another occasion she wrote, "How dad and I do hope that all our children will have the same good reputation our eldest son has. You have been a dear good boy . . . [and] have caused us little worry. How we do appreciate and love you."[8]

Sarah Benson also supplied motherly counsel. "I am happy to hear you are both so happy," she wrote. "Well, why shouldn't you be? . . . I just know if you will continue to be faithful our Heavenly Father will bless you that your love for each other will grow stronger as the years go by. It is a sad thing . . . to see husband and wife grow more distant . . . as time goes on. Oh, what a sad thing!"[9]

The university atmosphere encouraged a tolerant flow of ideas, and on occasion the subject of religion was raised. One evening Ezra attended a dinner for graduate students at which religion and its impact on college students was discussed. He took advantage of the opportunity to tell of the influence the Church and BYU had had upon his life. The students organized a religious discussion group, with Ezra appointed as a committee member.

As their year in Ames drew to a close, Ezra took every opportunity to learn from agricultural experts who visited campus. He was fascinated with the marketing side of agriculture, a facet of the industry he felt was commonly ignored.

By May 20, 1927, he received notification he would graduate with honors and was being inducted into Gamma Sigma Delta, the National Honor Society of Agriculture. Five days later his thesis, "The Beef Cattle Situation in the Northern Range Area in its Relation to the Iowa Feeder," was approved, and on May 31, he took his oral exams, which lasted two hours. One can sense his relief at getting it all behind him. "It's over. After all the very long and weary hours of preparation, it was only half as difficult and nerve wrecking as I had it pictured to be. . . . A warm congratulations followed from all, and an announcement that I had made a very creditable showing. Then home to tell the news to my best gal," he recorded.

Dr. Holmes offered Ezra a teaching position at Iowa State, but Ezra was anxious to return to Whitney. On June 13, he paraded to the gymnasium on the Iowa State campus for commencement, where he was awarded a master of science in agricultural economics. Two days later he and Flora packed the old Ford, took a final look around their first home, and headed north toward St. Paul, Minnesota. They intended to take a scenic route home, touring through Minnesota, North Dakota, Montana, and Wyoming so that Ezra could evaluate agriculture of the northern Midwest firsthand. Again they camped en route and took in sights and looked up friends and relatives along the way. Occasionally they stopped at mission homes; in Valley City, North Dakota, they posed as investigators and had "a good deal of fun" with the missionaries.

Ezra observed the soil conditions, the ratio of pasture to cultivated land, methods of irrigation, the numbers of dairy cattle, the condition of farm homes and rural schoolhouses, and uninterrupted expanses of wide open spaces unlike anything in the West. "Every few miles one passes a white one- or two-room schoolhouse with two outhouses painted to match," he noted. "I was led to wonder where people came from to occupy these buildings, as often a home could not be seen in any direction."

In Cleveland, North Dakota, he put Flora on a train for Dickinson, North Dakota, some 217 miles away. Heavy rains had left the roads rutted and treacherous in places, and just prior to leaving Ames they had learned that she was carrying their first child. Ezra chose not to leave Flora's health to chance. As she left, he headed across country to meet her train that evening. When they were reunited, he recorded that they "were so happy to meet, as though it had been a week." From there they headed across the Dakota Badlands, made famous by Theodore Roosevelt, and Ezra continued to be solicitous of his wife, who didn't complain about the hot, dusty ride but who tired easily. They stopped often so she could rest. Two weeks later they arrived in Whitney to a loud and boisterous welcome from family and friends.

"I always wanted to marry a farmer," Flora said, "because I knew they had to work hard for what they got." Ezra responded to his wife's devotion. Perhaps he realized then the force she had already become in his life. Certainly later the impact of her influence became fully evident when he said, "As always she had more faith in me than I had in myself. It was her prayerful, quiet planning and inspiration, in large measure, that encouraged me to complete college and graduate study before settling down on the farm." But Ezra's view of the future did not seem as long-range as Flora's. Back from Ames, he reflected, "We were home, and we expected to spend the rest of our lives there."

*"I am grateful that my lot has been cast
in large measure with rural people,
and I thrill as I have the opportunity
of mingling with them, working with them."*

Chapter 7

Return to the Farm

In June, Idaho is at its best. The harshness of a bitter winter is forgotten; trout are running in the streams and rivers; ditchbanks are lined with wild yellow and red roses; and the air smells of sweet clover.

If home is truly where the heart is, there's no question that the twenty-seven-year-old Ezra Benson felt he was finally home. To family and friends, who couldn't recall knowing anyone who'd gone "back east" to college and earned a prestigious master's degree, he returned a hero, almost bigger than life. And life couldn't have been sweeter. He was home in Whitney with his wife; they were expecting their first child; and after on-again-off-again university work, he could get back into farming and make all his book learning pay off.

Though Flora was no stranger to many in the small farming community of Whitney, there were some who wondered if a woman reared in more luxurious circumstances could tolerate rural life and exist on a farmer's income. To Flora's credit, she adjusted to her new environment, living up to the promise she had made her husband before they were married. She was not a complainer and didn't feel sorry for herself when her husband left at sunrise and returned past dusk, nor did she moan about their lack of funds.

On that score, despite booming nationwide prosperity, farmers were in the throes of an agricultural depression. Prior to and during World War I, the American farmer had enjoyed a steady increase in real income. But during the postwar decade, times were lean. In 1919 gross farm revenues accounted for nearly 16 percent of the national income; ten years later that share had decreased to 8.8 percent, or nearly $6 billion less than in 1919.

In large part, the depressed agricultural market was an outgrowth of the war. Responding to a huge wartime demand for food, farmers had increased their acreage and output. Some mortgaged heavily to purchase land at inflated prices. Meanwhile, cumbersome postwar surpluses, abetted by an agricultural revolution that brought with it improved varieties of fertilizers, livestock, seed, and pest controls, dramatically increased per-acre productivity. In short, the market was glutted; the price of farm commodities fell; and many farmers could not keep up with payments on land, equipment, and even livestock.[1]

Ezra and Orval suffered from the trend. They had purchased the farm in 1924 while land values were still inflated, and they still owed money on their property. It had been difficult for them to keep current with interest payments, let alone reduce the principal. (By January 1, 1930, for example, butterfat sold for seventy cents a pound; within the year it had dropped to seventeen cents. The bank was forced to liquidate Orval's herd, previously worth $250 a head, at $35 each.) Ezra also owed money on his school loans. And on October 11, 1927, Orval was set apart as a missionary to the Danish Mission. Ezra was expected to help support Orval out of proceeds from the farm. In a letter from the mission field Orval joked, "Received your letter . . . with the check. . . . Hope things are going along alright for it looks as if you will have to keep me here for four or five years to learn this language."[2]

Despite their financial challenges, Flora insisted that they make it on their own without dipping into what little inheritance she had retained after marriage. "My wife seemed to care little for material wealth," Ezra said. "Her one ambition was to support me in my efforts to serve my church, my fellowman, and to rear an honorable family. Always she found time to be helpful to my brothers and sisters."

Though the farm home had running water and electricity, there were few conveniences—no overstuffed furniture, carpeting on the floor, or air conditioning. Flora scoured milk buckets, washed clothes by hand until they could afford a second-hand machine, and cooked for the large group of threshers hired to harvest grain. She managed the household on a meager budget, constantly supplementing the funds with foodstuffs from the garden or using recipes that made meals go further.

Ezra worked long hours with his dairy herd and in the fields, hoping to increase production and therefore some margin of profit. His brother Valdo moved in with them to drive the dairy truck, delivering milk they bottled on the farm. They kept a flock of 250 chickens, traded eggs for groceries, and slaughtered a hog each winter for meat. There was respectable production from field crops—sugar beets, alfalfa, and a little grain—though prices were low.

In late 1927 the birth of Ezra and Flora's first child loomed near, as did accompanying doctor and hospital bills. They sold a cow they had just paid for to raise money for the doctor. They planned that a Salt Lake City physician, Dr. Earl Skidmore, would deliver the child, and as the time neared, Ezra drove Flora to the Utah capital. But several days passed without the birth, and finally, anxious about things at home, he returned to Whitney. While he was en route, Flora went into labor, and he arrived home just as word reached him that Flora was in delivery. He hurried back to Salt Lake City and learned that he was the father of a baby boy, born on January 2, 1928. They named their son Reed Amussen Benson.

"There's nothing quite like the thrill of becoming a parent the first time," Ezra reflected. "You know for nine months it's going to happen, but there's no way to anticipate the feelings. I just couldn't believe we had a boy."

When they returned to Whitney from Iowa, Ezra and Flora were immediately put to work in the Whitney Ward. "T," as everyone still called him, became a member of the stake Young Men's MIA board, and a short time after her baby was born, on April 29, 1928, Flora was sustained as president of the

Whitney Ward Young Women's MIA. Ezra also had a chance to refuel his fire for missionary work. On November 27, 1927, while attending a stake priesthood meeting in the old opera house in Preston, his name was announced as one of those to be ordained seventies. When he joined the others for the ordinations after the meeting, Elder Melvin J. Ballard of the Quorum of the Twelve said, "Oh, you are not the Ezra T. Benson we meant, but I feel impressed to ordain you a seventy." As a seventy, Ezra got another taste of missionary work, and he loved it.

Ezra farmed for two years on his 160 acres in southern Idaho and despite the skimpy profits, his thriving Holstein herd was talked about for miles and his trim acres attracted the attention of the county commissioners. They were looking for a new county agricultural agent, connected with the University of Idaho Extension Service, an office financed cooperatively by the county, state, and U.S. departments of agriculture.

One afternoon the Franklin County commissioners stopped at the Benson farm to visit Ezra. They knew about his educational background and were familiar with the agricultural record compiled by his father. And they were hoping to hire someone native to the area. Would Ezra accept the job as county agent?

Ezra, flattered at the overtures, indicated he would be happy to consider their proposal. In the meantime, word of the conversation reached Dean Iddings of the University of Idaho, who was the director of Extension Services. He was happy to give Ezra Benson the appointment as a county agent, but policy prohibited any agent from serving in his own county. At that point, Ezra refused the offer. He was obligated to oversee the farm while Orval was in Denmark, and didn't feel he could move from the county.

Days later the commissioners were back at Ezra's doorstep. The dean had made an exception, and if Ezra would accept the post, he could not only serve in his own county but also maintain his residence on the farm.

The offer was tempting—but also distressing. Since boyhood Ezra had wanted to stay in Whitney and farm. Despite the hard work and discouraging economic factors, he loved the land. On the other hand, this job carried a salary of $150 a month, more than he was currently earning and enough to help meet some of his pressing financial obligations—education and farm debts, plus a growing family. It would allow him to pursue his interest in agricultural marketing with local farmers. Flora encouraged him, bolstering his confidence that he could fill the post well. Ezra decided to accept, but on one condition—that he move to Preston, the county seat, to avoid a potential conflict of interest. He felt that it wouldn't sit well with farmers if he were drawing a salary from the county and still farming. On March 4, 1929, he was appointed county extension agent of Franklin County, and soon thereafter he hired Kenneth Olverson to run the farm, with Ezra providing some supervision until Orval returned.

In Preston Ezra purchased a small red brick home that was in a preliminary stage of construction. By doing much of the framing and other labor himself, he obtained the dwelling, for thirty-three hundred dollars, complete with a small apartment in the basement that could be rented for additional income.

It took several months to complete the home, which was just as well. Flora was again carrying a child, and on May 2, 1929, she bore their second son, Mark Amussen Benson. Flora had always said she wanted a dozen children, but Mark's birth, just sixteen months after Reed's, was hard on her health. Nevertheless, she and Ezra were delighted with their small family, and by the time she came home from the hospital with her new son, the home was ready for the family.

The home, located two blocks east of the center of town, put the couple in the Preston First Ward. Again they became active in Church activities. Flora was called to the stake Young Women's MIA board, and Ezra, whose Scouting reputation had spread, was asked to lead the ward's senior Scouts on an energetic hike.

Ezra thoroughly enjoyed working with the Scouts, but he had almost as much fun serving as county agent. Though he had an office in the Greaves Building, next door to Sheriff Bill Head, he spent scarcely thirty days at his desk the first year there, preferring to drive around the county "helping farmers solve a hundred and one problems," as he put it. He talked

Ezra shows a Percheron stallion at a county fair while serving as a county agent in Franklin County, Idaho

with farmers, and then assessed areas where a hard-working county agent could make a difference. He put in long hours to get programs introduced and functioning, as well as spent time at his own farm. His skills of observation and organization were invaluable in developing programs and administering them among dozens of farmers with diverse operations and schedules.

"He sure was a hustler," recalled D. G. Eames, a Preston dairyman. "He really got around the county and looked after things. He once went with me to Bear Lake and helped me pick out some purebred Holsteins. That started me in the purebred business." G. L. Wright, later county commission chairman, declared after Ezra had moved on, "The county would sure like to have him back."[3]

By and large, local farmers had four problems: first, they weren't taking advantage of new agricultural technology and procedures; second, the marketing of their products was left largely to chance; third, some farms suffered from poor management; and fourth, many young men were leaving the farm, and Ezra anticipated a shortage of well-prepared young farmers a few years down the road.

Ezra began to respond to his observations with self-helps for the farmer. He selected "demonstration farms," where one particular facet of farming—for example, irrigation—was operating smoothly, and organized field trips for other farmers to inspect and analyze the procedures being used. On demonstration days, farmers even competed with each other in contests that included everything from livestock to per-acre yield. He also invited specialists in poultry, dairy, and field crops from the University of Idaho to visit the county, where he took them from farm to farm, answering questions and giving instruction as it related to each farmer's situation.

During his two years as county agent, Ezra became an agricultural jack of all trades. He found there was no systematic rotation of crops, and some of the land was infested with nematode because beets had been grown without rotation. Ezra taught the farmers how and when to rotate their crops, including planting sweet clover to revitalize the soil. He helped them arrange for bank loans and taught them how to do their bookkeeping, how to forecast expenses and revenues, and how to play the volatile commodities market. He also introduced improved varieties of grains, fertilizers, and pest controls. When he convinced six farmers to try Federation wheat, yields were so encouraging that most of the production was saved for seeding the county the following year. He led a campaign to rid the county of rodents and eradicate weeds, persuading a county commissioner to allocate eight hundred dollars for the project, and organized a county competition herd composed of some of the finest dairy cattle in the area.

In time Ezra won over some of the older generation of farmers to the progressive farming techniques he had learned in school. For example, when he promoted open shed barns for dairymen, a cost-saving measure, many older farmers resisted, insisting that cattle preferred barns. So Ezra engineered a demonstration. Feed was provided in the barn and in the corral near the shed, and both shed and barn were bedded well. In the morning every cow had left the barn and was resting under the shed.

During his second year, Ezra became actively involved in the 4-H Club movement. He wanted to get boys enthused about agriculture so they would want to return to the farm, and then know how to make a living when they did so. His results were beyond argument. Enrollment increased dramatically, from one hundred to nearly five hundred. The program grew so large that approval was obtained to hire an additional agent to work with 4-H Clubs. He also organized the county's first 4-H Club fair. Over four thousand turned out to see the exhibits.

As he moved throughout the county, Ezra became increasingly convinced that one of the great weaknesses not only in Franklin County but throughout the agricultural industry was the lack of marketing. Even great products didn't sell themselves—not at profitable rates. Working individually, farmers were totally at the mercy of the markets; but working cooperatively, their marketing opportunities increased measurably.

From childhood Ezra had been trained in the principles of cooperation. Many of the early Mormon settlements, including Whitney, were founded on cooperative techniques. As he observed what was happening in Franklin County, he became convinced that one of the most effective ways for farmers to sell their products, and at acceptable prices, was to join together in cooperative groups.

On a limited scale he put his ideas to work. His first attempt was a pig project, where he directed the farmers to pool their hogs and classify and size them according to breed. The quantity was larger than any one farmer's herd, and the hogs were better classified than they ordinarily would have been. Ezra had them shipped to California and sold for a better price than the going rate locally.

Utilizing the same principle with a different product, wheat, Franklin County farmers organized their own flour mill and bypassed the middleman who typically absorbed much of the profit. Ezra promoted formation of the Franklin County Grain Growers, which by 1930 produced 80 percent of the county's wheat. And he continued his emphasis on farm management, organizing a two-day economic conference for local farmers. Three hundred attended, of whom two hundred secured livestock loans.

In the second year alone, Ezra held 147 meetings, many of them at night. Though he lived in Preston and was beginning to keep long hours, he made time to frequent his parents' home in Whitney. Younger brothers and sisters looked up to him, and he was conscientious about this stewardship. His youngest sister, Sarah, who at fifteen years his junior had few memories of Ezra, was amazed when he stopped by the home one evening after she had been left behind when her friends went to a dance at the Persiana Ballroom in Preston. "I was sitting home practically in tears when Ezra came by and said he'd drive me to the dance. He did—took me in to make sure I met up with my friends, arranged a ride home, and then left."

In Ezra's nearly two years on the job as county agent, word of his programs spread throughout the state. As a result, on October 15, 1930, he was given a promotion as agricultural economist and extension specialist with the University of Idaho Extension Division in Boise. The appointment form on file includes this statement regarding his qualifications: "Mr. Benson has excellent training. . . . We are very fortunate in securing a man of Mr. Benson's qualifications for this work at a time when men with such qualifications are in great demand."

By this time Orval had returned from his mission. Trying to make ends meet on his modest salary, with payments on the farm and their Preston home as well as providing for the needs of a wife and two sons, was difficult for Ezra. The brothers determined it best to dissolve their partnership, and Ezra sold his interest in the farm to Orval.

Ezra and Flora's decision to move their family to Boise wasn't nearly as difficult as deciding to move to Preston had been. Boise was the state capital, and Ezra saw opportunities there that he would never have in Franklin County. The short time he had spent as county agent had raised his sights, so in late 1930 the Bensons moved to Boise, 180 miles west of Preston.

*"I had a firm philosophy
that you cannot help people permanently
by doing for them what they can
and should do for themselves."*

Chapter 8

Agriculture Specialist

The early thirties found the United States in the throes of the Great Depression. In the summer of 1932, when the nation's economy hit bottom, one-fourth of the working force was unemployed. Perhaps nowhere were conditions as strained as among the chronically depressed farmers. While farm output dropped only 6 percent between 1929 and 1933, commodity prices plummeted a startling 64 percent.

The situation throughout Idaho was no different. And as the economist/extension specialist hired to direct the marketing effort of the University of Idaho's Extension Division, Ezra Benson came face to face with the stark realities of local agriculture.

As he saw it, conditions had never rebounded from the post-World War I slump. Young men returning from war had found a shortage of jobs. Rather than let their sons sit idle, many Idaho farmers divided their homesteads, giving each son a small portion. Now few owned enough land or livestock to sustain life. As a county agent Ezra had lamented that the typical farmer owned only a few acres, four head of horses, six cows, three sows, three hundred hens—and had a wife and six children. Yet it was Ezra's assignment to help Idaho farmers survive. In his pivotal role, he had the potential of affecting half the population of Idaho. He welcomed the challenge.

Ezra was soon on the road, spending little time in his basement office in the State Capitol. He was critical of those who believed the country's farms could be administered from a desk in Washington, and he wasn't about to plan programs for people he didn't know or determine solutions for problems he didn't fully understand. As he drove from county to county, he encountered sobering scenarios: farmers watching their life's work sold to the highest bidder in foreclosure auctions; granaries full of wheat and cellars filled with potatoes that weren't worth anything; farmers who were experts in the field and dairy, but strangers to a budget and uninformed about improved strains of livestock and crops.

And he observed situations that didn't make sense—farmers who raised grain yet scrimped to buy high-priced puffed wheat in a box; who bought the fruit the family ate rather than raising fruit on idle acres; who left valuable equipment outside to rust in winter without taking preventive measures. He cried with men whose homesteads had been in their families for decades and who knew nothing other than tilling the soil, but who couldn't afford to stay on the farm.

After his first tour of the state, Ezra came to appreciate more fully the Prophet Joseph Smith's counsel to the Latter-day Saints that men should be taught correct principles and then allowed to govern themselves. "I had a firm philosophy," Ezra said. "You cannot help people permanently by doing for them what they can and should do for themselves. I had to help the people stand on their own feet."

Based upon supply and demand, it was clear to Ezra that until crop surpluses were reduced, farmers would find no relief at the market. And the surpluses could be alleviated only if commodities were marketed more aggressively. Within his own domain, he attacked the problem areas vigorously.

Flora and the boys found they would often have to function without their husband and father, as the pressure and demands of his job took Ezra away from home nearly half of the time. For eight years he crisscrossed the state, giving demonstrations, speaking, conducting outlook seminars, and talking one-on-one with farmers. It wasn't uncommon for him to be away for two weeks, then return home just long enough to change clothes before going to a church meeting. Flora used to humorously say, "Well, when you are home, you're gone." She and the boys often stood alongside the track at the Boise train depot, waiting for Ezra to return. As a boy Mark had the impression that his father "moved fast. Whenever he was going anywhere, he didn't fiddle around—he moved. It taught us boys, subtly, that he was engaged in a good cause and was anxious to get the work done."

To Ezra's mind, there were few causes better, and his position with the Extension Division became more than a job. To really help the farmers, he had to gain their confidence and do what hadn't been done before—improve their situation.

Carol Youngstrom, then assistant agricultural economist and assistant professor at the university experiment station, remembered that "Ezra had the attributes required. He had the background and knowledge, but he also had the leadership qualities. He was a good extension economist. Among other things, he was confident and well respected among the people he worked with."

Hans C. Johnson sold farm equipment in the small community of Bancroft in Bannock County. One summer in the early thirties the county suffered a heavy infestation of ground squirrels, and Ezra Benson stopped to inquire about the availability of squirrel poison. Johnson's son, B. Clair Johnson, was in the store and remembers watching Ezra "stride confidently into my father's store. From a boy's viewpoint, he was excitement itself! He was perfectly dressed as a farm counselor and possessed an air of confidence felt by all who saw and heard him. His hi-top boots laced almost to the knee were, in the parlance of this day, the epitome of 'cool.' I was, as a young boy, so fascinated by his person that I paid little heed to his conversation with my father. He stayed only a short time, completed his business, and strode out as purposefully as he had entered. Somehow all assembled felt the truth of my father's words when he said, 'There is a young man who is really going places!'"[1]

Few who observed Ezra's obsession with getting relief to farmers would have disagreed. To accomplish this he became a combination teacher-administrator-analyst, preaching the doctrine of self-reliance as well as a variety of practical functions. He held classes from county to county, informing farmers on the outlook for prices and production and helping them determine how many acres to plant. He tracked the weekly market value of everything from eggs to apples, advising farmers when and how much to sell. He openly disagreed with New Deal farm measures, in which the government imposed price supports and production controls, but kept farmers informed on regulations and requirements for participating in subsidy programs. He traveled nationwide to study livestock marketing, helped farmers get loans, taught budgeting and financial forecasting, gave advice on crop rotation, interpreted government relief bills for farmers, and conducted farm management conferences. And he spearheaded or assisted with campaigns to develop markets for Idaho products nationwide, including an effort to make the baked Idaho potato famous on menus across America.

For farmers who had been purchasing puffed wheat, he calculated the savings in grinding their own for cereal. He showed farmers how to preserve their machines from rust by spraying them with crankcase oil, and teamed with engineers to instruct farmers in machinery repair. Ezra evaluated that "there were shortcuts that would save money in light of the fact that most had a minimum of cash in their pockets. Most farmers could be nearly self-sufficient, but were not doing so."

In time he became Ezra Benson the Expert, and local town newspapers chronicled his wide-ranging efforts. One paper noted: "Present relatively high beef prices probably will be maintained through 1938, Ezra T. Benson . . . predicted." The *Teton Daily News* of February 3, 1938, referred to him as one of several "prominent speakers" scheduled to participate in a community function.

When Roosevelt's New Deal promoted increased price supports and production controls through the Agricultural Adjustment Act in May 1933, it was Ezra's responsibility to administer the program, though he disagreed heartily with its premise:

that farmers would receive subsidies for reducing their herds or acreage. Millions of hogs were slaughtered and ten of the forty million acres planted to cotton were plowed under that year. Even Secretrary of Agriculture Henry Wallace, who concocted the scheme, admitted, "I hope we shall never have to resort to [it] again. To destroy a standing crop goes against the soundest instincts of human nature."[2]

The waste of food and fiber offended Ezra's sensibilities and was an outrage to his logic. "I never encouraged the farmers to join up, but I did explain the economics of the program," he said. However, when the hog program was announced, he opposed it openly, and the dean of agriculture called him in. "We had a friendly visit and talked for an hour," Ezra remembered. "I explained my philosophy, and he agreed with me. But he wasn't sure I should have been quite so vigorous in opposing it."

Ezra rarely toned down his comments, though he delivered speeches by the hundreds in churches and high school auditoriums. When the forecast for agriculture looked grim, he didn't try to mask the situation. In his 1938 outlook report, for example, he admitted that farm prices and the domestic demand for farm products were "the lowest since August 1934" with little hope for change.[3]

Though his message wasn't always positive, Ezra had wide acceptance. Dozens of Idaho's industry leaders acknowledged his influence, such as William E. Hess, vice-president of the Power County Grain Growers, who wrote: "[Thank] you for . . . your splendid talk at our annual stockholders meeting and picnic. Everybody I talked to said you hit the nail on the head."[4]

Through it all Ezra became convinced that farmers working independently of each other had no leverage on the market; but those who joined together, disposed of their crops in bulk, and exchanged knowledge and problems in a fraternal give-and-take atmosphere could accomplish much more.

The National Council of Farmer Cooperatives was encouraging the formation of state cooperative organizations nationwide, and by 1933 Ezra had done enough talking in Idaho to lead to the formation of the Idaho Cooperative Council (ICC), a federation of agricultural marketing organizations in the state.

The ICC's premise was simple: getting small cooperatives to work together under a unifying umbrella. His foresight in pushing for such an organization did not go unnoticed by national co-op leaders; only California had organized earlier. During the five years Ezra served as its executive secretary, the ICC became one of the most progressive organizations of its kind in the nation.[5]

In Ezra's judgment, the co-op concept made good sense. Farmers who were linked could pool their resources to purchase machinery at a discount, sell their commodities in larger quantities with increased bargaining power, buy fuel and other staples in bulk at lower prices, improve their marketing, and share industry knowledge. In addition, they could purchase stock in the enterprise and share dividends when the co-op turned a profit. Ezra's convictions about cooperatives became the stabilizing plank in his agricultural philosophy.

He helped organize small, specialized co-ops, such as the Idaho Potato Growers Association. Before he was through, hog producers, dairymen, and turkey and poultry growers had all organized. "We found that if we could discuss our common problems," Ezra explained, "it usually drew us closer together. We developed almost a fraternal spirit."

The practical results were measurable. Dairymen, for example, had their milk condensed and canned in Preston, then shipped to California, where it commanded a higher price. Though cooperatives had some struggles—jealousy and suspicion among members, and weak leaders at times—the net results in Idaho were positive. The results were, in all likelihood, indicative of Ezra's power of persuasion and his track record, which consistently worked in the farmers' favor.

Nevertheless, professional agriculture in a rural state always foments problems. In Boise Ezra had his first scrape with occupational opposition. With farming issues paramount in the minds of state legislators and other officials, almost any decision he made could arouse controversy. When he opposed the New Deal, some local Democrats were outraged; when he preached the view that the government didn't owe farmers a living, some Idaho farmers who depended on subsidies turned on him. After he published his findings on the effects of tariffs on Idaho agricultural commodities, a state legislator blasted him. Reed remembers his father, subdued and worried about the outcry, walking to the front door the next morning, with Flora at his elbow. After kissing and hugging her husband, she said, "Don't worry, T, you're right. Things will work out."

There were also colorful moments during Ezra's association with state officials. Idaho Governor Ben Ross enjoyed campaigning on agricultural issues, though, as Ezra said, "it wasn't the subject he understood best." Nevertheless, the governor was familiar with Ezra's accomplishments. During Ezra's stint as county agent, Ross visited Preston to dedicate a new dam. The services were held on the dam itself, and the governor spoke from a flat-bottom truck. Predictably he spoke on the agricultural potential of the Gem State, and, spotting Ezra standing in the audience next to the county sheriff, said dramatically, "I can see your county agent in the audience, the most valuable man in the whole county. If you can't afford a county agent and a sheriff, fire your sheriff and let the bootleggers loose." Ezra found it very embarrassing.

Ezra seldom slowed down. But when his mother's health started to deteriorate rapidly in early 1933, the worry almost overcame him. Sarah and her eldest son had always had an unusual bond. They had been each other's strength while George Benson served a mission. She had raised her other ten children to look up to Ezra. There was, she had quietly told her husband, something distinctive about their oldest boy. And how Ezra loved his mother! She was a stabilizing force in his life, a barometer and inspiration. In his eyes, she was without flaw.

When Ezra's younger brother George prepared to leave for the Southern States Mission, his father confided in Ezra that unless the Lord intervened, Sarah would probably not live more than a few weeks. As young George stood at his mother's bedside before leaving, she counseled, "George, no matter what happens at home, I want you to stay and fill an honorable mission."

On June 1, 1933, Sarah Benson died. Despite its inevitability, her death stunned her family. Before preaching a sermon at her funeral, Elder David O. McKay visited the Bensons. Ezra described the impact of his visit on the family: "Our father was bowed in grief, and ten children were weeping for the loss of mother. But he [Elder McKay] completely changed the atmosphere in our home. He literally lifted us and filled us with hope and assurance and had us counting our blessings as we attended the funeral of that angel mother."[6]

The following Sunday Ezra sang a solo in church, "O Mother of Mine." His cousin William Poole wondered how he could do it with so much sorrow. But from the time of Sarah Benson's death, Ezra gradually assumed more responsibility with the family. Margaret spent a lot of time with her father, who was heartsick at the loss of Sarah. In May 1934, following childbirth, Margaret was stricken with scarlet fever. On July 22 she wrote Ezra, "I was in such terrific pain and too sick to move. . . . Father sat by my bed with his head bowed for what seemed like hours, praying for my recovery. . . . I know I would never have walked, or been able to raise my head from the pillow, had it not been for the Priesthood."[7]

Then, just fourteen months after Sarah's death, Ezra's father suddenly became ill. By the time the doctor correctly diagnosed a ruptured appendix, George's condition had become critical. Margaret, still weak from her illness, visited her father in the hospital. "They needed someone to stay all night, how I wanted to stay with him, but he said, 'No my dear it would not be wise.' He had so much wisdom."[8]

On August 13, 1934, Barbara Amussen recorded in her journal, "We were made very sad when we got a long distance call from 'T' saying that his beloved father had passed away . . . and how sad to have mother and father both pass away while [young George] is yet on a mission."

George's death took his family by surprise, though he seemed to know it was coming. Before going to the hospital he drew up a will and consulted with the stake president on other matters.

More than a thousand people attended the funeral, at which Elder Melvin J. Ballard of the Council of the Twelve spoke. It was the largest funeral ever held in Franklin County.

The unexpected death of his father stung Ezra. From boyhood his father had been his hero, his model. There was no earthly person he wanted more to be like. The poignant circumstances took him back to the day some twenty years before when he had stood at the side of a dusty road and waved good-bye as his father left for the mission field. He remembered worrying that he would never see him again. But at least then, Ezra had had his mother to lean on. Now both were gone. The two people who had most shaped his early life had passed on. He doubted his life would ever be the same—especially as the head now of his family of ten brothers and sisters.

Pushing grief aside, Ezra corresponded immediately with LeGrand Richards, president of the Southern States Mission where George was serving. Ezra could only imagine how much harder all this must be on his brother. But Elder Richards assured him George was coping with the situation and counseled Ezra, "Now that [George] has no Father or Mother to write him it will of course be necessary that [you] write often to keep him encouraged. He must not be permitted to feel that he is alone in the world."[9]

George later told Ezra how much Elder Richards had done to salve his grief: "I'll never forget when Father died. President Richards came to Milton, Florida, where I was. As I met the train, I tried to think why he was coming to see me. . . . He came toward me and threw his arms around me and held me tight. And then he whispered to me of Father's passing. He insisted that I return to Atlanta with him, where I spent two glorious weeks."[10]

Despite the loss of his second parent in just a year, George completed his mission. Such family devotion to missionary work would later prompt Thomas S. Monson of the Church's First Presidency to say, "What else would you expect the outcome to be, with that kind of mother and father setting the example? The Benson family is the best example of missionary service which could be portrayed to the Church worldwide. We have none to equal it. Absolutely none."[11]

Nevertheless, all of George and Sarah's offspring had to cope with an emptiness. In a letter to his sister Louise, who was unable to attend the funeral, Ezra described the services and closed with words of comfort: "While Father has not left very much, fortunately I feel, in the way of material things, he has certainly left us more than money can buy, and the splendid life of service and integrity which he has lived is the greatest legacy which parents may leave to their children."[12]

It was a gospel-centered legacy that Ezra took seriously. Since moving to Boise, he had been deeply involved in the local Church organization. He had been called first to the Boise Stake's YMMIA board, and in late 1932, he was asked to serve as the stake YMMIA superintendent. Flora served on the stake YWMIA board, and their callings to work with youth suited the couple nicely. "The youth are our future," Ezra stated firmly, "and we placed great emphasis on them in the Boise Stake."

As in most generations, Ezra and his associates feared many young people were getting sidetracked, and they determined to provide quality activities to keep them involved. They held dances, such as Gold and Green balls, in the basement of the old Boise Tabernacle, and three-day fathers-and-sons' outings. Reed and Mark attended the campouts with their father. Ezra always provided a lot of infield chatter when he pitched softball. There were bow-and-arrow shooting matches, fathers versus sons softball games, peanut throws, and campfire programs, where Ezra entertained the boys with humorous recitations, such as "The Cremation of Sam McGee," led hearty rounds of singing (a favorite was "John Brown's Baby Has a Cold Upon His Chest"), and told stories about great men, heroes the boys could emulate. Mark and Reed looked forward to the outings with great anticipation, though Mark, who wasn't the healthiest child, nearly froze to death and inevitably returned home with cold sores from ear to ear. "Being with dad in the element he loved best, the outdoors, was worth it," Mark said.

Nowhere was Ezra's passion for youth more evident than in his work with Boy Scouts. From 1930 to 1933 he served as a Scout commissioner. He was one of Scouting's enthusiastic advocates.

As the little family grew in number, so did Ezra's pride and satisfaction. Five years after Mark's birth, the Bensons were blessed with a third child, their first girl. On June 20, 1934, Barbara Amussen Benson, a "lovely husky daughter," as her namesake called her, was born in Boise's St. Luke's Hospital. The delivery cost thirty-five dollars.

On January 13, 1935, the presidency of the Boise Stake was reorganized, and Ezra was sustained as first counselor to Scott S. Brown, with Mathias J. Benson (no relation) as second counselor. On the same day Ezra was ordained a high priest.

Because Scott Brown lived some eighty miles away in Weiser, Ezra carried a little more of the load than he might have otherwise. Typically, visiting General Authorities stayed with the Bensons in Boise, where travel connections were more convenient. The Bensons hosted many Church officials, including Rudger B. Clawson, Charles A. Callis, LeGrand Richards, Melvin J. Ballard, Rulon S. Wells, and Joseph F. Hardy. Flora's refined upbringing proved beneficial, for she knew how to make guests comfortable. From the beginning she counseled her husband, "You may invite anyone to our home that you wish, but when we serve meals the children will be allowed to join us at the table, not tucked away in the kitchen to get leftovers." Ezra agreed, and the children learned how to respond with guests present. Many visitors complimented Ezra and Flora on their well-behaved children.

Frequent visits from the Brethren led to memorable moments. One such occasion came in July 1936 when President Heber J. Grant and his wife stopped in Boise en route home from an Alaskan tour. The First Presidency had announced their intention to build a temple in Idaho, and stake presidencies throughout the state were hoping it would be in their city. "It was a big day for us to have the president of the church in our home," Ezra remembered, and news of the prophet's visit spread throughout the city.

That evening Flora had prepared a special meal and kept it waiting for President Grant. But, when the President arrived, he asked her if he might have just three slices of toast and a bowl of milk for supper. "I'll sit here in the breakfast room and eat while you put food on the table for the others. Then I'm going to bed. I know what's best for Heber J. Grant," he told her.

When he entered Ezra and Flora's bedroom, President Grant noticed a painting of Carl Amussen. "How did you become acquainted with this distinguished Danish gentleman?" he asked Flora. When she replied that he was her father, President Grant said, "You can't fool me! I knew that elderly gentleman as a boy." "Father was seventy-six when I was born," she explained, "and I was his last child." President Grant thought for a moment before saying, "That could be. That could be."

Just as President Grant was ready to retire, a knock came at the Bensons' front door. Fifteen prominent businessmen had come to pay their respects. Flora and Ezra hurried to find chairs for all, and President Grant joined them. The group's spokesman explained that the Boise Chamber of Commerce would donate any piece of land the Church wanted to build a temple. President Grant responded, "I'll make you a counter proposition. If all of you will join the Church and volunteer your services as missionaries, we'll build a temple in this valley as soon as the numbers justify it." Then President Grant prophesied, "Someday you will have a temple in this valley." (Ezra later said, "Flora and I kept that locked up in our hearts for years." The prophecy was fulfilled nearly five decades later, when a temple was dedicated in Boise in 1984.)

The Boise Stake was large in both distance and population. On June 30, 1937, the stake population was 7,651, and the needs of its people were widespread and diverse. Ezra continued to aggressively support the youth and was also sensitive toward those who weren't active. One experience is typical:

> We were trying to select a president for the weakest and smallest elder's quorum in the stake. Our clerk had brought a list of all the elders of that quorum, and on the list was the name of a man I had known for years. He came from a strong Latter-day Saint family, but he wasn't doing much in the Church. He would work on the chapel and play softball with the elders, and he did have leadership ability.
>
> I said to the stake president, "Would you authorize me to challenge this man to square his life with the standards of the Church and take the leadership of his quorum? I know there is some hazard in it, but he has the ability."
>
> The stake president told me to go ahead, and after Sunday School I went to this man's home. I'll never forget the look on his face as he opened the door and saw a member of his stake presidency standing there. He hesitantly invited me in; I could smell the aroma of coffee coming from the kitchen.

I asked him to have his wife join us, and when we were seated I told him why I had come. "I'm not going to ask you for your answer today," I told him. "All I want you to do is promise to think about it, pray about it, think in terms of what it will mean to your family, and I'll be back to see you next week. If you decide not to accept, we'll go on loving you."

The next Sunday, as soon as he opened the door I saw there had been a change. He was glad to see me, and he quickly invited me in and called his wife to join us. He said, "Brother Benson, we've thought about it and we've prayed about it, and we've decided to accept the call. If you brethren have that much confidence in me, I'm willing to square my life with the standards of the Church, a thing I should have done long ago. I haven't had coffee since you were here last week, and I'm not going to have any more."

He was set apart as elder's quorum president, and attendance in his quorum kept going up. He went out, put his arm around the inactive elders, and brought them in.

Years passed, and one day on Temple Square a man came up to me and said, "Brother Benson, do you remember coming to the home of a delinquent elder in Boise seven years ago? I'll never live long enough to thank you. I am now a bishop. I used to think I was happy, but I didn't know what real happiness was."

One of the stake's most dramatic changes came when it embraced the Church's new security (welfare) program. The Depression caught many Latter-day Saints unprepared. A 1935 survey revealed the distressing fact that nearly one-sixth of all Church members were receiving public relief. The welfare program was launched in April 1936 at general conference in Salt Lake City when the First Presidency outlined the principles of the new program: "Our primary purpose was to set up, insofar as it might be possible, a system under which the curse of idleness would be done away with, the evils of a dole abolished, and independence, industry, thrift and self-respect be once more established amongst our people. The aim of the Church is to help the people help themselves."[13]

Ezra was assigned to attend a regional welfare meeting in Burley presided over by Elder Melvin J. Ballard and Harold B.

Lee, managing director of the general welfare committee. What Ezra heard in Burley impressed him. Back home in a meeting with the stake presidency, high council, and bishops he said, "Brethren, this is economically, socially, and spiritually sound, and we want to get back of it."

But Ezra didn't realize how soon his stake would get involved. Not long thereafter, he received an urgent phone call from the bishop of the Emmett Ward, telling him that the previous night's rain had split the nearly ripe cherries and they would deteriorate quickly unless measures were taken. Ezra quickly organized volunteers to pick cherries, while Relief Society sisters gathered at the stake house to bottle them. By the end of that week the Boise Stake had sent thousands of quarts of cherries to the welfare storehouse in Salt Lake City.

This was just the beginning. Though Ezra found stake members generally "slow in getting on" with the program, in time they responded very well. Just two months after they first heard about the new program, numerous welfare projects were underway: one ward had planted a multi-acre garden, another had sown fifteen acres of sugar beets, and the Relief Society in another was canning food and making quilts and clothing. The Boise Third Ward even built a small cannery.

Two years later Ezra reported the stake's progress at a regional welfare meeting, attended by Harold B. Lee and Marion G. Romney of the general welfare committee. His report was impressive. Every Melchizedek Priesthood quorum in the stake had been involved. Twenty-five thousand quarts of fruits and vegetables had been processed, at least three cars of potatoes raised, two tons of dried fruit prepared, 450 bushels of apples gathered, and a large quantity of root vegetables, such as carrots and onions, raised.[14]

By September 1936, when Ezra took a leave to accept a graduate fellowship at the University of California in Berkeley, his impact on the welfare program and in other areas of the stake had been substantial enough that President Scott Brown refused to release him as his counselor, praising him later as having "filled every position of responsibility given him with honor and distinction."[15]

Despite his impact on Idaho agriculture, Ezra wasn't satisfied with his qualifications. At Flora's urging he applied for and received one of six fellowship awards offered by the Giannini Foundation for Agricultural Economics. "I have always felt education was an important asset," Ezra said, "and that this additional schooling would lead to greater opportunity. We expected to have a large family, and I wanted to provide for them as well as possible." On August 1, 1936, the Bensons moved to Berkeley, California in the interest of furthering his career.

As part of his course work at Berkeley, Ezra conducted the field work for a study on beef marketing, which took him from one end of California to the other. "I think I saw every slaughter and feed yard, every boat loaded with meat that docked," he recalled.

California was the most progressive state in organizing cooperatives, and Ezra visited dozens of cooperatives, sizing up their strengths and weaknesses. Avocado growers, orange growers, walnut growers—all and many more were functioning effectively. This broadened his vision considerably and put him in a position to meet with prominent leaders in the cooperative movement.

The statewide marketing study took Ezra away from class periodically, as indicated in his professor's remarks on an essay exam taken for Economics 209 on which he received an *A* grade: "Paper shows good grasp considering fact you had to be absent part of the time." It also revealed that, in a nutshell, Ezra understood the burgeoning agricultural problem and could express himself articulately.

The course work at Berkeley was demanding. "T is kept very busy with his school work," Flora wrote to her mother. "He gets up . . . at 5 o'clock and starts studying. Then he leaves shortly after and I don't see him until 6 o'clock in the evening and right after supper he is right at his studying again. . . . When Saturday comes he spends half of it at school. He [tries] once in a while to go [and] visit someplace of interest with the family."[16]

With Ezra studying heavily at his desk in a small office shared with other graduate students, and spending additional time on the road, the family spent many evenings and nights alone. It must have been a somewhat lonely time for Flora, who was now living in an unfamiliar city with only her children as company. She wrote to her mother often, thanking her for "words of encouragement and counsel." These letters no doubt focused on her loneliness.

But Flora forced herself to be independent. She was devoted to helping Ezra stretch himself to the limit, and she never regretted her role. In fact, she loved it. She lost herself in the lives of her husband and children. There were, of course, times when she struggled with rearing her children almost singlehandedly. In a letter to Ezra, she told how she had juggled finances to buy groceries when his paycheck didn't come on time and mentioned hiding Easter eggs for the children before admitting, "I don't know when I've ever felt so lonesome and just a bit discouraged. It seems I am such a flop."[17]

On another occasion Flora's letter was more typical, revealing her intense pride in her husband: "As usual the days seem like months since you left. . . . [But] if all men . . . loved and lived their religion as you do, there would be very little sorrow [and] suffering. . . . You're always so devoted to your family and ready at all times to give help to others in need."[18]

Overall, the nine months the Bensons spent in Berkeley were pleasant. For outings Ezra and Flora took the children on the ferry to San Francisco to visit Golden Gate Park. In early 1937, they learned they were expecting another child. Flora was so thrilled that she almost forgot her home- and morning sickness. The family also stayed close to the Church, attending the Berkeley Ward. Though Ezra was still officially a counselor in the Boise Stake presidency, the president of the Oakland Stake asked him to serve on the high council there. Flora was called to teach Primary.

In a letter to her mother dated September 5, Flora wrote that "T" had spoken in their ward's sacrament meeting, as well as in nearby Richmond, where he "spoke just grand." One Sunday the family attended a Sunday evening service in San Francisco, and during the meeting the bishop asked all returned missionaries to come forward. Flora and Ezra, with others, went to the stand, and the bishop called on several persons to speak. Flora wrote her mother about what happened then. "After all those had spoken he looked at T and said there is a man I want to hear from. . . . He said his [Ezra's] eyes have just been sparkling and he has looked so happy [and] enthused [and] interested. T got up and spoke very fine."

At the end of his nine months in Berkeley, Ezra requested a five-month extension of his leave of absence to complete his Ph.D. The application was denied, and in June 1937 the Bensons returned to Boise. Three months later, on September 20, their fourth child, Beverly Amussen Benson, was born.

The Boise Stake continued to grow. By early 1938 it had a membership of over eight thousand. In November of that year Elder Melvin J. Ballard divided the stake into three stakes, and Ezra was called as president of the Boise Stake, encompassing some 3,300 members in the Boise First, Second, and Third wards, the Glenns Ferry Ward and the Meridian Branch. He selected as his counselors Z. Reed Millar and Mathias J. Benson.

Though he had been warned by President McKay to expect a call such as this, Ezra was shocked when it came. Mark Benson, then nine, remembers the commotion the call caused at home. Flora gathered the children and told them their father had been called to be a stake president. Mark didn't comprehend the full significance, but he sensed "how pleased mother was and how anxious she was to share the news with us. She told us what a blessing it was for dad to receive that call."

As stake president, Ezra once again emphasized welfare and youth programs. He had an open-door policy with youth. Don Schlurf remembers trying to skip out with friends just before an afternoon session of stake conference. They started slowly down the hall toward the back door, keeping their eyes on the foyer to be sure their exit wasn't being detected. About then Ezra stepped out of his office, sized up the situation, and stretched his arms across the hall so that the boys fell right into them. "I'm so glad to see you boys," he said. "Let's go to conference together." He led them to the front bench, and later called upon them to bear their testimonies. Don never skipped out again.

Efficiency flourished under Ezra, whose penchant for organization quickly affected the entire stake. "No souls are saved after 9 P.M.," he insisted, instructing stake leaders to conclude meetings by that hour so that they could get home and see their children before bedtime.

As secretary of the Idaho Cooperative Council, Ezra was expected to attend annual meetings of the National Council of Farmer Cooperatives and of the American Institute of Cooperation (AIC). Gradually he attracted the attention of national agricultural leaders, including Raymond W. Miller, president of the AIC. An associate of Miller's repeatedly told him about the bright young marketing specialist in Boise, calling him "one of the coming men in America in the field of agriculture." Finally in 1938 Miller agreed to visit Ezra Benson in Boise. "He did not have much of an office—just a hole in the basement—but the charm and wisdom and dignity of the man made this visit for me one of the most exciting I had ever experienced," Miller remembered.

Ralph Taylor, executive secretary of the Agricultural Council of California, had also become acquainted with Ezra. As dean of state secretaries for the cooperatives, he invited Ezra to deliver the report of the state councils at an annual meeting of the National Council of Farmer Cooperatives. Ezra's presentation, said Miller, "won for him the respect of the delegates."

In the fall of 1938 word spread that the National Council was to be reorganized and that the position of executive secretary was likely to be open. The *Kiplinger Agricultural Letter* and other industry publications speculated openly about the appointee. Ezra Taft Benson's name was mentioned, but so was the fact that he had "no Washington experience." The *Kiplinger Letter* of August 6, 1938, categorically stated that "Dr. Benson" would not get the job.

Earlier that summer, however, Charles C. Teague, vice-president of the council and president of the California Fruit Growers Exchange, had approached Ezra about the position. Ezra had also visited with John D. (Judge) Miller, president of the council, and been candid about his priorities. "I told them plainly of my standards, activities in the Church, and advised them that any job which would involve the lowering of those standards would not attract me at any figure. To my joy and gratitude they approved my standards and indicated that one reason they'd come to me was because of my ideals." Ezra was offered the job.

Subsequently, a split developed in the nominating committee. Ezra withdrew his name from consideration, and during late 1938 he heard rumors that a new secretary had been hired. In the meantime he was called to be stake president, and he also received a salary increase from the University of Idaho.

As he left for meetings of the National Council in Washington, D.C., on January 8, 1939, Ezra noted in his journal that his family's future was in Boise. He had been stake president for little over a month, they had just painted their home and purchased a new lot, and they "felt settled for the future." He was surprised, therefore, when he arrived in Washington, to find that the nominating committee wanted to meet with him. Again he reviewed his religious affiliation, adding, "If this job in Washington will entail buying influence and goodwill by providing cocktails as a means of trying to gain influence, I'm not interested at any figure."

Judge Miller, ever gracious, responded to the frank young Idahoan: "Mr. Benson, we know all about your background and your principles. We've been checking you out for a year. You will never be asked to do anything that is in conflict with your standards. In fact, we'd be greatly disappointed if you did so."

Again Ezra was offered the post—this time at 25 percent more salary plus moving expenses. He declined to respond before conferring with Flora, Church leaders, and University of Idaho officials.

He placed the first call to Flora, and to his surprise she said that ever since he had left Boise, she had had a strong impression that they were going to move to Washington. She had even planned out their move. This settled the matter, and they agreed to permit Ezra's name to go before the meeting of the forty directors.

One of the directors, a Latter-day Saint, later told Ezra about the meeting, which comments Ezra recorded in his journal: "I could not hold back the tears as that group not only approved [you] but endorsed and commended the Mormon Church. . . .

One man said later, 'If you were to die tonight, your funeral sermon was preached in the meeting this afternoon.' "

Ezra also went to Salt Lake City to confer with Church authorities about the new job opportunity. "They were intensely interested in the entire matter and strongly advised that I accept," he noted in his journal. "Pres. McKay said the Church needed its people in such key positions."

With this assurance, combined with Flora's support, Ezra immediately made up his mind. "There is but one decision. We will go to Washington. I feel that the Lord has a hand in it, and the entire matter is a testimony to me that it pays to live Mormonism."

*"Life cannot be fully successful, no matter
what goals we attain in the material world,
no matter what honors of men come to us in our lives,
if we fail as fathers, mothers, and children."*

Chapter 9

Rearing an Eternal Family

Many of the qualities that took an Idaho farm boy
and fashioned him into an agricultural authority
of national repute—a deep trust in God, hard
work, an innate sense of values, and congenial
or cooperative living—spilled over into Ezra and Flora's home
life. Ezra found a sanctuary at home. "Some of the sweetest,
most soul-satisfying impressions and experiences of [my] life
are associated with home and family ties," he would repeat
hundreds of times.

In a favorite Edgar A. Guest poem, which Flora could still
recite with vigor years later, their philosophy about home life
was colloquially spelled out: "It takes a heap o' livin' in a house
t' make it home," the poem began. After thirteen years of marriage, Ezra and Flora still adored each other. There were the
inevitable money problems as they struggled to make payments
on Ezra's schooling and the farm, but they had little inclination
to quarrel, though they had frank discussions on many matters. Perhaps their biggest adjustment was coping with frequent
separation.

One Sunday while Ezra was visiting the Whitney Ward, the
bishop introduced him by saying, "Wouldn't it be wonderful if
we all had jobs like Brother Benson's. He travels this great state
of Idaho all the time." Just before that, Ezra had looked over

*Ezra and
Flora with
Reed,
Barbara, and
Mark in
front of their
Boise home,
1936*

the congregation and thought to himself, "Wouldn't it be wonderful to be home every Sunday with my family."

But with their own relationship providing a solid foundation, Ezra and Flora approached the task of nurturing their
family unit with energy and enthusiasm. Though their home
life was in some respects typical—budgeting problems, moves
and adjustments to new neighborhoods, illnesses, spats between
children—it was perhaps atypical in the intense unity and loyalty that prevailed. Ezra wasn't one to look for greener pastures
or to dwell upon regrets, and he taught his children it was best
to be happy where they were and with what they had.

Many visitors who observed the Bensons at home commented
on the friendly spirit in the home. After a visit in 1938, Flora's
half-sister, Julia Dalley, described them as "a perfect family,"

adding, "What on earth could be more ideal? I admire the simplicity of your mode of living but most of all I was impressed with the fact that in your home there dwelled the Spirit of the Lord."[1] Ezra and Flora worked hard to cultivate that spirit. The gospel set for them the standard for acceptable behavior and family priorities.

As with most families, the Bensons administered their share of discipline, but there was an open atmosphere in which expectations were clearly outlined. And the results were positive. Mark and Reed, though only sixteen months apart, got along unusually well. It was a relationship Flora actively fostered.

Almost from birth Mark suffered from severe asthma. Never as strong as his older brother, he was unable to splash in the shallow pool created when Ezra left the water running on their banked lawn, to run around the house, or to work outside with his father, without starting to wheeze and strain for breath. By age three he was well acquainted with doctors. One came to the house weekly to treat his clogged breathing passage. In his bedside prayers, Mark always remembered his osteopath, Dr. Anderson.

At age six Mark's condition became so serious that he almost died. Day after day Flora stayed at his bedside, applying mustard plasters to his chest and offering comfort. He wheezed so badly that he couldn't get his breath, and just when he would feel he might never breathe again, she would kneel at his bedside and pray. Relief always came. It was a constant, around-the-clock vigil that lasted for many years. There were good days, then bad days; weeks when he could play outside, then periods when he didn't leave his bed. During a visit to Boise, Grandma Amussen wrote in her journal, "Little Mark is not very well today. He isn't very strong, and the last two days he has been helping his daddy and . . . Reed . . . putting kindlings in the basement for winter. . . . We didn't take the necessary care in not letting him work too long."

Flora prepared special foods for Mark and nursed him conscientiously, but he felt that it was his mother's faith and prayers that made the difference. In a patriarchal blessing, he was promised strength of mind and body, and that he would "grow to be a stalwart, healthy man." Flora believed this, and she acted accordingly.

Many factors affected Mark's condition—weather, certain foods and pollens, and even the atmosphere in the home. Any quarrels among the children would set off an attack. Beverly remembers her mother quickly putting a stop to any bickering so that Mark wouldn't get sick. In particular, Flora elicited Reed's help. One day she said to him, "Mark does all he can to help, but he's not strong like you are, Reed. You and I might have to pick up the load and carry a little more responsibility, even if it means suffering in silence, but we can do it for Mark, can't we, because we want him to stay with us." In this and other ways Flora spent unusual time with her older son, hoping that he would then have a positive influence on the younger children. Even at a very young age, Reed was assuming a role of leadership among his brother and sisters.

Flora often told each son in confidence how much his brother loved him. The practice evidently paid dividends, for as unlikely as it may seem, neither brother later remembered ever arguing with the other. "Mother's attitude," Reed insisted, "created within me great love for my brother and a desire to work with her to protect him." Mark missed much of first grade, but on the sporadic days when he did attend, Reed stood by to defend him from the tauntings of classmates. He became Mark's hero, and over time they became inseparable.

Despite his frequent absences from school, Mark was an excellent student. His first-grade teacher, Grace Tucker, once gave him a book in which she inscribed, "To Mark, the student, the leader of his class. To Mark, the boy, his teacher's inspiration."

Such harmony set a pattern for the sisters who followed. Nevertheless, had Mark's health not demanded unusual cooperation among the children, it seems likely that Flora would have picked up the slack in other ways. She believed that home ought to be the place where children learned, developed, and had fun. Home was to be a sanctuary from the world. There were two vital areas—family loyalty and obedience—where she was emphatic. Both she and Ezra were firm about the children's not quarreling, stressing that they expected them to get along with each other. This was an eternal family unit, they emphasized over and over, and they wanted—and expected—no vacant chairs in the eternities. Even when the children were too young to appreciate the implications, the "no vacant chair" theme became part of their family culture.

Having spent much of her childhood alone, Flora felt strongly that children needed their mother at home—on their terms. Though in that day a relative few mothers worked outside the home, Ezra and Flora were particularly united in the view that Flora belonged at home. As an apostle many years later, Ezra would state emphatically, "One apparent impact of the women's movement has been the feelings of discontent it has created among young mothers who have chosen the role of wife and mother. They are often made to feel that there are more exciting and self-fulfilling roles. . . . This view loses sight of the eternal perspective that God elected women to the noble role of mother."[2]

In her own hand Flora wrote, "If you want to find greatness, don't go to the throne, go to the cradle. There is mighty power in a mother. She is the one who molds hearts, lives, and shapes character."

Flora felt strongly that she should be home when the children returned from school. She wanted to hear about their experiences, determine if they had had problems that day, and share in their achievements and sorrows. She explained, "If I'd gone to work I would have missed so much. You don't need the material things. The Lord will make it up to you in some way."

Of necessity, Flora became the anchor in the home. From the time the Bensons moved to Boise in 1930, Ezra's work took him away nearly half of the time, and Church obligations often took much of the time that was left. One Sunday as her father prepared to leave for an afternoon meeting, young Barbara stood on the front porch and exclaimed, "Good-bye, daddy. And come back again and visit us sometime."

Though Flora was often left alone with her small children, no child questioned her authority. "Mother taught us that the mother's role is to be strong and strict," Barbara said, "and that's what she was." When the need for discipline arose, she delivered on the spot, seldom choosing to wait until Ezra was home and the intensity of the moment had passed.

Reed described those uncomfortable times: "Mother had a way of punishing with the tone of her voice. When I did something wrong, she gave me a tongue-lashing with such power that I got physically faint and had to lie down on the floor. She was angry, though she didn't raise her voice. She let me know that she expected more of me. If I wasn't pleasing her, that was the punishment that hurt the most."

Physical punishment was rare. Neither Flora nor Ezra resorted to spanking very often. The discipline was more mental than physical. Reed explained, "Dad doesn't spend a lot of time regretting things. After you confess things and the problem is taken care of, he points your head to the sun." When a child had seriously misbehaved, the disappointment showed on Ezra's face, and he walked away, crestfallen. "That was punishment enough," Mark said. "I knew how important it was to my parents for me to do what was right, and none of us wanted to let them down. They always stressed there was greatness in being good."

Nevertheless, neither Ezra nor Flora defended or tolerated a child's behavior when the child was in the wrong. Once one of them took a classmate's pencil in kindergarten. The incident so upset Flora that when Reed arrived home, he found her in bed, physically ill.

By and large, discipline incorporated a denial of privileges. When Reed came home from school spouting a coarse word he had heard at school but didn't understand, Flora refused to let him see *Young Tom Edison*, a movie he had looked forward to seeing for weeks. Often when a child misbehaved, Flora sent him or her to the basement. The punishment was being isolated from the other children upstairs.

But punishment was meted out far less frequently than was praise. Praise struck a responsive chord in Flora's soul. She was an encourager, a supporter of anything praiseworthy. Even in later years, as the children left home, she would send them hundreds of letters full of compliments and inspiring stories she had heard. The positive-mental-attitude enthusiasts of subsequent generations would have paled in comparison to her homemade, albeit effective and enthusiastic, forms of encouragement.

The outlook on life that she and Ezra shared was positive. Their affection was open. Never did he leave for or return from work without kissing his wife and hugging the children. They both believed that it was hard for disharmony to brew if they never let a child leave home without a hug.

Flora carried the same open, positive attitude into other areas. Many days she prepared a concoction of milk and raw eggs, or orange juice, mixed with cod liver oil. She called her brew "the good drink." The children disliked it immensely, but Flora, convinced it was a deterrent to illness, prevailed.

On one occasion when Reed was performing in a piano recital at the Whitney Elementary School in Boise and having some difficulty remembering his piece, Flora called out from the audience, "Reed, you can do it. Keep going." When bullies from school waited in the ditch to harass him as he walked home, Flora advised, "The next time they try to hurt you, invite them home for watermelon." He did, and before he knew it, his mother had won them over to his side. She once wore an inexpensive brooch that Mark had given her for Christmas to a formal dinner. Mark didn't know if she wore it all evening or just when she left home, but it made him feel that he had given her something of value. When the children gave her cards on Mother's Day or small gifts for other occasions, she was effusive in her thanks but always added, "The greatest gift you can give me is to just be good."

If the children felt any resentment about their father's frequent absences, Flora quickly diffused it. Repeatedly she told the children, "Aren't we proud of our daddy, that he is helping the farmers." When his assignments were connected with the Church, she said, "Aren't we proud that our daddy is worthy to serve in the Church." When neighborhood children played outside on Sunday and the Bensons weren't allowed to, she explained, "Aren't we lucky that our family does things differently."

Constantly the children were told, "We're proud of you," "What a good job you did on that," "We have confidence in you," and the like. "Mother was never a faultfinder," Mark said. "I was disciplined, but never berated. She handled the situation when we misbehaved, but never in a way that took away our self-worth." Anything negative to be said to the children was discussed in private. Years later, when her children were older, Flora still took the same approach. She told one interviewer, "No one is perfect. In our family it is not our objective to magnify each other's shortcomings, but to encourage one another to improve."

Despite Flora's streak of optimism, the load was heavy for a woman who had four small children, one of whom was frequently ill, and whose husband was often away. Though none of the children remember her complaining, Reed sometimes found her crying while she ironed at night. He surmised, "I'm sure she was lonely for Dad, and perhaps worn out from working all day. But Mother was a natural motivator, a great encourager. We always had a sense that if Mother was behind us, we could do almost anything."

Flora's strategy built loyalty within the family. Home became the safety net. "I would have rather been home than anywhere," Mark said. "More than with friends or the Scouts. It was a refuge from the storm. Mother was the protective element, and Dad was there with his strength. When classmates gave me a bad time in school or I got a poor grade, I could go home, and there I was okay."

The children had disagreements, but never in public. Never did they criticize or belittle a family member in the presence of others. If a brother or sister ran into difficulty, the others came to the rescue. A pattern of the older watching out for the younger ones developed. Family came first. It was a theme that became a measuring rod for all they did. In later years Ezra would make an interesting comment, considering the breadth and scope of criticism he had faced by that time: "I think the one burden I could not have borne would have been a disloyal child."

Flora had a driving sense of purpose and allegiance. She felt that her greatest responsibilities were to encourage and support her husband, to rear righteous children, and to make home a haven that all wanted to return to. "Mother absolutely loved home," Mark explained. "And she loved us—not because it was her duty to, but because that was her life."

Flora took on her role with the zeal and aplomb of a chief executive. She felt that a woman needed to know how to shop prudently, feed her family properly, and keep a home clean and orderly—all of which were more central to family happiness than fine furnishings and expensive clothing. Of greatest importance was love—of the gospel, of family, and of work. "The home is the center of our mortal affections," she claimed. Accordingly, family members were to bear each other's burdens and inspire each other's ambitions.

Some may have felt that she and Ezra were overprotective. They carefully monitored their children's playmates, insisted that they know their whereabouts at all times, and required that they come home promptly from school. The children weren't allowed to see movies unless their parents had seen them or learned from reliable sources that the films were wholesome. And the children knew they must come running when they heard Flora's ear-piercing "family whistle," which could be heard for blocks. But Ezra and Flora's expectations had results. When Alice Marriott, wife of J. Willard Marriott, first met the Bensons in 1939, she thought they had the best behaved children she had ever seen.

Despite the rules, none of the Benson children felt that their home was a rigid, stifling place. Ezra and Flora selected their houses with care—first the seven-room house at 817 North 20th Street in Boise, with fruit trees, three screened porches, a large lawn, and sandboxes for the boys; and later a larger home on Owyhee Street on Boise's Whitney Bench, an acre lot complete with an expansive lawn, flowers, large vegetable garden, and swings in the backyard. Flora preferred that the children bring their friends home to play, and, following her mother's lead, she provided swings, sandboxes, and, when possible, a small basketball court for them. She wanted home to be more enticing than anywhere else.

Reed and Mark climbed trees around the house and played catch with their dad in the backyard. Ezra spent as much time with the boys as possible, often citing the story of a busy father who explained the hours he spent playing ball with his son by saying, "I'd sooner have a backache now than a heartache later." (In his day Ezra was a good baseball player. William Poole remembers a reunion in Whitney in 1935. During a baseball game at Willow Flat Diamond, Poole whispered to his wife that

Flora with (left to right) Mark, Beverly, Barbara, and Reed

if "T" could bat like he used to, the ball would go in the river. Just then Ezra hit a towering shot over the river into the weeds, and the game was stopped to find the baseball.)

The boys dug a pool in the backyard and filled it with muddy water. Ezra let them hollow out cucumber boats to sail down the irrigation ditch. When he flooded the front lawn with water, the boys lined up boxes to jump from. They built an airplane out of rough lumber big enough to sit in and made plans to sail it off a golf course hill, which Flora indulged but naturally never allowed to happen.

Flora and Ezra selected toys for the children that had some educational merit, such as erector and chemistry sets, books, Checkers and Domino games, and even a life-size tepee, which sat in the backyard for months. The children had a dog named Happy, a string of bicycles, and sleds during wintertime. On the Fourth of July, Ezra took the boys to Boise's "China Town" to purchase firecrackers, and Flora made root beer. For a while the family stabled ponies on their property, until they determined that Mark was allergic to the animals. Ezra did hang on to a chicken coop, and Reed has vivid memories of his father chopping off chickens' heads and placing the chickens in boiling water before plucking them.

Once a week or so, the family gathered for singing, games, piano solos, and stories. For part of the program the children entertained their parents with plays, and after Reed and Mark's version of "Cowboys and Indians" had been patiently endured for a generous amount of time, Ezra would ask, "Any idea, boys, when the fighting will end?" The whole family loved poems, particularly Edgar A. Guest's humorous rhymes, such as "Ma and the Checkbook" and "Ma and the Auto," which Ezra sometimes read to Flora while she did the dishes.

Flora placed good books around the house, even "planting" material geared for teenagers, with babysitters in mind, such as *If I Were Twenty-One*. Books on presidents of the United States, nature, and other topics were always available. The dinner table was a family forum. Ezra kept everyone posted on what he was doing at work. On Sundays they talked about the gospel. In fact, there were frequent gospel discussions. Though the family had no systemized program for studying the scriptures, Ezra and Flora read to them regularly, enough to give them a healthy familiarity with the scriptures. Barbara Amussen recorded, on one of her Boise visits, "We spent the afternoon reading the *Era* and other good books."

Ezra generally rose at five in the morning and worked for an hour or so in his home office, which he kept cool to stimulate his thinking. During the quiet morning hours, he scoured farm journals and magazines and material on current events and economics. When he was called as stake YMMIA superintendent, he undertook a program of regular scripture study.

Even on days when the children were sick, Flora had things for them to do, such as molding putty or papier-mâché objects while sitting in bed. She didn't like to see children idle.

Music was important to the family. In 1934 Barbara Amussen shipped her piano to Flora. Though Flora didn't read music, she played by ear and could accompany the family in "Springtime in the Rockies" and other favorites. Over the years various children took piano, voice, organ, art, dance, ice skating, swimming, and sculpture lessons. One summer Ezra took the girls on tours of various industries, including a local dairy, a soda pop bottling company, and a chocolate factory. He wanted them to see free enterprise at work.

Flora wanted the children to be comfortable in front of an audience. She taught them to raise a hand when volunteers were needed for talks, prayers, or school programs. They were to sit in the front row at school, if possible, and near the front in church, together. When a younger child was assigned a talk, Ezra usually wrote out a message and Flora took the child to the basement to practice. She sat on a chair and let the child rehearse in front of her. "When I gave a talk, the first person I looked for in the audience was Mother," Reed said. "And when I struggled and forgot what to say, I'd see Mother's head bow slightly. I knew she was sending up a prayer on my behalf."

Ezra and Flora were both hard workers. Flora prided herself in how long and fast she could work. Ezra, too, worked quickly, particularly on jobs he didn't enjoy, such as running the old Hoover vacuum. He didn't take much time off. Even on Saturdays he worked in the yard. He had a strong body and mind, and work gave him great satisfaction. When he was home, he made good use of his time. Particular about an immaculate yard, he and the boys spent Saturdays mowing and trimming, weeding and watering. They had a large garden in Boise, growing potatoes, watermelon, corn, many varieties of berries, and even peanuts, which everyone said would never grow in the cold climate. In the summer Mark and Reed went from door to door, pulling their green wagon full of fresh produce from their garden to sell. Their first summer they earned fifteen dollars which they split evenly with their father. Reed always enjoyed saying, "Dad was the first middleman I had to deal with." Ezra put his own share of the earnings toward mission funds for the boys. When Ezra left for work in the morning, he often gave the boys chore assignments to complete by day's end, and he would check them off when he came home in the evening. As the girls got older, they helped their mother: when Flora made a pie, they made small ones alongside her; when she dusted, they dusted. Sometimes the children fell short with their chores; other days they followed through.

Ezra also helped around the house, bathing the children, doing loads of laundry, and even washing dishes, though he had a reputation for leaving particles of food on the plates. "We'd say, 'Dad!' and he'd be disappointed that he'd have to do some of them over again," Reed recalled. Whenever possible, Ezra took one or more of the family with him on business trips.

When Mark became ill, Ezra took him to Salt Lake City to see a specialist, and despite his poor health, the trip was a highlight for Mark. "We stayed in a hotel and ate in a restaurant together. How fun it was to be with Dad, just him and me! We talked about anything I wanted to talk about. Even as a boy, I knew Dad loved me, because he was with me and helping me get better."

Extended family was very important, and several of Ezra's brothers and sisters lived with them at various times. Valdo lived with them on the Whitney farm for a year and spent another year with them in Boise. George joined them in Boise after his mission. Both Sally and Ross worked and lived with the Bensons in Boise for a time. Sally remembers Flora welcoming her with open arms and not getting flustered by additional mouths at the table. "She always wanted to have something tasty for Ezra T," she recalled. "He loved fudge, and those were in the days when you beat it by hand until it was creamy. Flora was very fussy. She'd have me beat it for hours."

From the beginning, Ezra enjoyed an amicable relationship with his mother-in-law. Whenever he drove to Cache Valley, he stopped to visit or stay overnight with Barbara Amussen, and often they talked into the night. After one visit she recorded, "We had quite a long talk 'til the wee hours in the morning, discussing the critical conditions that now exist all over the world."

Ezra was mindful of his widowed mother-in-law, whose financial reverses late in life forced her to take in boarders and cut corners to make ends meet. "Ezra . . . called on us today. He was on his way to Denver. . . . He fetched me a five gallon can of honey and a sack of dry beans," she wrote in a typical journal entry. In 1935 he supervised the remodeling and modernization of the kitchen in the old Amussen home in Logan, and Flora paid for the construction from dividends left by her father's legacy. "It has added greatly to the comfort and convenience of my apartment, and it never would have been so lovely if Flora and Ezra T. had not given such constant supervision," Barbara wrote. She kept Ezra's temple clothes laundered so he could go to a temple session whenever he was in Logan.

Following a trip to the East with Ezra in June 1935, Flora wrote her mother: "The first thing 'T' said when we arrived in Boise was call your mother and . . . thank her for all the sweet kind things she did. . . . 'T' thinks that you are certainly a wonderful example to follow. He is always saying, 'You are so like your mother, and certainly alright in most every respect.'"[3]

If Ezra felt Barbara Amussen possessed sterling qualities, he found that his wife embodied many of the same. Flora was a woman of unwavering faith. "When mother prayed, you knew her prayers were getting through the roof," Reed said. "She got very specific with the Lord in her prayers and talked out situations with Him; even as a little boy I felt that when she prayed for me, things would work out fine." He often looked throughout the house for his mother and finally found her in her bedroom on her knees. She would be praying for a child who had a problem or was facing something, such as an exam. She liked to be on her knees at the exact time the challenge was occurring. Family prayer was usually held at mealtime, where they turned their chairs around and knelt in family prayer at the table.

No detail was too small to take before the Lord. Flora's daughter Barbara remembered, "If someone else was leading in prayer and Mother didn't want something to be forgotten, she spoke right up and reminded the person to bless so and so. She believed the Lord was interested in every little thing that was taking place in our lives."

"Mother had more faith than any woman I've ever known," Mark said. "Faith in Dad. Faith in the children. Faith in the kingdom. Faith that the Lord would answer prayers. I've never seen more praying in my life. At the drop of a hat she'd be on her knees, praying for the children, whether it was about a test or a fight on the school grounds, it didn't matter. She and Dad both had that simple faith.

"When Dad knelt down to pray," Mark continued, "he didn't rush things. There was meaning behind his words. It came through loud and clear that he was communicating with our Father in heaven." In later years, the children reminded their parents that they prayed everywhere, even in the garage, to which Flora responded, "Of course I do. I pray wherever I feel like it."

With Flora's confidence in things spiritual came an abiding conviction that the gospel was all-important. If the children heard it once, they heard it hundreds of times that they should put their Church work first. Whether it was preparing a two-minute talk, going to meetings, or praying for Ezra when he had to speak, Flora's theme was "the kingdom first." Mark said, "From the time we were little, we saw Dad in leadership positions, and we were proud of him. But it was Mother who engendered a love of the gospel in our home."

When he was called as president of the Boise Stake in 1938, Ezra's family was young—Reed was ten; Mark, nine; Barbara, four; and Beverly, fourteen months—and his time at home was limited. "It must have been Mother who gave us a reassurance that Dad was where he'd ought to be," Mark said. "It's only in retrospect that I realize he was gone that much. It never occurred to me that some fathers were home more, and I didn't draw those comparisons. When he was home, it was great."

Things at home moved along even when Ezra was away. "That doesn't mean we didn't have struggles," Reed said. "We did. We didn't always get along. We didn't always do our chores. We tested Mother's patience to the limit at times. But, undergirding it all, was a sense of family unity that we were trying to pull together."

Over time Ezra and the children sensed that Flora had powers of discernment and often perceived when things weren't as they should be. She was a prolific note-taker, and as ideas occurred that might help her husband with a problem at work or a child who was having trouble at school, she jotted a note to discuss it that evening. Often the evenings found piles of notes in the bedroom or on the kitchen counter. She kept paper and pencil by the bed so she could jot down thoughts as they occurred during the night. She gave her husband insights on people he worked with and situations that weren't going well. He increasingly relied on her counsel. "I could see that I had a spiritually perceptive woman at my side," he said, "and I'd ought to listen." Sometimes he'd find notes to "Tell 'T' such and such" in his briefcase.

Flora was amenable to Ezra's direction in the home. But when she said she didn't *feel* good about something, he—and the rest of the family—paid attention.

"The word *feel* struck terror in me," Reed admitted. "That was the signal there was inspiration working. Mother may not have been always right, but the averages were on her side."

One day Ezra loaded Reed, Mark, and a neighbor girl in the car. Flora expressed some anxiety and lingered behind, standing in the road. Something didn't seem right. She watched as Ezra stopped down the road and let the girl out to cross the street to her home. The girl walked behind the car, paused, then dashed across the street just as another car darted up the hill. Flora, feeling uneasy, was still standing in the road and saw the accident take place. With Ezra attending to the girl, the boys hurried home and, at their mother's direction, knelt around the piano bench to pray. The girl's life was spared. "It was those kinds of experiences," Reed said, "that showed me Mother lived close to the Lord. Maybe it was just good judgment on some things, but I learned to honor her feelings."

In turn, Ezra was a support and strength to his wife. While on a short trip to Logan to visit her mother she wrote home, "One lady said I have never seen Flora look so well and happy before, and in order for her to look that way you know she must have a grand husband. I do appreciate and love you dearly 'T.' "[4]

One thing Flora felt strongly about was teaching children manners, which they had frequent occasions to practice, as General Authorities and others visited their home. The children could tell when a General Authority was a guest in their home, because Flora prepared creamed eggs on toast for breakfast, and for dinner, *bankekoed*, a Danish dish of steak and gravy seasoned with bay leaf. There was also fruit in Ezra and Flora's bedroom, which room they gave up for the visiting authority because it was the best they had. As soon as the official left, the children dashed into the room, hoping to find grapes or an orange left over. When Elder John A. Widtsoe of the Council of the Twelve came, Flora always had a box of candy to pass around after meals. "Sister Benson," he would say, "if you don't mind, I'd like another piece of that candy. I don't get much of this at home."

The children didn't get much of it either, for candy was expensive, health was important, and finances were tight, though the Bensons' standard of living increased during their years in Boise. At one point the family ate canned plums for months when Ezra found a good buy on the fruit. But perhaps more significant than surviving the Depression in respectable fashion was the impact Boise, with its opportunities and responsibilities, had on the young family. While they lived there, news of Ezra Benson's agricultural expertise had spread to Washington, D.C. Two daughters had joined the family. And all six Bensons had begun to enjoy a family culture built around unity and devotion to the Church, establishing a foundation upon which they could safely build.

"Though at the time I didn't understand the word, Dad was *tenacious*," Mark said. "He spared no energy to accomplish something he felt was right, whether it was for the family, the Church, or his occupation. And Mother was right there with him, picking up where he left off. She tied things together at home. She's the one who helped us understand where our loyalties should be—to the family and to the Church."

"It pays to live the standards of the Church and be true to the faith."

Chapter 10

Rise to National Prominence

At the end of a busy Sunday, on January 22, 1939, feeling confident in the decision to move to Washington, Ezra nevertheless lamented in his journal, "I wonder how we'll ever be able to get along without the good people of the Boise Stake." Five days later he notified Judge Miller that he accepted the offer to become executive secretary of the National Council of Farmer Cooperatives.[1]

Ezra's acceptance meant he must also resign as secretary of the Idaho Cooperative Council, and when E. S. Trask, president of the ICC, learned of the development, he wrote, "The resignation of Mr. Ezra T. Benson . . . will be considered by the members of the Council as a distinct loss to the organization. . . . We are positive that when our members realize he is no longer to be with us, the news will be received with keen regret. . . . He has always been true to the cooperative principle, and we bespeak for his future that he will go far in the cooperative leadership of our nation."[2]

On February 5 Ezra notified the high council of the Boise Stake that he had accepted the position, and the next day his promotion became public knowledge. He had not quite sixty days to culminate nearly eight years of activity at the extension office and effect a smooth transition within the Boise Stake. He and Flora also needed to sell their home in Boise and real estate holdings in Logan, and make arrangements for the two-month interim when they would be separated.

As confident as they were about their decision to move to Washington, it was difficult to leave Idaho. When he was released as stake president on March 26, he recorded that it was "the most difficult day I have ever experienced. . . . In my remarks I was greatly blessed of the Lord but had great difficulty controlling my feelings. There are no finer people in all the world [and] I love every one."

The stake held a testimonial in the Boise Tabernacle, which was filled to overflowing. On Ezra's last Sunday in Boise, the stake patriarch Mathias J. Benson conferred a blessing upon him in which he counseled Ezra to give freely of his time and means to forward the Lord's work on earth. Then he prophesied: "Men may try to persuade you to diverge from the course of right . . . but if you are humble and faithful before the Lord, they shall not have power over you. . . . Though you will have many perplexing problems and though there will come before you many things that will tax your judgment and ability to decide but yet, if you place your trust and confidence in the Lord, if you take your problems before Him, the solution will come unto you . . . and [you will have] no doubt as to the course that you should pursue."

Sleep would not come that night. The challenge ahead, he sensed, was enormous, the future uncertain. He was leaving a stable position in a state where he was known and respected, and joining an organization still in its administrative infancy. There were no guarantees. And he was uprooting his family and moving them three thousand miles.

But when he quickly sold their Boise home and three vacant lots they had purchased, he felt the Lord had opened the way. Just prior to the general conference in April, he said his last good-byes in Boise and headed for Washington, D.C., via Salt Lake City. "It was very difficult to leave my devoted wife and four children tonight for my new work in Wash. D.C. . . . The next 6 weeks we are to be separated will be long ones," he wrote in his journal.

He arrived in Washington the Friday after general conference. The next morning, though it was Saturday, he presented himself, with the anticipation of a nervous suitor, at 1730 I Street, headquarters of the National Council of Farmer Cooperatives, located centrally within comfortable walking distance of the White House. A letter from Flora full of encouragement was already waiting.

When Ezra Benson accepted his position with the National Council of Farmer Cooperatives, the council was celebrating its tenth anniversary; but though it was recognized nationally, it had not yet matured organizationally. Council staffing was minimal, funds for travel were insufficient, and the organization's influence was modest. In short, "the organization was anything but stable."[3]

The National Council was organized in Baton Rouge in August 1929, and at the close of its inaugural year, eighteen large cooperative organizations were listed as members. After a decade, some 4,000 cooperative purchasing and marketing organizations, representing almost 1.6 million farmers throughout the country and more than $1.2 billion worth of products annually, fell under the council's umbrella.

As executive secretary, Ezra functioned as the chief operating officer. He could not have foreseen how intimate his involvement with the highest levels of government would be. Still convinced that marketing was the key and cooperatives the vehicle to solving many of the farmers' woes, he would have preferred spending his early weeks in office assessing needs and determining areas where he could have the greatest and most immediate impact.

But the honeymoon was nonexistent. There was no luxury of easing into the job. Legislation that affected cooperatives was being introduced in Congress daily, and Ezra was thrust into the mainstream of agricultural politics. During his first full week in office he met with officials from the U.S. Department of Agriculture (USDA) and national farm leaders regarding a bill to amend the National Labor Relations Act; spent an uncharacteristic day in bed with the flu ("reckon I'm missing my wife"); lobbied against a bill to transfer the Cooperative Division of the Farm Credit Association (FCA) to the USDA because "some crack-brained attorney thot it'd be a good thing"; and hunted houses in the evening. At the end of his first week he wrote in his journal, "The job appears almost too large for me, but I expect to give it the best I have."

Ezra and Judge Miller, the council's president, enjoyed immediate rapport. An international lawyer of repute and dairyman from Susquehanna County, Pennsylvania, the Judge was considered dean of the farmer cooperative movement. On a subsequent occasion while visiting Senator Capper of Kansas, Ezra commended the Senator for passage of the Capper-Volstead Act (1922), the legislation authorizing farmers to organize cooperatives. Capper responded, "I just attached my name to the bill, and have been honored by so doing. The man who is with you, John D. Miller, wrote the act, prepared the bill, and saw it through Congress. To him should go the credit."

Ezra found his superior to be a man of intelligence and integrity. The respect was mutual. At the close of one annual meeting of the council, Ezra and the Judge relaxed after bidding the last delegate good-bye. Miller was fingering a cigar when he abruptly teased, "Ezra, you don't smoke, drink alcohol, use tea or coffee, or chase women. Just what is your redeeming vice?" (Several years later, at age ninety, Judge Miller indicated that he would like to travel one more time. His associates supposed he meant a trip to Europe and proceeded to dissuade him. Miller countered, "Oh, I'm not going East. I'm going West. I want to have one more good visit with my friend, Ezra Taft Benson, in Salt Lake City.")

Ezra's pace heated up, and during his second week he found himself on Capitol Hill lobbying, testifying in congressional hearings, and representing the interests of cooperatives regarding pending legislation. And amid it all he sandwiched in closed-door sessions with each member of the council staff. Hoping to head off the resignations that typically come with a change in command, he spoke frankly with each person, inviting each to voice concerns and ask questions.

Through 1939 Ezra's activities were manyfold. He represented cooperatives before committees of Congress, requiring him to be well apprised of numerous pieces of complicated legislation; furthered efforts to educate cooperative leaders nationwide about the agricultural outlook; prepared a monthly bulletin; and attended meetings throughout the country. He worked late into the evenings and most Saturdays, trying to get a grasp on what was an administrative juggling act.

Adjusting to his new post kept Ezra more than busy, but he longed for his family and spent what spare minutes he could looking for a home to buy or build. He finally located a comfortable home for rent in the Westgate section of Washington. Letters from Flora kept him going. "Received another lovely letter from my sweet and devoted wife," he noted after being away nearly a month. "Her unfailing loyalty is a great source of strength to me. It is extremely lonely here."

Though he had visited Washington many times, moving to the East was a culture shock, and he worried about the transition for his wife and children. "Coming here is a great change from Idaho. We will all have to make great adjustments, but the Lord will assist us if we do our part because His inspiration directed us here," he wrote in his journal.

Members of the Chevy Chase Branch of the Church at first seemed aloof, but they soon warmed up to the Idahoan, and before long he had met many who would become lifelong friends—Louise and Mervyn Bennion, Edgar and Laura Cowley Brossard, J. Willard and Alice Marriott, and others. They invited him to their homes, which relieved some loneliness.

Finally, on May 11 Ezra returned to Idaho to pick up Flora and the children. That weekend he spoke in a session of the Boise Stake quarterly conference, visited his former office in the state capitol, and helped Flora with final preparations. On Monday, May 15, the family boarded the train for Washington, D.C., occupying a drawing room and one lower berth. Three days later, at 8:00 A.M. on May 18, they arrived in Washington. After retrieving their baggage, they drove to their rented home, and by eleven o'clock Ezra was back at the office.

It was a volatile era for agriculture in America, and Ezra was immersed in the campaign to protect the interests of cooperatives nationwide. As executive secretary of the National Coun-

cil of Farmer Cooperatives, he was the authority on cooperatives, and he had to understand every phase of cooperative
agriculture well enough to defend and promote it. In the council's
1940 *Blue Book*, their annual report, he divided his
responsibilities into six areas: legislative concerns vital to all
co-ops, legislative activities pertinent to isolated co-ops, public
relations, field work, an information service, and bulletins. In
practice, his attention and energy were focused on two areas:
legislation and field work with local co-op officials.

The council itself employed standing committees on farm
parity, commodity exchange, land-grant colleges, legal and tax
problems, membership, production credit, and unfair trade practices. On any given day Ezra might cover half of these topics in
appearances before Senate or House committees or with other
key officials representing government agencies and even departments of the President's cabinet. Few days passed that he didn't
make appearances on Capitol Hill.

Ezra prepared voraciously for his encounters with congressmen. "I had to have the confidence of Congress, and I worked
hard at it, preparing as thoroughly as I knew how," he recorded.
One day he met for three hours in joint conference with representatives of farm organizations and members of the House of
Representatives regarding wage-and-hour legislation. He was
finding how political politics were, frequently recording his frustrations in his journal: "We had some rather weak and some
really fine men from the House in attendance. Political expediency and not service is paramount with some."

After subsequent meetings over the same bill, he noted with
disgust that one congressman, "because of backbone weakness,
refused to take the leadership in a continuation of the fight to
receive needed agricultural amendments. This would not be so
discouraging had he not promised to go ahead."

Ezra was dismayed when a man didn't stand by his convictions. And he became frustrated with politicians who looked
more to the next election than to the next generation. The tendency among politicians toward expediency and away from fiscal responsibility angered him.

Among other things, during his first year on the job he supported a federal seed bill and a fabric labeling bill that passed

the House; fought legislation seeking to change the definition of a "cooperative association"; and opposed a proposal to strip the Farm Credit Association of its autonomous status and transfer it to the Department of Agriculture. Almost overnight, it seemed, the fate of cooperatives rested in his hands.

The workload was unwieldy, the pressure intense. In late June, Ezra took Flora and the boys with him to New York City for meetings of the National Council's executive committee, which was composed of distinguished agricultural leaders. It was evident that these men, heavily committed in their own businesses, expected him to essentially run the council. "I feel the responsibility very keenly," he noted. "I hope I can merit the fulfillment of promises made me regarding this work."

While in New York the Bensons spent a day at the World's Fair. But even while relaxing, Ezra was preoccupied with matters of a larger scope. "The entire Fair is a marvel in the accomplishments of man and yet how little we know about the social, economic and moral problems of the nation," he recorded.

Back in Washington, Ezra increasingly learned how serious those problems were. On July 27, 1939, a day he called "my heaviest since I came to Washington" and one filled with conferences, long distance calls, telegrams, and hurry-up letters, he admitted, to himself at least, "Were it not because I feel our work is of great value to co-op marketing, it would be a dreary life."

But the principles basic to cooperation burned deep within Ezra. He saw them as a tool for the little man. Cooperatives, he was sure, helped the individual preserve and exercise his rights of free enterprise. It was an individual's God-given right to work and to have the freedom of choice.

This sense of purpose, along with his family, kept him going. During the summer, for the first time in eight years, Ezra had back-to-back weeks at home, something he enjoyed so much that when it came time for an extended trip in August, parting was "very difficult." But when he was discouraged or found himself standing alone on an issue, Flora was inevitably there, ready to back him up.

"Mother was a 'bucker-upper,' " Reed explained. "So many times I heard her say to Dad, 'I know you can do it. We're praying for you, T.' " And her role went further than an occasional pat on the back. Flora evaluated her husband's talks and advised him on parts that might better be left out. As the years went on, Ezra counseled with her more frequently. He learned, perhaps from sad experience, that her insights about people and events were usually right. Flora was a valuable counselor.

The family's first ten weeks in Washington together, though hectic for Ezra, were filled with family outings and decisions. Flora and Ezra softened the transition for the children, taking them to points of interest. On Memorial Day they toured the Smithsonian Institution and Arlington National Cemetery, and Ezra took Reed to his first Scout meeting. Another day they caught a glimpse of the visiting King and Queen of England, and other times they picnicked in nearby Rock Creek Park or at a beach.

Family home evenings were held frequently, with one child keeping minutes. A typical evening went something like this: a song by the family, minutes read from the previous meeting, a story read by Flora entitled "How I Became a Mormon," a scripture reading by Mark, a song by the girls, a clarinet solo by Reed, closing thoughts by Ezra on "The Meaning of Family Loyalty," and discussion of family problems. The problems discussed in this meeting included the decision on whether to purchase a dishwasher or recover the living-room furniture. The minutes recorded, "We all agreed to lighten mother's work, so it was decided we purchase a dishwasher now, but wait a while to recover the furniture. It was also agreed we would not take out membership in the Edgemoor Club [a swim and tennis club] unless the dues were reduced."

The children were consulted about major purchases, including the decision to build a colonial-style, four-bedroom home in Edgemoor, a section of Bethesda, Maryland, some eight miles from the council offices. The home was finished in one hundred days, and on September 29, after Ezra had checked every detail carefully, they moved in.

It wasn't long before the swing set and sandbox were in, a basketball standard set up, and a garden planted. At home the boys mowed, weeded, and took their turns with dishes. Ezra pitched in when possible, doing the laundry in the morning, vacuuming, and the like. With four children and a large new house, Flora carried a heavy load. In the fall of 1939 the Bensons learned another child was on the way, and Ezra was even more conscientious about relieving her when possible.

Because of his position, Ezra's family had many social responsibilities, and guests came for dinner often. Regardless of who was present, though, some things didn't change. One evening Judge Miller joined the family for dinner, and as Flora called everyone to the table, the children knelt around the table for prayer, as usual. Ezra invited Miller to join them, which he did. Barbara, age six, led in prayer, saying, "Bless Judge Miller that he will have a good time with us and return to his hotel safely."

Nothing was said about the incident. Some months later, while Ezra was attending conferences in Florida with Miller and thirty other industrial, business, labor, and agricultural leaders, the conversation turned to religion. Without warning Judge Miller recounted the evening he had spent in the Benson home. Referring to Barbara's prayer, he concluded, "Gentlemen, I have never had a sweeter experience in my life. I've often thought since that my children have missed something vitally important, and that probably [I am] to blame."[4]

"Dad used to tell us that prayer will keep you from sin, and sin will keep you from prayer," Barbara said. "And Mother prayed for us all the time—for recitals, exams, even for our friends. Some of my friends confided in Mother and Dad because they felt so close to them."

After the family moved to their home in Edgemore, Reed encountered trouble when a transfer student harassed him at school in the locker room of the gym. Reed responded by slapping the boy across the face. Students grabbed them both and took them to the gym teacher, who decided they would fight it out the next week in a boxing match with gloves and a referee. When Reed reported what had happened, his mother went to work. They bought a book on boxing, he worked out on a punching bag in the basement, and she coached him for a week. The day of the fight Flora fasted for Reed. As he left for school, she asked him when the fight would take place. She wanted to be in prayer at the exact time he stepped in the ring. Between rounds a friend, Roger Parkinson, read to Reed from the notes he had made from the boxing book, but Reed felt it was his mother kneeling in prayer that pulled him through. Round after round they went. Years later Reed would say he met the real victor when he came home that night and saw his mother. "When mother prayed for us, we knew things would be all right," he said. He won the match.

Ezra was rarely home for any length of time, but he took time for things that were important. "Dad was never too busy to talk with us," Mark said. "He often worked in his study early in the morning or late at night, but the door was always open." When Reed or Mark walked by, their father typically summoned them in and handed them a book or talk or some other document. "I'd like your opinion on this," he would say. "I'm thinking of using it in a speech." Often the materials were gospel-oriented; other times they were on freedom or love of country—even dating. "It elevated me," Mark said, "to think he wanted my opinion, and he'd ask questions about it later. Now I realize it was also his way of getting good material into our hands."

Because Scouting was a priority of their father, it became one for Reed and Mark, and earning their Eagle Scout awards was important. Each summer the boys attended the Boy Scouts' Camp Theodore Roosevelt on the Chesapeake Bay, and Ezra spent at least one weekend at the "Dad's Shack" there. The boys looked forward to these outings with anticipation akin to Christmas because they had their father to themselves. Other times they rose early and went to nearby woods to identify birds for a merit badge, or worked on other Scouting projects.

The older children were conversant with their father's work and interests. Ezra typically slipped articles into his briefcase to share at dinnertime. He marked articles in the newspaper every night, and it was Barbara's responsibility to cut them out. That spurred her interest in world events and politics, and years later she could remember talking about love of country and freedom from the time she was young. Ezra and Flora liked being the bearers of good news. They started the children collecting information and developing files at an early age. For a social studies

Ezra Taft Benson with sons Reed and Mark in their Scout uniforms, Bethesda, Maryland

class, Mark wrote an article on "Freedom for the Farmer" and defended it to his teacher.

Little time elapsed after their move to Washington before Flora and Ezra were again deeply involved in the Church. Flora was called as a counselor to Louise Bennion, the district Relief Society president, and Abe Cannon, the district president, called Ezra to the district council.

In an attempt to get better acquainted with the Saints, the Bensons held a few social functions at their home, where parlor games were played, along with table tennis and other activities. Flora was adept at getting everyone involved and enjoying themselves. Many would subsequently comment on the enjoyable time they spent in the Bensons' home.

In an area where a stake was yet to be formed, a former stake president was a valuable asset, and Ezra responded to numerous speaking requests. At President Cannon's behest, he prepared instructional materials for the district council and branch presidents on procedures relative to selecting local Church officers.

As he traveled throughout the country on co-op business, Ezra sought every opportunity to meet with the Saints, visiting small branches (and typically being called on to speak extemporaneously in sacrament meeting) and stopping in at mission homes. In Cleveland one Sunday he tried for four hours to find where the Saints met, even calling the police for help, but without success. On a trip through Florida he stopped in Tallahassee, where he met Saints who had known his brother George when George had presided over the district there just a few years earlier. The Saints sang George's praises.

Ezra was not a desk-bound administrator, and though the National Council funds were scarce, he traveled as much as possible to evaluate conditions within various agricultural industries, work on expansion of markets, and help improve packaging and processing. It was imperative that he be intimately acquainted with the full scope of agriculture. The breadth and depth of his briefing would prove invaluable years later and prime him for responsibilities of a greater scope.

In late November 1939 he took an extended trip through the South, stopping in Louisiana at New Orleans, where he watched cotton being loaded on boats for shipment to the Far East, and Lake Charles, where he visited the American Rice Growers Association. He rode through the cotton fields in Tennessee and met with officials from the tobacco co-op ("While I don't approve of the weed, the men showed me great respect," he noted).

Traveling by train and car was exhausting, but Ezra loved getting out among the farm leaders and driving through the country. During a trip through Connecticut in October he wrote, "Never before have I witnessed such inspiring, colorful beauty. No pen or brush could paint anything to compare with this, the handiwork of God."

He was always overjoyed to come home again. As much as he thrived on agricultural work, his frequent absences from home were hard on him.

By year's end the Bensons were solidly entrenched in the nation's capital. They had moved into a new home. Ezra and Flora were both busy in the Church. A fifth child was on the way. They had made new friends. And Ezra had been long enough on the job to sense what lay ahead of him: "Some momentous questions face the co-ops of this nation that will tax to the limit the leaders of the co-op movement." Nevertheless, on the last day of the year, Ezra evaluated 1939 as "the most valuable year thus far of our glorious married life. The Lord has blessed us with health and prosperity and wonderful new opportunities. At the end of 1938 we thot we were settled for the balance of our mortal days in Boise. May we strive more fully to be worthy of His bounteous blessings."

The year 1940 brought new opportunities, and with them increased challenges. The impact of the war in Europe presented the National Council with new problems. But in his 1939 year-end annual report Executive Secretary Benson concluded that the council was enjoying a "high degree of unity and understanding." He admitted that his greatest skill lay in achieving harmony among divergent groups. "We had some unification problems," he explained. "The cotton farmers were at odds with the sheep farmers. Or the peanut growers picked at the corn growers. If we pushed apples, the plum farmers wondered why we weren't doing more for them. If I had any skills, it was in getting groups to cooperate with each other."

Ezra saw that contention can divide a family; he was determined to prevent internal squabbles from destroying the council "family." "I emphasized that, while we represented different commodities, we must go before Congress unified. Internal differences posed the greatest threat to weakening our organization. I tried to keep peace in the family, and it was a big family."

Perhaps the most significant indicator of the council's effectiveness was revealed by its expenditures—or lack of them. Even though the council was allotted less than $16,000 in operational funds, perhaps no other organized agricultural group wielded such influence in proportion to expenditures. In 1940 the council worked on twenty-eight specific projects, nineteen of which involved legislative activity.

For some time rumors had circulated that the first stake of the Church in the East would soon be organized in Washington, D.C. The nation's capital was an area ripe for missionary growth.[5] Even on Ezra's sporadic trips to Washington in the 1930s, he had witnessed Church growth. In the early thirties, members of the Washington Branch met in the old Washington Auditorium, an arena that smelled of stale tobacco and perspiration from prize fights and wrestling matches held Saturday evenings. On one visit Ezra asked Senator Reed Smoot (a member of the Council of the Twelve) when the Church was going to get a decent place to meet in the city. Elder Smoot took a telegram from his pocket and explained, "We bought a lot on the corner of 16th Street and Columbia Road, but the people in the neighborhood weren't happy about it and offered to purchase it for $25,000 more than we paid for it. Here's the First Presidency's answer, that we didn't buy it for speculation and we're going to build a chapel."

The result was the Washington Ward building, a landmark to Eastern Mormons. Constructed of Utah marble, it had 16,404 stones, each quarried and milled in the West to fit its particular slot in the building. The building, which had an Angel Moroni statue atop its steeple, was dedicated on November 5, 1933, and soon became one of the city's sightseeing attractions. Thousands of visitors passed through its doors during the thirties and forties.

At quarterly district conference on June 29 and 30, 1940, Elders Rudger Clawson, the president of the Council of the Twelve, and Albert E. Bowen, a member of the Twelve, organized the Washington Stake from the Capital District of the Eastern States Mission. As Ezra walked through the door to keep an appointment with President Clawson, the apostle took him by the hand and said, "Brother Benson, the Lord wants you to be president of this stake. What have you got to say about that?"

"Brother Clawson, you can't be serious," Ezra replied, stunned. "I don't know these people. I've scarcely lived here a year."

"It was an awful shock," Ezra remembered, "one that took me totally by surprise." It was evidently less surprising to others. On July 8, 1940, President J. Reuben Clark of the Church's First Presidency wrote Ezra: "I was very much delighted with the organization of the Washington Stake. Ever since you visited us in the office of the Presidency, telling us of your expectation of moving to Washington, I have had you in mind as one who would be a splendid Stake President. I congratulate you, too, upon having Sister Benson, who is so thoroughly converted to the Church. . . . I think perhaps I can see a little more clearly than some how difficult your problems are going to be there, but I have complete confidence in your ability to meet these problems."

The problems were many and complex. With war looming, it was a difficult time, economically and spiritually, to mold a new stake into full operation. Ezra selected as counselors two strong, faithful men—Samuel Carpenter, secretary to the Federal Reserve Board, as first counselor, and Ernest L. Wilkinson, a lawyer (and the future president of Brigham Young University), as second. When Wilkinson told Ezra he had recommended someone else for the position of stake president, Ezra replied, "That's just the reason I want you. I admire your judgment."[6]

The stake, comprised of 2,013 members in four wards and two branches, was a far-flung unit, extending north into Pennsylvania and as far south as Richmond, Virginia. Most Mormons who lived in the area were young, bright, and eager, but most called to leadership positions were inexperienced in stake administration. As Ezra visited congregations, he noticed few bald or gray heads in the audience. He admitted, "I wished I might have heard a testimony from an old stalwart who had been through the fire." There was much to be done, and the providence of Ezra's short tenure as stake president in Boise seemed clear.

Ezra asked Roy W. Doxey to instruct the high council on doctrine and Church procedures. (Roy later became dean of religion at Brigham Young University.) Rarely has there been so much talent assembled in one region at a given time. Men such as J. Willard Marriott, David M. Kennedy, Cleon Skousen, and Harold Glen Clark filled key roles in the stake. Edgar B. Brossard, who would succeed Ezra as stake president, was a member of the U.S. Tariff Commission and bishop of the Washington Ward.

With Ezra's new calling, the word *busy* took on a new dimension. Constantly on the firing line at his work, he was now also challenged with organizing a new stake. And his and Flora's fifth child—Bonnie Amussen Benson—was born on March 30, 1940. They were delighted with the addition to their family, but times were busy. "It seems like the Lord always strengthens the back for the burden, if you're willing to take it," Flora said in retrospect of that hectic time.

Ezra was not only willing, he was also able. At the NCFC and in the stake, his administrative skills flourished. Sam Carpenter remembered, "Ezra was always prepared. He never went off half-cocked. And he was tireless. No one ever questioned his dedication. The stake grew under Ezra, and the Church became well established in Washington."

As stake president, he was forward-thinking. In a practice uncommon at the time, he published a pocket calendar for stake officers and had a small light installed on the pulpit in the chapel of the Washington Ward to inform speakers when their time was spent. After thorough review of his stake, Ezra became convinced that if all members paid tithing, there would be no need for additional Church donations. He suggested such a course to the First Presidency, recommending that such an emphasis on tithing would lead to a condition of financial preparedness for the entire church.

Great emphasis was placed on missionary work in the stake, with the Washington Ward becoming a focal point. Cleon Skousen was stake mission president. Ezra assigned Sterling Wheelwright to give organ recitals and conduct tours through the building, interspersing the music with a gospel message. He himself invited associates to visit church meetings. Ed Babcock, former president of the NCFC, attended one meeting. Afterwards he asked Ezra if the people didn't have anywhere to go— he had had a difficult time getting through the throng in the foyer at the close of the meeting. Ezra explained that Latter-day Saints enjoyed visiting with each other.

Ezra's new position weighed heavily upon his shoulders. Flora wrote her mother, " 'T' is so humble in his new appointment in the Church. There is nothing that brings to him more joy than that of doing Church work. He loves it so. It isn't the title that counts with him but it's the joy of being able to help as many as possible see the truth of the gospel."[7] He seldom traveled without a briefcase full of work and a copy of the Book of Mormon, which he read on trains and in motel rooms late at night.

Ezra's pace was pressing enough to catch the attention of Church authorities in Salt Lake City. J. Reuben Clark advised, "We hear . . . that you are working day and night, days on your own work and nights on your Church work. Remember such a course cannot go on indefinitely."[8]

But Ezra wasn't inclined to slow down. Always direct in his comments, he maintained an ongoing dialogue with Church leaders. To President Clark he wrote shortly after his call, "Suggestions and advice from you and other leaders at headquarters are much needed, particularly in this Stake, and we will appreciate your frank suggestions as we proceed with our new assignment." Sometimes his letters pertained to the cooperative movement or other political or national affairs that he felt Church leadership should be apprised of.[9]

On the national front, Ezra's war against subsidies and fight for freedom for the farmer continued unabated. Though he disagreed strongly with Roosevelt's New Deal, in July 1940 he recommended support of the Democratic Party platform planks on surplus management. Late that year he was elected to membership in the National Farm Credit Committee.

The year 1941 was a pivotal twelve months—for the nation, for the National Council. War in Europe intensified, and America responded by sending tons of supplies to the anti-Axis nations. At home government-mandated priorities threatened to cut down on vital supplies needed by farmers.

In response, in the summer of that year twenty-nine of the nation's leading cooperatives met in Chicago to discuss the esca-

THE NATIONAL MAGAZINE OF AGRICULTURAL COOPERATION

Ezra T. Benson (Page 4)   Jan. 1941
Secretary to 2,000,000 farmers

The January 1941 issue of Cooperative Digest *featured Ezra Taft Benson on the cover*

lating problem. Too many staples—everything from baling wire to canvas—were scarce. In September the National Committee for Farm Production Supplies was organized with Ezra as secretary. With the slogan "Food to Win the War," the committee determined to impress upon defense officials that for farmers to achieve increased production, they had to have supplies and tools. Discussions between farm groups and the government were often heated. In one session when the farmers' representatives were arguing the need for canvas for lambing sheds, a government official replied in exasperation, "Gentlemen, there is no canvas. You will just have to postpone the lambing." "That's about all some of those on Capitol Hill knew or cared about farm production," Ezra noted with regret.

During the war Ezra worked closely with Donald Nelson, director of the War Production Board, and Raymond Miller, later appointed president of the American Institute of Cooperation. In Miller's judgment, Ezra was a king-pin in keeping the food lines flowing while diverting labor and facilities to the manufacture of farm implements and fertilizers. "I know of no man who contributed more to the solving of these intricate problems," he said. "His cool head had as much to do with keeping our food lines flowing [during the war] as that of any other person in America."

Pulp production became a critical issue, and the War Production Board called upon agriculture to cut additional millions of cords of wood. The demand was immediate and imperative. "Lines of communication with the farm people were kept open largely as a result of the prior work of Benson," said Miller. "Millions of cords were cut and the essential pulp made possible. This is just one of innumerable cases of similar action for which someone else got the credit for work which was expedited by Ezra Taft Benson."[10]

Perhaps nothing demanded more of Ezra's time during 1941 than his vigorous campaign against price ceilings on farm products. In midsummer, as it became apparent that some form of price ceiling would receive Congressional approval, Ezra loudly insisted that no action be taken unless the wages of labor were also placed under control. His work on this legislation was impressive. Ed Babcock, the past president of the National Council of Farmer Cooperatives, told an associate, "It was a long, laborious job at which . . . Ezra Benson showed himself to be a top hand. The lion's share of anything which is eventually accomplished should go to him."[11]

As the war escalated in Europe, President Roosevelt organized a National Agricultural Advisory Committee, composed of the presidents of the four national farm organizations, to meet monthly with him. In addition to the National Council, these included the Farm Bureau, National Grange, and Farmers Union. Initially Judge Miller represented the National Council on this influential committee. Later, at Miller's request, Ezra replaced him.

Then disaster struck. On December 7, 1941, the Japanese bombed military installations at Pearl Harbor, and America was thrown into war. Reed remembers his father standing next to the radio that day, listening intently as the news broke. The implications for agriculture and the nation were devastating. In the National Council's 1941 annual report, Ezra gave his perspective: "For America, the immediate future is not at all cheery. The year 1942 will, without doubt, be one of the most fateful in the history of this great nation. Yet there cannot be one among us today who does not feel that through redoubled effort, unflinching courage, and, above all, with spiritual guidance in all we do, America will win through and still remain a land choice above all others."

But it would take a fight to keep it that way.

As early as January 5, 1942, Ezra began making war-related adjustments in stake activities. With tire and automobile sales curtailed, and following instructions in a First Presidency letter dated January 17, 1942, he reduced the number of meetings held in the stake. The stake presidency counseled members of the stake to put away a year's supply of food and clothing, and get out of debt.[12]

So many LDS service personnel attended meetings in the stake on weekends that the stake presidency opened up the Washington Ward gymnasium and provided bedrolls so they could have a place to sleep and could associate with one another. On Sunday each visitor had dinner at a member's home. "It was a way of keeping those people close to the Church," Ezra explained. "We had many testimonials from those servicemen that it was the nearest place to home they saw during the war." The Benson house became a second home to military men and women, who were welcome without advance notice. Flora prepared social activities and food; Ezra performed occasional marriages for those who couldn't go to the temple.

Missionary work was a priority, and the Washington Stake boasted one of the largest core groups of stake missionaries found in the Church at the time. Taking seriously the First Presidency's counsel at general conference in April 1942 that "no act of ours or of the church must interfere with this God-given mandate," Ezra dedicated the subsequent stake conference to missionary work. "Probably no stake," he assessed, "has greater missionary opportunities."

Fellowshipping took place with members and nonmembers alike. As Ezra traveled and met Latter-day Saints around the country, those who had family, especially children, in Washington inevitably cornered him to ask two questions: "Do you know my son or daughter?" and, "What are they doing in the Church?"

One of Ezra's highest priorities was keeping the youth active. Gold and Green balls and athletic events were carefully orchestrated. Repeatedly Ezra reminded stake leaders that the future of the Church lay in the youth.

Ezra's stake came to regard him as a caring man who stood firm when he needed to. As Alice Marriott explained, "He was a lovable, personable man." She related how he would put his arm around his brethren and ask how they were. "But he had a mind of his own," she said of him. "Right was right, and wrong was wrong, and there was nothing in between." Ezra would later say, "Be right and easy to live with, if possible, but in that order."

As problems arose, he addressed them. When, for example, one ward developed an "East-West" mentality—that is, that both parts of the country had to be equally represented among the leadership—he was firm: "I told the priesthood I never wanted to hear anything about East and West when they were selecting officers. This is a world church. We are all one great family."[13]

In time Ezra's high profile in government circles brought awareness of, and later recognition to, the Church in Washington and elsewhere. A corporate official from Chicago called on him one day and asked for names of young men with integrity. Someone had suggested that the man hire a returned Mormon missionary, so at his Washington hotel he had inquired if there were any Mormons in the District of Columbia and was told to contact Ezra Benson. The man did so, and asked Ezra if he could supply the names he needed. Ezra replied, "Not only can I give you three or four names, but I can give you dozens." Often thereafter Ezra commented that "it pays to maintain the standards of the Church and be true to the faith."

As he became better acquainted with members of his high council, Ezra established a deep friendship with J. Willard Marriott, who had parlayed a root beer stand into an impressive chain of restaurants. After many high council meetings, he and Ezra would stop at one of Marriott's Hot Shoppe restaurants for a snack. They talked about everything from politics and religion to business. They thought much alike and enjoyed each other's company. And the two families mixed well. Young Bill Jr. and Richard Marriott played with the Benson boys, and Alice Marriott and Flora got along well. Marriott even invited Ezra to join him in business. "Bill, I'm committed to two million farmers," Ezra responded, "and I know nothing about the food business, except that I like to eat."

As Bill began to prosper, Ezra had to watch him. "He'd want to pay the whole Church budget. Of course I wouldn't let him, but he was always very generous." The two men became very close. "No man ever had a better friend than Bill Marriott," Ezra said many years later.

Few men had more challenges during those years than Ezra Benson. While the Washington Stake of the Church increased in efficiency and growth, problems in agriculture stimulated by the war were never-ending.

Roosevelt set up a number of emergency agencies during the first half of 1942, too many in Ezra's estimation, as he believed that existing agencies would have sufficed. The old saying that there is nothing quite so permanent as a temporary government building seemed frighteningly accurate, and the size of government grew like a rolling freight train out of control.

What little remained of a normal economy vanished after Pearl Harbor. It takes a lot of food to win a war, and the possibility of massive food shortages became a reality, though the Administration was slow to believe it. Judge Miller resigned as National Council president and was replaced first by H. E. Babcock and then by Charles C. Teague, president of the California Fruit Growers Exchange and Fruit Growers Supply Company. The war ended twenty years of agricultural depression. Between 1940 and 1945 farm prices and income doubled; by 1944 total farm income exceeded $20 billion, compared with less than $5 billion in 1932. Increased demand abroad and at home pushed prices up. In October 1942, when Congress granted the President authorization to freeze prices, rents, and wages, Ezra went on a national radio hook-up to vigorously oppose price controls and price fixing. He felt that the best regulator of prices was the free market. "Farmers need more freedom, not more control," he explained.

During 1942 and early 1943, the four major national farm organizations cooperated to keep America's wartime agriculture healthy. In 1942 Ezra was named a member of the executive committee of the American Institute of Cooperation, an educational aggregate of cooperatives, land-grant colleges, and other farm organizations.

In all, the net effect was that Ezra, in behalf of the National Council, attained prominence as a spokesman for the growing segment of cooperative agriculture. In an unprecedented move and flattering vote of confidence, the council's executive committee declared that Ezra was "capable of assuming the burden here in Washington which has formerly been borne by our [council] presidents," and passed a resolution empowering him "to speak and act with full and complete authority." Ed Babcock wrote Ezra that the change wouldn't have been made had the council not been absolutely sure of Ezra's "integrity and ability to speak for the Cooperatives of the United States. I am no amateur in selecting and working with men of quality and I am not inexperienced in judging men. . . . You furnish the Council with the dignified, poised, intelligent and Christian direction to which a great social and economic movement is entitled." The council budget and staff were also increased, giving Ezra an assistant and the council legal representation—Ernest L. Wilkinson.[14]

The year 1942 brought a major change in Flora's life. Barbara Amussen had been planning to visit her daughter's family in Washington, D. C., but unexpectedly, in early September, she wrote that she would not be coming. She also revealed an impression she had received that Ezra would "be called to a high and important calling in this Glorious Church in due time."

It was but a few days later that Barbara Amussen's deceased husband appeared to her in a manifestation and indicated she would die and join him on the following Thursday. When she described the experience to her daughter Mabel, who also lived in Logan, Mabel responded, "Oh, Mother, you're in good health. You've been worrying about something. Are you ill?" Barbara insisted she was fine, but that she would leave mortality on the following Thursday. Mabel could not believe her at first, so she did not contact Flora immediately. The following Sunday Barbara bore strong testimony in her ward, so strong that when she concluded, the bishop closed the meeting though there was time remaining.

On Monday Barbara withdrew her savings, paid her bills, and had the lights and telephone disconnected. She paid the boy who took care of the lawn, had the plumber turn off the water, selected her own casket and paid for it, and went to stay at Mabel's home. On Wednesday evening, after visiting with Mabel and with her son Charles, she said, "Now, Mabel, I feel drowsy. Don't disturb me if I sleep until the eventide." Those were her last words. She passed away early Thursday morning.

Flora, with Bonnie and Beverly, arrived from Washington around noon that day. When she entered her mother's home, Flora found a jar filled with seventy-five birthday pennies for the Penny Parade of the Primary Association, wooden blocks waiting for the children, and cookies in the cookie jar. "It was as though she was there with us, which eased the pain," Flora wrote. Later, Mr. Baugh, the plumber, told Flora of his last encounter with her mother: "She told me she was going to die soon. Her words of love, counsel and advice were most glorious. I have never been around a more beautiful, spiritual lady in my whole life."

Nevertheless, her mother's death was a great shock to Flora, and it was many months before her daily sobbing subsided. Years earlier Barbara Amussen had assured Flora that as long as Flora needed her, she would remain alive. Yet now she was gone.

By early 1943 the National Council of Farmer Cooperatives had grown significantly. "The Council continues its growth and

I am enjoying my work," Ezra wrote, "altho working long hours and under considerable pressure." He continued preaching the doctrine of cooperation, insisting it provided a means of self-help through mutual help, rather than dependence upon state aid.[15]

But with war raging, all was not well on the farm front. On repeated occasions, Ezra, with Albert Goss and Edward O'Neal, had warned the Administration of pending food shortages. Acres of crops had gone unharvested due to lack of machinery, yet it seemed to him that the Administration continued to coddle labor. High wages in defense plants lured farmers away from their fields.

In February 1943, Ezra unleashed his frustrations in his journal: "Government controls and regulations have increased almost daily. The morale of the people, laboring under impossible directives, seems to be at low ebb. Bungling and delay and red tape is having a bewildering effect. Altho internationally the war seems to be progressing satisfactorily, on the 'home front' all is not well. Conditions call for vigorous, courageous action. I fear, however, we haven't the political courage to meet the issue squarely."

On March 12, Ezra, with Babcock and Goss, spent thirty-five minutes with President Roosevelt. Conducting the meeting from behind his large, old-fashioned desk laden with trinkets and symbols of the Democratic Party, the President was congenial. He expressed concern about the food production outlook and requested recommendations for corrective measures.

On March 31 the group met again to discuss the question of food production. Though the conference was constructive, Ezra noted that each time "the question of food prices was raised, the President dodged the issue. It appeared he was afraid of the demands of organized labor."

A third session was scheduled for April 7, causing Ezra to miss the Church's general conference, his first in a long while. But after the meeting he recorded that finally "the Administration is food production conscious, which tho belated offers encouragement. Cooperative leaders were laughed at when last September we emphasized this country faced a serious food

*Ezra and Flora Benson
outside the home
they lived in when
he served as
Secretary of Agriculture*

situation unless certain fundamental policies were adopted." In this meeting Ezra presented a five-point program designed to resolve the pending food crisis, and all endorsed his plan. But it seemed little more than a Band-Aid on a gaping wound.

Ezra seldom agreed with the President's programs or policies. But despite the friction, Roosevelt once remarked that he would rather talk with Ezra Benson than any farm leader because of his "knowledge of the subject."[16]

While the pressure of work and Church seemed to never diminish, Ezra spent as much time as possible with his family. Flora, convinced the children needed constancy at home, rarely accompanied her husband on trips out of town, but she and Ezra spent as many evenings together as possible, sometimes joining the Marriotts for dinner or going to a movie.

He had his own way of keeping in close touch with the children. Huge amounts of mail passed between him and the family, and when possible, family members traveled with him. When he was home, some of his and Flora's most satisfying associations were with members of the Church. In a reflective tone Ezra recorded, "I don't know what Heaven will be like [but] I want nothing finer than the associations of the fine . . . Latter-day Saints that constitute the membership of this stake. . . . Some, it is true, have wandered afield, but we are gradually winning them back, to their great joy and our deep satisfaction."

Perhaps few men would have been as well suited to lead the Washington Stake through the war. He had unusual rapport with Latter-day Saint servicemen and -women. And he counseled his flock on temporal matters, advising them to be frugal, conserve and store food, and get out of debt. But the war put a drain on resources, manpower, and patience. "Practically all of our people are working long hours and have very little free time," he noted of stake members. "This is affecting our Church work some, but through better organization and planning the work of the stake is actually improving. The Lord seems to be pouring out His blessings upon us as never before."

In early May 1943, the same day he received a letter from *Who's Who in America* requesting a life sketch, Ezra heard from President J. Reuben Clark of the First Presidency, asking when he and Flora would next be in Salt Lake City. President Clark added, "I hear only good reports of the work which you are doing, not alone for the Church but on behalf of the industry which you represent." The comment might have served as an omen, but Ezra modestly noted, "Pres. Clark, like all others of the General Authorities, is very kind and generous."

For nearly a year Ezra had had a standing offer from the Southern States Cooperative to manage that influential organization at a salary much higher than his current compensation. The job would mean moving his family to Richmond, Virginia, and perhaps a release from his assignment as stake president. He decided to make an extended farm trip throughout the West and consult with Church authorities while in Salt Lake City. In keeping with his promise to the boys that when they became

Eagle Scouts they could accompany him on a major trip, he arranged for Reed, the first Eagle Scout in the Washington Stake, to travel with him.

On June 21, 1943, Ezra and Reed boarded the B&O in Silver Springs, Maryland, bound for Chicago. Ezra looked forward to time alone with his eldest son and a visit with cooperative leaders and Church officials. His mind was preoccupied with matters at hand—postwar agriculture and his future. He could not have known that those decisions had already been taken out of his hands.

*"The foremost responsibility of the Twelve Apostles
is to bear witness to the divinity of Jesus Christ
and to the restoration of His gospel
in these latter days."*

Chapter 11

The Call to the Apostleship

Ezra wasn't much of a worrier, but as he set out on his month-long trip, he was preoccupied. The world was engulfed in war; the prospects of a devastating food shortage had never been greater; the welfare of members of his stake, many of them young and away from home for the first time, played on his emotions; and an attractive job offer had dangled before him long enough that he wondered if he was foolish not to accept. Too many facets of life seemed unsettled.

Nevertheless, as he and Reed headed West, they enjoyed the companionship of traveling together. Though Reed was but fifteen, there was a deep bond between the father and son. As they traveled first to Chicago, then through Texas and Arizona, and subsequently the length of California, visiting as many cities and cooperatives as there were numbers of days, they talked into the late hours, did a little sightseeing, and took in an occasional movie. After seeing one Western, Reed reported to his mother in a letter, "It was so comical about farming that Dad nearly burst his belt. There were some old-fashioned horse races and Dad nearly beat in the chair in front of him for fear the bad men might win. I had more fun watchin' Dad than the movie."[1]

On the food front: Farm leaders O'Neal, Benson, and Goss carry fight against food subsidies to the White House.

BUSINESS
WEEK

BUSINESS WEEK INDEX

PUBLISHED BY THE McGRAW-HILL PUBLISHING COMPANY, INC • TWENTY CENTS

Reprinted from Business Week, October 30, 1943, by special permission. © 1943 by McGraw-Hill, Inc.

Ezra Taft Benson on the cover of Business Week

For sixteen days they toured cooperatives in California—everything from Sunkist to the California Rice Growers. And they also spent an evening with Charles C. Teague, newly appointed president of the National Council of Farmer Cooperatives, at his ranch in Santa Paula.

Teague, a prosperous citrus farmer, had served as president or chairman of some sixteen agricultural organizations. As Ezra was driven onto Teague's spacious grounds, he gasped at the largest, most beautiful home he had ever been in. During Ezra and Reed's twenty-four-hour visit, Teague drove them throughout his vast holdings of lemon and orange orchards, all the while relating the history of the citrus industry in California. Later that evening, presumably in response to rumors that had circulated throughout the industry, he pulled Ezra aside and told him, "I know you have been offered greater opportunities financially than we are paying you, but we don't want you to leave the cooperative movement. It's no longer a question of salary. You can set your own salary."

Ezra was taken aback by this generosity and confidence. He wasn't comfortable making long-term commitments until he had discussed alternatives with Church officials, but he responded that he had "no desire to leave the cooperative movement."

While in California, Ezra toured housing facilities and labor camps of workers who had migrated to California from the Dust Bowl sections of the Midwest. He had heard horror stories about inhumane treatment of migrant workers. What he saw pleasantly surprised him. "The facilities seemed very satisfactory. . . . I found farmers had a good attitude toward labor, and the relationship between employer and employee was satisfactory. It seemed to be the outside agitators which caused the trouble."

In San Francisco, Ezra addressed two groups of agricultural, city, and state leaders, including some of his former Berkeley professors. Though he was nervous about facing his instructors, his fear left as he began talking, and he spoke freely and frankly at both meetings, making frequent reference to prayer and other spiritual values that influence progress. The response was gratifying.

On July 15, 1943, Ezra and Reed arrived in Utah, and the following day Ezra met with David O. McKay, now a member of the First Presidency. Their reunion was sweet and, as always for Ezra, inspiring, though it aroused the lament, "How I wish we had [men] at the head of this great country of his stature and character."

Then it was off to Idaho for a long-needed visit with family and friends. In Idaho Falls Ezra received a personal tour of the nearly completed temple. Tears welled in his eyes as he contemplated what the imposing structure situated by the falls would mean for the Saints there.

In Idaho, and for the first time since his mother's funeral ten years earlier, Ezra walked through the doors in the old Whitney Ward building. It was a nostalgic occasion that aroused deep emotion and reflection. "Many sweet and never-to-be-forgotten memories surged thru my mind as I sat in the little church and looked into the kindly faces I had learned to love," he wrote. "Here much of the training which has been of great value thru the years was received. These sacred and fundamental principles, instilled into my young soul by faithful and unselfish teachers, will ever be a great blessing to me."

On July 26, he and Reed returned to Salt Lake City and learned that President McKay's office staff had been frantically calling hotels throughout the city trying to locate Ezra. President Heber J. Grant wanted to meet with Ezra at his summer home in a nearby canyon.

"Oh, I can't go up the canyon," Ezra began to explain, "I have a train to catch shortly." After being assured President Grant was just a few minutes away, near the mouth of Emigration Canyon, Ezra relented, and he and Reed were driven there. Ezra was immediately shown into President Grant's bedroom, where the aged prophet was resting. At the President's bidding, Ezra closed the door and approached him, sitting down on a chair next to the bed. President Grant took Ezra's right hand in both of his and, with tears filling his eyes, said simply, "Brother Benson, with all my heart I congratulate you and pray God's blessing to attend you. You have been chosen as the youngest member of the Council of the Twelve Apostles."

The shock registered in Ezra's face. He felt as if the earth were sinking from beneath him. He had had no premonition of the calling. Later he recorded his feelings: "The announcement seemed unbelievable and overwhelming. . . . For several minutes [I] could say only, 'Oh, President Grant, that can't be!' which I must have repeated several times before I was able to collect my thots enough to realize what had happened. . . . He held my hand for a long time as we both shed tears. . . . For over an hour we were alone together, much of the time with our hands clasped warmly together. Tho [he was] feeble, his mind was clear and alert, and I was deeply impressed with his sweet, kindly, humble spirit as he seemed to look into my soul.

"I felt so utterly weak and unworthy that his words of comfort and reassurance which followed were doubly appreciated. Among other things he stated, 'The Lord has a way of magnifying men who are called to positions of leadership.' When in my weakness I was able to state that I loved the Church he said, 'We know that,' and the Lord wants men who will give everything for His work.'

"He told of the action taken in a special meeting of the First Presidency and the Twelve two weeks before and that the discussion regarding me had been enthusiastically unanimous. . . . I feel confident that only thru the rich blessings of the Almighty can this ever be realized."[2]

The President asked Ezra to attend general conference in October, when he would be sustained and ordained. He also told him that his great-grandfather and other faithful progenitors were rejoicing at this appointment of a descendant to the apostleship. And he advised Ezra to continue with the National Council until arrangements for a smooth transition could be made, even if it took a year or longer.

At the conclusion of the visit, Ezra found Reed outside, and they were chauffeured back to President McKay's home. They rode in silence. Ezra was still in a daze when Elder McKay greeted him at the door with outstretched arms and an embrace. President McKay then told Reed what had happened, and father and son embraced.

That night, aboard the train, Ezra retired before midnight, but rest did not come. His thoughts raced from one concern to another. He had always revered the Twelve. Was he worthy to sit in that council? Was he capable? What were the financial implications? He had just paid off their home and for the first time in his married life was out of debt, but they had no savings. How would he afford the children's missions and schooling? What about the impending food shortage and the condition of cooperatives—could he relegate such crucial matters to someone else? How would the children adjust to Salt Lake City? How would this lifetime call affect him? Even forty years later, as he relived the moment of his appointment to the Twelve, tears would well in his eyes as he recalled, "It was the most humbling, overwhelming moment. I couldn't believe it, that the Lord would choose me."

"Slept very little but prayed, wept and did much sincere thinking regarding this great thing which has come to me, a humble weak farmer boy," he wrote in his journal that first night. "With heart full of gratitude I pledged my all to the establishment of the Kingdom of God on the earth and pled with the Lord to give me strength to ever be worthy of this high and holy calling."

When the train arrived in Grand Junction, Colorado, Ezra placed some overdue calls. The first was to Flora. She registered little surprise at her husband's emotional news, admitting she had had a strong impression that something of magnitude would happen on this trip. "She said how wonderful she felt it was and expressed her complete confidence I could measure up," Ezra wrote. "It was reassuring to talk to her. She has always shown more faith in me than I have myself."

Perhaps Flora was less surprised by her husband's call than anyone. While she had never discussed her feelings with anyone, she had had premonitions about her husband's potential and his life mission and had worked to help him to that end. She later recorded, "It's been a lot of hard work and sacrifice and encouragement giving him faith in himself. . . . He wasn't all ready-made when I got him." One Church authority subsequently said, "If we had more women like Sister Benson, we would have more men like Apostle Benson."

Ezra's second call was to Charles Teague, whose words were reassuring: "God bless you. This is a great honor, and you will have our full support."

In the meantime, word of Ezra's appointment had been released to the press. The Church-owned *Deseret News*, noting that he was descended from Ezra T. Benson and calling him a "national authority" on farm problems, broke the news on July 27, and word spread rapidly from coast to coast. While Ezra and Reed continued their journey home, congratulations poured in to the Bensons' Bethesda home. By the time they arrived home on July 31, the whole world knew, or at least so it seemed.

The call may have taken Ezra by surprise, but others insisted that they had seen it coming. Ernest Wilkinson said that "those of us in Washington who have worked close to him were not surprised." At a stake presidency meeting held after Ezra's departure for the West Coast, stake clerk Don Crowther confided to Wilkinson, "I would not be a bit surprised if the Presiding Officers chose Brother Benson for the other vacancy in the Council of the Twelve." Wilkinson admitted that while he had also felt so impressed, he had supposed the call might be several years hence. "I had become so accustomed to having men of riper years appointed to that Council that I had almost forgotten the age of the Prophet Joseph."[3]

On August 3, Ezra directed a press release to the board of directors of the National Council of Farmer Cooperatives:

> Many of you have no doubt seen the press account of my appointment as a member of the Quorum of Twelve Apostles of the Church of Jesus Christ of Latter-day Saints. This high and holy calling came as a tremendous and almost overwhelming surprise to me. . . .
>
> I, of course, am deeply grateful for this great honor and, because of my deep religious convictions and love for the church, accept gladly the responsibility. . . . Please be assured, however, that acceptance of this appointment does not mean immediate severance of my relationship with the National Council. . . . Needless to say, it will be with deep regret that I sever my active connections with this unusually fine group of men and this excellent organization.

Ezra's peers responded immediately. Two are representative. C. D. Bennett, editor of *Washington Farm Reporter*, wrote: "It is amazing to find in a city like Washington, where men become engrossed with affairs of business and government, an executive so identified with his spiritual convictions." A. H. Lauterbach, general manager of the Pure Milk Association, wrote on August 9, 1943: "In many of my talks I have said that world peace will come only through (first) a greater church following and (second) a world-wide cooperative movement. We will miss you and you will be hard to replace but we will have the knowledge that on the council of one of the great churches will sit a man who knows the cooperative movement and who will aid and guide it in its future activities."

Many were openly concerned about the impact of Ezra's departure on the National Council. R. N. Benjamin, executive secretary of the Pennsylvania Farm Bureau, wrote that Ezra had done much to iron out difficulties between cooperatives and that they faced critical tests in the future that called for unity, concluding, "I hope . . . [you will be permitted] to remain in your present position for at least another year."[4]

Howard Cowden, president of the Consumers Cooperative Association in Kansas City, Missouri, admitted that, because of Ezra, he had "come to have a high regard for the Latter-day Saints. They are as near a truly cooperative body as one will find among religious sects." And from the president of the Farmers and Traders Life Insurance Company, "The Mormon Church will seem a little nearer to me."[5]

Miller Shurtleff, a member of the Washington Stake who was stationed in the South Pacific, wrote: "A man who can walk with the wealthy of the nation, counsel with the powerful of the nation, carry a full share of the responsibility of feeding the world at war, conduct a home such as yours, serve the Church as I've seen you serve, enjoy the Spirit of the Lord, hoe corn in a welfare garden on a hot Saturday afternoon, and be at all times patient, humble and considerate is a man worthy of being called a . . . servant of God."[6]

LeGrand Richards, the Church's Presiding Bishop, wrote that if the Presiding Bishopric had been asked to make the selection, Ezra would have been their choice: "No one who knows you can question the sincerity of your testimony and your love for the truth." Members of the Council of the Twelve sent personal congratulations. John A. Widtsoe counseled that service in the Twelve "is not entirely an easy life, for the Church calls upon its servants unremittingly."[7]

Elder Widtsoe made a strong point. Ezra wondered what toll the move west and his new responsibilities would take on the family. His children were still young. Reed (fifteen), Mark (fourteen), and Barbara (nine) in particular would be uprooted from friends and schools. "Extensive travel on Church work will take me from my family to a great extent," Ezra noted in his journal. "Often this is the beginning of less interest in Church matters by families of Church leaders. I sincerely trust I may be true to my family, keep them close to the Church, and yet fulfil my obligations as one of the General Authorities. This I know will be no easy matter."

But from the outset, there was no lack of family support for Ezra's call. His Aunt Carmen told him that years earlier she had picked him to follow in the footsteps of his great-grandfather. Ezra's boyhood hero, Uncle Serge, wrote just two days after his call, "We do not fear for your success. You have always made good and failure is not for you."

At home, in the confines of their close-knit family unit, the Bensons discussed the honor and responsibility that had come to their husband and father. And many nights Ezra and Flora lay awake. Often she wiped away his tears as he confided fears and lingering feelings of inadequacy. But, as he had already done before—twice when called as stake president, when he had assumed his position with the University of Idaho Extension Division in Boise, and later in a demanding post with the NCFC—he forged ahead. It had become his pattern that if the Lord called, he would rise to the task, and his family provided him the underlying drive and strength to move on. As Barbara remembered, "There was a lot of praying and fasting for daddy."

J. Willard Marriott wrote, "We have all been talking about you and your family and can't tell you how thrilled we are about your appointment. . . . Allie says you are the backbone of the whole stake and she doesn't know how you can be replaced."

On the evening of August 15, 1943, Ezra related the events surrounding his call to the members of his stake high council. His associates' "sincere assurances that the Lord had inspired his prophet to call me was a source of real strength and satisfaction. It was an evening long to be remembered, and I couldn't hold back the tears as I told my wife of it near midnight."

Though the initial shock had subsided, questions of a practical nature prompted Ezra to consult the First Presidency. How soon should he move to Salt Lake City, and should he plan to assume the cost of moving? What was the housing situation in Utah? Should he plan to maintain outside interests to sustain his family financially? How soon would the Washington Stake be reorganized?

The First Presidency responded, point by point. Ezra was responsible for his moving expenses, might consider renting a home until after the war, would receive a modest living allowance, and should continue as stake president until informed otherwise.[8]

On August 1, 1943, Ezra took the boys to Camp Roosevelt on the Chesapeake Bay. He had intended to spend several days with them, but with the new pressures he stayed only long enough for dinner in the camp mess hall. Later that month he took Barbara with him on an overnight business trip to New York City, and they enjoyed a sightseeing trip on a double-decker bus.

Over Labor Day weekend Ezra and Flora spent four restful days as guests of the Marriotts at their summer home at Lake Winnipesaukee in New Hampshire. Ezra knew coming weeks would be stressful, and the respite was delightful. They swam, cruised the beautiful lake, and talked into the night about the gospel.

In mid-September Ezra prepared once again for meetings with President Roosevelt and other farm leaders at the White House. Their concerns focused around the problem of high postwar unemployment. Business enterprises with war contracts were paying nearly 90 percent of their profits in taxes and would face serious consequences if there were no monies available to retool and convert their industries from war to peacetime operations. The same dilemma faced farmers, and Ezra was concerned about reserving funds to ease the shock of postwar adjustment. Afterwards he noted, "I fear the present leadership has neither the political courage nor the vision to do an adequate job. Every decision seems to be directed toward political expediency and 1944 votes."

Ezra's interaction within the stake offset his frustration on political matters. Quarterly stake conference, held on September 19, was "glorious," and he wondered how he could leave the people in Washington. But he looked forward to new opportunities. As Spencer W. Kimball indicated in an August 2, 1943, letter to Ezra, "I shall look forward to seeing you at the October Conference and it will be my great joy to sit with you and work with you the rest of our lives in the great work to which we have been called."

On September 26, he and Flora left for general conference in Salt Lake City. Among other shortages, wartime had depleted the ranks of available domestic help, and when they could not locate a sitter it looked as though Flora might not be able to accompany her husband. The crisis was averted when one of

Ezra's secretaries volunteered to spend her vacation tending the children.

The first day of the 114th semiannual conference of the Church was one of the most significant of Ezra's life. In the opening session Spencer Woolley Kimball and he were sustained as members of the Council of the Twelve Apostles. When Ezra was called upon to address the conference, he was almost overcome with emotion. He managed to deliver a brief message, giving some indication of the spirit with which he assumed his apostolic ministry: "I am grateful beyond my power of expression for the . . . great honor that has come to one of the weakest of your number. I love this work. All my life I have had a testimony of it. . . . I know something of the honors which men can bestow, but I know that there is nothing that can compare with the honors which come to us as servants of the Lord."⁹

That evening Ezra and Flora gathered with other General Authorities at the home of Elder Stephen L Richards for an evening of music, storytelling, and conversation. They also heard from home that Ezra's secretary was being charmed by her five charges. "I never saw such well-behaved and happy little faces all the time," she reported in a letter. One evening the children surprised her with a birthday cake. "After dinner Reed came out in the kitchen and suggested that I take some milk bottles out, and when I went out he brought in the cake and they all chimed in and sang 'Happy Birthday.' I was really so touched I felt like crying. . . . I spent one of the happiest birthdays I have ever had."¹⁰

As the conference proceeded, Ezra and Flora were overwhelmed with the enthusiastic response from friends and family, and were made to feel so welcome that many of their jitters fled. At the end of three days, Ezra's right hand was bruised and sore from shaking so many hands.

On the morning of October 7, after meeting with the Twelve in the temple, all gathered in the office of President Grant. There he first ordained Spencer Kimball an apostle, and then Ezra knelt before the ailing prophet. As the rest of the Twelve and members of the First Presidency placed their hands on Ezra's head, President Grant ordained him as one of the "Twelve Spe-

*Elders Spencer W.
Kimball and
Ezra Taft Benson,
who were sustained
as members of
the Council
of the Twelve
in October 1943*

cial Witnesses of the divine mission of the Savior," a calling
"paramount to everything else upon the earth." He counseled
Elder Benson to "from this very moment resolve to make His
cause and His labor first and foremost in all your thoughts,"
and blessed him with "power to make friends for the Church
and to accomplish every desire of your heart in righteousness."
Then, for nearly an hour afterwards, President Grant counseled
the new apostles as they joined the body of men that, with the
First Presidency, directed the affairs of the kingdom.

The kingdom at that time consisted of 837,000 members in
144 stakes, most of them in the United States. World War II
had retarded missionary work, sacrament meeting attendance
was 19 percent, and priesthood attendance was 31 percent. The
Brethren usually traveled in pairs to stake conferences. Ezra's
calling was not only spiritual in nature but also an administrative assignment, as part of the governing body of the Church.

It had been an overwhelming week, and as Flora and Ezra returned to Washington, they reviewed the events again and again and planned out the next few months. Spencer Kimball had already moved from Arizona to Salt Lake City, and Ezra, too, longed to join the Brethren. But he knew that he must follow President Grant's counsel to sever ties with the National Council only after an orderly transition had been made. As he explained to one associate, "I am deeply grateful for [my call to the Twelve], but as I contemplate severing my active connection with farm cooperatives, I find my feelings very much mixed. The work with the Council has been pleasant from the beginning, not only because I believe wholeheartedly in the movement, but because of the great opportunity of associating with [the] men who constitute its leadership." Nevertheless, he determined to push for a quick but effective transition.[11]

Back in Washington it was one round of meetings after another. The brisk slap of political reality was in sharp contrast to the spiritual warmth of general conference. Ezra was increasingly sensitive to the differences, as he tried to hold down assignments as stake president, General Authority, and farm executive.

Perhaps as a result of his firsthand observation of the interworkings of government on the highest levels, Ezra's love of freedom burned with increasing intensity. And so did his commitment to men and women in the service, with whom he spent time at every opportunity. On October 17 he filled his first assignment as an apostle when he visited the Annapolis Branch, formed to enable midshipmen of the U.S. Naval Academy and their families to be active in the Church. Ezra felt strongly that there was an army of Latter-day Saint men— "missionaries in uniform," as he called them—stationed throughout the world whose spiritual impact could be dramatic. He told the midshipmen so and encouraged them to serve the Church while they served their country.

In a subsequent letter to servicemen from the Washington Stake Military Committee, dated June 2, 1944, Ezra wrote, "You . . . are the greatest missionary force the Church has. . . . The Church's mission is to renounce war and proclaim peace. . . . [But] there are some things more dear to us than life itself. You are serving to preserve many of these God-given liberties. And, although war clouds are hanging heavy and all seems dark, be assured that God is still at the helm. We are proud of your dual efforts as representatives of the United States of America and soldiers of the cross."

In late October, Ezra was the featured speaker at meetings of the board of directors of the Eastern States Farmers Exchange. In introducing him, the Exchange manager noted Ezra's recent appointment and was highly complimentary of the Church. The force of President Grant's admonition that Ezra "make friends for the Church" began to hit home.

Later George Albert Smith, president of the Council of the Twelve, reinforced this charge, writing Elder Benson, "Your opportunity to mingle with large groups of non-Mormons and people who are influential should be availed of wherever possible. Your mission from now on is to find ways and means to disseminate the truth and warn the people that you come in contact with in as kind a way as possible that repentance will be the only panacea for the ills of this world." President Smith also offered some practical advice: that Ezra sign his name in full, *Ezra Taft Benson*, to minimize confusion with his great-grandfather, Ezra T. Benson. President Smith spoke from experience—his grandfather was George A. Smith, a former apostle and counselor to Brigham Young.[12]

During November and December 1943, Ezra's schedule became more hectic as he traveled for both the National Council and the Church. En route to his first stake conference in New York City, he was preoccupied with his assignment: "All day I have worried about it. Only with great difficulty have I been able to center my mind on the work at hand."

There was good news, though. Ezra and Flora were elated to learn that she was carrying another child. Though she was ill and threatened to miscarry, all were delighted at the prospect of a baby. For over a year they had been hoping and praying for additional family.

In late 1943 Ezra learned that he had been elected to the National Committee on Rural Scouting. The honor came as a total surprise, though the nomination was a natural outgrowth of Ezra's longtime support of the Boy Scouts. With his appointment, two members of the Twelve now held national Boy Scout positions. The other person, George Albert Smith, had been a member of the National Boy Scouts of America Executive Board for fifteen years.

At year's end the Bensons were in transition. Flora was struggling with pregnancy-related illness, and some of the children were nervous about moving to Utah. But that didn't dampen their holiday spirit, and after the children lined up single file, youngest to oldest, and marched into the living room Christmas morning to see their gifts, Ezra spent two hours calling bishops, stake officers, branch presidents, widows, and others in his stake to wish them a Merry Christmas.

The new year's first business was the National Council's annual convention in Chicago, Ezra's fifth and last as executive secretary. During a marathon meeting of the executive committee, he recommended that, for the first time in council history, "America" be sung and an invocation offered. The committee agreed.

At this convention Ezra delivered his last annual report to the National Council delegates. Throughout the three-day convention he was deluged with messages praising his five years of leadership. And at convention's end, the delegates passed a resolution that read in part: "During the years that have passed since we first knew [Ezra Taft Benson] we have been privileged to witness the unfolding of his talents and capabilities in a manner which culminated in the universal recognition of him as a man without peer in his field of activities. We have drawn on his resources of energy and have profited by his unerring judgment in meeting the ever-mounting problems facing the farmers of the nation and their cooperatives. His sincerity, resourcefulness and complete honesty of purpose have endeared him not only to us but to everyone with whom he has come in contact, no matter what their station."[13]

Considering the volatile position he had occupied, Ezra was grateful for the appraisal of his services. The September 1943 issue of *Cooperative Digest* reported on the National Council's growth during Ezra's tenure—to some 4600 associations representing 2.3 million farmers—which they evaluated as "directly traceable to Benson." The article concluded that selection of a successor would be "extremely difficult." *Agricultural News*, in the January 22, 1944, issue, editorialized, "Friends and associates of Mr. Benson will be sorry to lose this hard-hitting, clear-thinking farm leader."

Leaders of various member associations assessed and praised Ezra's service. The following, from the American Rice Growers, is typical: "You came into the Council at a time when the outlook was extremely gloomy, and I think very few of us had much real confidence in the future until we saw the way you were taking hold of the situation. . . . Few other people in the cooperative field could have . . . built the Council as efficiently and as rapidly as you have done."[14]

With the annual convention concluded in Chicago, Ezra hurried to Salt Lake City for quarterly meetings of the Council of the Twelve. He returned home on January 16 at 7:45 A.M. and was there less than an hour before leaving for a conference of the Baltimore Ward. "There was no complaint from my devoted wife and I left and returned at midnight," he noted at day's end.

This kind of pace was one that Flora, Ezra, and the children got used to. Though Ezra had accepted an ecclesiastical calling, his affiliation with agricultural groups would never end, though it would wane. By the end of February he had attended the National Postwar Planning Conference and traveled to meetings in Columbus, Buffalo, and Albany. In Albany he met with New York Governor Thomas E. Dewey at the governor's request. For over an hour Ezra discussed national problems and the Church with Dewey, who seemed fascinated by the Church's welfare and youth programs. Dewey was amazed that, at age forty-four, Ezra would turn his back on a promising future in Washington in favor of a position with the Church. But, looking Ezra straight in the eye, Dewey added, "I'm worried about our youth. They're getting away from us." Ezra responded, "Last week I attended a [Church] dance . . . [with] several hundred young people . . . which was opened and closed with prayer. There wasn't a bottle, a cigarette, or any evidence of vulgarity whatever." Dewey paused momentarily before replying, "Mr.

The Benson family at the time of Elder Benson's call to the apostleship: Ezra and Flora with (left to right) Bonnie, Mark, Barbara, Beverly, and Reed

Benson, that's one of the most difficult things I've ever been asked to believe, knowing the world as I do." Ezra left after discussing such things as family prayer and the Constitution.[15]

On March 5, 1944, in an emotional session of quarterly stake conference, Ezra was released as president of the Washington Stake and succeeded by Edgar B. Brossard. Later that month Ezra took Mark, as a reward for obtaining his Eagle Scout award, on a business trip to Florida. They returned home long enough for Ezra to repack and board the train for another three-day trip to Salt Lake City and his second general conference as an apostle. Her health precarious, Flora remained behind.

Prior to conference Ezra attended meetings of the Twelve in the Salt Lake Temple. The Brethren spoke freely. To the youngest apostle, the meeting reinforced in him "the great adjustments required in the lives of each of the brethren. All bore strong testimony to the truth and humbly prayed for the power to do more and for the advancement of the kingdom."

In those days, the Brethren were not advised prior to conference which session they would speak in. In the third session, President J. Reuben Clark announced Ezra as the first speaker. Elder Benson talked about juvenile and parental delinquency and noted that it was a thrill for him "to face that body of 5,000 priesthood leaders and to feel the power of the Lord's Spirit." During the trip Ezra located a home in Salt Lake City on Military Drive for the family to rent until they could find a suitable home to purchase.

Back in Washington, it was largely a matter of clearing up odds and ends. On April 28, 1944, the Washington Stake held a testimonial for the Bensons at the Washington Ward. It was an emotional event. "We were all crying, every member of the family," Ezra remembered. "I had to remind them that when we boarded the train to leave Boise our oldest daughter Barbara, with her big brown eyes filled with tears, had looked over at me and said, 'Daddy, do you think we'll ever find people we love as much as we do the people in Boise?' It was the same experience all over again."

At Ezra's last meeting with the executive committee of the National Council, he was presented with a gold watch. Bidding his colleagues good-bye, emotion choking his voice, he said, "You are the best group of men in this nation outside the Mormon Church, and I wish you were all in it." Tears flowed liberally as each person embraced Ezra and thanked him for his service. In his farewell statement to the National Council he said, "There are no better, more unselfish or higher principled men in any industry than those who make up the leadership of the farm cooperative movement."

The Bensons' send-off from Washington, D.C., was warm. J. Willard Marriott drove them to the train, and as he and Ezra embraced, both had tears in their eyes. Three days later the family arrived in Salt Lake City and spent their first night across the street from their rented home sleeping on Spencer and Camilla Kimball's living room floor. It took three days to unpack their household goods and get the house in order. Ezra then began full-time work in the Church.

One of Elder Benson's first quorum assignments was to serve as executive secretary of the Melchizedek Priesthood committee, which entailed supervising development of the priesthood handbook and evaluating the question of a Churchwide home evening program. Another assignment was adviser to the general boards of the YMMIA and YWMIA, a role that delighted him.

He took on a full load of visiting stake conferences, assignments that, though somewhat intimidating at first, were not foreign to him. He had hosted numerous General Authorities in his home and stake, and thus felt some confidence in presiding over these conferences. Church procedure was deeply ingrained. In his role as apostle, however, he learned how essential it was to rely on the Spirit for direction.

To prepare for a stake reorganization, Elder Benson reviewed in advance the roster of those serving in the stake. On one occasion, while studying a list of the high council, he received a strong impression that the junior member of the high council was to be the new stake president. Initially he shrugged it off, but the impression persisted. The following day, as Elder Benson and Elder S. Dilworth Young of the First Council of the Seventy, who was with him, interviewed priesthood leadership in the stake, every man, when asked to suggest who might lead the stake, named the junior member of the high council. "I've had many experiences since along the same line," Ezra later said, "and all of them are different. But that was the first experience, and it made a very deep impression on me. I've never had any doubt but what the Lord was directing this work."

Still, there was some "learning the ropes." In June he made his "first mistake in Church procedure" by setting apart a new stake president incorrectly. "The First Presidency were most kind and assured me I was not alone in making such mistakes."

Ezra also learned that he didn't always have the answers. While presiding at a priesthood leadership meeting at a stake conference in Orem, Utah, he was asked some detailed questions about the welfare program. He didn't know all the answers, but bore his testimony that the Church was guided by revelation through a prophet, and that in due time all would see the wisdom of the welfare program. (It would be only a few months later that Elder Benson would understand in a personal way that the words he spoke were true.)

Ezra joined Mark at Scout camp, canned peas at Welfare Square with Elders Harold B. Lee and Spencer W. Kimball, and took the children to local canyons for picnics. Flora, despite her pregnancy, did her best to get the house in order and help the children adjust to Salt Lake City. Reed spent many evenings talking with his mother as she sprinkled clothing for ironing. She seemed to sense when he had things on his mind, and even when there was cause for motherly reprimand, she would conclude with, "I love you, Reed, and the only reason I've told you these things is to make you a little better man." None of the children doubted their mother's devotion to them, and they regularly showered her with letters, cards, and poems.

On August 12, 1944, Flora, after a difficult labor, bore her sixth and last child, Flora Beth Benson. Ezra was elated. He wrote in his journal, "Flora is recovering splendidly and the baby, the largest in the hospital, is perfect."

One of the choicest experiences for the young apostle was the Twelve's weekly meeting in the temple. In their room on the fourth floor, the apostles sat according to seniority in large chairs surrounding an upholstered altar. After dressing in temple clothes and forming a prayer circle around the altar, they changed into street clothes and conducted business. Elder Benson began to understand the intense affection that bonds members of the Twelve. It was a brotherhood he had never experienced previously, and soon these men became almost as dear to him as his own family.

Slight of build and with a slender face and goatee, the apostle who sat in the first chair, George Albert Smith, was, to Ezra, one of the kindest men on earth. Though the elderly president had been an apostle since Ezra was four years old, he welcomed Elder Benson as an equal and made him feel comfortable among the imposing group of men.

"It is a moving thing to go into the temple every Thursday, join with the Brethren there, and enjoy the prayers around the altar," Ezra said. "Often tears flowed as I sat there and contemplated the blessings which were mine." With each week his love

Courtesy of Deseret News

*The Benson family in
Christmas photo that
appeared in the*
Deseret News,
December 23, 1944

for his Brethren increased. On one occasion he explained, "I don't think there's a body of men anywhere on the face of the earth who are as close to one another as the Twelve. We have differences of opinion, certainly, yet there's such a spirit of oneness and unity. It's impossible to describe."

Because Ezra had always traveled extensively, his frequent trips out of town were perhaps less an adjustment for him and Flora than for other families whose circumstances differed. Nevertheless, it was a balancing act—taking the girls for a swim in the Great Salt Lake one day, traveling out of town the next—and the constant coming and going was difficult, sometimes more so than others. The afternoon Ezra brought Flora and Beth home from the hospital, he left on a conference assignment in Idaho. Three weeks later, after giving Beth a name and blessing at church and enjoying Sunday dinner with the family, he left on his first extended trip as an apostle.

The tour of the East Central States Mission, combined with meetings of the American Institute of Cooperation (where he was elected vice-president and a member of the executive committee), took him to visit the Saints in twenty-eight cities in just twenty-six days. At a stake conference session in Wilmington, North Carolina, he suffered from the stifling heat and humidity. While speaking at the pulpit he removed his coat and invited the audience to do likewise. Fifty minutes later, his clothing was wet through. Nevertheless, he thrived on intimate association with the Saints, particularly those who made their living from the soil.

The trip took Ezra through Washington, D.C., and he stopped at their old Bethesda home. "I've surely missed you today, especially as I have viewed old scenes where we spent so many happy hours together," he wrote Flora. "I love you dearly and miss you greatly whenever we are separated. I love you even more since Flora Beth has come and am grateful for your willingness to have a family, no matter what the sacrifice might be."[16]

Ezra wasn't oblivious to the strain his lengthy absences placed on Flora. A few days later he wrote her, "My being away places a double responsibility on you, dear, but I know the Lord has and will bless you. It is my constant prayer that you will be given strength sufficient to keep close to the children."

In the same letter Ezra told his wife about a surprising telegram he had just received; he was to deliver a talk on the "Church of the Air" broadcast during general conference. "I feel so weak and the time is so short . . . that it seems an almost impossible task."[17]

These broadcasts were regular features at general conference. In his address, entitled "America, a Choice Land," Ezra outlined the spiritual foundations of America, praised the Constitution as an inspired document, and preached doctrines of repentance and freedom. Quoting a revered U.S. president, he pleaded, "Let us yield then to Lincoln's fervent appeal, 'to humble ourselves before the offended power, to confess our national sins, and to pray for clemency and forgiveness.' As a nation we have been kept as in the hollow of God's hand. But what of the future?"[18]

Elder Benson's spiritual treatment of a secular topic provoked widespread praise. Many who did not belong to the Church requested copies of his talk. He was pleased with the response. Through subsequent months he continued, in keeping with George Albert Smith's counsel, to pursue agricultural and national interests as his time allowed. He spoke to dozens of Scout groups, attended meetings of the five-man Agricultural Postwar Committee in Chicago, and was retained as a director of the National Council of Farmer Cooperatives. When he was named as a candidate for president of Utah State Agricultural College, he kindly declined, citing the important work to which he had been called.

His assignments in the Twelve increased proportionate to his experience, and the pace intensified. There were missionaries to be set apart, marriages and sealings in the temple to perform, and hundreds of people to counsel in his office. He chaired a committee to issue stake conference assignments, advocated formation of an office of research and statistics, which he observed as being past due, and continued as executive secretary of the Melchizedek Priesthood committee.

Elder Benson also served on a committee to review Elder Joseph Fielding Smith's proposed priesthood course of study. When Elder Benson replied that he would be happy to approve anything "Brother Joseph Fielding writes," he was mildly reprimanded: "That will not satisfy Elder Smith. He insists on a review committee. Please read each lesson as he drafts it, then take it to him with any comments you have." Ezra agreed.[19]

Elder Benson was determined, at first, never to turn down a request to speak, but that proved unrealistic. Nevertheless, he responded equally to invitations from small high schools or national associations. As he toured missions and attended stake conferences, he looked past the relentless administrative functions to meet the people. "My right hand ached from shaking hands with about 700 people," he reported after one stake conference.

His counsel was always practical. In Cedar City, Utah, he directed local leaders to build a recreational center for the youth rather than leaving their entertainment in the hands of others. In Great Falls, Montana, when leaders requested permission to spend $10,000 on an underground drainage system, he inspected the property and advised them to simply slope the surface grading away from the chapel. When he noticed, during a conference in a small Utah town, that the people were taking the Church for granted, he told them so and called them to repentance.

On May 8, 1945, Germany surrendered, and Elder Benson felt confident that fighting in the Pacific would soon end. Another milestone of major importance occurred the following week when, on May 14, 1945, President Heber J. Grant died. Ezra couldn't believe the President was gone. He had known that the prophet was weak, but the suddenness of his death shocked him. This was the man who had gently, kindly called him to the Twelve. Heber J. Grant had been president of the Church for twenty-six years. Many Saints remembered no other prophet.

Thousands filed past the casket in the Church Administration Building. After the doors closed to the public, the General Authorities, with George Albert Smith and George F. Richards, the senior apostles, leading them, filed in double columns past President Grant for a final look at their beloved leader. The Tabernacle was filled to overflowing for the funeral. Following the services, the Authorities rode through throngs of people to the cemetery. As the procession passed the Catholic Cathedral of the Madeleine, the bells tolled. Elder Benson found the display of affection "most fitting."

It now fell upon the Council of the Twelve to select, sustain, and ordain a new president of the Church. On Monday, May 21, three days after the funeral, Elder Benson went fasting with the other apostles to their council room in the Salt Lake Temple. David O. McKay and J. Reuben Clark, who had served in the First Presidency under President Grant, resumed their positions of seniority, third and ninth respectively, making fourteen apostles in all. Ezra sat in the thirteenth chair. During the meeting, George Albert Smith was ordained president, and he selected Elders Clark and McKay as first and second counselors, respectively. George F. Richards was sustained president of the Twelve.

Elder Benson was impressed with the orderly transition, which was conducted in an atmosphere of harmony. He had seen nothing like it in the secular world, where expediency and politics motivated too many individuals.

In May, Reed injured his foot, and, while hobbling on crutches, obtained a job herding turkeys at his Uncle Valdo's farm. As Ezra was preparing to drive him to Logan, Reed pulled out several books he had selected to read that summer and asked his father's counsel on them. Ezra told him to put all those aside and take only the Book of Mormon. The Book of Mormon was Elder Benson's first scriptural love. He read it on trains and planes and late in the evening before retiring, and consulted it frequently for answers to gospel questions. Wherever he went, he bore testimony of the book.

In June Elder Benson traveled to Alaska, the first visit to that territory by an apostle and a trip so noteworthy that even the *Anchorage Daily Times*, on June 30, 1945, announced his coming. In Juneau he called on the mayor and governor. In Fairbanks and Anchorage he held standing-room-only meetings in small makeshift chapels and even filled an Episcopal church, where the meeting was attended by the minister and many of his congregation.

As he had done in years previous, Elder Benson planned his itinerary when possible to take him through cities where family members lived. On a trip to San Francisco, he drove to nearby Santa Cruz for a visit with his brother Ben. After Reed entered BYU, Ezra often left early for conferences in the Provo area so he could spend time with his oldest son. When he traveled through Idaho, he stopped to see Margaret or Orval. With his parents gone, he felt responsible for keeping the family together.

On August 14, 1945, word reached Salt Lake City that Japan had surrendered unconditionally. The nightmarish war was over! Horns honked, people danced in the streets, bonfires erupted all over the city, flags flew. The celebration in Salt Lake City— as in the rest of the country—lasted most of the night. Elder Benson, too, was overjoyed. On September 4 he and his family attended a meeting held in the Salt Lake Tabernacle that was sponsored by all Salt Lake churches to give thanks for the cessation of hostilities.

Ezra loved general conference, though it was different when he had to worry about speaking. In the October 1945 conference he suffered "a long period of anxious anxiety" waiting to be called to the pulpit. It was not until the final session that his name was announced. "The fear and overwhelming responsibility of speaking in the Tabernacle and on the air, as six of the sessions were broadcast, almost overpower[ed] me," he wrote in his journal. The next day dozens of visitors seeking advice on spiritual and agricultural issues stopped by his office. In just a short time he had come to be recognized as a man who spoke with power and clarity and who wouldn't pull a punch. The Monday evening after conference, he and Flora entertained some twenty of the Brethren and their wives in a social at their home.

Ezra was mindful of Flora, and when he was home he tried to alleviate some burden by helping her as much as possible. With Reed at BYU, there were still five children at home, ranging in age from one to sixteen. Flora had never fully recovered from complications relative to Beth's birth, and when they purchased and moved to a home on Harvard Avenue, she had been called to the Yale Ward Relief Society presidency, which created more demands on her time.

Ezra took the children for picnics in nearby canyons and parks when possible, helped prepare meals at home, babysat when he could arrange it so she could attend meetings without the responsibility of young children, and helped the children with talks and school lessons. Admittedly, his assistance was sporadic. Flora attended the children's school programs, met with their teachers, and generally tried to provide the support of two. There was never enough time.

It all started to take a toll on Flora. In late November 1945 Ezra noted that she didn't seem at all well, though she resisted the idea of bringing help into the home. "I am away so much that it places an added burden on her, altho I try to help when I'm home as much as my heavy Church duties will permit," he noted.

And the burden was soon to intensify dramatically.

*"In 1946 I visited thirteen countries of Europe.
I saw nations flat on their backs economically.
I saw people who were near starvation. It is heartrending
to see people who have lost their freedom."*

Chapter 12

Mission of Mercy

All of Salt Lake City was in a holiday spirit. For the first time in four years people looked forward to Christmas without the pall of war clouding the season a dismal gray.

Three days before Christmas 1945, President George Albert Smith convened a special meeting of the First Presidency and Council of the Twelve. With World War II over, it was necessary to reestablish contact with the Saints in Europe and distribute much-needed welfare supplies, he said, and the First Presidency had determined that a member of the Twelve should go to Europe for an undetermined length of time to supervise this delicate assignment. As the Brethren listened, each wondered who would receive the appointment. Elder Harold B. Lee later said that as he scanned the room, the first man he eliminated was his boyhood friend, "T" Benson. "He had the largest and youngest family," Elder Lee said. "I felt he would not be selected."

No sooner had Elder Lee reached this conclusion than President Smith announced that after careful and prayerful consideration, Ezra Taft Benson had been chosen to preside over the European Mission. Elder Lee was not the only apostle taken by surprise. To Ezra the announcement came as a shock. There was little time to indulge that emotion, however. He was to

197

travel promptly to Washington, D.C., to obtain necessary passports and visas. Civilians had not yet been admitted into the areas occupied by the Allies in Europe, and red tape hampered all travel on the European continent.

There were advantages in calling Elder Benson to this assignment. He was young and vigorous, had strong administrative skills, and was experienced in dealing with government agencies. He knew how to cut through red tape.

That evening Ezra broke the news to Flora. "In a sweet and impressive talk, sanctified by tears," he wrote in his journal, "Flora expressed loving gratitude and assured me of her wholehearted support."

The following weeks went by quickly. The Bensons enjoyed what Ezra felt was their happiest Christmas ever, and the first of January he traveled to Washington, D.C. He had been warned it would take three months to make the complicated arrangements (it was taking that long just to book overseas transportation), but after three days he returned to Salt Lake City with the necessary arrangements completed for himself and the young man who would accompany him as his secretary, Frederick W. Babbel.

When the Benson family filed into sacrament meeting in the Yale Ward the Sunday evening before Ezra's departure, they were surprised to find the chapel filled to overflowing. A smiling President George Albert Smith was seated on the stand. The meeting was a farewell testimonial for Elder Benson, and afterwards all the family except the baby, Beth, stood in the foyer while the congregation filed by to shake hands.

On Monday, January 28, 1946, President Smith set Ezra apart as president of the European Mission, blessing him with safety, energy, and the ability to break down prejudice. He promised: "There is not anything desirable that you will not be able to do with the aid and the help of the Lord . . . if you do your full part." In a letter from the First Presidency, Ezra was further told that his influence would be felt for good by all, and people would sense there was "a power and spirit accompanying you not of man."

Flora witnessed the blessing, and President J. Reuben Clark, recognizing her sacrifice, praised her when he said, "There is none better than you." That night Ezra wrote, "How true he spoke, for truly in all my acquaintances I have never met a more completely devoted woman with greater faith in the purposes of the Almighty."

The evening of January 29, Elder Benson gathered his family around him one final time for prayer. As he kissed and said good-bye to the five younger children, each cried and clung to him. He also called Reed at BYU and talked until they both choked up. "Leaving my children in tears pulled at my heartstrings," Ezra wrote, "but there was not a murmur." As he and Flora were preparing to leave for the airport, President Smith stopped for a final farewell. Tears streamed the length of the prophet's long, slender face as he embraced and kissed his young associate.

At the airport Elder Benson found Elders Harold B. Lee, Mark E. Petersen, Spencer W. Kimball, and Matthew Cowley waiting to give a fitting send-off. It was snowing heavily, and the gloomy night seemed an ominous beginning for what everyone sensed would prove a demanding, perhaps even dangerous, mission. Emotions ran high.

Flora Benson had learned to live with a man who was often away from home. But this time, Ezra would not return in a few days. In fact, no one knew how long he would be away.

As other passengers boarded the United Airlines flight, Ezra stayed behind with Flora, his arm around her protectively. Finally there was no more time. He embraced his Brethren one by one, then turned to Flora. Tears filled their eyes as they held each other for a final moment. Then he was gone.

"It was most difficult to tell my sweet and ever loyal wife good-bye," he wrote in his journal. "I'll never forget looking down as that plane took off and seeing my Brethren standing there in a circle, with my wife. . . . I quietly shed tears as we soared eastward."

Though Ezra and Flora had talked for hours during the preceding weeks, planning and reassuring each other, neither had belabored the probable danger he would encounter in Europe. As he contemplated what 1946 might bring, Ezra recorded, "I go with no fear whatsoever knowing that this is the Lord's work and that He will sustain me." As for Flora, an unusual calm

Elder Benson and Frederick Babbel board plane in Salt Lake City en route to London, January 1946

overcame her. "It was a peaceful feeling which came over me when I fondly kissed and said good-bye to my devoted and loving husband." As difficult as their parting was, Flora felt strongly about her husband's assignment in Europe. In her journal she wrote of his "exceeding great call."

But things didn't begin smoothly. If the first leg of Elder Benson's trip, from Salt Lake City to New York, was any indication, this mission promised to be a test of faith and endurance. A blizzard grounded their plane in North Platte, Nebraska. Weathermen forecasted unchanging conditions for two days—an impossible delay if Ezra and Fred Babbel were to make their transatlantic connections. Ezra suggested that they pray for direction. Several long-distance phone calls later, he had secured two seats on a train to Chicago. There, though the storm had caused a three-day halt in air traffic, the sky cleared briefly and they boarded the only plane that departed that day. Elder Babbel would come to understand why some would say of Elder Benson that, with God's help, he accomplished the difficult immediately. The impossible took a little longer.

The storm in Salt Lake City raged on also, and Flora was confronted with chores her husband often performed, such as clearing the driveway of snow. The morning after he left she had a flat tire. "I am beginning to realize that our daddy's absence will be greatly missed in so many ways," she wrote.

The separation tugged at Ezra as well. From New York, he called Flora one more time. "It was so good to hear her sweet voice and feel of her undeviating spirit of faith and encouragement," he noted. "How I miss her and my sweet children. The separation pulls heavy on the heartstrings."

The morning of February 3, Elder Benson and Fred Babbel departed New York City. With transatlantic air travel in its infancy, passengers and flight crew shared the same cabin. Two motors were running rough, and the pilot landed in Newfoundland to check and replace sparkplugs before starting across the Atlantic. "The ride was rough in spots," Ezra recorded, "and caused a bit of anxiety, especially as the captain would turn his light on the motors occasionally as tho all was not right."

But a few moments of anxiety were nothing compared to what the apostle found in Europe. Even in London, where he and Fred Babbel were met by President Hugh B. Brown of the British Mission, and where life had regained a measure of normalcy, Ezra felt he had been transferred to another world.

The first evening President Brown briefed him about conditions in England. The Saints there had weathered the strain of war, and many had remained loyal, though the English people generally were downcast and apprehensive. Food and clothing were being strictly rationed. Ezra would find that everything was in short supply, including patience.

The next few days were hectic. Ezra was anxious to get to the Continent, but he couldn't leave London until he had set up an office. There was an acute housing shortage, and rents were exorbitant; yet the European Mission office needed to be in a respectable district and, for efficiency's sake, preferably near agencies he would deal with frequently. Despite a warning that he would probably not find housing for months, the first day out he rented a ground floor flat at 6 Horseshoe Yard, just a block from the American Embassy.

His next step was to call on government officials, including agricultural attachés, the European news manager of the United

Press, and embassy officials, who would help him procure a food ration book and priorities for air travel to Paris. Supper one of the first nights consisted of food allowed by the ration book—bread, butter, cheese, jam, milk, and one-third of a candy bar.

On the morning of February 11, Elder Benson flew to Paris. It was the beginning of travel that would take him, during his first 150 days in Europe, to 102 cities in 13 countries, some of them in the occupied areas of Germany. Complicating what would have been a staggering schedule even under favorable conditions were the facts that highways throughout Europe that had been bombed and strafed with gunfire were nearly impassable, bridges had been demolished, telephone and telegraph facilities were restricted, food was scarce, and all priority space on trains and planes was reserved for military personnel. The challenge of traveling throughout Europe appeared to be a strategical nightmare.

In Paris Elder Benson was met at the airport by a group of Latter-day Saint servicemen, who were elated to greet a General Authority for the first time in several years. An LDS chaplain, Howard C. Badger, secured permission to escort him on his initial tour of the European missions.

In the meantime, Fred Babbel was making travel arrangements in London for their first trip to Scandinavia. He was then to meet Elder Benson at The Hague in the Netherlands. When he arrived in The Hague, he found a telegram waiting with details on Elder Benson's incoming train. Babbel hurried to the station, but the stationmaster insisted the train in question was a local shuttle service, and any passenger arriving from France would come into another station a mile away, where a train from Paris was due. Babbel hurried there, but Elder Benson was not aboard that train. Back and forth he went between the stations, looking for Elder Benson.

Finally he called the Hotel des Indes and learned that Elder Benson had arrived. "How did you get here?" Babbel asked, amazed. "On the train about which I wired you," Ezra replied. "But the stationmaster insisted no passengers from Paris could possibly be aboard that train." "Yes, I know," Elder Benson answered, "they told me that in Paris."

In Paris, Ezra had learned that he and Chaplain Badger would be delayed a full day getting to the Netherlands. Just then he noticed a train preparing to leave for Antwerp, Belgium. The stationmaster warned him against taking the train, as all connections between Antwerp and the Netherlands were cut off. But Ezra felt otherwise, and he and Chaplain Badger boarded the dilapidated train with cardboard windows and wooden slats for seats.

In Antwerp an angry stationmaster insisted the two Americans must backtrack. Again Ezra spotted a train preparing to leave. This one was to stop at the Dutch border, where the Maas River Bridge had been demolished. Again Ezra felt prompted to take it, and over the stationmaster's protests he and Chaplain Badger boarded. As warned, at the Maas River all passengers were forced to pile out, but before long an American Army vehicle approached, and the driver was persuaded to take them to a small village just inside the Dutch border. There they found the local shuttle train leaving for The Hague.

Fred Babbel was amazed at the events, though he would learn to take such developments in stride. During coming months he would see Elder Benson's faith and determination at work countless times.

In the Netherlands, Elder Benson got his first close-up of war's aftermath. The Dutch people had survived terrible conditions during five years of German domination. Entire blocks of homes and offices were rubble. Bridges and wharfs had been bombed. The Germans had confiscated almost everything the Dutch people owned that could be used for the war effort. To escape capture by the Nazis, many young men had lived on the Underground. In a meeting with the Netherlands Mission presidency, Ezra learned that some of the Saints had even placed their lives in jeopardy in order to continue Church activities and save Church properties from being confiscated. The chapel in Rotterdam, however, had been destroyed, and the former mission office in The Hague seriously damaged.

In the meantime, Fred Babbel learned that their flight reservations for Denmark had been cancelled and they couldn't expect passage for at least ten days. Ezra insisted they must leave immediately, and he retired to pray about it. The next morning he contacted officials of the Dutch Military Airlines, the only airline with planes to Copenhagen, who insisted there were no seats available on any outbound flight. "You Americans seem to forget that we've had a terrible war over here," he was told. Ezra headed for the American Embassy, where his credentials gained him immediate audience with the ambassador. He explained that a plane was leaving at noon for Copenhagen and it was urgent they be aboard. The ambassador called airline officials, who finally relinquished two seats, but insisted that they could not provide a third. Undaunted, Ezra hurried back to the airport. Again airline officials insisted only two seats were available, but Ezra smiled and said firmly, "But we *must* all go." A strange look came over the official in charge, who said, "Well, then, you'd better hurry!" All three hurried to the waiting plane and climbed into bucket seats.

The welcome for the apostle in Copenhagen was enthusiastic. The people of Denmark had survived the war perhaps better than those of any other European nation. The Danish Saints had even sent welfare packages to distressed Latter-day Saints in Holland and Norway. Membership had steadily increased, and tithing receipts in the Danish Mission had more than doubled. Ezra was astounded at the faithfulness under the conditions. The Danish Saints considered their circumstances a direct fulfillment of a prophecy that Elder Joseph Fielding Smith had made at the outbreak of the war—that because Denmark had allowed missionaries being evacuated from Germany and Czechoslovakia to enter, its people would not suffer for lack of food during the war.

Members and nonmembers alike came to hear the apostle speak. As he entered the chapel that Sunday, the entire congregation stood while the mission Relief Society president gave him a bouquet of red tulips and white lilacs. Elder Benson was overcome with emotion at the thought of a people ravaged by war presenting *him* with a gift, and in his journal he wrote, "I shall always have sweet memories of this day with the Saints in Copenhagen. Never have I witnessed greater devotion to the Work and deeper love for the leaders of the Church."

From Denmark, Ezra and his companions boarded a train for Stockholm. With the temperature onboard near zero, the ride was extremely uncomfortable. They were met at the Stockholm railway station by Eben R. T. Blomquist, president of the Swedish Mission, and Einar Johannson, president of the Stockholm Branch. The Saints in Sweden had also survived the war in respectable fashion. Tithing had increased by 300 percent, and they had maintained nearly twenty full-time local missionaries throughout the war. Convert baptisms had also increased. Food and clothing were plentiful, though fuel was in critical supply. The day before Elder Benson's arrival, the people had been permitted to bathe in heated water for the first time in several years.

Though he was in Sweden less than forty-eight hours, Elder Benson held three press conferences, visited with the U. S. Minister and the agricultural and military attachés, presided at a public meeting, and held a missionary conference. Elder Fritz Johannson's opening remarks touched President Benson deeply, and when he rose to speak, he felt impressed to issue an unexpected call: "As a servant of the Lord I call upon you, Brother Fritz Johannson, to go to Finland as a missionary to open the way for the preaching of the gospel." Only one small branch existed in Finland, and President Benson felt that many in that country were ready to accept the truth. Elder Johannson accepted the call and departed soon thereafter.

Returning to the train station, Ezra found a large contingent of Saints waiting. They formed a large semicircle and sang, in English, "Farewell to Thee," waving handkerchiefs until the train was out of sight. Ezra's brief stay in Sweden touched him deeply, and he wrote that night, "Never have I become more attached to any people in so short a time."

Next stop, Norway. The Norwegians had endured severe restrictions imposed by the Germans. Elder Benson did what he could to uplift their spirits. His impact on the Saints was immeasurable. Chaplain Badger wrote his wife, Eleanor, "Have seen lots of tears of joy shed this last week by members of the Church in being privileged to meet with Elder Benson, after they had been separated from Church Headquarters . . . for so long. Elder Benson has untiring enthusiasm in the work."[1]

During his first month with Elder Benson, Fred Babbel observed the apostle's ability to confer comfortably with heads of state and Church members alike. He concluded that he had "never met a man of God who was so humble . . . a man who has such an all-consuming love for the children of our Father. Since our arrival he has been able to do more in less time, and that more thoroughly and effectively, than I had ever dreamed to be possible."[2]

Even several decades later, the European Saints who had been present when Elder Benson visited them could remember vividly the dramatic effect his visit had upon them. Many of them felt that he was an emissary of the Savior.

The three Americans returned to Copenhagen in an unheated plane with metal flooring and sides, and as it reached seven thousand feet, the temperature inside plummeted to 20 degrees below zero. "Our ride from Oslo to Copenhagen" Ezra noted, "was the coldest I ever expect to make. . . . Some of the men took their shoes off and rubbed their feet to keep the blood circulating. I kept my feet moving constantly for two hours and fared fairly well."

Their return flight to London wasn't much better. Fred Babbel recorded, "When we finally landed . . . we were a sad-looking lot. At each step our knees would buckle under us. Each foot felt like a large block of ice, and there was virtually no feeling in our legs. Never had I experienced such difficulty in walking. By bathing our legs in cold water . . . we were gradually able to restore some feeling in our limbs."[3]

The European Mission history summarized their initial tour of northern Europe: "During the past two or three weeks we have ridden in unheated trains, trucks and airplanes . . . but in every instance we were greeted upon arrival with such love and warmth of spirit that any hardships encountered in our travels were soon forgotten. Probably the gospel has never been so fully appreciated by the Saints in Europe as during the recent war period. Already we have come to love them deeply."[4]

Back in London an armload of mail, including Valentines from Flora and the children, captured Ezra's attention. Tears filled his eyes as he thought of home. But there was much to be done in preparation for traveling into the occupied areas of Germany. Just five days later, after working through mounds of red tape, the trio left for France.

With the assistance of LDS servicemen, Elder Benson made his first purchase of a surplus military vehicle

Ezra was appalled by what he saw as he arrived in Dieppe, France. "We saw on every side the ravages of war—bridges, highways, cathedrals, homes laid waste," he wrote in his journal. "We could see countless islands of black and holes in the green pastures where bombs had missed their railway target. Rebuilding has started but years will be required to do so." He was told that the destruction in France was mild compared to what he would find in Germany, but it was difficult to imagine anything worse.

Elder Benson's primary objective in Paris was to gain access to the occupied areas of Germany, but when he requested permission from the U.S. colonel in charge of communications with Germany to enter those areas, the officer blurted incredulously, "Mr. Benson, are you *crazy*? Don't you realize there has been a war here? *No* civilian travelers have entered these areas. All travel is restricted for the military."

Nevertheless, Elder Benson quietly asked if he could have permission for travel if he arranged for his own car. Cars were impossible to purchase in America, let alone Europe, the colonel retorted. Ezra countered, "If I *could* arrange transportation and military permission, do you think we might make it?" Annoyed but amazed, the colonel agreed. In a matter of days Ezra had purchased two of the first Citroen autos off the production line and arranged for everything else the colonel required—as well as leased a commodious home to serve as French Mission headquarters.

In the small but new auto, Elder Benson, with Chaplain Badger and Fred Babbel, drove to Basel, Switzerland, and from there, with Max Zimmer, president of the Swiss Mission, set out for Karlsruhe, Germany.

As they crossed the German border, the men found sickening scenes, like a vivid horror movie. Freiburg lay in blackened, twisted ruins, with haunted-looking people shuffling along its streets. Children fled in terror as their car approached.

In Karlsruhe, which was reduced to rubble, Elder Benson finally managed to park next to heaps of twisted steel and concrete. He climbed over the debris and hurried in the direction of faint strains of "Come, Come, Ye Saints." The Saints knew that he might arrive in time for their meeting, and inside a badly scarred building he found three hundred people. Most were dressed in rags; some were emaciated and in the advanced stages of starvation; and all were visibly shivering from the cold, as they had waited for hours for Elder Benson. "As we walked into the meeting," Ezra wrote in his journal, "every eye turned to us. I shall never forget the look in their faces as they beheld for the first time in [seven] years a representative of the General Authorities. It was not me, but the fact that a representative from Headquarters had arrived."

Elder Benson was so deeply moved that he found it difficult to speak, but he managed to preach a sermon of hope, love, and endurance, promising that supplies were coming soon. And he bore testimony: "As I look into your tear-stained eyes and see many of you virtually in rags and at death's door, yet with a smile upon your cracked lips and the light of love and understanding shining in your eyes, I know that you have been true to your covenants. . . . You—many of you—are some of the Lord's choicest witnesses of the fruits of the gospel of Jesus Christ. . . . God is at the helm. He is leading us. He will not permit His Church and kingdom to fail." Elder Benson shook hands with everyone—some of the Saints getting in line two and three times.[5]

As he did throughout Europe, Elder Benson pronounced many blessings—on women whose husbands were missing, on children, on many who were on the verge of starvation. In many cases he was the first priesthood holder the Saints had seen in a long time, and he ministered to their spiritual as well as temporal needs. Through it all he heard no bitterness, though the Karlsruhe Saints had lost almost everything. Instead, they insisted that the Saints in Berlin were worse off. After a tearful good-bye, Elder Benson and his party returned to Switzerland. They were silent as they drove. In a letter to the First Presidency Elder Benson admitted, "The job of taking care of our Saints even as to their most meager needs is overwhelming, and as we contemplate their rehabilitation it becomes staggering." But, he added, "The Lord is blessing our efforts, and I am sure he will continue to do so if we do our best."[6]

Back in Basel, everyone went to work. An agreement was reached with the International Red Cross to supervise the movement of Church welfare supplies into the occupied areas. On March 14, Elder Benson cabled the First Presidency to rush the first shipments through the port of Antwerp.[7]

On March 15 the foursome—Elder Benson, Max Zimmer, Chaplain Badger, and Brother Babbel—left for Frankfurt. This time their small car was loaded with as much food as they could carry. Though Frankfurt had not been listed among Europe's worst-bombed cities, they were shocked at what they found. The city was in sickening shambles.

Permission to proceed further into the occupied zones had to be obtained. In Frankfurt, Elder Benson drove to headquarters of the United States Forces, European Theatre, to seek audience with Joseph T. McNarney, the four-star general in charge of American forces in Europe. When an aide rudely denied Ezra's request to see General McNarney, by saying it would take at least three days to arrange such an appointment, Elder Benson went back to the car and suggested that they pray for guidance. Moments later, he returned to the general's office, where a different aide received his request. Within fifteen minutes he was ushered in.

It was evident, however, that General McNarney was annoyed at being disturbed. And when he heard of Elder Benson's proposed itinerary throughout Germany, Austria, and Czechoslovakia, he looked incredulous. But as his visitor continued to speak with conviction and feeling, the general softened visibly. Finally he said, "Mr. Benson, there's something about you that I like. I want to help you in every way I can." When Ezra explained that the Church had storehouses bulging with foodstuffs and clothing that could be shipped within twenty-four hours, the general was amazed. "Mr. Benson, I have never heard of a church with such vision," he responded, agreeing to authorize the Church to distribute supplies through its own channels. He cautioned Ezra that he and his companions would be the first American civilians to travel to Berlin by car, and that the military could not be responsible for their safe passage. But he also approved the Church's bringing two mission presidents into Germany, pending approval of the United States State Department and Joint Chiefs of Staff.

On March 19 Elder Benson proceeded further into the occupied areas, stopping in Hannover. "People walking about in the ruins," he recorded, "seem almost as tho they were from another world. My heart grows heavy and my eyes fill with tears as I picture in my mind's eyes these scenes of horror and destruction." With only two hours' notice he held a meeting with the Saints in a partially bombed schoolhouse. "The spirit of the meeting was marvelous to feel and behold. How I longed for power to lift these good people from their heart rending state," he wrote. That night he slept on a straw tick covered by a smelly blanket. In some of these meetings the Saints could find nothing but potato peelings to use for the sacrament.

Then it was on to Berlin. What he found there was indescribable. Miles of the city lay in utter waste. "Drove through once beautiful Berlin," he wrote the first night. "The wreckage . . . cannot possibly be understood unless seen. My soul rebels as I attempt to describe it. Truly war is hell in all its fury."

Months later, after witnessing dozens of similar scenarios, he wrote to Flora, "I'm so grateful you and the children can be spared the views of the terrible ravages of war. I fear I'll never be able to erase them from my memory."

In three days of meetings with military officials in Berlin, Elder Benson secured permission to resume the Church program there. Over seventeen hundred Latter-day Saints in Berlin were unaccounted for, and he marveled that anyone had escaped war's wrath at the epicenter. His journal observations are descriptive: "I witnessed scenes that seemed almost outside this world. . . . I saw the pomp and beauty of once proud Berlin at one time heralded by God-less leaders as the product of the 'master race' that would throw the principles of Christianity out the window and conquer the world by force, now a mass of sad wreckage. . . . I smelled the odor of decaying, human bodies. . . . I saw old men and women with small hatchets eagerly digging at tree stumps and roots in an effort to get scraps of fuel and then pulling them home for miles on anything that would roll. . . . Later I faced in a cold half wrecked 3rd floor auditorium off a bombed street 480 cold half-starved but faithful Latter-day Saints. . . . It was an inspiration to see the light of faith. I heard their harrowing experiences including murder, rape and starvation of their loved ones. Yet there was no bitterness or anger but a sweet . . . expression of faith in the gospel."

Next stop, Nuremberg, where the Nazi war trials were in process. The scenes of devastation persisted, and the group's travel was seriously retarded as they dodged shell craters in roads, made tiresome detours around bombed bridges, and routinely spent over a dozen hours a day in a cramped car plagued with flat tires. They stopped only to meet with Saints wherever they could find them and to negotiate with officials.

Often their only food was the K-rations they carried in the trunk; more than once they made breakfast, lunch, and dinner of the Army cuisine, which made up in nourishment what it lacked in flavor. They rose early and worked late, seldom getting more than five hours' rest a night, and were usually so tired by day's end that a flimsy cot or the floor sufficed for sleep. In a letter to his wife, Fred Babbel wrote, "All in all we are having it really rough . . . to see members of our Church in the last stages of starvation, eyes bulging out, legs and ankles swelling, and becoming so listless that it is a major effort to

THIS AREA IS BEING RETAINED AS A SHRINE TO THE 238.000 INDIVIDUALS WHO WERE CREMATED HERE PLEASE DONT DESTROY

Elder Benson at Dachau, World War II concentration camp in Germany

speak. . . . The pace we are keeping is terrific. . . . When one sees all the starving and suffering . . . he is driven to work day and night."[8]

The element of danger, though ever-present, seemed to concern Elder Benson only occasionally. Despite warnings that caused him anxiety, he and his associates traveled into Czechoslovakia, where Russian guards stopped them repeatedly but each time allowed them to proceed.

Once his plane plowed through a thunderhead and was struck by a large bolt of lightning. A fireball about the size of a basketball bounced between the metal sides of the plane as it lost control, hurtling toward the ground. But the pilot brought it under control just in time to avoid the treetops.

Some things were even more frightening. Dachau, where the Americans saw the crematorium where 238,000 Jews were exterminated, was one of them. "The scenes and statistics given made us shudder to realize how far men will go in evil and sin when they discard the eternal truths of the gospel," Ezra wrote in his journal.

Flora wrote her husband frequently, often several times a week, and her letters were encouraging and optimistic. She also sent packages filled with everything from gum and hard candy to needles and thread.

Because he was seldom in one place very long, Ezra's mail was often delayed several weeks. One day he stopped at the mission home in Basel after a lengthy trip through Germany and found a large pouch of mail waiting. One of Flora's letters struck instant fear in the apostle. Their daughter Beth was critically ill with pneumonia. The letter had been written two weeks earlier.

He remembered, "I was scheduled within two hours to be the main speaker at the beautiful new chapel in Basel. Hundreds of people from many parts of Switzerland would be there to learn about our visit [to Germany, Austria and Czechoslovakia] just completed. I was torn with such anxiety that I felt unable to participate unless I could be assured of my child's welfare. Yet to get word at this late hour was a practical impossibility. Previous phone calls to the United States had required one to two days to complete. . . . Faced with such a problem I realized I must seek my guidance and assurance through my Heavenly Father. As I prayed at my bedside in the quiet of my room, I received the overwhelming impression to place a phone call without delay. Much to my joy, and somewhat to my astonishment, the call was completed in less than ten minutes. My wife's voice was as clear as though she were in the room at my side. What a sense of gratitude and relief I felt to learn that the crisis had just passed! Our beloved baby daughter would live."[9]

At home, Flora had had her hands full. For days and nights she had given the baby sulfa and administered mustard plasters every other hour. With little sleep, the ordeal had taken its toll on her. President George Albert Smith had administered to the baby, and when President J. Reuben Clark called Flora's bishop to ask what compassionate service the Relief Society might render, he learned that Flora was a member of the presidency. "How much do you think one woman can take?" President Clark asked. "Release her. She's carrying a burden twice that of most women."

The greatest burden was the long separation from her husband. Never had Flora been separated from Ezra for such a long time and without means of adequate communication. Calls to Europe were expensive and connections usually poor. Her great source of sustenance was in writing to him, and often she wrote late into the night. Her letters were those of a woman deeply in love with her husband and devoted to helping him in his difficult assignment. And they were the writings of a woman with faith.

"I have been given an abundance of added strength during Beth's sickness from our Father in Heaven," she wrote. "I have felt His Spirit so close to me at times in protecting, directing, guiding and comforting me that I have marveled at it."

Ezra's letters home were an elixir to her. "T dear, you and your letters mean everything to me," she wrote him. "I couldn't carry on without them. Life to me is so worthwhile having you as my husband." After receiving two letters the same day, she wrote back, "I've just been walking on air today since I received them. I have read [and] reread them—just can't get my work done [and] I don't seem to care."

Constantly she reassured her husband that all was well at home. "May you have a peace of mind always, T, and know that things are going well with us. Don't worry about us," she told him.

And she left no doubt about the source of her confidence and strength. "Honey dear, if we do our part, the Lord never fails us."

And yet there were lonely, difficult times at the home on Harvard Avenue, times when one of the children would find her crying silently as she ironed at night. Elder Levi Edgar Young of the First Council of the Seventy once told Flora that "the wife and mother who stays home and watches over the career of her little children is the bravest character in the world."

Some of Flora's everyday activities demanded a quiet kind of bravery—providing comfort to the children, though she herself at times was in need of comfort; juggling finances and sending Ezra money as she could; carrying the load of teaching and disciplining the children; rallying the family, trying to be both father and mother. Beverly, then eight, wrote her father, "I miss you very much but I know you were told to go to London. We are doing a play in school and inviting our Mother's and Daddy's. I wish my Daddy could see the play in school."

One of Barbara's friends asked if her father would be home for Christmas. When she replied she didn't know, the friend advised, "Tell your daddy to work day and night so he can come home sooner."

Ezra *was* working nearly day and night, and the results were showing. When general conference convened in April 1946, frequent mention was made of his activities in Europe.

Following the concluding session, Flora wrote him, "Yesterday was the happiest day I've experienced since you left, because we heard so many good things about you the whole day. . . . Were we excited and thrilled when Pres. Smith announced that Brother Badger had just arrived that morning at 3 o clock [and] that he had been with you just three days ago."

Chaplain Badger visited with Flora, and afterwards she wrote her husband that the officer had told her Ezra was "working too hard—both day [and] night. He said when you get a big job accomplished you never stop for rest—but continue on with greater determination. He couldn't say finer [and] grander things of a man. I told him it wasn't new, how grand you were, to me."

And others from the Continent sent word to Flora. Tessy Vojkuvka from Czechoslovakia wrote her: "We must thank you in our broken English for the sacrifice you make in giving your husband . . . to us foreign people in Europe. . . . Br. Benson brought to us so much happiness, he encouraged us so, that we have now new strength again to work for our Heavenly Father."[10]

Eben R. T. Blomquist, president of the Swedish Mission, wrote: "No matter where [your husband] has gone, as he has watched the little children, he has picked them up, he has talked to them, he has shown them pictures of his own family; and where these dear ones would remind him of his own at home, I could see the smile on his face and also the longing to be with his own again. . . . I doubt there could be anyone who could endear himself so much in the hearts of all the people in Europe as your husband has done."[11]

After April conference, Flora told Ezra that President Smith worried that he was working too hard. How hard was too hard, Ezra wondered, when the Saints were suffering—physically and spiritually? It drove him to work nearly around the clock.

Elder Benson at site of what was formerly a bank in Offenbach, Germany

There were so many kinds of problems to handle. In one area so many false practices had slipped into local Church units during their years of isolation from headquarters that Ezra lamented that if the war had persisted much longer, there would have been "crowns and crosses" on every pulpit.[12] In remote areas of Scandinavia and Germany, the sacrament hadn't been administered for over a year due to lack of priesthood authority. Throughout the Continent there were mission homes and land to purchase, chapels to rebuild, construction materials to procure from somewhere. National welfare organizations in Norway demanded that the Church distribute some of its supplies to the people at large through their networks, though there was evidence of improprieties in their manner of distribution. It took lengthy conferences, but Elder Benson changed their minds.

There was a struggle with bureaucratic red tape in nearly every country. Some governments allowed the missionaries to reenter; others would not. With the food shortages in Great Britain, visas were limited to a few weeks, virtually halting the missionary program until Elder Benson persuaded officials to grant more visas. In large part, his mission was a constant challenge of diplomacy.

The food shortage was a prime topic all over Europe, and at the urging of the First Presidency, Ezra accepted an invitation to represent the National Council of Farmer Cooperatives at the International Conference of Agriculture Producers in London in late May. Many delegates from European nations subsequently invited him to contact them further when he visited their countries. In September, by special invitation, he joined the American delegation to the Conference of Food and Agriculture Organization of the United Nations in Copenhagen. From there he wrote Flora, "I am mixing in a good bit of church work. . . . I spoke to the [American delegation] re my observations in Europe. We were together for 4 hours . . . spent discussing spiritual and moral problems and our church."

Ezra was strong. Those traveling with him struggled to keep pace. After several months in Europe, Fred Babbel was down to 130 pounds. But at times, the privations of the Saints were almost too much for even Ezra to bear. He missed the weekly temple meetings with his brethren, and as the weight of his errand wore on him, he frequently suffered from insomnia. "From my observation," wrote Fred Babbel, "he not only talked matters over with the Lord, but the Lord was not unmindful of him and was pleased to reveal to him things beyond the normal comprehension of man. After each such experience he appeared to gain new strength."[13]

Letters and packages from Flora and occasional phone calls home also sustained him. Flora counseled him, inspired him, and gave him increased confidence in himself. As time passed, though separated, their love deepened with the sweet affection born of absence. Both were of strong spirit and mind, but Ezra's continued absence was never easy for Flora. One of Barbara's letters revealed that sometimes her "mother was pretty sad," but we "all try to cheer her up the best we can."

Usually, though, Flora cheered herself on. When loneliness closed in, she wrote to Ezra. And he responded in kind. "Darling girl, I love you with all my heart and ever miss you and doing for you. Sometimes I wonder what people do who are separated from their wives and not engaged in the work of the Lord." In another letter he acknowledged her effect on him: "I could never have accomplished what I have with anyone else. We've done it together. . . . To you who [have] remained in the background goes most of the credit for anything we accomplished. Your love and constant devotion mean more to me than life itself."

Many times Flora's support was manifest in very practical ways. In Hamburg Elder Benson found five hundred Saints thin, weak, and hungry. Near the conclusion of one meeting he asked the children under eight to line up in the middle aisle. As they walked past, he distributed gum, candy, and fruit from Flora's packages, breaking pieces in two to make it go around. "These sweet, eager, but polite little ones almost broke my heart as they looked up with their large eyes and pale faces," he wrote to Flora. "Then I had all mothers with babies come up and I distributed a bar of soap to each and a few safety pins, needles and thread. . . . Flora dear, you'll never know how much those few little things mean." In his journal that night he wrote, "Surely when the Lord chooses the most faithful these His suffering children will be among those most blessed."

On another occasion, as Elder Benson and his associates drove toward Kiel, Germany, they saw dozens of people combing the ditch banks. He described the scene in a letter home: "Some take ordinary grass and weeds and cut it up to mix with a little chicken feed and water which is their meal. I noticed between meetings some would take out of their pocket a little cup partly filled with chicken feed or cereal and water which they would eat cold. . . . I didn't intend to write all this sad picture. I have tried to spare you at home most of the heartrending scenes in Europe today. But somehow I just couldn't hold it this morning. It's terrible to contemplate. I know the Lord permits the righteous to suffer as he pours out His judgments on the wicked."

On June 21, 1946, the first shipments of welfare supplies for the Saints in Germany and Austria arrived in Geneva. With the needs so acute, every precaution was taken to insure maximum security and efficiency in distribution. Ezra insisted that there be no concentration of large quantities of food or supplies in the occupied areas. An ongoing stock of supplies was

*Elder Benson
and Max Zimmer
inspect boxes
of welfare supplies
in warehouse
of International
Red Cross
at Geneva*

to be maintained in Geneva. And he closely monitored products being shipped, adjusting quantities of foods, types and sizes of clothing, and so forth.[14]

When the first shipment of welfare supplies arrived in Berlin, Elder Benson took acting mission president Richard Ranglack to the battered warehouse that, under armed guard, housed the precious goods stacked nearly to the ceiling. "Do you mean to tell me those boxes are full of food?" President Ranglack asked. "Yes," Ezra replied, "food, clothing, bedding, and a few medical supplies." To prove his point, he pulled down a box of dried beans. As Ranglack ran his fingers through the contents, he broke down and cried. Ezra opened another box, this one filled with cracked wheat. Ranglack touched a pinch of it to his mouth. When he could finally speak, he said, "Brother Benson, it is hard for me to believe that people who have never seen us could do so much for us."[15]

On Monday evening, June 24, Elder Benson witnessed the most poignant scene to date when he stopped in Langen (near Frankfurt) to meet with ninety Latter-day Saint refugees who had fled Poland and East Germany. His heart went out to them, living as they were in the most unfavorable conditions imaginable—four families in a thin-walled one-room frame structure with a leaking roof. There were no sanitary facilities or water nearby. A small stove in the middle of the rough floor provided the only heat, and everyone slept on the floor.

Technically the refugees were in Langen illegally, but they had already planted gardens and shown a desire to help themselves. Elder Benson received permission for them to stay, and he tried to better their condition. He recorded his plans to help: "I hope we can in spite of military restrictions, get some lumber or barracks and more food, blankets and clothing to provide at least one room for each family. We'll try and purchase immediately in Basel . . . curtain material and wire for dividing the large rooms into a bit of privacy."

Elder Benson dealt with many people who had been abandoned and destitute, but there were many outpourings of the Spirit as he and his companions attended to physical as well as spiritual needs. One Sunday morning in Herne, Germany, a children's chorus set the tone for a memorable meeting. Elder Benson walked to the pulpit and, referring to the children, said, "I hope you were listening carefully as the children were singing. Let me assure you they were not singing alone. The angels were singing with them. And if the Lord would touch your spiritual eyes and understanding, you would see that many of your loved ones, whom you have lost during the war, are assembled with us today."[16]

The war exacted a demanding price from the Finnish people. The Germans entered Finland the summer of 1941 and remained there until 1944. At first, the Finnish people saw the Germans as protection against neighboring Russia, but now they were paying dearly for three years of German domination. Ezra found that there was an acute food shortage, communications and transportation were unreliable, and the people suffered from anxiety over the future.

On July 16, 1946, at a site not far from Larsmo, Elder Benson dedicated Finland for the preaching of the gospel. He described the events in his journal: "We formed in a half moon on the large flat rock, from which we could see in all directions for long distances. As in the quiet of early morning the glory of God's sunlight shown thru the trees. . . . During the prayer we were overjoyed in our humility to feel powerfully the Spirit of the Lord as we were all moved to tears. Several sobbed like children."

The Finns won Ezra's heart. The group of fourteen faithful Saints there, though ravaged by war, had been 100 percent tithe payers and had 100 percent attendance at church. The morning of his departure many gathered at the train station at 4:30 A.M. to bid him farewell. More tears were shed as they sang "God Be With You" and the dilapidated old train rolled down the track. About his departure Ezra noted, "As I waved a final goodbye as they went out of sight I thought silently, these are the kind of saints I should like to associate with in Eternity."

For several months Ezra sought permission to enter Poland, but repeated attempts to secure visas from the Polish embassy had been unfruitful. After yet another failure, Fred Babbel recorded the following: "I sensed deeply with him that we were faced with a seemingly insurmountable problem. After moments of soul-searching reflection, during which neither one of us broke the silence, he said quietly but firmly, 'Let me pray about it.' Some two or three hours after President Benson had retired to his room to pray, he stood in my doorway and said with a smile on his face, 'Pack your bags. We are leaving for Poland in the morning!' At first I could scarcely believe my eyes. He stood there enveloped in a beautiful glow of radiant light."[17]

The two men made their way to Berlin. There the ranking general at Polish Military Mission Headquarters said it would take at least fourteen days to clear visas to enter Poland. Ezra asked if he might call on the general again, and the officer agreed. Two days later, when Ezra returned, he procured the necessary security clearances within ten minutes. Soon thereafter the Americans booked passage on the one plane a week that flew to Warsaw.

In Warsaw Elder Benson and his companion stayed at the Polonia Hotel in a small room shared with seven other men. The pillage and devastation they saw seemed almost too much to bear. Ezra wrote to Flora, "As one walks about the city the most sickening odors meet you from debris, dead bodies in the ruins and filth. Because of the lack of sanitary facilities the people generally are filthy. . . . Cripples are everywhere. . . . One feels so helpless amidst it all, that you find yourself wanting to leave or shut yourself from it in your room."

In Warsaw a missionary representing a Protestant church was incredulous when he heard that Ezra intended to visit scattered Latter-day Saints throughout Poland in a week's time. This man had been in Warsaw for over a month and hadn't been able to so much as secure a Jeep to take him beyond the city limits. But Elder Benson was determined, and U.S. Ambassador Arthur Bliss Lane proved sympathetic, promising to help secure transportation if he could.

Through one means or another Ezra and Fred Babbel traveled throughout Poland. On Sunday, August 4, accompanied by Francis Gasser, an LDS military employee from Berlin, they left by Jeep for southern Poland in an attempt to locate members. At dusk they arrived in the village of Selbongen (now Zelbak). The streets were deserted, but they spotted a woman cowering behind a tree. She was terrified until Elder Benson identified himself. Suddenly she exclaimed, "The elders have arrived from Zion!" kissed his hands, and ran from door to door, crying, "The Brethren are here!"

Within minutes the nearby church, what was left of it, was filled with overjoyed Saints who were hugging each other and crying. The small group had prayed and fasted for "the Lord to send the Brethren," and after handshakes all around, Elder Benson spoke to them. During his remarks two armed Polish soldiers entered the door. Elder Benson could see that the people were instantly filled with fear. He paused long enough to motion the soldiers to front-row seats, then continued speaking on freedom. The soldiers left without disturbance.

Ezra recorded in his journal: "We listened to the most harrowing accounts of the dastardly deeds of Russian soldiers. . . . Women and even little girls . . . were ravaged. . . . Cases were reported where as many as 10 soldiers one after the other forced relations with young girls . . . and in some cases while parents looked on at the point of a bayonet. . . . Never in all my life

Elder Benson meets with a group of Saints in Poland

have I heard of such terrors, many of which included cold-blooded murder of husbands as their wives looked on helplessly."

Ezra did what he could for these and other isolated groups of Saints before leaving Poland. When he again ran into the Protestant missionary at the Warsaw airport, the man was astonished to learn how extensively Elder Benson had traveled throughout the country.

Months later, when a second trip to Poland was cancelled, Ezra realized how miraculous his trip to Poland had been. Again he wrote Flora: "I'm not going [back to] Poland. The authorities advise against it and the Polish military officials here seem to be against it. In fact, they've told me that I shouldn't have traveled freely in Poland contacting our German Saints as I did before. . . . When I talked with my good Polish friend who is head of the Polish Military Mission, he tells me that the officials in Poland are surprised I traveled about the nation without being stopped. And apparently they are somewhat displeased. But as our Ambassador said to me yesterday, 'Mr. Benson, it's fortunate for you, I suppose, that you were not familiar with all their restrictions or else you would not have been able to contact your people in Poland at all.' So again the Lord has worked things out for us in a most peculiar way."

In early August Elder Benson learned that Elder Alma Sonne, an Assistant to the Twelve, had been called to succeed him in Europe. The news was unexpected. He had planned to be in Europe for another six months and believed there was much left to do. But he was delighted to be going home. In a moment of rare reflection, he admitted that the previous months had been "a bit rough and rugged, but the Lord has sustained me in a most remarkable way."

But because word of the change came so suddenly, Elder Benson wondered if his performance had been acceptable. Then an unusual experience allayed his fears, and he recorded it in his journal: "Last night, in a dream, I was privileged to spend, what seemed about an hour, with Pres. George Albert Smith in Salt Lake. It was a most impressive and soul-satisfying experience. We talked intimately together about the Great Work in which we are engaged and about my devoted family. I felt the warmth of his embrace as we both shed tears of gratitude for the rich blessings of the Lord. . . . The last day or so I have been wondering if my labors in Europe have been acceptable to the First Pres'y and the Brethren at home and especially to my Heavenly Father. This sweet experience has tended to put my mind completely at ease, for which I am deeply grateful."

Shortly thereafter Elder Harold B. Lee wrote Ezra, "The brethren are united in the feeling that you have performed a glorious mission and a work that could hardly have been accomplished by one of lesser courage and ability . . . and with undaunted faith in the power of the Lord to overcome obstacles."[18]

At home Flora had driven herself to exhaustion. Before Ezra left for Europe, they had learned she needed an operation— complications from childbearing. Then the call to Europe had come, and the doctor had agreed to postpone surgery. But in mid-October he warned that because of the strain of the previous months, her condition had deteriorated. He insisted on operating immediately.

Flora took the news fairly well, but when Ezra received word, he was distraught. It took two days to get a call through to his wife, and then the connection was so poor that they could barely understand each other. "We could hardly talk for crying," he wrote, "but her last words were, 'Don't tell the Brethren, but stay and fill your mission.' "

Ezra felt extreme concern over an unfinished mission and his wife's condition. He told Bill Marriott by letter, "I fear it would almost break her heart if she felt that I was called home before my mission was fully completed." He worried that if he left Europe without orienting Elder Sonne, sensitive contacts with government agencies might be jeopardized.[19]

Ezra fasted and prayed for guidance and then called Elder Lee to ask if he would talk with the doctor and also administer to Flora. Neither man could hold back the tears as they struggled to make themselves understood long distance. The next day Ezra received a sad letter from Flora, written in a moment of loneliness. "How I wish I could be close to her!" he lamented that night.

It was several days before Ezra learned that Elder Lee had given the blessing, and a few more days before he heard that the doctor had agreed to delay the operation until he could return home.

With each week the pangs of separation were eased by the knowledge they would soon be together. "Mark Petersen said in a letter that he saw you and you were looking fine and counting the days until I return," Ezra wrote to Flora in late September. "The days are being well counted, dearest, because I'm doing it too."

Elder Sonne arrived in London on November 16, 1946, and three days later he and Elder Benson left for a three-week orientation tour of the nine missions. It was Ezra's last visit with the European Saints, and everywhere he went they showered him with affection. In Frankfurt, a tear-filled audience listened to him deliver his last address. "I had some difficulty in speaking because of the emotion that welled in my bosom," he said later. He shook hands with each of the four hundred present before leaving, though his arm was already sore from days of handshaking.

In a final message, Elder Benson bid his beloved Saints farewell: "Here we have found faith, loyalty, and devotion unsurpassed in the annals of Church history. Only through a testimony that God lives and has . . . established His Church can men and women stand amidst the rubble, which was once happy homes, with hope and courage. Only with a faith in the ultimate consummation of the Lord's purposes can people, with all their earthly possessions swept away, continue with spirits sweet and hearts free from bitterness. . . . I promise you the richest blessings of eternity inasmuch as you continue faithful."

On December 9 Ezra wrote Flora one last time from Europe. "I'm constantly singing and walking on air in contemplation of our sweet meeting. . . . Sweetheart, I thank the Lord for you and thank you for your undeviating loyalty and support. . . . I love you so very much—more than when I left, if such a thing is possible."

Elder Benson departed London for New York City on December 11. In ten months he had traveled 61,236 miles by plane, train, ship, automobile, bus, and Jeep. Mission presidents were functioning in most European Missions; some ninety-two boxcars full of food, clothing, and bedding had arrived in Europe; missionaries were proselyting in many countries; and the Saints had a renewed spirit of hope.[20]

The night of December 12, Flora made the final entry in her "mission" journal: "I can hardly wait for my adorable husband to arrive. I don't believe I can sleep all night." She was waiting when he stepped off the plane at 6:00 A.M.

Six years later, in general conference of October 1952, Elder Benson told how the experience in Europe had changed him and how he appreciated even more deeply his testimony, the priesthood, and the gospel. And he reflected on memories, many of which went nearly beyond his power to describe: "I presume you have never had the great and trying experience of looking into the faces of people who are starving when you are unable to give them even a crust of bread. We faced that as we first met with the Saints in parts of Europe. But when the welfare supplies came, it was a time never to be forgotten. . . . I can see them now in tears, weeping like children. . . .

"The aftermath of war is usually worse than the actual physical combat. Everywhere there is the suffering of old people, innocent women and children. Economies are broken down, the spirits of people crushed, men and women bewildered. . . . It is a saddening thing to see people who have lost their freedom. . . .

"[But] the Saints. . . . taught me a deeper appreciation for this intangible thing we refer to as a testimony—this thing that provides an anchor for men and women during times of great stress, trial, and hardship. . . . I saw people peacefully happy in their hearts, while standing amidst the ruins all around them. I heard people bear testimonies to the goodness of the Lord unto them, although they were the sole remaining member of a once prosperous and happy family. . . . I came to know. . . that men and women who have a testimony of this work can endure anything which they may be called upon to endure and still keep sweet in spirit."[21]

It was nine months after Ezra's return that Elder Harold B. Lee summarized the significance of his associate's emergency mission: "I think the most signal thing he has done in his present career is his mission to Europe. . . . The hazards of this mission, the obstacles that had to be overcome . . . all called for a particular kind of missionary service. Ezra Taft Benson performed all that and more in a mission that took him away from a little family at a time when his absence entailed the kind of support that only families such as his were prepared to give."[22]

*"The outlook for the world is not encouraging,
but we know what the answer is. There is
only one answer, and that is the gospel of
Jesus Christ."*

Chapter 13

Young Apostle

For the same reason missionaries proclaim their era of full-time proselyting the best years of their lives, Ezra's ten months in Europe was the most growing period of life for him and his family. Never before had his faith, endurance, and energy been so greatly put to the test. As a diamond is formed under great pressure, so was this "diamond in the rough," as Flora had called her rough-hewn farm boy, refined under pressure of another sort.

And while he had met the challenge in Europe, Flora had done the same at home. As they talked, planned, and dreamed until near daybreak his first night back, they were elated to be together, immensely thankful for each other's support, and grateful to Him who had given them the assignment and then helped them prove equal to the challenge. As much as they had cared for each other before, both sensed something wonderful had happened to their relationship. It was nothing they could describe, but the feeling was overwhelming. Between them, there was a new bond.

Flora hoped Ezra would slow down now. He was much thinner than before. Aunt Carmen said her nephew "looked bad. . . . I could have wept for him. But when I mentioned it he insisted, 'I'm fine.' " The First Presidency felt the same, and after Ezra had given preliminary reports, they advised him to take some time away from the office for relaxation and to see Flora through her surgery, which was scheduled after Christmas.

With Mark and Reed tending the girls, Ezra and his wife stole away to Cache Valley for a four-day retreat. They visited relatives, read and wept over each other's journals from the period just past, and relaxed.

On Christmas Eve they returned home to find the house spotless, tree trimmed, presents wrapped, and children anxious for their return. Coming after so many months of separation, this Christmas was indeed a joyful holiday. And, as Ezra and Flora anticipated the departure of their eldest son for the mission field, they knew it would be some time before the whole family would enjoy Christmas together again.

With the celebrating behind, Flora entered LDS Hospital in Salt Lake City on December 29. Her operation the following morning, which lasted three hours, was successful.

On New Year's Eve, Ezra reflected in his journal on the year just past: "As I close this volume I sit in my lovely home in the quiet of a peaceful winter night. It is a bit lonely with Flora . . . at the hospital. . . . This has no doubt been the most eventful year of my life to date. . . . Altho I have been put to many inconveniences and hardships, so called, because of the devastation of war, yet I feel sure my ever-faithful and devoted wife has had the hardest end of the mission. She has been true blue in every respect, and I'm grateful for her, the unity in my family, and their constant support."

As though the scenes weren't still vivid in his mind, letters from European Saints flooded Ezra with memories of all he had seen. One from Czechoslovakia is typical: "Our English is not very good, but we hope you can understand all the desire of our hearts and souls, to make you feeling happy and contented after the many hardships and sorrows you have had on your many trips in Europe. We will never forget you and the sweet spirit we felt in your presence."[1]

Flora returned home on January 8, 1947, and while she was convalescing nicely, Ezra had never regained his strength since returning from Europe. For months he had run on raw energy and nerves, and the strain had finally caught up with him. Even news on January 21 of his appointment to a three-year term as a trustee of the American Institute of Cooperation didn't perk him up.

It was difficult to find time to relax. But when his energy had not returned by February, and Flora was still recuperating, the First Presidency insisted he take time off. The doctor prescribed three weeks. Ezra consented to a week's vacation in Arizona with Flora and without meetings, speaking engagements, or paperwork. It was their first real vacation together since Reed was born. They soaked up the desert sun, rested, and listened to Book of Mormon records. Ezra returned to Utah physically and spiritually refreshed.

It was a good thing, because he was in demand on all fronts. In February 1947 he was one of the few American civilians who had seen the occupied areas of Europe firsthand. It seemed that everyone—from organizations to universities—wanted his time. Members of the press dogged him; speaking requests came in by the score. Above all, he was anxious to resume a full load of church work.

The Church was surging forward with unprecedented growth and vigor. In 1946 the number of missionaries in the field was 2,244; by 1950, over 5,100 were serving. In 1949 nearly two hundred meetinghouses were completed; just three years later the total reached nine hundred. With postwar social trends and a sharp increase in the number of marriages (and hence, divorces) placing stress on families and youth, the Church emphasized a regular "family hour" and bolstered its youth programs. (In October 1947, in "Responsibilities of the Latter-day Saint Home," Elder Benson had delivered one of the few conference addresses in decades on the value and importance of home evening.) And 1947 was a benchmark year—the centennial of the pioneers' entry into the Salt Lake Valley. Every effort was made to pay fitting tribute.

On February 20, 1947, Ezra left for his first extended trip since Europe, traveling to stake conferences in Chicago, New York, Florida, and Washington, D.C., where Flora joined him. The pace was hectic. In Chicago he presided over his first stake conference in over a year, and after speaking at four meetings, performing ordinations and blessings, and inspecting Church properties, he called it a "glorious experience." In Rochester, New York, he toured the Peter Whitmer, Joseph Smith, and Martin Harris farms, which the Church owned but which were unprofitable as agricultural enterprises. After observing the operations, he forwarded recommendations to the First Presidency.

When Elder Benson had returned from Europe, one of his first recommendations had been formation of a mission in Finland. The Brethren agreed, and President McKay assigned him to find a mission president who could speak Finnish. But thus far the search had been unsuccessful. As Ezra and Flora left Washington, on a rare trip when she accompanied him, their train stopped in Indianapolis. The conductor assured them they had ten minutes before it departed, so they left to get a newspaper. When they returned five minutes later, the train was pulling out of the station with all of their belongings onboard. Ezra had only a few dollars in his pocket. Then he remembered a friend from his farmer cooperative days, placed a call, quickly obtained a short-term loan to purchase plane fare to Chicago, and wired the Chicago Stake presidency of the change in his itinerary.

A counselor in the presidency met them at the airport, and through Flora's friendly questioning they learned that he had lived in a small Finnish community in Colorado, was of Finnish descent, and spoke the Finnish tongue. At stake conference Ezra called on the counselor to speak; afterwards he wired President McKay, "I've found the president for the Finnish Mission." It always amazed Ezra how the Lord intervened to move the Church forward.[2]

In mid-April 1947, Ezra resumed the role he had held before his 1946 mission as executive secretary of the Melchizedek Priesthood committee. Throughout the summer the committee prepared a new Melchizedek Priesthood handbook, a project that required sensitivity and scholarship. Ezra was concerned about it from inception to completion, but he was pleased with the finished product.

On June 22, 1947, he recorded in his journal that his six-week lapse in entries was due to the fact that "never have I experienced such a busy period." In addition to visiting stake conferences in several states, he had given addresses at high school and seminary graduations, Boy Scout meetings, BYU graduation, the MIA's June Conference, and Idaho Pioneer Day in Franklin, among others. June 22 also marked the day of Reed's missionary farewell to Great Britain.

President George Albert Smith made an appearance at Reed's farewell and spoke briefly. A member of the Bensons' ward, he said there was no more exemplary family in all the Church than the family of Ezra Taft Benson. Ezra was pleased, but he noted in his journal that night, "Most of the credit goes to my ever devoted wife."

As the pace continued, Elder Benson was seldom home for more than a few days at a time. After an extended trip to the Pacific Northwest, he made it back to Salt Lake City in time to take Flora to dinner on her birthday. In early July the family spent five days vacationing at Yellowstone National Park and Jackson Hole, Wyoming. But even there, his evenings and weekend were filled with speaking assignments.

On July 24, 1947, however, the centennial anniversary of the pioneers' entry into the Salt Lake Valley, Ezra's attention was focused strictly on the celebration. He felt that his life was personally intertwined with the lives of the pioneers. As he and Flora joined 50,000 others for the dedication of the *This Is The Place* monument at the mouth of Emigration Canyon, he thrilled at the inspiring services. He was but three generations removed from his great-grandfather, and his mind was filled with thoughts of the Church's progress during its first century. Ezra T. Benson, his great-grandfather, had been in the first company of pioneers to enter the valley; just the year previous, he (Ezra Taft Benson) had directed the first efforts to reestablish ties with the Saints abroad. Would his great-grandfather be pleased with his efforts? He hoped so.

It was a rare trip out of town on Church business that didn't include assignments to speak at agricultural meetings. Ezra was highly respected in national agricultural circles. Elder Richard L. Evans of the First Council of the Seventy relayed a comment his brother made after speaking at the National Institute of

Animal Agriculture at Purdue: "Wherever I go in such circles I find that Ezra Taft Benson is held in high esteem, that he enjoys influence and personal prestige and confidence and acceptance."[3]

In late August, with Mark traveling with him, Ezra delivered the concluding address at the annual meeting of the American Institute of Cooperation in Colorado. He did not seek to entertain his audience. What he had just seen in Europe, and what he had previously observed in the nation's capital, worried him. He feared Americans were gradually losing their freedom, and he sounded a bold warning: "More attention . . . should be given to those eternal principles of freedom and liberty, those inalienable rights vouchsafed in the Constitution. In other words, more attention to the fact that this is a choice land. . . . We should guard against a spirit of indifference and false security. . . . The outlook for world peace and security is darker now than at any time since 1940. The gravity and seriousness of the International situation seems to be increasing almost daily. . . . The days ahead will demand the faith, prayers, and loyalty of every American."[4]

Regardless of his audience, Ezra was unafraid to preach spiritual values, particularly as they related to America and the Constitution.

The last four months of 1947 passed quickly, with Ezra continuing to honor as many speaking requests as he could handle. The speech making and traveling were taxing physically, mentally, and emotionally, but he seemed to thrive on it. He worked incessantly—on trains and planes, in hotel lobbies and rooms, and for short snatches between meetings. For example, en route to Kansas City to speak to the 2,000-delegate Consumers Cooperative Association, he worked on the train; when he arrived at eight A.M. he prepared his address. By eleven A.M. a stenographer from the co-op was assisting him, and by three P.M. his remarks were finished. At four o'clock the next morning, when he couldn't sleep, he wrote Flora, "I [can't] go back to sleep so here I am thinking of the loveliest, most devoted wife and sweetheart in all the world. My! but I miss you. The speech is over. It is a real relief."[5]

With Ezra's heavy travel schedule, Flora continued to receive dozens of letters from her husband. They came on stationery from across the country—from New York City's Waldorf-Astoria to the Hotel Durrant in Flint, Michigan. But at least they came. In late November, from Gallup, New Mexico, he wrote, "I love you a bit more each trip away and each journey home, so it's really mounting up."[6]

It seemed there was never enough time for family. His children were growing, and he worried about being there when they needed him. When he was home, he attended their school activities and PTA meetings and talked for hours with them.

With Reed serving a mission in England, Mark began preparing for his mission and compiled pages of questions about the scriptures. Ezra spent many hours answering the questions and outlined a six-week study plan for his son. He loved teaching youth—and though, hour for hour, he perhaps spent more time with the young couples who came to his office seeking counsel than he did with his own children, still nothing delighted him more than one-on-one time with family members.

On March 2, 1948, Ezra left for agricultural meetings in Omaha with seven-year-old Bonnie in tow. Members of the media in Nebraska were fascinated that Ezra Benson would babysit. Prior to meeting the press, he helped Bonnie get ready the best he could. After the interview, photographers asked if they could take photos of her. To Ezra's surprise and delight, a photograph of her made front-page news. After his address, he was asked to bring Bonnie to the speaker's table and introduce her. She received a round of applause.

Ezra had to snatch moments with his children when he could, and traveling with them was often the best way for meaningful interaction. He was holding down not only his share of church assignments but also a demanding secular schedule that would have fatigued many men. His description of the events of one day is typical: "I can't remember when I've been more tired. I have spoken in four different meetings on different subjects, and each talk was listed as a principal talk. At 8:30 I spoke to the Ricks College studentbody and Leadership Week visitors; at 9:30 to Scout leaders; at 1 p.m. to the agricultural meeting and at 2:10 to a general meeting in the tabernacle. Drove to

Idaho Falls tonight and . . . spent the evening working on the paper I am to present . . . in Omaha."

He spoke to poultry groups, chambers of commerce, Boy Scouts, and sacrament meetings and stake conferences from coast to coast, constantly switching gears from agricultural to religious settings, from audiences of thousands to those of fewer than a hundred. During his travels, he attended firesides, softball games, priesthood meetings, and essentially every range of meeting and activity the Church had to offer. He was comfortable giving administrative and spiritual instruction to leaders, but he was happiest among the general membership. There was always time to bless a child, counsel with an unhappy couple, or comfort those who were ill. His journal contains hundreds of brief notations about stopping at hospitals to visit the sick.

Elder Benson's responsibilities at Church headquarters steadily increased. In January 1948 he was appointed chairman of a committee to review all reports and statistics. He was also senior advisor to the YWMIA and YMMIA programs.

On March 18 he noted that his stomach had been bothering him for several weeks and "seems to become more distressing. It is especially noticeable when I am under nervous strain. The Dr. after a preliminary examination expressed fear of an ulcer." But Ezra pressed on.

The April 1948 general conference was the first to make use of television, and a screen was installed in the Assembly Hall on Temple Square for overflow crowds. Ezra, despite extensive experience in front of audiences, was anxious about it all. He noted in his journal, "This is a great blessing to the people. To me it adds to my worry and anxiety to realize that I am not only on the air during my remarks but being photographed also. The strong television lights directed toward the pulpit are a constant eye strain."

In late April, while eating breakfast, Ezra suddenly felt sharp pains in his back, shoulders, and chest. With difficulty he made his way to the couch until the doctor arrived. Three days later he submitted to extensive tests. The doctor concluded it was only a warning to slow down.

That spring Mark received a call to serve in the Eastern States Mission. On Sunday, May 2, the day he turned nineteen, a testimonial was held in his behalf, with the largest attendance Ezra had witnessed for a missionary farewell. Ezra left early to speak at another farewell, but he returned in time to greet those gathered at a reception at his home. Nine days later Mark spent his last evening with the family. "There came a bit of a lump in my throat as I realized it is his last night with us for two years," Ezra wrote.

But there was little time to be homesick for either of his sons, as there was much to be done, not the least of which was Ezra's ongoing support of anything that built youth. In the fall of 1949 a conflict developed between the Boy Scouts of America, which changed its age groupings in a way that affected the Primary, the Church's organization for children, which supported the Scouting programs. Elder Benson was very concerned, as he noted in his journal, that "the entire Scouting program may be abandoned." He often said, "It's better to build boys than mend men." No effort was too great if it related to Scouting. He even took time to write an Eagle Scout recommendation for his paperboy. Ezra's devotion to the Boy Scouts had not gone unnoticed. On May 23, 1949, he was elected to the BSA National Executive Board, and Flora joined him in New York City for his installation.

While in the East, the Bensons paid a courtesy call on President Harry S Truman, extending LDS President George Albert Smith's greetings and talking about the importance of the family unit. Later they enjoyed a serene moment in the Sacred Grove, scene of Joseph Smith's vision of the Father and the Son in upstate New York. "As Flora and I were left alone in the Sacred Grove," Ezra recorded, "the peace of heaven seemed to pervade. There was borne in upon our hearts the influence of the Holy Spirit to such a degree that tears of gratitude filled my eyes as we stood silent arm in arm in this sacred spot where the most glorious vision ever given to man transpired."

Tender moments such as these strengthened Ezra's growing commitment to the gospel, his family, and his country, which he considered inseparable. Following Joseph Smith's experience in the Sacred Grove, the gospel had been restored—not insignificantly, Ezra felt—in a land of freedom where men were able to choose their own destiny. In an article titled "Survival of the American Way of Life," published in the *Improvement Era* in June 1948, he outlined the precarious political and social paths America was taking: "It is heart-rending to see people who have lost their freedom of choice . . . who feel no security; who have no home they can call their own . . . ; whose hearts are filled with hatred, distrust, and fear of the future. . . . With all of its weaknesses, our free enterprise system has accomplished in terms of human welfare that which no other economic or social system has even approached. . . . Good government . . . guarantees the maximum of freedom, liberty, and development to the individual."

Elder Benson's desire to protect the Constitution, and to defend, at all cost, individual freedom, fueled his patriotic interests. He monitored national developments almost daily and was a keen observer of political climates. He supported Thomas Dewey for U.S. president, though he felt Dewey was a middle-of-the roader whose ideologies were perhaps closer to the New Deal than the planks of Dewey's own party. As early as 1944 Dewey had asked Ezra to outline a national agricultural program, and four years later he requested Elder Benson's service on an agricultural advisory committee. Ezra discussed the matter with the First Presidency and also told them about a rumor he had heard that Dewey, if elected, would offer him a Cabinet post. The First Presidency approved his serving in the government if the opportunity arose.

Ezra did not lust for office. He had often said, "Blessed is he who expecteth nothing, for he shall never be disappointed." And he wrote in his journal, "I have no political ambitions except as such activities might redound to the good of the work of the Lord and this great nation preserved to permit the Restored Church to become established and fill its great mission."

Dewey evidently held Ezra in some regard. He visited the Benson home on a campaign swing through Utah (Mark remembers police cars in front of the home and reporters waiting outside), and accepted Ezra's advice that he add a spiritual emphasis to his messages.[7] At a later date, Ezra met in Chicago's Stevens Hotel with Governor Dewey and the agricultural advisory committee. Dewey asked for suggestions on the farm aspect of his campaign. But when Ezra offered one, an aide interrupted, "Don't rock the boat."

All indications pointed to Dewey's victory over Truman. After the meeting in Chicago, Dewey told Ezra he would like to talk with him about a Cabinet position. A member of the Republican National Committee also contacted Ezra about the possibility, but Ezra suggested they wait until after election results were in. The man laughed and said, "It's in the bag." For years thereafter that expression made Ezra shiver. It was indicative of complacency—something he feared could cost America much more than an election, perhaps even its freedom.

From Chicago, Ezra traveled to New York City to complete negotiations on purchase of a mission home for the Eastern States Mission. When he had first been assigned to find property there, he had asked George Albert Smith, teasingly, "Where do you want it—on Fifth Avenue?" But, in fact, that is where Elder Benson did locate property. At 973 Fifth Avenue, across from Central Park, stood an elegant, six-story mansion that the State of New York had considered making a historical site. The asking price was $175,000. Ezra indicated that the Church couldn't pay that price but might be interested at a lower figure. The property was finally offered at $105,000 cash, which Ezra accepted. A subsequent appraisal valued the property at double that amount.

On November 2, still in New York City, Ezra listened to election returns in his hotel room. He even strolled over to Dewey headquarters, where the mood was festive. That all changed, however, when, in one of the great political upsets in American history, Truman emerged the victor. All talk—and worry—about a Cabinet position was suddenly irrelevant. In many ways Ezra was relieved. There was no uncertainty now about his future.

Without further political concerns, Ezra stepped up his pace— speaking, speaking, and more speaking, missionary interviews, committee work, temple sealings, priesthood ordinations, and weekend trips to stake conferences. And he continued to have great interest in the European Saints. He checked on members there and worked long-distance with government agencies. To the deputy chief of the Religious Affairs Section in Germany, for example, he insisted that the German people needed spiritual reeducation and requested permission for Latter-day Saint representatives to enter Germany "to promote not only the Church program as such, but to teach the principles of freedom and liberty."[8]

Many Saints from Europe emigrated to the United States, and others visited Utah to go through the temple. In December 1948 Ezra and Flora spearheaded a reunion for Saints from Europe who had relocated in Utah and arranged for President George Albert Smith to attend. The Bensons shook hands with each person. "Many of them have just arrived . . . and were almost overcome by this get-together and the joy of being in Zion," Ezra wrote.

Had Ezra not been well organized, it is doubtful he could have managed his schedule. But he seemed to have a knack for sizing up situations, making quick decisions, and getting things done. When each of the Twelve was asked to respond to one particular assignment and Ezra's report was the first submitted, Elder John A. Widtsoe quipped that Elder Benson could go to the head of the class, adding, "Your comments are excellent."[9]

It was Ezra who realized that responsibilities of the Twelve had become so unwieldy that a full-time executive secretary was needed. He got the idea approved and helped hire and train the man selected for the position. Few things escaped his attention. Yet he also had the common touch. He went out of his way to praise and reassure those he met in his travels. After a mission tour through the South, for example, he wrote to a couple in North Carolina, "Of all the branches we visited . . . none impressed me more deeply than what I saw and heard in Elizabeth City. It is putting it mildly to say that I am proud of both of you."[10]

Being a General Authority sometimes exacted its price. Ezra worried about his finances, as the living allowance he now received was significantly less than his former salary. With two sons on missions, his savings were being rapidly depleted. "Since we. . . moved to Salt Lake," he recorded in his journal, "it has been necessary . . . to draw on our small savings each month at the rate of well over $1,000 per year. If this continues for long we'll not be able to help the children with their college." At years's end, with the situation unresolved, the Bensons only sent Christmas cards to family and very close friends. After moving to Salt Lake City, the Benson children noticed fewer presents under the tree.

Elder Benson was also worried about having to be away from home on church assignments so frequently. As he prepared to leave for a stake conference in Monticello, Utah, Flora hovered over him, finally admitting, "I've never felt so strange about you leaving on a church assignment." En route, Elder Benson came within a foot of being killed by a runaway semitrailer, which hit his car so hard that the force of his body against the seat broke the welding loose.

Few assignments were so dangerous, but all were demanding. They required sensitivity to the people and receptivity to the Spirit. In one Colorado stake, new facilities were needed, which required relocating stake headquarters. The stake president feared disunity in the stake because of the problem, so he had not yet broached the subject with his high council. Elder Benson called the group together, and within forty-five minutes he received unanimous approval for the change.

Neal A. Maxwell, then a young missionary in Canada, was influenced by Elder Benson in a way that affected him for many years. He recorded the events of a district conference: "Elder E. T. Benson asked me my age and if I'd had any service experience. Thought it rather unusual. As they sustained new officers I was stunned by the reading of my name to be a new District President. . . . Set apart under the voice and hands of . . . Apostle Benson. Received splendid blessing."[11] (Neal Maxwell would later serve as a counselor to Reed Benson in the Washington D.C. Stake mission presidency, and Mark Benson would be called as a counselor to Bishop Maxwell. Elder Maxwell would then serve with Elder Benson as a member of the Council of the Twelve Apostles.)

In an effort to help youth, Elder Benson got behind a proposal for a Churchwide softball tournament and, with the help of many others, saw it through. "Something miraculous happened today," he wrote Flora from aboard the Los Angeles Limited. "I tried to call [Oscar] Kirkham this A.M. in Salt Lake [regarding the softball tournament]. We were stopped in the R.R. station in Rawlins, Wyoming. I was thinking of the softball program when I looked out of my window into the club car across the platform and saw only the back of the head of a man who I felt impressed was Bro. Kirkham. Without being sure I rushed out and rapped on his window and sure enough it was him en route home. We had a short visit [talking softball] before our trains left in different directions." The first all-Church softball tournament was held in September 1949, with President George Albert Smith throwing out the first ball.

Things didn't always work that smoothly. Asked to deliver his second CBS "Church of the Air" radio address in connection with April 1949 general conference, Elder Benson was informed by radio officials that his talk was too forceful for a national radio audience. "I revamped it somewhat—to my disappointment," he lamented. "Apparently they wanted me to say that which will please everyone, including the offenders of the moral code." His address, entitled "Our Homes—Divinely Ordained," strongly outlined the critical effects home life has on society.

Ezra Taft Benson didn't care to mince words. In the keynote address to the American Institute of Cooperation's summer meetings in Madison, Wisconsin, he delivered a powerful and clear message in support of free enterprise. One observer wrote his reaction to Ezra's remarks: "If no other address than Mr. Benson's were delivered before the Cooperative Conference . . . it must have been an epoch-making event, not only as regards Cooperative Marketing but as a crystal clear call back to sane thinking, for every American citizen."[12]

In September 1949 the Twelve determined that, due to the rapid increase in Church membership, General Authorities would attend stake conferences semiannually rather than quarterly. The First Presidency, presumably concerned that Elder Benson's never-ending pace would eventually take its toll, also insisted that he take some days away from the office. He relented. He spent one Tuesday at home working twelve hours in the yard, and found time to relax occasionally with the children. He made stilts for Bonnie's birthday, took the three oldest girls to the state fair, saw *Little Women* with his wife and daughters, and took them all to outings at a local amusement park and to the beach at the Great Salt Lake.

Ezra felt it was also important that his extended family stay close to one another, and he visited his brothers and sisters as often as he could. Once, while on the way home from a church assignment in Idaho, he felt impressed to detour to Mink Creek to see his sister Margaret. He didn't know that earlier in the day, with her husband out of town, she had become seriously ill, leaving her small children largely unattended. "I prayed desperately for help to come," Margaret later told her brother in a letter. "I was so relieved to see you. You gave me a blessing and I was much better the next morning. You stayed overnight and next day about noon went on your way home."

Ezra was proud of his family, particularly his children. He noted every achievement, large or small. If they took the tiniest part in a roadshow or school play, he made mention of it. When Barbara earned the Church's "individual achievement award" and was singled out in sacrament meeting as the only girl with 100 percent attendance in all of her meetings, Ezra recorded it in his journal as though she had won national recognition.

Perhaps nothing touched him more, however, than his sons' service as missionaries. In late December 1949, Flora accompanied him to New York City, where they went to a concert by the Utah Centennial Chorus, a missionary choir of which Mark was president, at a meeting of the National Association of Manufacturers in the Waldorf-Astoria Hotel. Then, just days later, Ezra and Flora stood at Pier 98 as the Queen Mary docked from England. "We were thrilled to get a glimpse first thing . . . of our son Reed returning from Europe after 2½ years . . . as a missionary. . . . We were soon on the ship with our passes and embracing our wonderful son whom we are so proud of." During his mission Reed had opened a branch at Oxford and was supervising elder over the Newcastle District, the same district his father had presided over in 1923. There were Saints who still recalled the earlier Elder Benson, whom they considered one of their own. When he arrived in New York, Reed was called by President George Albert Smith to serve a short-term mission. He was assigned to be a companion to Mark to help establish full-time missionary work in Washington, D. C., where Mark was serving as district president.

In 1950, with the beginning of a new decade, Elder Benson's varied involvements persisted. Speaking requests continued to arrive at his office, many of them invitations to come back a second time. He enjoyed telling the story of one livestock association in Utah that he had addressed the year before. When the officers invited him to again keynote their annual meeting, Ezra sent his regrets, indicating that it would probably be better to find another speaker as he hadn't kept record of his remarks and wouldn't want to be repetitious. A few days later the association president replied, "We have checked with a number of our members and we find there aren't any of them who remember anything you said last year, so you come right along."[13]

With all the speaking and other assignments, Elder Benson was in Salt Lake City scarcely half the time. Frequently he arrived home in time only to pack for another trip. From Idaho he wrote to Flora, "Forgot to tell you, I took your apples from the utility room, also 2 bananas and a piece of cheese. These will serve several breakfasts."

At a stake conference in Los Angeles, two close relatives, neither of them active in the Church, came at his invitation. "As I saw them enter I prayed silently for strength to speak powerfully and if possible touch their hearts," he noted. "I have never been blessed with greater freedom and they seemed impressed."

He centered his remarks to graduates of Utah State Agricultural College on building spiritual values: "It is a basic principle that you cannot help a man permanently by doing for him what he could do, and should do, for himself. Dependence upon the state for sustenance means the eventual surrender of political freedom." The president of the Northwestern States Mission wrote Elder Benson after reading a copy of his talk, "I was pleased to note that you did not hesitate to quote the word of the Lord. . . . What you presented was given in such a way that no one could take offense."[14]

To Ezra, there was no dichotomy between speaking of fundamental gospel principles and warning of forces threatening the American way of life, and he made that clear. His practical messages frequently reinforced the theme that America is a land of destiny, and that a resurgence of spiritual values among its citizens is the only sure way to preserve freedom. At an annual cooperatives banquet in Spokane, he addressed the same theme. "I was deeply grateful," he recorded, "when some of the leaders later spoke of my humble offering as 'spiritual statesmanship' where as a matter of fact it was nothing more than Mormonism unlabeled."

To the Saints, he was even more direct. "The outlook for the world is not encouraging," he said, "but we know what the answer is. There is only one answer, and that is the gospel of Jesus Christ. Peace must come from the heart. Men's hearts must change, and righteousness must rule in the lives of the people of the world before peace can come."[15]

There was rarely any let-up. After stake conferences in Ogden, during which he performed thirty-nine ordinations and settings-apart, he wrote, "This and public speaking is the most exhausting work I have ever done, not excluding thinning beets, pitching hay, or heaving 120 lb. sacks of grain. My labors in the Church, joyous as they are, take something out of me which is different in effect. I wish I could do it without limit and not tire." Later he lamented, "I find myself wishing the days were longer and less sleep was required for my health."

It was hard to be separated so frequently from his family. From Philadelphia, where he attended national meetings of the Boy Scouts, he wrote Flora, "Last night at the dinner I was really homesick for you as I saw so many of the men with their wives. . . . I went to my box and to my joy there was a letter from the sweetest girl in all the world. . . . I went to my room and thought of you for hours and again when I awakened this morning."

In April 1950, Flora returned to the hospital for a second operation, "a part of the price for bearing six children and working so hard for our family," Ezra observed. He spent an anxious day while she was in surgery, and was grateful that only five days later she was sufficiently recovered to go home. But

The Bensons in front of their home on Harvard Avenue in 1950: from left, Beth, Bonnie, Beverly, Barbara, Flora, Elder Benson, Reed, Mark

her strength was not sufficient in June to allow her to accompany him to the East Coast to bring their sons home from their missions. Barbara and Beverly made the trip, however, and while their father attended BSA national meetings and visited over a thousand LDS Scouts at camp, the girls stayed with Ed and Laura Brossard in Washington. Laura later wrote Flora, "I shall always remember a beautiful picture I glimpsed as I went through the hall to the kitchen one night and saw the two little figures kneeling at their beds in prayer, far from home, but the teachings of their home always with them. . . . You know how some pictures we never forget? I knew this was one of those I would always carry with me."[16]

En route home, the five Bensons visited LDS historical sites in Kirtland, Ohio, and Nauvoo, Illinois. Reed and Mark read Church history as they drove. At the Kirtland Temple, which the Saints had built in the 1830s before they were forced to leave that city, Ezra noted that in his "mind's eye," he "pictured the transcendent beauty and magnitude of what transpired"

245

there—the Savior's appearance to Joseph Smith and Oliver Cowdery. In Nauvoo the travelers tried to imagine where Ezra T. Benson's home would have been, and in Carthage they reviewed events leading to the martyrdom of Joseph Smith and his brother Hyrum. "It is a real joy to travel, visit historical points, eat and pray with the four children," Ezra wrote. "The trip is proving of the utmost value to the girls with whom the boys talk about the church and discuss the gospel." As they traveled, he jotted ideas that might help the Church's proselyting efforts.

When they arrived home on June 11, it was the first time in nearly three years that the family had all been together. "It seems so good," Ezra noted simply, "to all be together again, especially as we knelt in family prayer."

In early August 1950, Ezra and his sons took a saddle-pack trip into the high Uintah mountains of eastern Utah. They planned to fish, hunt rocks, and hike, but they had scarcely arrived when a messenger reached them with word that George F. Richards, president of the Twelve, had passed away. The vacationers cut their trip short and returned to Salt Lake City. Elder Benson had often referred to President Richards as a man who nearly approached perfection, and he had never forgotten the tender, fatherly kiss he had received from him as he left for his relief mission in Europe.

As the years passed, Ezra became increasingly bonded with his associates in the Twelve. He often said that when he was in Europe, or away from Salt Lake City on Thursday, when the Twelve met, he could feel the strength and warmth of his colleagues praying for him. Outside of his family, he missed them more than anyone. On January 12, 1951, after a sweet testimony meeting of the Twelve in the temple, he noted, "It has been a glorious meeting in which the Spirit has been richly in evidence and we have been drawn close together. . . . I have, I believe, never enjoyed 5 hours more. I thank the Lord for my Brethren. I love them and am grateful for their association, love and confidence. Today I believe we all could say with John of old, 'We know that we have passed from death unto life, because we love the Brethren.' "

The health of the prophet, George Albert Smith, deteriorated in 1950 and 1951, and he was able to attend temple meetings less frequently. At the President's request Ezra administered to him twice in early 1951. On April 2, the two counselors in the First Presidency, J. Reuben Clark and David O. McKay, visited President Smith at home, but he did not recognize them. Two days later, on his eighty-first birthday, President Smith passed away. As soon as Ezra received word, he walked over to the Smith home, just two blocks away. Peace pervaded the home, but it was an emotional time for Ezra as he reminisced about the man who had administered to his sick baby daughter while he was an ocean away.

On April 8, the apostles met in the temple to reorganize the First Presidency. David O. McKay, as senior apostle, took his place in the first chair around the semicircle. He was ordained president of the Church, and he subsequently announced his selection as counselors—Stephen L Richards as first counselor and J. Reuben Clark as second. The room was suddenly deathly silent, for Elder Clark had served as first counselor to two presidents. The next day, in the solemn assembly where the new officers were presented to the members of the Church, President McKay asked President Clark to handle the procedure of sustaining the First Presidency. Later in his remarks President Clark said that in the service of the Lord it is not where you serve, but how.[17]

After the proceedings, Ezra wrote: "Some . . . had expressed . . . deep concern over placing Pres. Clark . . . as second counselor. There was expressed a feeling 'It will kill Brother Clark' and also 'The people will not be reconciled.' Some questioned the wisdom of Pres. McKay making any explanation of seniority in the Twelve as a factor. However, thanks be to God, Pres. McKay went ahead as he was first impressed to do, and the people not only approved unanimously but the most powerful witness of the Spirit literally melted the audience to tears and all left reassured and confident God's will had been done. Such a spirit of loyalty and love I have never seen exhibited before."

With every year, it seemed, Ezra Benson's influence and reputation spread, both within and outside the Church. He received the Boy Scouts' highest regional award, the Silver Antelope, on April 24, 1951; the University of Wisconsin awarded him one of six honorary citations for agricultural leadership on February 6, 1952; and the American Institute of Cooperation elected him chairman of the board of trustees on August 14, 1952. Consequently, as he carried out his assignments as a member of the Council of the Twelve, he, and in turn the Church, attracted media attention. Everything from small hometown newspapers to national wire services reported on his comings and goings. For example, the Syracuse (New York) *Post-Standard* of September 10, 1951, called him "the famous Mormon leader." The Minneapolis *Morning Tribune* dated September 13, 1951, reporting on his dedicatory address for a chapel there, headlined an article "How Does Mormon Church Differ From Other Faiths?" and outlined basic gospel principles. From the Topeka (Kansas) *Capital* of September 17, 1951, came the headline "Mormons Set Examples" and an accompanying article about Ezra Benson's message on free enterprise.

In June, after Ezra received an honorary degree from the College of Osteopathic Physicians and Surgeons in Los Angeles, a man who attended the graduation wrote Elder Richard L. Evans, "One of your apostles, Ezra T. Benson, delivered the commencement address last month for the graduating class of my alma mater . . . and he definitely stirred the. . . cerebrations of the profession as I've never seen it stirred before in the field of moral ethics. Men of science need to be often reminded of moral values."[18]

The Brethren were aware of Ezra's high profile. Regardless of his audience, he didn't hedge on incorporating gospel principles, frequently quoting scripture, in his message. Often his text was the Book of Mormon, and he drew liberally from its message about America's destiny. After a national training conference of Scout Executives, Elder John A. Widtsoe wrote, "I have scanned your address. Congratulations. You are doing a splendid work for the Cause of the Church. . . . Such services as you give will establish us in many important places." His postscript concluded, "As I read your address, my pride in you increased."[19]

Flora's pride in her husband also continually increased, though neither she nor Ezra enjoyed being separated so frequently. When he traveled with Elder and Sister Mark Petersen to Hawaii to dedicate the Kalihi Ward chapel, Flora remained at home, and Ezra lamented, "Hawaii just doesn't seem as I'd hoped without you here. I fear the people notice my lack of enthusiasm."

When Elder Benson left on November 15, 1951, for an extended tour of the Southern States Mission that would keep him from home on Thanksgiving, he asked if the children would stagger their letters so he would receive one every other day. After Thanksgiving he wrote, "The Thanksgiving letters were perfect and a real inspiration." When he arrived in New York City on December 6 and found no letter from Flora, he chastised her slightly: "Am disappointed not to have word from you here as there was none in Wash. D.C."

But despite their frequent separations, Ezra made no attempt to adjust what he had come to view as his lot in life. On February 19, 1952, after a hectic month in which he had let his journal lapse, he noted he had been too busy to write, adding, "It has always been of more interest to me . . . to do things . . . than to write about them."

He relied heavily on Flora. He wished she could travel with him more often, but he was also grateful that she was so devoted to the children. It was difficult balancing a demanding church and secular life with the rearing of a young family—a trying life-style for anyone—and he realized that her judgment, energy, and commitment were the keys to their stable family life. Apparently Ezra and Flora's efforts were noticed. President George F. Richards of the Council of the Twelve had told Ezra, "I remember my visit to your home in Washington. . . and the favorable impressions I received as to your home life. I do not remember having such impressions in any other home."[20]

The children also recognized their mother's influence. Mark wrote from the mission field, "As I grew into young manhood it was you who encouraged me on, who gave me self-confidence, who told me again and again that I could succeed. . . . You've always kept plugging, mom. You've always kept me plugging."

As the children grew older, even with their typical adolescent growing pains, they stayed in line. They excelled in school and other activities. Reed was freshman class president at BYU, won the extemporaneous speaking contest there, and was voted the friendliest man on campus. During the Korean War, he served as a chaplain in the Air Force. Mark was Junior Prom chairman at BYU, won the Heber J. Grant Oratorical contest, and chaired BYU's homecoming festivities (which Reed emceed). He received the Henry Newell scholarship, and went to Stanford University, where he obtained his master's degree. Barbara and Beverly were both presidents of girls organizations at school, and during her first year at the University of Utah, Barbara was elected class vice-president. Later, at BYU, she was elected homecoming queen and named "friendliest girl on campus." Bonnie would serve as an eighteen-year-old Relief Society president at a BYU ward.

It was not always easy for the Benson children to live in their father's shadow. They came to realize that everything they said or did would not only be a reflection on him, but on the Church as well. Years later a General Authority gave insight into what it must have been like to grow up in the Benson home when he commented about one of the daughters: "She is not an ordinary woman. She was reared in a home with a father who is a prophet, seer, and revelator. She had to be an unusual spirit to get into that home. It's not easy being born into a family like that. . . . She's had to be perfect ever since she was a little girl."[21]

Ezra loved being with his family and drew strength from them. After one stake conference during which he had spent two days soothing hard feelings among some of the priesthood leaders, he realized how blessed he was to have a loyal family. "It must be most difficult to serve as [stake] president without the full support of your leaders. . . . It is a feeling closely akin to that experienced by parents when their children fail to . . . give them full support."

His family's support was becoming increasingly essential. As he continued to speak out on the future of America and its freedom, some Latter-day Saints began to question why a religious leader was addressing what they considered to be politi-

cal topics. President Clark had stated the government was stray-
ing into so many areas affecting the lives of Church members
that it was becoming almost impossible for a Church leader to
stay out of "political matters." Ezra agreed.

In fact, Ezra's philosophies fell much in line with President
Clark, who regarded the New Deal as anticonstitutional. Across
the top of a *Church News* article reporting one of President
Clark's addresses, one that criticized the United Nations for
limiting the United States's sovereignty, Ezra penned, *"This I
believe."*22 In his address President Clark outlined his frame of
reference: "I am . . . pro-liberty, pro-freedom, . . . pro-local
self-government, and pro-everything else that has made us the
free country we have grown to be in the first 130 years of our
national existence. It necessarily follows that I am anti-
internationalist, anti-interventionist, anti-meddlesome-busy-
bodiness in our international affairs. In the domestic field, I am
anti-socialist, anti-Communist, anti-Welfare State. I am what
the kindlier ones of all these latter people with whom I am
denying any association or sympathy, would call a rabid reac-
tionary (I am not, in fact, that)."

Ezra might have been classified in a similar manner. He
repeatedly spoke out against the United Nations, though this
outlook was not widely accepted in the early 1950s.23

Elder Benson's love for America burned deep in his soul.
Rarely did he visit the nation's capital but what the spirit and
feeling in that city didn't move him. One evening in October
1952, while in Washington, D.C., he walked the mall between
the Washington Monument and the Lincoln Memorial. A feeling of deep reverence burned within him, a feeling of love and
loyalty. He later related: "Suddenly the history of this country
seemed for a moment to merge into one great whole for me:
Our beginnings as a nation under Washington, our preservation under Lincoln. . . . As I gazed on that great statue of Lincoln, sitting upright in his chair, . . . I read and pondered the
inscription on the wall behind and above his head. . . . I went
to the other plaques inside the Memorial and read each. One
contained the Gettysburg Address, another the words of the
second inaugural. As I pondered those beautiful phrases, there
came into my heart a surge of gratitude such as I had never

known before, for the privilege of being a citizen in this land, for the priceless blessing of being an American."[24]

At general conference in April 1952, Ezra's message, entitled "America, What of the Future?" warned against threats to America's freedom. Though he felt the message was well received, he knew that some might criticize him. "However, I could not do otherwise and follow my impressions. If I come in for criticism, so be it," he wrote in his journal.

Criticism was the least of his worries. Popularity was not a priority, but principles were. Elder Benson believed the Church was moving into a new era, as he told a gathering of BYU alumni, an era in which it must fearlessly take its message throughout the world and an era in which America must solidify its commitment to free enterprise, freedom, and the sanctity of man's agency to choose for himself rather that be limited by government dictums.

Though in his formative years Ezra Taft Benson had not imagined himself venturing much beyond the farm, his life had already taken uncharted paths. And though he had never sought appointment or acclaim, both had embraced him. He had no way of knowing what honors of men would soon come or that the attention of an entire nation would push him and his family into a spotlight that would focus international attention upon the Church.

"No real American wants to be subsidized."

Chapter 14

Welcome, Mr. Secretary

On November 4, 1952, Dwight David Eisenhower was elected president of the United States. The World War II military hero defeated Adlai Stevenson soundly, collecting 442 electoral votes to Stevenson's 89, and bringing with him a Republican Congress (though by a slim margin).

During his two terms as Chief Executive, Eisenhower was to enjoy immense popularity, establishing himself solidly in the affections of middle-class, mainstream America. The General inspired confidence. Colleague Bernard Law Montgomery surmised, "He has the power of drawing the hearts of men towards him as a magnet attracts the bits of metal. He merely has to smile at you, and you trust him at once."[1]

That trait, among others, served Ike well as he selected his cabinet. Not one appointment was a personal friend. His choice for Secretary of Labor was, in fact, an Adlai Stevenson-supported Democrat. Some of his most prominent appointments were men he had never met.

On Thursday evening, November 20, 1952, Elder Benson received an unexpected call from Utah Senator Arthur V. Watkins informing him there was a sudden ground swell of support that he be named Secretary of Agriculture. The news came as a complete surprise, and when the Senator inquired if he would be available to accept the post, Elder Benson replied that only President David O. McKay could answer that question.

The following morning, he encountered President McKay in the Church Office Building parking lot. The prophet, too, had received a phone call the night before about Elder Benson's availability for a cabinet post. "My mind is clear in the matter," he told his associate. "If the opportunity comes in the proper spirit, I think you should accept." Elder Benson shook his head and replied, "I can't believe it will come. If it were Dewey asking, it would be different. But I've never even *seen* Eisenhower, much less met him."[2]

On Saturday, Ezra and Mark E. Petersen traveled to Provo to divide the Sharon Stake and form what would be the Church's 200th stake. It was there that Flora reached Ezra by telephone. President-elect Eisenhower was trying to contact him. Ezra quickly found an empty room, spent some moments in solitude and prayer, called President McKay to confer with him, and then returned the call to New York City.

Milton Eisenhower, the president-elect's brother, asked Elder Benson if he could interview with Ike on Monday afternoon at two. Ezra agreed, called President McKay again, and hurried home. He and Flora called their sons. Reed, a chaplain, was stationed at Lackland Air Force Base in San Antonio. Mark was attending Stanford. Ezra asked the boys to fast with the family—not that he would get the appointment, but that he would make the proper decision. Then he left for the East Coast.

On Monday afternoon Ezra sat in the outer office of Eisenhower headquarters at the Hotel Commodore in New York City. Earlier he had lunched with Milton Eisenhower. Ezra had assumed he was one of several being interviewed for the cabinet post, but Milton made it clear that he was Ike's choice for Secretary of Agriculture.

As he waited to meet Eisenhower, Ezra perhaps asked himself, *What am I doing here?* His agricultural work had thrust him into political circles before, but he had never been politically ambitious. He was acutely aware that the farm situation was explosive, and the next Secretary would inherit a hot seat. How much power would he have to change farm programs?

Would he be dealing with a Congress motivated more by political expediency than principle? Would he be expected to rubber-stamp programs or policies he didn't endorse? Most importantly, he was completely devoted to his calling as an apostle. Why give up that peaceful association for what promised to be a turbulent experience? Only at President McKay's instruction was he here at all. The mixing of farming and what Ezra considered to be unsound economic policies in recent years had built up farm surpluses, reduced farm income, and in general created a political dilemma.

On the other hand, Ezra believed that Americans had a duty to serve their country. And President McKay had counseled him to assess the spirit of what Eisenhower had to say. These thoughts were rushing through his mind as the door opened. He was unprepared for his first impression of Eisenhower. He wrote in his journal that day, "I saw a powerfully built person, a little under six feet, with a smile fresh and warm as a sunny summer's day. . . . I liked him immediately."

Eisenhower quickly came to the point. Would Ezra accept the appointment as Secretary of Agriculture? Rather than answer directly, Elder Benson enumerated reasons why he shouldn't be appointed. First, he had supported his distant cousin, Senator Robert Taft, who ran against Eisenhower for the Republican nomination. Second, all other things being equal, he did not favor having a military man in the White House. Third, he came from a comparatively insignificant agricultural state, and a Secretary of Agriculture from the Midwest would perhaps be more acceptable—and he even knew three men who *wanted* the job. And finally, he was an ecclesiastical leader, and he wondered about the wisdom in calling a church official to the cabinet.

On the last point, Eisenhower looked directly at Ezra and replied, "Surely you know we have the great responsibility to restore the confidence of our people in their own government, and that means we've got to deal with spiritual matters. You can't refuse to serve America!"[3] There it was. Eisenhower's statement was compelling to a man with deep spiritual and patriotic loyalties. President McKay had said that if the request came in the proper spirit, he must accept. In Ezra's judgment, that condition had been met. But there was one more question he must put to Ike: Would he ever be expected to support legislation he didn't approve of? Eisenhower assured him that that would not be expected of him.

Scarcely twenty minutes after the interview had begun Eisenhower accompanied his selection for Secretary of Agriculture into an adjoining room and announced the appointment to the press.

Ezra hurried back to the hotel and called his wife. "Flora," he said, "General Eisenhower has asked me to be in his cabinet, and I've accepted." There was no hesitancy in her voice as she responded, "I knew he would, and I knew you'd accept. It must be the Lord's will. How do you feel?" "I feel more like praying than anything else," he replied.

Ezra's second call was to FBI director J. Edgar Hoover. "Run a complete security check on me," he insisted. When Hoover replied that wouldn't be necessary, Ezra responded, "I'd appreciate it if you'd do it for me and all of my top appointments. There must be no question about my background."

By evening newspapers from coast to coast headlined the news that Ike had named the first clergyman in a century to a cabinet post (Edward Everett, Secretary of State in 1852, was pastor of Boston's Brattle Street Unitarian Church), and reporters scrambled to learn more about this dark-horse appointee from Utah. By the time Elder Benson returned to Salt Lake City, writers from *Time, Life, U.S. News & World Report*, the *Christian Science Monitor*, and other publications were clamoring for interviews.

Though the Mormon apostle was an unexpected choice, his selection was greeted with almost universal approbation. Some writers even glamorized his pioneer, dirt-farmer beginnings. And there were inevitable comparisons between him and the last ranking Mormon official to occupy political spotlight, Reed Smoot, an apostle and U.S. senator.

While most analysts agreed with the *Washington Post* that few cabinet appointees would "face a bigger challenge," most also predicted Secretary Benson would prune the U.S. Department of Agriculture's sprawling bureaucracy.[4] The press evaluted him as politically inexperienced but agriculturally astute and a breath of fresh air in Washington, even if he was one of the biggest post-election surprises. Paul Friggens, western editor of *Farm Journal*, one of the most respected agricultural publications, wrote, "It will be interesting to see the new secretary manage the U.S. Department of Agriculture by principle rather than political expediency."[5]

Others were cautious. The *Cincinnati Post* warned that Eisenhower may have made a "grave misstep" by naming a religious leader to his cabinet and thereby breaching the sacrosanct barrier between church and state. But even that writer concluded with a qualified endorsement: "Mr. Benson will make a good secretary of agriculture, and . . . if he introduces old-fashioned Mormon polygamy into the nation's farmyards it will be a refreshing change from the birth prevention policies for pigs popularized by . . . [former Secretary of Agriculture] Henry Wallace."[6]

A few observers were openly critical. The general secretary of the American Council of Churches, for example, was indignant, though misinformed, when he said, "Informed Christians are perfectly aware that . . . pagan religions are no more hostile to the Biblical evangelical Christian faith than is Mormonism. . . . I think it is rather unfortunate that the President named him as a member of his Cabinet."[7]

There was, however, universal agreement on one thing: Ezra Benson knew agriculture, and for the first time in many years the Secretary of Agriculture was more than a political appointee. He knew what it meant to work from sunup to sundown, and then tighten his belt when flagging farm prices didn't pay the bills.

The *Denver Post* of November 26, 1952, reported that Ezra's appointment had already spawned something of a miracle. "President Allan B. Kline of the American Farm Bureau Federation and President James G. Patton of the National Farmers Union agree that his qualifications are splendid—the first time for years these two gentlemen have agreed on anything." The executive vice-president of the National Farm Grange said, "We think that Benson's high character will make him one of the great, if not the greatest, agriculture secretaries."[8] And Raymond W. Miller added, "Ezra T. Benson is not and never can become a

politician, but he is a statesman and a man of rare integrity. . . .
It augurs well that he has been set aside for national service at
this critical time. Surely he is a man of destiny in the hands of
God."[9]

Latter-day Saints watched with great interest and pride. Perhaps most important amid all the excitement was President
McKay's quiet but full approval of the appointment. He stated,
"The appointment is a distinct honor to him and one he will fill
with credit to himself and to the nation. We are happy that a
prominent member of the Church has received this position."[10]

Bill Marriott told his good friend that everyone he had talked
to was "beaming with enthusiasm" at the appointment, and
George Romney wired, "You have brought honor to the entire
church." People from his hometown were also buzzing. "Golly,
T," wrote Tom Heath, "no need to tell you how well the
announcement was received in Franklin County. Over at the
Whitney Store and in town [there was] . . . nothing but praise.
How proud your dad would be!"[11]

Ezra was still in a state of shock. It was all so overwhelming! Suddenly his well-ordered though fast-paced life was turned
upside down. On December 1, he told students at a BYU devotional assembly, "I didn't *want* to be Secretary of Agriculture. I
can't imagine anyone in his right mind wanting it." It was a
statement he would repeat hundreds of times during subsequent
years.

In the meantime, he faced a number of unanswered questions. In less than eight weeks he would take the oath of office.
Where did he begin? How should he select a staff? The first few
nights, sleep came only in fits and starts. Often he arose hours
before dawn to write notes to himself.

Early on, Elder Benson sought a blessing from the First Presidency. Assisted by J. Reuben Clark, President McKay
pronounced words of comfort and counsel on the apostle's head:
"You will have a responsibility, even greater than your associates in the cabinet because you go . . . as an apostle of the
Lord Jesus Christ. You are entitled to inspiration from on high,
and if you so live and think and pray, you will have that divine
guidance which others may not have. . . . We bless you, therefore, dear Brother Ezra, that when questions of right and wrong

come before the men with whom you are deliberating, you may see clearly what is right, and knowing it, that you may have courage to stand by that which is right and proper. . . . We seal upon you the blessings of . . . sound judgment, clear vision, that you might see afar the needs of this country; vision that you might see, too, the enemies who would thwart the freedoms of the individual as vouchsafed by the Constitution, . . . and may you be fearless in the condemnation of these subversive influences, and strong in your defense of the rights and privileges of the Constitution."

The prophet's words were comforting, the declarations insightful. Elder Benson did feel that his appointment was an evidence that "people have come to recognize [Mormons] for what we are, our standards, our ideals, our philosophy."

Two thousand congratulatory telegrams and a similar number of letters arrived at the Church Office Building the first two days following the announcement. The response was as intimidating to Ezra as it was heartwarming. So many people expected so much of him. And while he wasn't talking policy yet, his philosophies were already on public display.

In the media reports, a common thread emerged. As one prestigious farm periodical stated, "Ezra Benson is going to shock Washington. He's in the habit of deciding everything on principle."[12] The *Wall Street Journal* (November 25, 1952) indicated that the Secretary's views appeared to be vague, but others scanned his recent addresses for clues to his agricultural philosophies. As early as October 1945, in a general conference address, he had preached the principle of self-reliance, counseling the Saints to avoid the temptation to "run to a paternalistic government for help" and admonishing, "Let us Latter-day Saints stand on our feet. . . . The principles of self-help are economically, socially and spiritually sound." And he had gone on record against subsidies ("I don't think any real American wants to be subsidized") and for free enterprise ("Nobody owes [farmers] anything for crops they don't grow, or goods they don't produce, or work they won't do"). Throughout his term, Ezra would staunchly defend the free enterprise system. "We are a prosperous people because of a free enterprise founded on spiritual, not material, values," he said. "It is founded on freedom of choice—an eternal, God-given principle. The founding fathers, inspired though they were, did not invent the priceless blessing of individual freedom. That gift to mankind sprang from the God of Heaven and not from government."[13]

In 1848, while on a mission to the East, the first Ezra T. Benson observed firsthand how Congress appropriated funds. "They have been in session ten weeks, and have spent $500,000," he wrote a fellow apostle, frustrated at the slow pace and government extravagance. His great-grandson had little more patience with bureaucracy.

For a man who opposed big government, Ezra was taking the reins of an enormous department. The USDA housed one-tenth of its 78,000 employees in the combined Administration and South buildings in Washington, D. C., containing between them nearly five thousand rooms and eight miles of corridors. The remainder were scattered in ten thousand locations throughout the United States and in fifty countries. His 1953 budget, $2.1 billion, was, next to the Treasury, the largest for any civilian department. He and his staff would oversee food needs for 160 million Americans.

Ezra's responsibilities were mind-boggling. It would take months, even years, for him to grasp everything that fell under the USDA umbrella. After he had been in Washington several months, his chauffeur drove him home one day by way of the National Arboretum. It was spring, and brilliant azaleas were in full bloom. Impressed, Ezra asked who was responsible for the establishment. After a pause the chauffeur responded, "*You* are, Mr. Secretary."

The department had many divisions that Ezra would direct. He was responsible for the nation's largest money-lending agency, the Commodity Credit Corporation, making him the "biggest butter, cheese, and dried-milk man" in the country, as he described it. He was also responsible for the largest conservation operation in history; for protecting the nation against insects, diseases, and crop failures; for inspecting meat, insuring crops, grading, and classing commodities. The USDA employed 350 scientists to develop improved strains of crops and breeds of animals, as well as hundreds of economists, and ran one of the country's largest adult-education programs and electrification projects. Above all, he would bear the yoke of bailing farmers out of a mess that was threatening the survival of American agriculture.

Why was American agriculture in precarious shape? In short, Ezra believed, there was too much "big brother" in government. During World War II the government, to encourage peak production of food, guaranteed to protect prices of farm products at an artificially high level. Price supports were, simply, a government buy-back guarantee—the amount the government would pay for commodities if farmers couldn't get that much on the open market. Accordingly, a compulsory fixed price support of 90 percent of parity on basic crops was instituted.

(The concept of parity was developed during World War I as a balance between the prices received by farmers and prices paid by them. Such a balance, it was assumed, existed between 1909 and 1914. This became the base period. The price of wheat, then, would be 100 percent of parity when the selling price of a bushel of wheat would buy as much of other goods as it did during that period. Ezra explained, "As good a [definition as] I've ever heard came from a farmer who said that if a bushel of corn would buy a work shirt in the period 1909 to 1914, then a bushel of corn should still buy a shirt today.")

After World War II, food demands fell sharply while production actually increased, causing commodity prices to fall steadily in relation to the economy. Yet the Truman administration extended high fixed price supports through 1954; as a result, by that year the government had accumulated so much surplus cotton, wheat, and other staples that it could have filled America's market needs for a full year. When Ezra took office, the government owned a startling 37 million pounds of butter, 7 million pounds of cheese, and 56 million pounds of dried milk.[14] To complicate the situation, the government had trouble selling the crops without losing great sums of money and disturbing world markets, so they stored the commodities, costing taxpayers millions of dollars annually. (It cost $66.9 million in 1953 alone to store USDA's surpluses.) The precarious balance between supply and demand was mercilessly out of control. Agriculture, as Ezra described it, was a Grade A mess.

Ezra knew he couldn't solve the dilemma by himself, and he was anxious to consult with as many agricultural experts as possible before assuming office. On December 2, 1952, he left on a twenty-day tour of the United States to confer with farmers, educators, marketing and commodity experts, processors, economists, and retailers. He wanted to hear the farmers' complaints himself, ask questions, and begin to sort through the chaos. He also hoped to select an agricultural advisory committee and to staff his office.

Hundreds of top men came to his hotel rooms—from Los Angeles to Atlanta—for interviews. Ezra asked detailed questions, making copious notes in longhand. In New York he met with former President Herbert Hoover and General Douglas MacArthur. Hoover showed great interest in Ezra's plans to reorganize the Department of Agriculture (later giving it a boost by announcing his endorsement to the press), and talked to him like a father to son. "MacArthur was an eagle," Ezra wrote in his journal. "Majestic in bearing, direct and piercing in facial expression, he was about the youngest seventy-two-year-old I have ever met. . . . He was, in a moment, expressing feelingly his love for the United States . . . and his conviction of the immense values of free enterprise and the dangers of big government." He also commented that if he could ever be of service to Ezra, he was but a phone call away and would go to Washington or anywhere else to help him on a moment's notice. MacArthur's generosity and confidence moved Ezra deeply.

In city after city Ezra worked sixteen-hour days. Despite the schedule and pressing demands, he returned to Salt Lake City to perform the marriage of his son Mark to Lela Wing from Raymond, Alberta, Canada, in the Salt Lake Temple. Mark was the first of Elder Benson's six children to marry there.

Back on the road Ezra looked for staff members. His team came from varied backgrounds. Though his personal assistants— Arthur Haycock, Milan Smith, Lorenzo Hoopes, Daken Broadhead, and Miller Shurtleff—were Latter-day Saints, most of the staff were not.

Ezra had his own way of conducting job interviews with those whose professional credentials spoke for themselves. He was interested in character and values. When he met with Dr.

Don Paarlberg, professor of Agricultural Economics at Purdue, for example, Ezra asked just three questions: Are you happily married? Are you active in your church? Do you like your job? When Paarlberg answered yes to all three, Ezra invited him to join his team as staff economist.

The travel paid off. After a month on the road Ezra's view of agriculture was more comprehensive, though his initial judgment was reinforced—that a healthy dose of free enterprise was just what U.S. agriculture needed.

The cabinet appointment plunged the Bensons into Washington's circle of social elite. They were expected to attend the inaugural, and Ezra was shocked to learn that boxes at the inaugural ball were going fast—at three hundred dollars each. He and Flora decided against purchasing one. A reporter wrote that the cabinet consisted of "nine millionaires and a plumber," but Ezra found that curious. He was no plumber, but he came closer to that than a millionaire.

Another telegram requested Ezra's attendance at a pre-inaugural meeting of the new cabinet on January 12, 1953, in New York City. During a rare moment of privacy prior to the luncheon, Ezra and Eisenhower exchanged comments about the spiritual aspect of their challenge, and Ezra was impressed to ask if it might not be fitting to begin cabinet meetings with prayer. Ike didn't commit himself, but moments later, as the meeting convened, he looked at Ezra and said unexpectedly, "I am asking our Secretary of Agriculture to open this first meeting of the cabinet with prayer."

Maxwell M. Rabb, secretary to the cabinet, later recalled in a letter to Ezra how "electrifying" it was when Eisenhower called on Secretary Benson to open that meeting. "There was a murmur of approval and then several of your colleagues crowded around you at the conclusion of the meeting to tell you how moving your words were."[15]

All too soon it was time for Secretary Benson to move to Washington. Flora joined him for the inauguration, and Reed, a chaplain in the Air Force stationed in San Antonio, flew in to be with his parents. But Flora and the girls would remain in their Utah home through the school year. Mark was continuing his graduate studies at Stanford.

Reed, Flora, and Secretary Benson attend Eisenhower's first inaugural ball

President Eisenhower looks on as Supreme Court Chief Justice Fred M. Vinson administers the oath of office to Ezra Taft Benson

Nearly 750,000 people, including President David O. McKay, gathered for the inaugural festivities. Ezra and Flora, riding in a convertible, took their places in the procession down Pennsylvania Avenue after the formal inauguration at the Capitol. With hundreds of thousands waving to them, Elder Benson found it all exhilarating—and overwhelming. "It seemed to be a dream," he wrote later. "Yet even in the exciting spell of the moment the awareness of the responsibility that had come to me hovered like a shadow overhead. There would be a time when the crowds were gone."[16]

The following day, Reed and Flora accompanied Ezra to the Gold Room in the east wing of the White House. There, at 5:30 P.M., Ezra Taft Benson stood behind Abraham Lincoln's cabinet table as Chief Justice Fred M. Vinson administered the oath of office. President Eisenhower then shook Ezra's hand, smiled, and remarked, "Hello, Mr. Secretary. Welcome to a tough assignment."

It was that simple. In just minutes Ezra had become the fifteenth man to serve in his post.

The next morning Flora and Reed rode with Ezra to the USDA headquarters in the black Cadillac limousine provided for the Secretary. Reed was due back in San Antonio, and Flora would leave the following day, but Ezra wanted them both with him his first moments on the job. As they entered his spacious office, he stopped and stared at the large leather chair behind an imposing desk. Slowly he crossed the room and sat down. As he fingered the phone with dozens of buttons and intercoms, tears came to his eyes. What did the future hold? He told Reed he would be happy if he could go back right then to Salt Lake City. "I felt like somebody who was suddenly asked to take over a train hurtling through the night at ninety miles an hour with the throttle stuck open and the brake lever thrown out the window," he said. There were two and a half billion dollars' worth of surpluses on hand, another four billion dollars' worth coming in, and almost three billion more in prospect before he could get a handle on things. On his first day a staff member hurried in with a foot-high stack of requisitions for extra government storage bins.

Too soon Ezra was driving Flora to the airport. It would be five months before she and the girls would join him. After they said good-bye, he watched for some time as the plane rolled to the end of the runway and took off. Finally he returned to the apartment he had rented. He could think of nothing but Flora. "Everywhere I turned I saw evidences of her thoughtfulness: the way she had arranged my clothes, . . . brought in food, placed family pictures, . . . and the loving note she had written. And then, for the first time, it was suddenly more than I could bear. The job ahead seemed too big, the load too heavy, loneliness too sharp a pain. I broke down and wept aloud."[17]

Thus began one of the most strenuous and lonely periods of his life.

Most cabinet members enjoy a short time when elected officials and even the press observe a wait-and-see period. But for Ezra, the honeymoon was short.

Even during his confirmation hearings prior to the inauguration, his reception on Capitol Hill had been less than warm. When Senator Milton R. Young of North Dakota tried to pin him down on his views on price supports, Ezra refused to respond until he had more time to evaluate present legislation. The senator made it clear that Ezra's silence was affecting his willingness to vote for confirmation. Senator Allen J. Ellender of Louisiana blasted Ezra for criticizing the current program without offering solutions. But Ezra wanted time to devise the right solution and not be stampeded into action that would compound the problem. The confirmation hearing, which lasted almost two hours, was fairly unpleasant, but in his closing statement, Ezra left no doubt about his perspective: "I do not expect to spend my time trying to protect my job, because any time the . . . President is through with my services I will be greatly relieved and happy to return to what I was doing. But I am determined to use my every energy in the interests of agriculture and in the interests of the Nation."[18] The *Wall Street Journal* gave Ezra high marks on his performance: "The Mormon dignitary answered the senators quietly, slowly, deliberately. Whatever his feelings, his outer calm was never ruffled. And he very definitely stuck to his guns."[19]

In fact, during his first week in office Secretary Benson came out with guns blazing. On his first day he revealed detailed plans to rein in the sprawling USDA bureaucracy and reorganize the department's twenty agencies into four administrative units, each headed by a staff officer who reported to him. In the same memo announcing the reorganization (this and other interoffice communications were dubbed "Epistles from the Apostle" by USDA staffers), he jarred USDA staff members by stating that the people of America had a right to expect of public servants "a full day's work for a day's pay."

USDA employees were at once fearful that the reorganization would eliminate jobs and miffed at what they considered criticism of their working habits. The press hopped on the statement, which exacerbated the problem. Under a headline "Mr. Benson Enters, Swinging," the *Richmond News Leader* on January 26, 1953, reported, "These moves are as encouraging as they are unexpectedly swift. . . . It's been a long time since anything like [this] has been heard in Washington, and it is sweet music to the taxpayer's ear." When he learned that some employees were angry, Secretary Benson explained that he had intended only to stress his feelings on the work ethic rather than criticize past performance. He was learning that every word had to be twice weighed.

There were many adjustments, such as getting used to being called "Mr. Secretary" and increasingly finding that politics was a rough-and-tumble arena. In a matter of weeks he had come to almost expect to find his name, not always treated kindly, in almost any major newspaper or magazine. (Throughout his term he would receive extensive press coverage. He appeared on the cover of *Time* twice, as well as on the covers of *U.S. News & World Report* and other leading magazines.)[20] His job, it seemed, grew bigger with each day. On January 25, 1953, after eating breakfast in a lonely apartment, he wrote Flora, "I just can't keep the tears back, and yet I realize it's all so unnecessary when I stop to count my blessings." He added, "The papers have more about me today. There are some who are trying to smoke me out on several issues that are most controversial."

Ezra selected his team carefully and prayerfully. Joining Paarlberg on the staff were True D. Morse, Under Secretary of Agriculture; J. Earl Coke, assistant secretary; John H. Davis, Ezra's hand-picked successor at the National Council of Farmer Cooperatives, as president of the Commodity Credit Corporation; and Clarence M. Ferguson, administrator of the Extension Service. A believer in the scriptural injunction to "pray oft," he asked his staff when they gathered for their first session if anyone objected to opening their meetings with prayer. No one dissented. And so began a practice that Ezra perpetuated for eight years. He invited each staff member to take turns offering the invocation. Only once in advance did an aide decline. And even then, the man later told the Secretary privately that he was ready to take his turn.

How did Ezra's associates regard the practice? Some may have initially been put off by an observance considered unorthodox, if not provincial, and out of place in a business office. But one assistant wrote: "Some of us hadn't prayed aloud since our 'Now I lay me down to sleep' days. We stumbled and fumbled for words. But the Boss never let on that he noticed. And after a few trials everybody was at ease. Has it helped? Well, I'd say that when you start a meeting that way, people aren't stuck up with the pride of their opinions. You pretty quickly come to an agreement as to what *ought* to be done in any situation."[21]

Secretary Benson had other habits his associates perhaps found unusual. Barring emergencies, he refused to work on Sunday, and he was reportedly the first dignitary to have his interview for "Meet the Press" prerecorded rather than appear in person on the Sunday news program. Also, he would not be photographed holding a glass that gave the appearance of alcohol.

His behavior apparently inspired modifications in the actions of others. Often a top aide would come dashing through the outer office to keep an appointment with him, douse a cigarette in an ashtray, and explain, "I can't smoke in the Secretary's presence." Others remarked they were trying to cut down on smoking or drinking coffee, because if the Secretary could abstain, they could too. When a third-level employee developed a drinking problem and his work suffered, his supervisor recommended dismissal. Secretary Benson called the man in and talked at length about his responsibility to his family, his job, and himself. The man became a productive employee.

Not all of the Secretary's innovations took hold so quickly. When the cabinet convened for their first session at the White House, Eisenhower plunged into the agenda without calling for an invocation. Ezra was "deeply disappointed." The omission bothered him for days. Finally he wrote the President and suggested that each weekly cabinet meeting be opened with prayer. Ike responded that he was quietly investigating other cabinet members' feelings about the practice.[22] At a subsequent meeting, the President said simply, "If there is no objection, we'll begin our deliberations with prayer," and that practice was followed throughout his presidency.

Ezra felt strongly about prayer, and his associates came to appreciate that quality in him. Said one, "He spends as much time on his knees as he does on his feet."[23] And on Thursday mornings Ezra's thoughts often turned to his colleagues of the Twelve, who were meeting in the Salt Lake Temple. He knew they would be praying for him, and he could count on their

The Eisenhower cabinet in session. Secretary of Agriculture Benson is second from right in the photo

Ed Clark, Life Magazine. © Time, Inc.

Secretary Benson regularly began staff meetings with prayer

strength. From the beginning of his USDA tenure, he and his staff would need that strength, for they were fighting an uphill battle.

If Secretary Benson had agreed in principle with the policies established by his predecessor, his job would have been largely administrative. But he didn't. He was convinced that government intervention in and control of agriculture threatened to undermine the moral fiber of farmers. "It just isn't good for government to do for people what they can and should do for themselves," he said again and again. In this vein, his economic philosophies were strictly in line with those of his spiritual leader, President David O. McKay, who had said, "We are placed upon this earth to work. . . . No government owes you a living. You get it yourself by your own acts."[24]

"Any country which pursues policies that cause the self-reliance, initiative, and freedom of its people to drain slowly away is a country in danger," Ezra said.[25] He believed, as he always had, that farmers were the backbone of America—the figurative salt of the earth. Frequently he stated that he was

Secretary Benson holds his first press conference, the first member of the Eisenhower cabinet to do so

delighted his lot had been cast with the rural people of America. And it was time to relieve the farmer of government regulations—particularly high rigid price supports—that undermined individual initiative and let the free market regulate trade.

Yet Eisenhower had temporarily saddled his Secretary of Agriculture with high, rigid price supports. During a campaign speech in Kasson, Minnesota, Ike had stated flatly that his administration would stand behind the existing price-support legislation guaranteeing 90 percent of parity through 1954. To complicate matters, Ezra realized that farmers had come to depend on these federal subsidies.

On February 5, 1953, fifteen days after taking office, Secretary Benson held his first press conference (he would hold more press conferences than any other cabinet member). Nearly a hundred reporters filled a room in the USDA's Administration Building for what promised to be the Secretary's first statement on price supports. Ezra didn't let them down, delivering a carefully worded statement on his agricultural policy. He indicated the USDA would make good on Eisenhower's campaign promise to uphold rigid price supports through 1954, but then stated his view that such supports should be used only to protect the farmer against disaster and to stabilize the volatile commodities market—not to guarantee the farmer a living. He would support flexible price supports based on market performance, but not rigid supports. He expressed his belief that freedom was more precious than life itself, and that no person who depends upon the state for sustenance is free. "The supreme test of any government policy," he stated, "should be, 'How will it affect the character, morale, and well-being of our people?' "[26] Most reports of the press conference were favorable.

Secretary Benson then turned his attention to his first major speech as Secretary of Agriculture, an address before the Central Livestock Association in St. Paul, Minnesota. The price of beef had been sliding for months, and this crowd of cattlemen could be hostile. On February 11, nearly three thousand crowded St. Paul's municipal auditorium.

The Secretary ad-libbed generously, extending his prepared thirty-five-minute address to an hour. He stated candidly that cattlemen should produce meat for the free market and not for government bounty, and concluded with a stirring plea that he would sound again and again: "We must return to the fundamental virtues that have made this nation great. There is a Force in the universe which no mortal can alter. This nation does have a spiritual foundation."[27]

The ovation was warm and the next morning's newspaper report congratulatory. Even Senator Edward J. Thye, who had given him some trouble in his confirmation hearing, admitted, "Ezra, this talk had everything you could ask for."

But when Secretary Benson flew back to Washington, the roof fell in. He was soundly chastised on Capitol Hill. Many Democrats, incensed about his firm views on price supports, were furious. Senator Eugene McCarthy jibed sarcastically, "Benson is like a man standing on the bank of the river telling a drowning man that all he needs to do is take a deep breath of air."[28]

Even some Republicans joined in. Senator Frank Carlson of Kansas called Ezra's St. Paul speech a political blunder and claimed the Secretary had shaken the confidence of farmers.

The congressional outrage puzzled Ezra. The parts of his speech criticized most were those lifted verbatim from the policy statement he had read at the press conference just six days earlier—from which there had been no backlash. Evidently the depth of feeling attached to price supports went far beyond what he had imagined. He was beginning to see that while the economics of the farm situation were straightforward, the politics of the problem were not.

As the first cabinet member to arouse controversy, Ezra and his views filled the press by the end of February. One of the nation's most prominent journalists, purportedly quoting a White House aide, called him "expendable" and predicted that he would be "promoted" to an ambassadorship. He went so far as to say that the Secretary of Agriculture would be the first cabinet member to resign. Headlines such as "Too Much Corn, or Too Much Benson" (*The Nation*) and "Elder Benson's Going to Catch It!" (*Saturday Evening Post*) appeared in nearly every major publication.[29]

But there were also favorable reports. Said *Barron's* on February 16, 1953, "[The Secretary] has been talking some very positive good sense about farm policy. . . . After twenty years of Henry Wallace & Co., it's time!" In addition, two organizations that represented the lion's share of American farmers—the Farm Bureau (with 1.6 million members, the largest of the general farm organizations) and the American Cattleman's Association—consistently backed him.

Even more significant than the views of the press were those of farmers themselves. Incoming mail at the USDA was running fifteen to one in Ezra's favor. In fact, throughout his term, his mail always heavily favored his policies. For example, a young couple who had invested all they had in a farm wrote to say it was good "to hear somebody talk to us as tho we had some intelligence. We don't think the farmer has been riding a gravy train, as we hear said [but] . . . we are 100 per cent for any man who has the courage to tell us we are capable of standing on our own feet rather than merely surviving with Government aid." As a *Life* magazine editorial put it, "The politicians have been complaining . . . Benson is no politician, which may mean he is qualifying for higher honors."[30]

© Time, Inc. All rights reserved. Reprinted by permission from Time

Secretary Benson was on the covers of many national magazines, including Time (this one is dated April 13, 1953)

AGRICULTURE SECRETARY BENSON
"No real American wants to be subsidized."

Nevertheless, the intensity of the debate that raged around him was discouraging. Ezra couldn't remember ever feeling so low. He was being attacked daily in Congress, Washington insiders were placing bets on how long he would last, and he was working fifteen to eighteen hours a day—which was better, however, than coming home to an empty apartment. He longed for Flora and made no bones about it. On one television appearance in which new cabinet members were introduced, he mentioned how much he missed his family. One viewer wrote Flora, "Nothing he could have said, even if he had a dozen top flight public relations men, . . . would have been so effective as his simple and truthful statement that you were at home with your children . . . and that he was a lonely man."[31]

Letters flew back and forth between them. In one, Ezra said, "[Your support does] so much [to] encourage me at a time when the load and worry seem almost too much to bear." When he was especially down, he would call home. Flora did her best to keep his spirits up. "You mustn't worry," she would say. "The President is still behind you, isn't he?"

What did the president think about the controversy? Was Ezra an embarrassment to his administration? Finally the White House called. The president wanted to see him. As Ezra walked into the Oval Office, Eisenhower took off his glasses and looked at him sternly. Then he broke into a chuckle and said, "Ezra, I believe every word you said at St. Paul. But I'm not sure you should have said it quite so soon."

Presidential advice notwithstanding, Ezra didn't wait long to say it again. He felt he spoke the truth, and it needed to be said now. On February 21 in Des Moines, where he was greeted by picketers, he spoke to a packed ballroom with hundreds standing in aisles. Again he pulled no punches, stating that rigid price supports should be used only to protect farmers, not to guarantee them a living. The *Des Moines Register* farm editor wrote that "he sold himself to his audience even though some of those present probably differed with him politically."[32]

One thing was clear: Ezra had the proverbial—and in his case fitting—long row to hoe. While some hailed his plans to decentralize agriculture, there were those who did not. Ahead of him lay the immense task of reeducating much of the public, Congress, and even the president.

Ezra's was a spartanlike existence. He arose by five-thirty every morning, put in an hour of homework, and was at his office by seven-thirty. He usually spent two hours dictating correspondence for his two secretaries. His days became so hectic that he begrudged time to eat, and he began holding staff meetings two evenings a week. Unless he was obligated to attend an official function, he left for home between seven and nine P.M., stopping for a quick meal and then working before retiring. One evening he wrote in his journal, "The pressure of work continues heavily with emerging problems arising daily. I only wish we didn't have to sleep. We are making headway, however, and I am encouraged the Lord is blessing our efforts."

But just as often it seemed that he was doing little more than hanging on, with an incessant round of emergencies, meetings, decisions, politics, social responsibilities, more decisions, and pressure, always pressure. When he could, he slipped out to Bill Marriott's Virginia ranch for horseback riding and a few hours of solitude. There was little he enjoyed more than a hard ride in a Western saddle astride a high-spirited Tennessee Walker named Trigger, a horse nobody else seemed to be able to handle.

Secretary Benson only wished he could handle the immense agricultural problem as easily. If it wasn't one segment of agriculture demanding government help, it was another. Dairymen, for example, were in as precarious a position as cattlemen. But he held firm to his line, proclaiming that it had become too easy "to merely spend taxpayers' money to bolster markets," and calling on farmers and ranchers to look to other solutions. Ezra himself was always on the lookout for marketing opportunities. When he found no milk available during a flight to Wisconsin, he wrote every airline president and urged each to remedy the situation. At Pennsylvania State College he could find no vending machines on campus that dispensed milk, mentioned the fact in his address to the National Dairy Science Association, and received the promise that machines would be installed. (Comedian Bob Hope joined Ezra in helping promote the American Dairyman's Association. He quipped, "There may be an organization with more branch offices, but there are none that have more outlets.")

The political crossfire exhausted Ezra and stood in sharp contrast to the spiritually rejuvenating work he had done for the past ten years. On March 1, Elder Harold B. Lee sensed his colleague's needs while visiting stake conference in Washington, D.C. In his remarks to the Saints, he put the situation in perspective: "There will be many who will belittle [Brother Benson] and will try to destroy him and destroy his reputation and destroy his influence in his high place. . . . Those who do will be forgotten in the remains of Mother Earth, and the odor of their infamy will ever be with them. But the glory and majesty attached to the name of Ezra Taft Benson will never die so long as Brother Benson continues to live the gospel of Jesus Christ. . . . And you and I who are in this congregation will live one day to see what I have said verified."[33]

In his journal that evening Elder Lee recorded, "Brother Benson was needing the uplift of the conference, and I did all I could to build him up before the people." His comments bolstered Ezra, who two days later wrote Flora in good spirits, "All is well, darling. Please don't worry about me."

A continuous stream of letters from his children also buoyed him up. Reed wrote, "Just a brief note to tell you how proud I am of the work you're doing. . . . Stay with her, Dad. The heart of America is . . . beating for you."[34] Mark wrote after reading one of his father's latest speeches, "It's full of spiritual and patriotic meat that ought to wake some Americans out of their lethargy. . . . Lela and I saw you in the newsreels . . . last night. You looked superb—I was so thrilled I started clapping."[35] (It was also in this letter that Mark broke the exciting news—Ezra and Flora were going to be grandparents.)

The news from home wasn't always so good. On March 3, Ezra was awakened at two in the morning by a call from the family physician in Salt Lake City. Flora and Barbara had been in a car accident. Flora was still unconscious, and Barbara had a broken shoulder and lacerations. Ezra immediately arranged for both to receive blessings, and he called Reed to ask that he take emergency leave from his chaplain duties and hurry home. Then, following a period of prayer, he tried in vain to sleep. The following day he kept a full round of appointments, though fasting. That evening he returned home to await word. At nine-thirty the call came. Both were doing fine. "It was the longest night and day I spent in Washington," he wrote.[36]

Ezra's family's support was felt in many ways. He knew that they prayed for him constantly and in all situations. At one general conference, when he rose to speak, the message "Pray for Dad" automatically swept down the row from person to person where his family sat.

In April Elder Benson returned home for his first general conference since leaving for Washington. Being with his family and the Brethren rejuvenated him. How he had missed them all! After conference he wrote, "I have wished many times that the conference might go on for five or ten days. It is almost like going into another world to leave the activity and pressure of Washington . . . and enter upon the peace and quiet of a general conference of the Church."[37]

Back in Washington, Secretary Benson and his staff pushed doggedly ahead. They continued to implement their reorganization of the USDA, streamlined the Soil Conservation Service, and established a Foreign Agricultural Service. On a bizarre note, a nest of counterfeiters was found operating within the Department. "This was definitely carrying free enterprise to an extreme," the Secretary joked. "We had no desire to see headlines . . . claiming that Agriculture was reducing the cash depletion of the Treasury by printing its own." And when he found, to his dismay, that he sat on the board of directors of the Virgin Islands Corporation, which among other properties operated a rum distillery, he urged the corporation to divest itself. "Being in the liquor business, even thus remotely and involuntarily, was too much for me," he wrote.[38]

In one of his first appearances before a congressional committee, Secretary Benson was accused of sidestepping questions on price supports. After the first go-around he noted, "My personal commitment to the President was for two years' service, but there were signs that I might not be around that long." He would have many confrontations with Congress. Don Paarlberg later assessed these sessions: "The essence of Secretary Benson was religious belief and ethical conduct. The essence of most people in the legislative branch was political pragmatism. In testimony before the committees he and the congressmen would sail by one another like ships that pass in the night."[39]

One of the first senators to attack Ezra on the Senate floor was James Eastland of Mississippi, who called the Secretary an enemy of the farmer. Ezra subsequently told his staff that he wanted to accept the first invitation that came to speak in Mississippi. His aides objected, but he didn't hesitate to face his detractors so long as he was armed with the truth. He always felt that if the truth were given equal time, it would fare well. In April 1953 the invitation came—to address the Delta Cotton

Council in southern Mississippi. Ezra accepted, and Senator Eastland invited him to stay at his plantation home.

The evening prior to the speech, Secretary Benson invited the senator to review a copy of his address. The next day, with twenty thousand gathered to hear him, the Secretary faced the coldest crowd on the hottest day he could remember. But in introducing him, Senator Eastland said, "My friends, today you're going to hear something you won't like, but it will be good for you because it's the truth." Ezra could not believe what he had heard. He later said he had never been so shocked in his life. He appreciated the senator's courage in making this reversal; Eastland would become one of his best defenders and closest congressional friends.

While Secretary Benson stood firm in his views, his messages did not bear the mark of an unreasonable man. His first interest was to improve conditions for the farmer. He was unencumbered by other motives. In an address to the National Conference of Christians and Jews on May 11, 1953, he explained: "My position on subsidies has been made very plain. . . . I do not think the American farmer is satisfied to depend on subsidies as a way of life. He wants a fair price at the market. But there is a tendency to dramatize agricultural subsidies because they are out in the open where everybody can see them. . . . But let us not overlook the nonfarm subsidies we taxpayers are charged with and the danger that they present to a free economy. . . . Perhaps many of them are still needed today. All I am saying is, 'Let's take a look at the whole picture.' "

Ezra was a convincing speaker. Lorenzo Hoopes, his personal assistant, said that the Secretary was his own best representative. He prepared tirelessly for presentations and often ad-libbed, sometimes at length. Don Paarlberg felt that Ezra was most effective when he laid his prepared speech aside and spoke from the heart, "with eloquence, about our wonderful farm people, about America, about freedom, the Constitution, individual responsibility—all of which he called our heritage. . . . The audience would listen attentively."[40]

Secretary Benson shows Eisenhower a purebred Holstein at the Beltsville (Maryland) Research Center, May 26, 1953

Ezra Benson was not a wishy-washy leader. He delivered hard facts that he believed farmers wanted to hear. And whether they agreed with him or not, many farmers sensed his sincerity. Sometimes his audiences were intimate—a few persons gathered on courthouse steps in small communities; other times he addressed thousands, such as in Eau Claire, Wisconsin, where an audience of sixty-five thousand gathered to hear him speak at the National Plowing Contest.

In the summer of 1953 the Midwest was suffering from a drouth so severe that some farmers were going out of business. During June, Secretary Benson toured Texas, a state almost immobilized by the lack of rain. One Texan quipped that it was so dry and dusty where he came from that when it did rain, only 60 percent of it was moisture. In Lubbock, Ezra spoke to an audience gathered under a large building with a tin roof. With the TV lights focused on the speaker's platform, it was "almost literally hot as Hades." He took off his coat and tie, rolled up his sleeves, and did his best to talk despite the oppressive heat.

He had been warned to expect hostile crowds in Austin, but before leaving the area, he felt impressed to suggest to the governor that he declare a day of fasting and prayer, and assured him that rain would be forthcoming. Three days later San Antonio had two inches of rain. A local paper reported, "Secretary of Agriculture Ezra Taft Benson apparently has contacts that are literally out of this world. When Benson left San Antonio on Sunday he promised south Texas farmers and ranchers immediate drouth aid. Less than 24 hours later it rained for the first time in months."

Chapter 15

Calm in the Crucible

I n June the Benson family moved to Washington—Flora's
tenth move since her marriage. Barbara stayed in Utah to
attend BYU. It was such a relief to have his family close
by again. Ezra relied on Flora's encouragement and her
judgment. And she helped him in practical ways. She often sat
up nights when he could no longer stay awake, reading folders
of material he couldn't squeeze into his eighteen-hour days,
and writing constructive ideas. Next morning orderly digests of
the material would be in his briefcase.

Others were relieved to have the Secretary's family close at
hand. He seemed easier to get along with. His aides noticed
that when Flora stopped by the office, it was as though a new
light turned on inside him. They came to understand that when,
after discussing an important matter, the Secretary said, "I'll
not decide now; I'll sleep on it and decide tomorrow," that meant
there would be a talk with Flora and prayer that evening. In
retrospect Ezra wrote, "Having Flora . . . nearby gave me new
confidence. . . . I became more decisive, surer of myself, more
willing to tackle the tough challenges."[1]

Before leaving Utah, the family had discussed what kind
and color of car to purchase. Ezra indicated any color was fine,
as long as it was black. He put it to a vote in one of their

regular family councils, and lost. They flew to South Bend, Indiana, and picked up a bright red Studebaker Champion. "Somehow, I couldn't get comfortable in that machine," Ezra said. Neighbors and friends remarked how out of character it seemed to see the Secretary of Agriculture driving a red car. As a joke, someone sent Ezra a pair of bright red suspenders to wear while motoring in the Studebaker.

The Bensons settled into a modest red brick home near Rock Creek Park. Prominently featured in the living room were an old spinet piano and a leatherbound volume of the Book of Mormon. The home also had chandeliers that used to be in the home of the individual who wrote the lyrics to "Home Sweet Home."

Some privileges that went with Ezra's position didn't set well with Flora—such as the chauffeur assigned to provide transportation for the family. She didn't like the idea of her children being chauffeured to school or of herself being driven around Washington. For months she drove the children everywhere. But the chauffeur was sitting at the office with nothing to do, so Flora finally relented. "Our demands were so pressing," she said. "A chauffeur could get you places quicker, better and safer. I could be driven to the doors of embassies and other functions [and not worry about parking]. . . . [Being] late is an unpardonable sin socially in Washington."[2]

Barbara, home from BYU, cried when her father said she had to ride in the Cadillac. "We look like something we're not. People will think we're snobs and rich, and we aren't either." She ducked her head the entire way. None of the children liked being driven to school, and they made the chauffeur let them out blocks away. Said Beth, "I was proud of who I was, and proud of my parents, but I wanted people to like me for me and not because of who my father was."

As time went on, the Benson children became the focus of frequent social attention. Photographs of the girls filled the *Washington Post* and the *Evening Star* society pages, but when they were approached about being debutantes, Flora said no. She did, however, allow Beverly, following vocal training in New York City, to make her formal singing debut at a private concert for dignitaries and congressmen in the Anderson House.

The Benson family visits President Eisenhower in the Oval Office. Left to right: Bonnie, Lela, Mark (holding Stephen), Flora, the President, Ezra, Beth, Barbara, Beverly, and Reed

Afterwards her parents kissed her on both cheeks, and this expression of affection was caught by press photographers. Photos appeared the following morning in a number of newspapers around the country. Ezra and Flora were particularly touched by a response from Emma Ray McKay, wife of David O. McKay, who wrote Beverly: "Is it fair to the rest of us that some are born with . . . a good voice and lovely character, and enough common sense not to be spoiled by it all? You are one of those lovely beings." At school the children intentionally maintained a low profile. Beverly attended Roosevelt High School for a year before her teachers realized who her father was.

Schools in Washington were vastly different from those in Utah. Most dignitaries sent their children to private schools, but Ezra and Flora did not follow suit. The Benson children found themselves attending public schools with peers they didn't know. But the girls participated fully, and Bonnie was even voted "friendliest girl" in her high school.

The transition was demanding for Flora as well. She insisted on maintaining the house herself without hired help, despite a demanding social calendar. She often sent Beverly or Bonnie as their father's partner at embassy dinners and receptions, but there were some appearances she couldn't avoid. "I was trying to do all the jobs of a good homemaker . . . and at the end of the day look rested, poised, relaxed, and properly groomed," she said. It was something Ezra appreciated. Her support would be invaluable to him in the days ahead.

By early fall 1953, reports in the press about Secretary Benson were mixed. Some applauded his hard-line policies. Others blamed him for Eisenhower's drop in the polls and claimed he was single-handedly jeopardizing Republican chances in the 1954 congressional elections.[3] Rumors that he was on his way out persisted. When the House Agriculture Committee released two resolutions demanding that the Secretary put price supports under livestock, Eisenhower was furious. This was an open break with Ezra and hence the administration. While the President staunchly backed his cabinet member, the choir of strident newspaper voices sang forth. "Eisenhower Faces Task of Saving Benson," cried the *Christian Science Monitor*, representative of dozens more.[4]

Washingtonians weren't the only ones interested in Ezra Benson's battles. Latter-day Saints around the country watched with keen interest, many of them understanding little more than that their apostle was under fire. There were those who disagreed with his agricultural policies and others who couldn't get used to their ecclesiastical leader getting battered about on Capitol Hill for all to see. Apparently Ezra was sensitive about this. In his general conference address in October 1954 he admitted, "My one anxiety is that I may inadvertently do something . . . that will cast an unfavorable light or bring discredit upon the Church. . . . I pray that this may never happen."

On November 8, 1953, after a stake conference in Orem, Utah, Barbara wrote, "Elder Harold B. Lee was the speaker. . . . Most of his talk was about you and the wonderful job you're doing and how we should all pray for you and be behind you 100%. He really scolded those that were critical."[5]

Presumably worried about the impact his activities might have upon those close to him, Ezra wrote his brothers and sisters on November 9, 1953: "I hope you will not become unduly depressed when you read items deeply critical of me. . . . This seems to be a part of the office and will be so, particularly during the ensuing year."

After they returned to Utah in the early sixties, Flora acknowledged how the strain had affected their immediate family: "Politics can be brutal. . . . Our family had many a cry and heartaches with fasting and earnest prayer, but the rewarding and sunny days came often."

Late in 1953 Ezra gave Eisenhower a graceful out, indicating that he would resign if the president saw fit. "That will never happen," Ike snapped. "I don't want to hear any more about it."[6]

The pressure leading to a Benson resignation intensified in October 1953 when a caravan of 350 cattlemen, most of them "suitcase" cowboys who had gotten into the cattle business to make a fast dollar when prices were high, and who now moaned at dropped prices, marched on Washington to demand that Ezra place price supports under beef. The USDA auditorium bulged with protesters, the press, and curious department employees. Despite the extensive media coverage of the cattlemen's caravan, the Secretary would not be stampeded. After hearing out the group's spokesmen, he addressed the problem at length, outlining sound principles that would benefit cattlemen in the long run. The department was subsequently flooded with letters from cattlemen nationwide who insisted those in the caravan represented no one but themselves, and who said they had seen fluctuating prices before and were willing to weather the storm. The crisis ended as suddenly as it had begun—but not before the media, Congress, and farmers across the country saw Ezra Taft Benson stand for principle rather than bow to political expediency.

The day before the cattle caravan invasion, Ezra and Under Secretary True D. Morse spent an hour during a cabinet session presenting a detailed report on the agricultural situation. For months Secretary Benson had worked to convince Eisenhower that flexible price supports were the answer to the surpluses, and finally the president endorsed his views. It was the most significant date in his first year as secretary.

Before the fickle political pendulum swung again, and with Ike solidly in his corner, Ezra determined to get in his punches. At his prodding, President Eisenhower agreed to outline the administration's farm program in a message to Congress on January 11, 1954.

Ezra wanted Eisenhower to make a strong speech. But getting it past White House aides, who wanted to tone down his policies to make them more attractive to Congress, was a task laced together by endurance and strategy. However, after repeated battles with the president's staff, Ezra had his way. The address called for flexible price supports on major commodities, a gradual shift to a modernized formula for figuring parity, and no change in the policy on perishable commodities.

A blizzard hit Washington, D.C., on January 11, but inside Congress the temperature was considerably warmer as the president delivered, point by point, the administration's new farm program. Secretary Benson had wanted the farm program to be regarded as the administration's rather than his, and that strategy paid off. Response to the address was surprisingly favorable. An editorial from the Chicago *Sun-Times* is typical of others: "The program makes a lot of sense to us, and we urge Congress to take Ike's advice and give it early approval."[7]

Round one was over. But it would take a long fight to get the program through Congress. One evening soon after, Ezra and Flora had a talk. He felt that if he could educate farmers, they would back the president's program. But that meant traveling to every agricultural state and talking with anyone who would listen. Flora encouraged him to take his message to the people, and she would keep things on an even keel at home. One reporter wrote, "Although Flora Benson is extremely retiring in public, in private she is considered to be the pivot on which the family moves. . . . Friends of the family agree that she acts as the leavening influence on her husband. Said a friend, 'Every once in a while, when it's needed, . . . she says, "Now, look here, T!" and that seems to do the trick.' "[8]

Immediately Ezra embarked on an exhausting tour. He made dozens of major speeches throughout the country, testified before congressional committees, gave radio and television interviews, and made it home for only a few nights before heading out again.

The strain of having her husband away so much was difficult for Flora. She explained, "It's a killing job but the Lord will see us through. If my husband's services are going to benefit our country, then we can make a contribution by sacrificing his company without complaint."

Repeatedly he preached the doctrine of self-reliance and freedom—that an individual's freedom to choose for himself, as outlined in the Book of Mormon, was God's greatest gift: "Ye are free; ye are permitted to act for yourselves; for behold God hath . . . made you free." Often he spoke to antagonistic farmers who resented the threat of losing government guarantees for growing crops. To those who said his policies were poor politics, he appealed to their sense of right and wrong: "Do you seriously believe that the American farmer . . . [is] so foolish . . . that [he] cannot, or will not, choose what is right over so-called political expediency? I refuse to believe that what is right is *not* good politics."[9]

But Ezra's principled, single-minded farm program had trouble in Congress. A newsletter of wide circulation reported that "things are looking bad for Benson and company on Capitol Hill—to put it mildly. Their farm program now stands less chance than ever for approval."[10]

Finally, Eisenhower went on television to appeal to the people, declaring, "Many have told me that it would not be good politics to attempt solution of the farm problem during an election year. The sensible thing to do, I have been told . . . was to close my eyes to the damage the present farm program does to our farmers. . . . In this matter I am completely unmoved by arguments as to what constitutes good or winning politics. . . . Though I have not been in this political business very long, I know that what is right for America is politically right."[11]

Despite the president's plea, only four days later the House Agriculture Committee voted to raise price supports on dairy products. The break with the administration was complete.

In the meantime, Secretary Benson continued to take his program to the people. Against advice from his staff, he went to Denver to speak to the National Farmers Union, whose 750,000 members consistently opposed his policies on price supports. Even the president asked if he were ready to face a "bunch of rebels." But after a hard-hitting address, the Secretary received a rousing standing ovation. It was all he could do to hold back the tears as farmers gathered around him afterwards.

While at Pennsylvania State University to deliver a speech, Ezra toured the dairy barns. When members of the press challenged him to milk a prize Holstein, he took his position, grinned, and told them to move back or he'd squirt them. As they backed about ten feet away, he overheard one reporter boast, "He'll never reach us here." Ezra recorded, "When I got going pretty well I suddenly shot a spray of milk and got him good."

Despite such lighter moments, the controversy over the farm program raged on in Congress, and subtlety was not Secretary Benson's forte. Then President Eisenhower gave him a lesson in strategy. He marked a square and an X on a piece of paper. The X was their objective, and the square their forces. "It might seem that the simplest thing to do is to go straight toward the objective," he explained. "But that is not always the best way to get there. You may have to move around some obstacle. You may have to feint and pull the defense out of position. Sometimes you just wait and catch the enemy when he isn't expecting you. That may have to be the way you work at this farm problem."[12]

As it turned out, Secretary Benson was forced to employ various tactics, including compromise, when he couldn't get all he wanted. On August 9, 1954, the vote on what had become known as the Agricultural Act of 1954 went to the Senate. The Bensons fasted that day; Reed sat in the Senate gallery, sending hourly reports to his father; and Ezra spent hours on the telephone with Senators rallying votes. At seven-thirty that night word came that the Senate had passed, by a vote of 49 to 44, flexible price support legislation.

The next day, under the headline "Foolish Ezra, They Said of Mr. Benson—But He Beat the Farm Bloc," Scripps-Howard columnist Howard Lucey wrote: "They . . . called him stupid

Secretary Benson was the subject of numerous editorial cartoons in the nation's press

and denounced him as the worst Secretary of Agriculture in history and demanded that President Eisenhower fire him. But Ezra Taft Benson stood his ground and took the pounding. Today he has emerged as hero of the biggest legislative victory the Eisenhower administration has had." *Collier's* saw it as a moral victory: "It would have been easier for the Secretary . . . if he had been willing to let the rigid 90 per cent of parity support remain operative. . . . But the issue as Secretary Benson saw it was not wholly or even mainly political. It was first economic, and ultimately moral."[13]

As the fickle arena of politics will have it, Ezra Taft Benson was suddenly a champion, and election-year candidates came to his office seeking endorsements and photographs. His farm program was the hottest election issue in farm states, and welcoming the opportunity to expound upon the principles involved, he hit the campaign trail. From early September until November 2, he made speeches daily, except Sundays. "Such campaigning is a terrible ordeal," he wrote, "but it is so exhilarating while going on, you don't know how tired you are until you stop."[14]

In the meantime, Secretary Benson had a run-in with Eisenhower's chief of staff, Sherman Adams. Ezra refused to stand behind price supports for eggs, and Adams chided him to get off "his puritanical white horse." At this the Secretary instructed an assistant to prepare a letter to Ike stating he wouldn't back down—"and make it strong." When a White House staff member suggested Ezra was still a political liability, Eisenhower responded, "Ezra is the shining star in the firmament of my administration."[15] (In due time Adams would inscribe on a picture that Ezra was "Rugged and Right.")

There were some who believed Eisenhower retained Secretary Benson because he functioned as a political lightning rod and drew attention away from other Eisenhower policies that might have harmed the president's appeal. But it seems clear there was mutual respect between the two men. The only criticism Ike is known to have made publicly about Secretary Benson is what was written in his memoirs when he recorded that the Secretary's views were "earnestly held and argued, though not always with the maximum of tact."[16]

Ezra sat out election day in 1954 with some anxiety. The farm program was a principal issue on trial in rural areas. The Republicans lost control of Congress, but the returns from agricultural states were surprisingly favorable. Senator Guy Gillette of Iowa, an eighteen-year Democratic veteran considered invincible, had opposed Secretary Benson. He was unseated. Republican strength prevailed in major Midwestern farm states. Senator Clinton Anderson, a Democrat from New Mexico who had supported the new program, was decisively reelected.

On the day after the election, the *Wall Street Journal* proclaimed that the biggest election victory went to "Ezra Taft Benson and his farm program. . . . Rural America made it plain amid all the other confusion . . . that it was not repudiating Mr. Benson." The *Chicago Sun-Times* headlined, "Benson Gets the Last Laugh," and NBC commentator Lloyd Burlingame concluded, "Hundreds of politicians won victories for themselves . . . but Secretary Benson won a victory for the United States of America."[17]

After the election, Ezra wondered if it wasn't time to return to Salt Lake City. He felt that the elections had vindicated his program and significant legislation had passed Congress—and he had only promised President Eisenhower two years. In a November meeting he told the president that he would be happy to be relieved of his responsibilities. The president quickly shot back, "If you quit, I quit," adding, "If it is necessary I'll go to Salt Lake myself to urge that you continue as my Secretary of Agriculture."[18]

As some of the most prominent Mormons in the nation, the Bensons and their religion were repeatedly in the spotlight. As the embodiment of family, home, and the American way, the Bensons were the focus of perhaps the most positive attention the Church had ever received throughout the country. A lengthy *Saturday Evening Post* article, published on March 28, 1953, retold the Joseph Smith story in its entirety, elaborating on doctrines such as the eternal nature of man, the Word of Wisdom, and the building of Zion on the American continent. Literally hundreds of news reports included in-depth discussions of the Church.

The Secretary seized every appropriate opportunity to talk about the gospel and the Church. When a university radio station in the Midwest asked if it might broadcast his favorite scriptural reading, he selected the Joseph Smith story, which is found in the Pearl of Great Price, one of the Church's standard scriptural works. Ezra sent Eisenhower lengthy excerpts from the Book of Mormon prophesying about America's destiny. After receiving one such letter, Ike responded: "Thank you for drawing on your wide knowledge of the Book of Mormon to send me certain prophecies and revelations. The quotations I have read with the greatest of interest, with special applications to the growth and the problems of America."[19] Dozens of world leaders received copies of the Book of Mormon—heads of state, ambassadors, even newspaper editors.

Perhaps another reason Ezra Benson continued to attract media attention was because, after a year of intense fire (one reporter called it the "hardest pounding any Administration official ever took in his first year of office"), he had remained surprisingly calm. Observers didn't know what to make of his serenity. A fellow cabinet officer told him, "Every night when I go to bed I thank God I'm not the Secretary of Agriculture!" But with Ezra, peace came in doing what he felt was right— and letting the consequences follow. As Flora reminded him frequently, "Don't worry about the world's opinion of you as long as you're right with the Lord."

Inevitably, the boiling cauldron of farm politics spilled into the Benson family life. Beverly often attended press conferences and congressional hearings, many of which blasted her father. It tore at her heart. But she, with her brothers and sisters, had implicit confidence in him. "When you know your dad is right, you know he's going to rise above it all," she said.

Beth was young enough to not understand everything, but old enough to dislike the criticism. "It hurt me deeply," she recalls. "Home should be peaceful, an escape. But some pressures couldn't help but come in. Dad put on a lot of weight, which was part of his stress relief."

In fact, Ezra's position put the entire family under strain. When, for example, gunmen from Puerto Rico opened fire in Congress, wounding four, police officers were immediately assigned to all cabinet members and their homes.

But Flora created a sanctuary to which Ezra could retreat. The social invitations she received could have taken her out of the home constantly, but she often sent one of the girls with Ezra to White House dinners or embassy receptions so she could stay home, where she felt she was most needed. At these receptions, the Bensons met some of the world's most renowned personalities, including Queen Elizabeth and Prince Philip, Winston Churchill, and the King and Queen of Greece.

When a young Army private, James Parker, began to court Beverly, he observed the Bensons firsthand. Beverly's first date with him was to a July Fourth celebration where Secretary Benson was the speaker. Parker felt somewhat intimidated by the chauffeurs and police escort. Afterwards, as the family returned home, he worried about feeling comfortable in the Secretary's home. They had barely stepped inside when the Secretary invited him into the kitchen, and Jim thought he was in for an interrogation. However, he breathed easier when the Secretary set things out on the counter and asked him if he would like some bread

The Benson family at J. Willard Marriott's ranch. Back, Barbara, Flora, Bonnie, Ezra, and Beverly; front, Reed, Mark, and Beth

and milk. The following Sunday Jim was invited to dinner. After the meal Sister Benson said, "Okay, T, it's your turn to do dishes. Jim, you can help." Another date was also memorable: "I came to pick Beverly up for a date, and she wasn't quite ready," Jim remembered. "Sister Benson pulled out the vacuum and asked if I'd mind cleaning while I waited. It was that kind of family environment."

The principal stabilizer for the family was the gospel and the priorities and focus it gave them. Regardless of how intense the pressures became, their lives were rooted in something much greater than politics and Washington. The gospel message gave them an eternal purpose and perspective. "We did a lot of praying and fasting," Beverly recalls. "We must have spent four of the eight years on our knees. We needed each other, and had to pull together."

There were other pressure valves. Beth and her father often took walks through nearby Rock Creek Park. She loved the private time with him, and he relished the solitude and surroundings. Occasionally at night Beverly gave her father a private organ recital at the Washington Ward chapel. The music seemed to soothe his nerves.

The Marriott ranch was also a refuge. Occasionally the family went there for the weekend. Ezra rose early to ride horses, and Beth sometimes stayed up all night so she wouldn't oversleep and miss those early-morning rides with him. They did him wonders. He felt that he had to get away from Washington to maintain his perspective.

Perspective was hard to come by at times, when he was constantly being labeled as a moralist, a do-gooder. Political cartoonists had a heyday with him. Yet Ezra maintained his composure. Don Paarlberg usually accompanied his boss to testify before congressional committees. One of his responsibilities was to "hold the book," a compilation of facts and statistics, tabbed and indexed for ready response. He sat directly behind the Secretary and communicated by notes and whispers. He recalled, "Committee members sometimes badger a witness. They bear down especially while television cameras are rolling. Sometimes, when the treatment got rough, I could see the red color rising above Secretary Benson's collar. He would pause, swallow, wet his lips and answer in calm tones. Coming back in the Secretary's car after one experience, an aide commended him on his poise. The Secretary said, seemingly more to himself than to others, 'A soft answer turneth away wrath but grievous words stir up anger.' "

Ezra's humor surfaced at unexpected times. At a congressional hearing Senator Hubert Humphrey, an outspoken critic, said, in words to this effect: "Secretary Benson, we hear much about exploration in Antarctica. Your stocks of surplus wheat would probably keep very well down there where it is so cold. Have you thought about shipping your wheat down there for storage?" "Yes I have, Senator," Ezra replied. "And I've thought of sending you down there to oversee the operation." Senator Humphrey laughed louder than anyone else.[20]

It was such behavior that caught the fancy of the press. In an article entitled "The Benson Formula for Success," the *New York Times Magazine* explained the Secretary's inner calm: "One reason is his religion. . . . He acts like a man whose conscience is always clear—his testimony today will be the same next week or the week after or a year from now. He doesn't have to remember what he said to an opposition Senator at their last meeting. This is a built-in ulcer-saving device not always found in Washington."[21]

A reporter from *American* magazine followed Ezra around his office and was unprepared with what he found: "Many high executives, I've noted, strike an attitude of outward calm during interviews, but it's easy to sense the unleashed powder keg underneath. . . . [However, Benson] wasn't fooling; he *was* calm. He spoke in a quiet, confident, unruffled voice. His brow never knotted up at the knottiest questions. . . . There might have been a touch of Pollyanna about the man, but there was no pomposity. And if he had little emotion, he certainly had warmth. I marked him as a man who'd never feel the sting of an ulcer."

The magazine reporter asked the Secretary his secret. "It's easy to keep calm," Ezra replied, "if you have inner security and peace of mind. . . . I try to do the thing I believe to be right and let the chips fall where they will." The reporter concluded that it was obvious the Secretary's " 'inner security and peace of mind' came largely from his religion."[22] Indeed, Ezra's inner stability and strength came from his reliance on the gospel and the teachings of the Savior. As the Book of Mormon taught, "Peace be unto you, because of your faith in my Well Beloved."

Years later Ezra would counsel his eldest grandson, who by that time had become a nationally syndicated political cartoonist, "We pray that in spite of the barbs that are directed your way, you will keep that sweet, humble spirit of the gospel mixed with your usual good humor." He knew whereof he spoke.[23]

The First Presidency followed with keen interest the activities of their apostle in Washington. In his personal journal under date of August 19, 1954, President McKay recorded his remarks to a meeting of the Council of the Twelve: "I expressed gratitude to the Lord for the success that has attended . . . Brother Benson. . . . I suppose it is not overstating the fact when I say that only the present responsibilities of the President himself exceed those which Brother Benson is carrying. . . . Out of it all stands before the American people Brother Benson's integrity and honesty of purpose. Even those who have opposed him in his policy admit that nobody can question Brother Benson's honesty . . . and in that declaration and radiant manifestation of character he has brought great credit to himself, the Council, and the Church."

On another occasion President McKay attended a meeting in the State Department. A senator made special mention of the administration's spirituality and attributed it in part to the influence of Secretary Benson. President McKay told Ezra he had hardly been able to hold back the tears.

A letter from Elder Mark E. Petersen to his colleague counseled him to not become discouraged, declaring that he was doing more good "than one hundred missionaries in the field."[24]

The Benson family hadn't been in Washington long before they realized how potent their missionary opportunities were, but Flora was determined to keep her children insulated from the pageantry of her husband's high-profile position. That, of course, was virtually impossible. But she wanted six children who had their feet on the ground and their heads out of the clouds. There were unusual social experiences, however. They had a standing offer to use the White House swimming pool, occasionally spent a day on the "Susie E," the presidential yacht, and enjoyed a few weekend trips to Camp David. Flora approved of her children having growing experiences, but she resented intrusions that drew them too far into the limelight.

For that reason, when Edward R. Murrow approached Secretary Benson about featuring the family on his popular Friday night television show, "Person to Person," Flora responded with a flat refusal. Ezra dropped the subject, but Reed sensed a missionary opportunity and doggedly promoted the idea of showing America an inside look at an LDS family's home evening. Finally Flora conceded.

The show was televised live on September 24, 1954, with only an informal run-through—no rehearsal. Three television cameras were set up in the Bensons' living room and library. The garage was filled with electronic equipment, and a production crew of ten was on hand. On the show, Flora introduced the family. The girls sang "Sittin' on Top of the World," Barbara sang "Italian Street Song," Beth tap-danced and sang, Reed and Mark explained the Church's missionary program, and the family sang "Love at Home."

With time winding down on the program, and realizing this as her last opportunity to cover a few salient points, Flora responded to Murrow's question, "Do you have any domestic help?" with a spirited reply: "No, we do not have a maid. We feel that we learn by doing. We prepare all of our own meals, and plan them. . . . We play together, sing together. We're a very religious family. We have daily prayer—individual and together—because we feel that a family that prays together stays together. I feel that's true of a nation." It was a typical home evening, as the Bensons saw it. That, however, is not how several million viewers perceived it.

Murrow called from New York later to say it was his finest show. Eisenhower told Ezra, "Besides all the rest of it, it was the best political show you could have put on." The December 1955 issue of *Look* reported, "The best shows often come from homes where one least expects to find them. The visit to Secretary of Agriculture Ezra Taft Benson turned out to be one of the most popular. . . . It made a moving family portrait that was much more entertaining than most calls on show-business celebrities." United Press International reported that the show featuring the Bensons brought Murrow more fan mail than any other in history. Hundreds of letters came to the Secretary's office. One read: "May a Catholic priest tell you and your family how inspiring and wholesome your visit was via television tonight? I never expect to live to see one of my own faith elected President. I would like to see candidates of your timber, and indeed you would be assured of my vote." A man who identified himself as being from the grass roots wrote Milton Eisenhower: "My resolve to write you was crystallized this morning when one of the men in our office asked me if I saw the program. . . . He said, 'I didn't realize there was anyone in Washington like that.' I think the wholesome picture presented of a Christian, close-knitted family serving their country in a high post was a sobering sight to many."[25]

Many letters were addressed specifically to Flora, such as one that read, "Your sincere warmth and spiritual attitude of family must have endeared you to many listeners. . . . I prayed that very night that I might be the mother you are." And another stated, "Did you stop to realize that your television performance, seen by millions of people, was a stroke of missionary work of the first magnitude?"

In addition to the show's missionary impact, it boosted Ezra's popularity in the South, where the conservative population responded enthusiastically. A short time later, a Republican party official from the South said that Ezra Taft Benson was so popular he could be elected to any office there.

The Murrow show brought the Bensons front and center as spokesmen for conservative religious thought. Unusual incidents followed, such as one at a banquet in Chicago. Just before the Secretary rose to speak, a waiter whispered, "Mr. Secretary, would it be helpful to you to know that thousands of people are praying for you?"

Many letters referred to the Bensons' sincerity. Elder Benson attributed it to genuine family loyalty that showed through. Regardless of how busy he was, he kept Wednesday nights open for family nights. When he could, he cancelled obligations that conflicted with family events—such as an important social function the same night as Bonnie's daddy-daughter party. Residents near the church were perhaps startled that evening to find the Secretary of Agriculture and his daughter collecting green toothpicks and shoelaces for a scavenger hunt.

After several years in Washington, Ezra worried that he wasn't spending enough time with his children and even noted in his journal that Flora had talked to him about freeing up more time. He tried to do better.

At home the kitchen was the center of the family's activity. Ezra had a favorite dish—whole wheat bread and honey, covered with milk, and topped off with raw onions. It was a family tradition for him to bite into an onion and begin, "You know . . . " The children would chime in and repeat, " . . . the onion is the most neglected vegetable in the world." Then Ezra would take another bite and say, "Glad to see you're finally learning. Here, have an onion," and everyone would laugh.

Ezra and Flora's first grandchild, Stephen Reed Benson, was born during the cabinet years

Metro Group Photo, Chicago Tribune

After Reed was honorably discharged from the Air Force and he joined the family in Washington, D.C., he spent much time with his sisters, and even held early-morning classes with them where he taught gospel subjects and shared notes he had used in his lectures as a chaplain. He also bought each a number of Church books to help them begin their individual libraries. The girls formed a Book of Mormon club—complete with a theme song, which they wrote.

Benson family nights opened with prayer and scripture reading. Frequently the meetings ended with the family all laughing until tears came to their eyes. Flora often turned on the record player for dancing. She and Ezra loved to dance. Flora said they danced their troubles away. A Washington columnist noted that at a White House reception, the Bensons were the first to take the dance floor.

In family council the family discussed finances, who was dating whom, how late the girls could stay out, how much time could be spent in front of the TV, time limits for phone calls, and so forth. The children agreed among themselves that they wouldn't date until they were sixteen and that any suitor had to be approved by the family. There was no dating out of the Church for the Benson girls.

While Flora was loathe to plunge her family into the Washington social scene, there were some obligations she couldn't decline. She hostessed her first luncheon for cabinet wives in May 1954. Though most such luncheons were catered, she deter-

Secretary Benson (right) enjoys a hard ride at the Marriott ranch with his close friend J. Willard Marriott (center)

Reprinted from Saturday Evening Post. © 1955 The Curtis Publishing Company

mined to invite these women to her home and, with the help of her daughters, prepare everything herself. Flora's preparations were painstaking. Reed even flew in from San Antonio to assist. When Ezra protested at the fuss, Flora insisted that it was her chance to host an enjoyable gathering with appropriate standards.

When the women arrived, she greeted them warmly and explained that things were different in her home—that there were no cocktails, playing cards, smoking, or tea and coffee—but then added, "We'll try to make it up to you in our way, and we hope you enjoy our home."

The girls helped serve the meal, and all of the children performed. BYU's Madrigal Singers were in Washington on tour, and they also sang (with Barbara as soloist). Mamie Eisenhower was so taken with the BYU group that she promptly invited them to the White House that afternoon, accompanied them on the tour of the mansion, and waved from the front porch as their Greyhound bus drove away. Later she wrote Flora her thanks: "This is just a note to tell you again how much I enjoyed your beautiful luncheon. . . . The food which you and your daughters prepared was delicious, it was all so good that my dinner was very unattractive to me that evening. I loved seeing your little house. The atmosphere of peace and love abiding within made all of us come away with a deep feeling of joy."[26]

The Bensons had other opportunities to mingle socially with the Eisenhowers, usually at formal White House dinners. One exception took place on December 21, 1954, when the Eisenhowers joined the Bensons at the Marriott ranch. After dinner, the family put on an hour of old-fashioned entertainment. The Secretary even led the group singing "John Brown's Baby Had a Cold upon Its Chest," complete with hand actions.[27]

That night, as the family was driven home, Secretary Benson contemplated the more serious side of his work and the president's recent assurance that he wanted him to stay in Washington. Ike's words of support were encouraging, but he wondered if he could hold up under two more years.

"I feel it is always good strategy
to stand up for the right,
even when it is unpopular.
Perhaps I should say, especially when it is unpopular."

Chapter 16

Respect Comes
the Hard Way

After literally climbing and, to a certain extent, conquering the mountain of opposition surrounding the farm program, Ezra hoped he might enjoy, for a period at least, some relative peace. But this was not to be. After the November 1954 elections, Congress was now controlled by the Democrats, and it remained to be seen how much success Ezra would have on Capitol Hill.

In the meantime, Secretary Benson's attention was focused beyond Washington, D. C. For some time Eisenhower had encouraged him to travel internationally on goodwill missions and expeditions to increase agricultural exports abroad. On February 19, 1955, the Secretary left on an eighteen-day tour that would take him to Cuba, Puerto Rico, the Virgin Islands, Trinidad, Costa Rica, Venezuela, Colombia, Panama, Nicaragua, Guatemala, and Mexico. In each country he met with presidents, ministers of agriculture, ambassadors, and U.S. businessmen. As he toured experimental livestock stations, farms, canneries, and the like, he discussed ways to increase U.S. exports without upsetting the balance of trade—always assuring his hosts that the U.S. would not dump its huge surpluses abroad.

An experienced traveler, the Secretary knew how to arrange an efficient, effective itinerary. When his hectic schedule of diplomatic responsibilities allowed, he met with Church groups of Latter-day Saints ranging from 450 in Mexico City to four in Barquisimeto, Venezuela, where the members drove 250 miles to be with him in an informal Sunday worship service in his hotel room.

Elder Benson reported his visits with the Saints to President McKay. Regarding this trip, President McKay recorded in his journal: "Received a letter yesterday from Fred Schluter, who has been down in Central and South America and went with Brother Benson on some of his appointments. Brother Schluter in his letter praises Brother Benson very highly. Said he was delighted with the way in which he met those audiences and gave the answers to their questions, and there is no question in his mind . . . that the people of . . . those countries . . . will recognize Brother Benson as the strongest man in President Eisenhower's Cabinet."[1]

Upon the Secretary's return, Eisenhower was similarly pleased with his report, holding him for an hour after a luncheon honoring Prime Minister Robert G. Menzies of Australia to discuss Ezra's observations.

The drouth lingered on in the Great Plains and in the South with severity reminiscent of the Dust Bowl in the 1930s. In April 1955 Ezra, accompanied by True Morse, Ken Scott (director of Credit Services), and his assistant Harvey Dahl, inspected the disaster firsthand. In Denver they met with governors from six Midwestern states, and then boarded buses to travel through eastern Colorado, Kansas, and New Mexico.[2]

In Lamar, Colorado, where Ezra was to address a meeting of some fifteen hundred farmers, they learned that dissidents from the Farmers Union intended to break up the meeting and embarrass the Secretary. No disturbance occurred, but the demonstrators followed them to their next meeting in Tucumcari, New Mexico. Concerned, Ezra asked Harvey Dahl (as a Latter-day Saint) to find someone in Tucumcari to offer an invocation and conduct music so the group could sing "America." The meeting began on such a patriotic note that the protesters were completely disarmed. That evening, after giving a midnight telephone interview to *U.S. News & World Report,* Ezra retired, closing his hotel window to keep the dry sand from blowing in and covering everything.

It was Dahl's responsibility to make recommendations on counties in the drouth-stricken plains to receive government aid due to agricultural disaster. Dahl later recalled the Secretary's instructions to him on his first day on the job: "If you err, Harvey, err on the side of mercy."[3]

In August 1955 Ezra left on a second international trip, this one to Europe, accompanied by Flora. They visited Scotland, England, the Netherlands, Denmark, France, Italy, and Switzerland, calling on governmental officials and reviewing the state of agriculture throughout those countries.

Several events were memorable. The Bensons spent a day in Köge, Denmark, the home of Flora's father. It was her first visit to the little community, and as they toured the home where Carl Amussen had lived, she struggled to hold back the tears. Later she wrote her brothers and sisters, giving a vivid description of the surroundings. That evening in Copenhagen they spoke to a congregation that filled the LDS chapel to capacity.

In Rome the Secretary delivered the keynote address to representatives of seventy nations at the International Federation of Agricultural Producers. A luncheon in Ezra's honor followed the morning session. During the hour when cocktails were usually available, he noticed that no liquor was being served and mentioned the omission to his host, Dr. Sen of India. Dr. Sen replied, "Mr. Secretary, today we honor you and respect your standards." At the banquet table only soft drinks and fruit juices were available, and Ezra again told Dr. Sen, "Surely the men expect to have their usual hot drink." "No, Mr. Secretary. I am the host. You are the honored guest, and at this luncheon we honor you and respect your standards." The tribute touched Ezra deeply.[4]

The trip's highlight, however, came on Sunday, September 11, in Bern, Switzerland, where Ezra spoke in dedicatory services for the Church's new Swiss Temple. He recited some of the history of his great-grandfather, Serge Louis Ballif, and as he spoke he had the impression that some of his ancestors were present in spirit. He later said he had never felt the veil any thinner.

As they flew back across the Atlantic, Ezra pondered how much Europe had changed since 1946, when he had seen the continent reduced to rubble. He recalled the touching moments when the Saints had cried as they saw the boxes of welfare supplies shipped from the States. The Church's welfare program, he felt, was literal evidence of Solomon's prophetic statement, "Where there is no vision, the people perish." Thousands would have perished had there been no vision and hence no welfare supplies.

But how ironic, Ezra thought, to have worked so hard to stave off starvation among the European Saints, and to now face the problem of huge surpluses sitting idle in government bins. Nine years earlier he had seen people eating chicken feed. Now he was overseer to enough foodstuffs to feed Americans for a year. He felt like the proverbial Joseph of Egypt, except he had had too many years of plenty without any famine in sight. Not that he was hoping for famine, but he knew something had to be done about the surpluses, and done quickly.

Through aggressive marketing programs implemented by Secretary Benson and his staff, between July 1953 and fall of 1955 the Department of Agriculture moved into the open market commodities valued at $4 billion. They sold oil, butter, and cheese at breakneck speed. But what they dispensed in dairy products was more than offset by rapidly growing quantities of grain, primarily wheat and corn. By 1955 the government owned enough wheat to provide for two years' domestic consumption, and the writing was on the wall—the Secretary had to seek additional legislation to deal with the surpluses.

When he couldn't get Congress to adopt realistic price supports, Ezra was forced to seek other solutions—some of which called for compromise. As he and his staff reviewed alternatives, they returned again and again to a solution Ezra found reprehensible: paying farmers for not producing. For a long time he couldn't bring himself to accept the idea, much less recommend it. But in August 1955 he set economist Don Paarlberg to work evaluating the possibilities with instructions to find a solution as unobjectionable as possible.

While Ezra's popularity was a constant roller-coaster ride, there was no question that he was having a positive effect on the administration. A June 1955 Gallup poll indicated that should Eisenhower run for reelection the following year, he would have 57 percent of the Southern vote. Eisenhower's popularity in the South was due in large measure to Ezra Taft Benson, according to Dr. Omer Clyde Aderhold, president of the University of Georgia. Pressed to explain, as most Southern states had opposed flexible price supports, he answered that the popularity was due to the Secretary's personal character, his family, and his belief in God and religion as portrayed on Edward R. Murrow's TV show "Person to Person."[5]

Ezra spent Saturday, September 24, 1955, at home with Bonnie and Beth. Flora was in Utah with Beverly, who was entering BYU, and helping Barbara make preparations for her forthcoming marriage. About five o'clock in the evening, John Foster Dulles called. President Eisenhower had had a heart attack.

Ezra was shocked at the news, but after contemplation and prayer, he felt unusually confident that the president would recover. Miller Shurtleff remembers the Secretary making that prediction to his staff on Monday. "I don't know if he would consider that instinct or inspiration, but the Secretary assured us Eisenhower would regain his health."[6] The public wasn't so sure; the following Monday the Dow Jones share index fell by over thirty points—its worst day since the 1929 crash.

The next day Ezra and the girls flew to Salt Lake City. Barbara's wedding plans had been covered widely by the press, and Washington socialites were still buzzing that this eligible young woman had opted for such a quiet, simple wedding. "Barbara Benson . . . will be married this month without the society crush and protocol problems that have marked weddings of daughters of other high government officials," wrote the *Chicago Daily News*.[7] Even so, her announcement list, which started at twelve hundred, escalated rapidly from there. On September 29, 1955, Ezra performed the marriage of his eldest

Flora Benson (left) with Mamie Eisenhower and Patricia Nixon at a luncheon given by the cabinet wives in honor of Mrs. Eisenhower on January 26, 1954

daughter to Robert Walker, a Canadian physician, in the Salt Lake Temple.

The Bensons were becoming distinguished for their unique social standards. When Mamie Eisenhower invited Flora to lunch at the White House, aware that Flora didn't play bridge, she penned a personal note on the invitation: "Dear Flora: Won't you come and join me for lunch. Maybe we will play Scrabble or Bolivia. I would love to have you come to lunch even if you don't play [card] games." At another White House luncheon Flora's placecard read: "She's as busy as can be, with family and Church/At singing and cooking she's famed/It's lucky for us that what Utah has lost/Our National City has gained."[8]

On October 26, 1955, Flora was honored by the National Home Fashions League as Homemaker of the Year. She responded that the award was a "wonderful recognition of one of the highest callings a woman can hold." Ezra and Reed witnessed the presentation. Secretary Benson's presence was considered unusual, for not in five years had a husband of the recipient been present.[9]

A month later, at Fitzsimmons Army Hospital in Denver, Secretary Benson saw President Eisenhower for the first time since his heart attack. Ike seemed pleased to see him. During their half hour together, Ezra relayed President McKay's greetings and mentioned that prayers in his behalf had been offered in every session of the recent general conference of the Church. "In fact," he said, "I guess no man living or dead within my memory has had so many prayers ascend to heaven as you, Mr. President." The president expressed his deep gratitude.[10]

Ezra found it natural to talk with the president of the United States about such things as prayer. Those who associated daily with Ezra saw how frequently he turned to prayer. As he left one morning to fill a potentially explosive appointment in Minnesota, an associate handed him a letter that read in part, "As you enter into a very difficult weekend, we want you to know that a lot of us are hoping and praying for you. Remember always that many of your friends feel that a great source of your personal strength is that you walk beside God, whereas most of the rest of us only report to Him."[11]

Another reason Ezra was successful in turning hostile audiences into inquisitive, even sympathetic ones, is that he spoke the farmers' language. Prior to the meeting in Minnesota, he toured several farms operated by Farmers Union members who opposed his program. He walked into barns, picked up handfuls of mixed feed, inspected and smelled it, and asked the farmers about their rate of gain on livestock. Invariably they were amazed that the Secretary knew what he was talking about. Ezra overheard one farmer tell his wife, "He knows as much about the dairy business as I do. We compared production records of our Holsteins with those he used to milk in Idaho."

One flabbergasted Iowa farmer was cultivating corn when the Secretary climbed a barbed wire fence and waved him down, stopping to visit beside his tractor.

In Deadwood, South Dakota, the Secretary was taken in a four-horse stagecoach to the fairgrounds, where he was to speak. He took over the reins, and as they entered the grounds he loosened the line and let the horses run at full speed around the track—to the delight of the audience and "probable terror of the driver. No matter how poor the speech might be, I had established myself with this group," Ezra said.[12]

One evening in Beloit, Wisconsin, when a dairy farmer invited the Secretary to inspect his farm, Ezra replied that he would be out to help with the milking. At 5:30 the next morning the headlights from Secretary Benson's car threaded through the darkness. When he found no activity around the barn, he walked over to the house and knocked on the door. An embarrassed farmer soon made his way out to the barn with the Secretary of Agriculture.[13]

At the conclusion of a trip to South Dakota, a farmer who had visited with the Secretary said afterwards, "I have been against Benson, but he made a believer out of me today."

Ezra's success one-on-one with farmers was so high that some close aides believed that if he could have met all of America's farmers in person, there would have been a public outcry of support for the administration's farm policies.

Unfortunately, that wasn't logistically feasible. Ezra was constantly trying to convince Congress to fill large gaps in the farm program. In early December 1955 a cabinet meeting convened at Camp David, with agriculture the predominant item of discussion. Ezra and his top aides carefully outlined the situation and explained the need for additional farm legislation. They recommended that Eisenhower's first special message to Congress in 1956 be on agriculture. The president agreed.

On January 9, 1956, President Eisenhower made nine recommendations to bolster the farm program, including one that revolved around a new concept, the soil bank. The premise was simple. A farmer would take X amount of acres out of cultivation and calculate what his net return, in bushels, would have been. He would then receive in compensation the normal net return, in bushels, from surplus stocks or its cash equivalent. The objective was to use up the surplus and not create more. The USDA estimated that the soil bank would reduce total cultivated acreage by 12 percent, cut the surplus, and lead to an upsurge in commodity prices. But critics labeled it a Benson gimmick, one certain never to get through Congress.

In truth, the Secretary wasn't the soil bank's strongest advocate. He too had doubts but for different reasons than congress-

Secretary Benson talks one-on-one with farmers in Nebraska

men who seemed to make a holiday of sending the Secretary of Agriculture back and forth between the wood shed and the doghouse. While admitting that the soil bank was the proposal most likely to pass Congress and dispose of the surplus, Ezra added, "I could not get as enthusiastic about it as some of my staff. Maybe just the idea of paying farmers for not producing—even as a one-shot emergency measure—outraged my sensibilities. The only real justification was that the government itself had been so largely responsible for the mess farmers were in."[14] And Congress had not passed the legislation that might have precluded having to resort to the soil bank.

It was fallacious to talk about the farmer as though he were a single type. Crosscurrents swept agriculture from all directions and affected farmers in various parts of the country differently. For example, research conducted by *Farm Management* magazine showed that two-thirds of the 50,000 Western farmers polled thought Secretary Benson was doing a good job. But in Iowa, where declining hog prices had hurt farmers, a poll in *Wallace's Farmer* at the end of 1955 indicated only 7 percent felt he was on track.

On January 25, 1956, nineteen Republican congressmen from the Midwest arrived unannounced at the Secretary of Agriculture's office to demand that he place price supports under hogs. Ben Jensen, a representative from Iowa, pounded the desk and told Ezra, in words to this effect, "If you don't put supports under hogs, not one of us will return to Congress next year." Ezra almost responded that he could think of worse things, as he reflected on an inscription he had placed on his appointment stand: *Oh, God, give us men with a mandate higher than the ballot box.* "We're not asking, we're *demanding* that you take action," Jensen continued. "If you don't, we're going to the White House."

Everybody was going to the White House, Ezra thought to himself. He told them that that's what they'd have to do, because he refused to place supports under a perishable product. The congressmen stomped out.

The day didn't get much better. Edward R. Murrow was doing a segment on the farm problem on a "See It Now" program, and Ezra was invited to comment at the end. The show reached an emotional pitch, leaving the impression that the administration's policies were forcing farmers off the land. One scene portrayed an Iowa family selling everything, down to the baby carriage. As the show wore on, Ezra fumed. This was, he felt, carefully planned television drama, not fact; and in the five minutes allotted him at the end, he called the show "demagoguery at its worst." (Upon checking on the farm family, Ezra found they were actually doing well and were leaving the farm only to accept a new job. They left for California in a new Pontiac. There had, in fact, been a greater exodus off the farm during the previous administration than during Eisenhower's.)

The day after Murrow's program, the Republican National Committee demanded equal time, and CBS acquiesced. But the rebuttal, which subsequently aired on Murrow's show, was anticlimactic. The USDA's elaborate presentation, with graphs and charts, ended up on the editing-room floor when CBS had to cut four minutes from the program. And the teleprompter malfunctioned while Ezra was speaking. "[The program] wasn't exactly a turkey," he surmised, "but it completely convinced me I was no TV star."[15]

From there, the climate regarding Ezra and the USDA went from lukewarm to icy cold. The shift in temperature was aided by an ignominious blunder within the USDA.

Late the previous year the Secretary had publicly invited farmers to send him suggestions on how to improve the farm program. The response was overwhelming, and secretaries were assigned to read and classify each letter, then prepare the appropriate form-letter acknowledgment.

John Fischer, editor of *Harper's Magazine*, wrote a letter in which he enclosed an editorial he had written calling farmers "our pampered tyrants," adding that too often they sold their votes to the highest bidder. The letter was tossed into the wrong pile by mistake, and it received the following acknowledgment: "I have read the article by John Fischer in the December issue of *Harper's* with a great deal of interest. It is excellent." The letter went out over Secretary Benson's signature.

Fischer was no doubt astonished when he received a letter from the Secretary of Agriculture agreeing that farmers were "irresponsible feeders at the public trough," and he promptly published it in the February 1956 *Harper's*. Republicans were outraged; the Democrats howled. Again, the "Fire Benson!" cries went out. But Ezra marched up to Capitol Hill, explained the blunder, and diffused the controversy.

While some politicians did not feel it was expedient to openly agree with Secretary Benson, others rose to his defense. In a radio address on the "Facts Forum" program, Senator Everett Dirksen of Illinois delivered a dignified defense of the Secretary, stating: "Last year while I was abroad I noticed that one of the favorite indoor sports was to pan America. At home the favorite political indoor sport is to pan Ezra Benson. . . . It would, in my judgment, be stark tragedy to lose Ezra Benson. . . . Anyone can direct the affairs of the Department of Agriculture in a time of high prices when war and the corpses of young men are the foundation for such prices and high prosperity, but it takes the consummate moral courage of an Ezra Benson to wrestle with the farm problems now on our doorstep, which he did not create but which he inherited. . . . To lose his conscience, his moral stamina, and his determination to find right answers would be tragedy indeed."[16]

It was unfortunate that some congressmen didn't agree with Dirksen's appraisal. Just days later Ezra was ambushed while testifying before the House Agricultural Committee. Columnist Roscoe Drummond reported that as soon as the hearing convened, it was clear the committee was after Benson. Boos, catcalls, and other disturbances were permitted from the audience during the five hours he was on the stand. An exchange student from Oxford University who observed the proceedings commented, "In England we treat our prisoners with more respect than this committee extended to a member of the United States Cabinet."[17]

On February 29, 1956, Eisenhower had announced his intention to run for reelection. Just three days later Ezra visited with President McKay, who advised him to stay in Washington as long as Eisenhower wanted him.

Ezra spent March and April that year fighting to save his agricultural legislation of 1954 and push through additional measures that the president had proposed in his message to Congress on January 9. All of the politicizing about the farm program frustrated Ezra. He repeatedly declared, "I abhor the efforts to place agriculture on the political auction block. Farmers' votes cannot be bought by the highest bidder. Our agriculture is neither Republican nor Democrat—it is *American. And it is not for sale.*"[18] On March 19 the Democrats, trying to kill the administration's legislation, passed a bill in the Senate that Ezra felt was the "worst piece of farm legislation ever approved by either House of Congress." Despite his lobbying and campaigning among GOP leadership, less than a month later the House passed a similar version of the 1956 Farm Bill, a bill that would likely undo nearly everything Secretary Benson had accomplished legislatively during his first four years.

In his mind, the only recourse was for the president to veto the bill; and during subsequent days, he and Under Secretary Morse tried to convince the White House staff of that. Sherman Adams, the president's chief of staff, couldn't believe Ezra would recommend that the president veto a farm bill in an election year, though earlier Eisenhower had told his aides, "The Democrats are going to do a very simple thing—write a bill that has something for everybody, and if I then veto it, a lot of people will be mad."[19]

The entire issue was so critical that Secretary Benson flew to Atlanta, where the president was vacationing, to discuss it with him personally. While he hadn't said as much, Ezra knew this was an issue over which he might well resign. His only hope was appealing to Ike's sense of morality. Just days earlier an article in *Fortune* had compared the two men: "Benson has more characteristics of the President, and in his outlook is more like the President, than any other man in the Cabinet. . . . Both have a deep faith. . . . The Boss and Ezra have the same ability to stand up to an answer dictated by conscience and faith; no other men in the Cabinet are the equals in that respect."[20]

When Ike saw Ezra, he immediately said, "I've been opening my mail, and there's not one letter here recommending that I veto the farm bill." Ezra asked if there were any letters from farmers. There weren't. Then he explained his vehement opposition to the bill: "This isn't a bill for farmers. It's a political gesture. Most farmers are too smart to fall for it."

The president disliked going against his staff, but Ezra was persuasive: "This bill is *not* right. It's not right for farmers. It's not right for the country. The only right thing to do is veto it."[21]

Ike agreed to veto. His staff, chagrined, advised that he at least wait until after the Republican National Committee meeting, which was being held in Washington, D.C. Again Ezra intervened, arguing that it was unfair to spring such an action on his own party after they had left town. And again the president decided against his staff and in favor of the Secretary's judgment.

On April 16 Eisenhower sent his veto to Congress. However, presumably to soften the blow, he raised minimum price supports on wheat, cotton, corn, rice, and peanuts. "This was the first, and I guess the only, time I was really disappointed in the President," Ezra wrote. "His veto was an act of raw political courage. Why negate it in part by putting off the inevitable dropping of support levels?"[22]

Immediately support for the president began to filter in from farmers across the country. However, Congress was stunned.

Senator Ellender warned that he would have Secretary Benson in front of the Senate Committee to defend the president's veto within forty-eight hours, and he made good on his threat. Seldom had the Senate Agricultural Committee drawn such a crowd. Every chair was filled. TV cameramen jockeyed for position. There were so many spotlights that one reporter got sunburned. A Washington reporter wrote that when Ezra walked in, he "looked as if he was loaded for Senatorial bear. He wore his gray testifying suit, his dark red cravat. . . . Then the Secretary began reading an 8-page statement. 'I appreciate the opportunity to come before this committee . . . ' This brought on laughter." Despite testifying for over three hours, Ezra said the confrontation "wasn't too bad."[23]

In late May Congress passed the Agricultural Act of 1956, a piece of administration-supported legislation providing for a soil bank. While the bill was far from what Secretary Benson or President Eisenhower wanted, both agreed it contained more good than bad. While he was anything but a political pragmatist, the Secretary was learning that, at times, half a legislative loaf was better than none. Perhaps there was some value in getting Congress to agree to a "lesser law," with the hope of progress from there.

In the meantime, he had unwittingly bolstered his ranks. One day in March, bad weather delayed his flight to Chicago. Realizing that he would not make it back to Washington in time for a speech to the National Federation of Republican Women, he called Reed, who was now working for the National Republican Congressional Committee, and asked him to pinch hit.

When Reed was introduced, the audience groaned in audible disappointment. But the response when he finished was markedly different. One newspaper reported, "Second only to the pandemonium that broke loose when President Eisenhower made his surprise appearance at the conference was the thunderous applause which greeted the young Benson at the end of his talk. He had wowed them." Departing from his father's prepared speech, Reed struck out on his own, explaining the farm problem in terms everyone could understand and saying things about his father that his father couldn't say about himself.

"Reed," continued the reporter, "is a stirring speaker with a wonderful sense of timing. He injects just enough humor (and his jokes are good) to balance the serious side of the subject he is discussing." Ezra personally observed his son's success, arriving at the meeting just after Reed took his ovations and hundreds of women were swarming around him.[24]

Reed preached farm doctrine while keeping his audience entertained. One of his typical quips: "Dad gave the President five reasons why he shouldn't be Secretary of Agriculture. . . . The number has increased since then."

Speaking requests for Reed began pouring in. Five hundred came from California alone. By May he had so many requests, he couldn't have filled them all if he were to speak three times a day, six days a week, until the November election. As it was, he logged nearly 100,000 miles in some forty states between March and November 1956.[25] (On August 30, 1957, Congressman William S. Hill of Colorado placed one of Reed's talks in the *Congressional Record*.) After reading news clippings on Reed's activities, President McKay wrote Ezra, "I share your pride in (Reed's) success! He is a credit to his distinguished parents and to the Church!"

As Reed became increasingly involved in political activities, he and his father developed a unique bond born of shared concerns, experiences, and convictions. In many ways Reed echoed his father. They thought alike and they trusted each other implicitly. Ezra wrote in his journal, "[Reed's] understanding of me, my strengths and weaknesses, and my desires for a free agriculture coupled with some of the wisest counsel I've ever received, made him a most valued political adviser."

Flora also began accepting a few of the speaking requests that came her way. She, too, had a very down-home approach. In April she traveled with other cabinet wives to Toledo for a state GOP convention. After reading her prepared speech, she said, "Now, let's start talking. I'm a farmer's wife," and she proceeded to tell stories about cooking for threshers and living on the farm. "We may live in Washington now but I don't have a maid," she said. "And when Mamie Eisenhower comes for dinner, the girls and I just pitch in and cook it." The audience cheered.[26]

A columnist from the *Cincinnati Enquirer* said Flora had done a better job tackling the farm problem than any Republican who had stepped forward to date, adding, "It might be a good idea for Mr. Eisenhower to get the Benson family a maid and send Mrs. Benson out to spread the gospel for the Republican farm program."[27]

At a luncheon in Ohio, Flora sat next to the editor of the *Toledo Blade*, a paper that had been highly critical of the administration's farm program. After she gave him a vigorous short course on her husband's policies, the editor admitted that she had changed his mind.[28]

Ezra was grateful for all the support he could get. Election years seemed to bring demands for his scalp. The Democrats saw the farm problem as their ticket to election success, and prior to the November 1956 election, they played the farm issue at campaign pitch. The Democratic Party platform expressed devotion to farmers and called for guarantees of prosperity. Ezra recorded in his journal, "It left me disgusted. It was a tossed salad made up of inaccuracies, half-truths, platitudes and promises impossible to fulfill."

Eisenhower apparently later told Earl Butz, then dean of agriculture at Purdue, that "high Republican after high Republican" came to him during 1956 demanding Ezra's resignation. Through it all the president supported his embattled Secretary of Agriculture. At a press conference on September 27 Eisenhower said, uncategorically, "I have never thought of him as a political millstone. . . . [He is] one of the finest, most dedicated public servants I have ever known, a man who is thoroughly acquainted with every phase of agriculture, and puts his whole heart into doing something that he believes will be good for the long-term benefit of the farmers of America."[29]

Evidently some farmers didn't feel that way. At a gathering of farm families in Eldora, Iowa, about thirty farmers seated on the front row got up in the middle of Ezra's remarks, made crude gestures, and marched through the audience. At a speech in Spencer, Iowa, a heckler hollered, "You're one of 'em," three times when Ezra mentioned that some people didn't like to see farmers make any money.[30] Adlai Stevenson, the Democratic presidential candidate, quipped, "The only way to break up the

New York Yankees is to get Ezra Taft Benson to manage their farm system." Nevertheless, many farmers gave the Secretary credit where credit was due. As one Iowa farmer indicated after a face-to-face meeting with him, "You've got to give him credit. He sticks to his guns. He doesn't back down." After hearing the Secretary speak to a group of 175 from the front porch of a farmhouse, another farmer said, "He sure shows a lot of guts. I thought it was as good a speech as I've ever heard. I'm voting for Eisenhower."

As the election neared and political temperatures heated up, the entire Benson family hit the campaign trail. The girls sang at rallies. Ezra raced around the country at breakneck pace; by October 1956 he had traveled 312,000 miles, more than any other cabinet member with the exception of Secretary of State John Foster Dulles. Reed stumped and ripped previous farm policies with statements such as, "Any political party . . . that wants to take credit for the high farm prices during the war better take credit for the war also." When Flora campaigned with cabinet wives, they were dubbed the "Kitchen Kabinet." One major news magazine reported that when Bonnie Benson said her prayers in the morning, she prayed for her father, who was campaigning; her brother, who was campaigning; and her mother, that she would "do and say the right thing today."[31]

Again, Flora's message was persuasive. "Not only has my husband been under strong pressure, but the children and I have shared those pressures too," she told one audience. According to one report, "Three times she brought the house down." "Isn't she marvelous?" exclaimed a woman near the speaker's table.[32]

On election day, Ezra and Flora visited Ike and Mamie at their suite in the Sheraton-Park Hotel in Washington. When it became clear Eisenhower would defeat Stevenson by a landslide, Ezra tallied the Republicans' losses and gains in farm states. Some Republicans who had supported the administration's farm program were defeated; others were reelected. But by and large, the president's team won solidly in the farm bloc. There was no change in the numerical division in the Senate, and the Democrats picked up only four seats in the House. Ezra regarded the election as a victory for his policies.

Two weeks later another event of major significance to the Bensons occurred. Barbara delivered her first child, and as Flora made preparations to visit her daughter and granddaughter, Ezra quietly chuckled at his wife's elaborate planning. She left the refrigerator loaded with food, precooked many meals, and left detailed instructions for the younger girls, who would have to prepare Thanksgiving dinner. Yet even with warm memories of a successful election and a new grandchild, all was not well.

On October 23, 1956, in the Hungarian capital of Budapest, two thousand university students initiated a march protesting Communist domination. Thousands of shopworkers joined them until eighty thousand moved through the streets. When police fired shots into the throng, a bloody revolution erupted. First it was bare hands and stones versus revolvers and machine guns. When it appeared the freedom fighters would win, Soviet tanks and heavy artillery rolled in and the "revolution" failed.

Weeks went by, and Ezra was ashamed of the United States' apathy toward the Hungarian revolutionaries. "We had encouraged the captive nations to believe that we would spring to their defense if and when they made a real surge for freedom," he wrote. "Now when the Hungarians had seemed almost on the verge of successful revolt, we had simply stood aghast while the Communist juggernaut rolled over the freedom fighters. I was sick at heart." When he encouraged Eisenhower to respond to Russia's brutality, Eisenhower asked him to draft an appropriate statement, and with minor changes Ezra's blistering denunciation was released. There was no government project he helped initiate outside of the Department of Agriculture that gave him more satisfaction.

As 1957 dawned, with the emotion of election year passed, the USDA entered an era of good feelings. Secretary Benson had minor disagreements with Congress, but most relations were courteous, if not conciliatory. It wasn't until the end of February that he had a confrontation with a congressional committee, this one a grilling from the House Committee on Appropriations, but little was accomplished. Don Paarlberg left him a short note afterwards: "It would be a hard pull without your leadership."[33]

Flora attended most of her husband's press conferences and also sat through what other cabinet wives considered the next thing to purgatory—an unfriendly congressional committee. "[Ezra] often says when he looks down on me it gives him strength," she told *Newsweek*. "I pray for him to remember what he should and give the answers he should. I go through all the emotions with him. When I come home I'm pretty worn out," she admitted.[34]

The spring and summer of 1957 were a welcome and calm respite from the storm for the Bensons. In April, Ezra took Beverly and Bonnie on a week's trip through Virginia and further South. Mark graduated from Stanford with a master's in educational administration and, though he had a scholarship offer to attend Boston University, opted for a commission sales job. Ezra was delighted his son took a route that immersed him immediately in free enterprise.

Then shortly after Labor Day, Ezra had unexpected contact with President McKay. One morning the White House called to say the Church president was in Washington and wished to see Eisenhower. The prophet's purpose, as it turned out, was to request Ezra's release from the cabinet.

Later, President McKay described to Elder Benson his meeting with Ike. Eisenhower had indicated that he and Secretary Benson were "just like this," he said, interlocking the fingers of his hands, and Eisenhower didn't know where he could find a suitable replacement. President McKay then agreed that Eisenhower should have first call on the apostle's services: the Church could make adjustments easier than the country could.

Nevertheless, Ezra confronted Eisenhower about returning to Utah. The president asked him to remain at least another year, when they would again review the situation. "I would like you to stay to the bitter end," the president said. "Do you think the end will be bitter?" Ezra asked, smiling. "Not one bit," Ike answered. "Just wait and see."[35]

It was only a matter of time before Secretary Benson found that the president's "bitter-to-the-end" comment held some truth. At a corn-picking contest in Sioux Falls, South Dakota, while the Secretary was making a speech, several eggs sailed over the speaker's platform, one of them splattering slightly on the suit of the South Dakota governor and another on Ezra's hat.

The story made headlines. In the end, Secretary Benson felt in debt to the marauders. He had learned that abuse typically rallied fair-minded people to his cause. In this case, the audience had been cold prior to the incident, but warmed up considerably afterwards. Hundreds of letters arrived at the USDA, with 90 percent running in favor of the Secretary. One woman from San Francisco wrote, "From now on I will pray harder for you and other sincere representatives of our great government. . . . P.S. I'm a Democrat."

Ezra later wrote that the egg incident wasn't as bad "as one might guess. Of course, no one in his right mind wants to be publicly flayed regardless of how strong his convictions may be."[36] Beth was more upset than anyone that someone would throw eggs at her father.

Despite these periodic run-ins with angry farmers and those with members of Congress and members of the press, there were other occasions when Secretary Benson won the expressed admiration of observers. Broadcaster Paul Harvey autographed a copy of his book *Autumn of Liberty* to Ezra, "To my friend Ezra Taft Benson—who makes it feel good to be an American." Inside the book Harvey had written, "Ezra Benson is a rare man in politics, thoroughly sincere, uncompromising, and above all, a good man."

Inevitably, when Ezra was introduced on television or radio talk-show programs, the announcer acknowledged, even praised, his stamina, integrity, and staunch defense of principle. On the "Longines-Wittnauer Chronoscope," a television interview program, on August 2, 1954, the moderator introduced Ezra by saying that, in the opinion of many, "no member of the Eisenhower Cabinet has shown more political courage than our guest tonight. For a time he was the most criticized member. But he stuck to his guns and never wavered in his convictions."

At an address before the National Press Club on March 23, 1956, Ezra was introduced as follows: "We have high respect for a man who started behind the plow and worked up. . . . The Secretary of Agriculture is known as a man who says what he thinks. A public official who does that makes news. . . .

The Secretary of Agriculture draws a full house when he speaks from this podium." And two years later, at another National Press Club luncheon, the man introducing him said, "Despite the heat [Secretary Benson] has taken, he has . . . stood his ground. Surely it can be said he is a man of great integrity. And he has guts."

In these situations with members of the press, Ezra was articulate and convincing, and he responded calmly but firmly to repeated questions and used humor to win over the audience. At his first National Press Club luncheon on March 24, 1953, at which time he was to make an address and then submit to a grilling from the audience, he began, "When I was persuaded to come to this occasion, I was told I wouldn't need to make a speech. But now I'm convinced to speak through the whole time allotted so there will be no questions."

And at times the press supplied their own humor. Secretary Benson inadvertently called a press conference one spring day that coincided with President Eisenhower's ceremonial first pitch on the opening day of baseball season. Ezra didn't realize his error until the morning of the press conference, and he wondered how many reporters would attend. The first reporter who walked into the press room teased Ezra, "What's the matter, Mr. Secretary, couldn't you get tickets?"[37]

In October 1957, Ezra, Flora, Beverly, and Bonnie left on a four-week, around-the-world trip. Sometimes the children groaned when a new excursion came up, as these journeys were anything but vacations. Flora admitted, "A trip with my husband meant few hours rest, no relaxation, and a constant rush with heavy schedules every day. I told him if he wanted our daughters to go, that we girls should at least be given a little time to see places of historical interest. He said we'd have to do it at 6:00 A.M. before the day's work began." The trips, however, were educational. The Bensons literally circled the globe, gained an increased appreciation for the worldwide nature of the Church, spoke and sang in countless meetings, were honored at numerous state dinners and receptions, and made new friends for America and the Church.

Top: Ezra and Flora enjoy a Bedouin-type feast hosted by the Jordanian Minister of Agriculture in Amman, Jordan. Bottom: Bonnie and Beverly Benson join Flora and Ezra in meeting Prime Minister Nehru of India

U.S. Information Service

The purpose of the October 1957 tour was to develop additional opportunities for agricultural trade throughout the world. The family visited twelve nations—Japan, India, Pakistan, Jordan, Israel, Turkey, Greece, Italy, Spain, Portugal, France, and England, as well as Hong Kong. Whenever possible, they stayed in Latter-day Saint mission homes. On Sundays, when no government business was conducted, they met and worshipped with the Saints.

In Amman, Jordan, Ezra conferred with King Hussein, and later the Bensons were guests of Minister of Agriculture 'Akif al-Fayiz at a feast under a goats' hair tent on the Jordanian plains fifteen miles from Amman. Bedouins indicate their wealth by the size of their tent and the number of poles required to support it. This lavish banquet, held in a nine-pole tent, consisted of sheep smothered in rice and toasted almonds, served in large vats around which ten or so persons sat on beautiful rugs and cushions.

The Secretary and his party visited a kibbutz in Israel; a refugee settlement near Karachi, Pakistan, which he described as one of the most poverty-ridden areas in the world; and landmarks such as the Acropolis in Athens. In Japan he operated a rice-threshing machine.

For Ezra, a highlight occurred in Israel, where he met with Prime Minister David Ben-Gurion. Their visit took place in the hospital, where Ben-Gurion was recuperating from a bombing injury. They discussed world conditions and, when Ben-Gurion directed the conversation that way, Old Testament prophecies. Ezra elaborated on scriptures in two of the LDS standard works, the Doctrine and Covenants and the Book of Mormon, that related to the gathering of the Jews, and referred to Elder Orson Hyde's dedication of Palestine in 1841 for the return of the descendants of Judah. When he returned to the United States, Ezra sent Ben-Gurion a copy of the Book of Mormon, to which the Jewish leader responded, "The sudden emergence of Mormonism was for me a deep enigma—and still remains so. Apparently the ways of the Lord are unfathomable."[38] Ezra couldn't help but think of the prophecy that the gospel would be "brought out of obscurity and out of darkness." (2 Nephi 22:12.)

Ezra Taft Benson visits with David Ben-Gurion in Jerusalem, where the Israeli leader was recovering from injuries received in a bombing incident in the Israeli Parliament

It is no wonder that Ezra was taken with Ben-Gurion. The Israeli leader embodied many traits he considered basic to enlightened leadership. He wrote, "He impressed me also as a man who has a clear insight into what Israel needs to do. He was not groping for answers. . . . He was not afraid to oppose his own people, or his Cabinet, or anyone else. . . . You knew exactly where he and you stood."[39]

The Secretary returned from his tour pleased with the results and confident that he had opened new avenues for selling U.S. agricultural products. He also sent a seven-page letter detailing his activities to President McKay and recounting his experience with Ben-Gurion. In his April 1950 general conference address, entitled "Jews Return to Palestine," Ezra had stated that the post-World War II migration of Jews to Palestine was a fulfillment of prophecy. Many civic leaders and Jewish people had requested copies of the talk. He now told President McKay, with no false modesty, his confidence that his family had been "effective ambassadors of good will" for the Church, as they had been for the United States.

When their plane touched down on November 16, Beth was waiting on the tarmac. As soon as she saw her parents step out of the plane, she started running toward them, tears on her cheeks. Ezra reached her first and pulled her up into a big bear hug. "With all the wonders of the world," he wrote, "that moment was suddenly the best of the entire trip."

The Secretary caught some flak for taking family members along on government trips. But he knew Eisenhower felt otherwise, and had even requested that Ezra take them for the good-will it created. No one could question that under Ezra's direction and, presumably, as a result of his international travel, U.S. farm exports had multiplied measurably. In the year beginning July 1, 1954, they increased by $200 million; in 1955–56, by another $350 million; and in 1956–57, by $1.33 billion. At times in 1956 and 1957 there were scarcely enough ships available to transport farm products abroad. On April 10, 1957, Ezra was awarded the High Cross of the Order of Merit of the Italian Republic, the highest decoration of the Italian government, in recognition of his assistance in helping Italy solve its food shortages with U.S. surpluses.

Nevertheless, there was no welcome home party from his trade trip. Prior to his leaving, the anti-Benson campaign had been revived when William Proxmire, campaigning, among other things, on an anti-Benson theme in the heavily Republican state of Wisconsin in an election to replace the late Senator Joseph McCarthy, defeated his opponent. Fearing erosion of further farm bloc states, congressmen pleaded with Eisenhower to replace Secretary Benson. Senator Karl Mundt wrote Sherman Adams, "I am completely convinced that we cannot even come close to electing a Republican House of Representatives or a Republican Senate in 1958 unless Secretary of Agriculture Benson is replaced by somebody who is personally acceptable to the farmers of this country."[40]

These constant calls from certain politicians for his resignation had no doubt become wearisome to Ezra. Until the end of

November he spent many sleepless nights. Was anything worth all this turmoil? It was one thing to resign willingly, but quite another to quit under pressure. Such a departure would be tantamount to admitting his farm program had failed. He later wrote, "There followed some ten days of soul-searching and prayerful consideration. . . . Everything I did, everywhere I went, seemed to put the question to me—which is right, to stay and fight on in a cause in which conceivably I had outlived my usefulness, or to return to the sphere in which I knew lay my true vocation?"[41]

On December 3, 1957, Ezra called a press conference to announce that he intended to continue as Secretary of Agriculture. He restated why he persisted in advocating policies that were not necessarily popular or expedient: "I do not believe one bit that telling the truth ever hurt any political party. I intend to continue to tell the truth."[42]

On a happier note, Secretary Benson sent a special Christmas message to all USDA employees describing scenes he had witnessed on his recent trip—Japanese schoolchildren eating lunch made from American farm products; a modern wool and cotton laboratory in Karachi, made possible through American assistance; boys in Turkey who proudly displayed their 4-K pins. The Secretary was proud of his department's work. "I hope you will forgive my reminiscences," he explained in the Christmas card. "I wanted to share them with you because I wanted you to feel that we each have a share in the future and we each have an unuttered though sincere gift of appreciation from our friends in other lands. The hope of the future lies very simply in the spirit of brotherly love."

As 1958 began, Ezra was still smarting from recent attacks. He had become the Eisenhower administration's most popular whipping boy. Typically, those who were loudest in their criticism were politicians, not farmers or agricultural leaders. But though major organizations such as the Farm Bureau continued to back the Secretary, there were always those farmers who attacked him as soon as commodity prices fell. And because the farm bloc states wielded power at the ballot box, he once again got caught in the web of election-year politics. It was one of Washington's most baffling political mysteries that he continued to face, and triumph over, the cries for him to resign.

Each new year brought the inevitable for Ezra—wooing Congress and devising strategy. And in January 1958, for the third time, Eisenhower sent a special message on agriculture to Congress. Again he called for lower price supports.

The day after Eisenhower's address, Secretary Benson appeared before the Senate Agricultural Committee. He had prepared a twenty-four-page statement, but committee chairman Ellender dispensed with procedure and encouraged the committee to feel free to pin the Secretary down. The heckling began before Ezra could finish page one. Ellender accused him of being a liar, Hubert Humphrey called his claims "false advertising," and Stuart Symington labeled him "insincere." When one committee member returned to the hearing after an hour's absence, he interrupted to ask where they were in the text, adding that when he left they had been at the bottom of page two. They were then at the bottom of page three, and so it went all day. One reporter observed, "Through all this Benson kept his temper, although a close observer might have noticed when the firing was heaviest the secretary's lower lip was thrust out a fraction of an inch and the back of his neck reddened. But his voice usually remained calm and patient."[43] Beverly watched from the audience as her father was grilled from 10:05 A.M. until 5:34 P.M.

If Ellender and his cohorts felt they had come out on top, they were soon disillusioned. Headlines cried that the Secretary had been cruelly pilloried. Then in February, reports circulated that twenty or so influential Republican congressmen had met in emergency caucus to plan strategy that would force his resignation. Representing the group, Minnesota's Walter H. Judd and Nebraska's Arthur L. Miller found the Secretary in his office and spent forty minutes imploring him to resign.

President Eisenhower again stood up for his Secretary of Agriculture, saying: "When we find a man of this dedication, this kind of courage, this kind of intellectual and personal honesty, we should say to ourselves, 'We just don't believe that America has come to the point where it wants to dispense with the advice of that kind of a person.' "[44]

But the opposition didn't back down. The very next day, February 27, 1958, Ezra received a demanding letter from Congressman Miller: "The 30 Republican members of the 11 Midwest farm states are asking that you present your resignation to the President. Will you do this?" Ezra didn't mince words in his reply: "I assume that you would not be pursuing your opposition to me and to the Administration's farm program so diligently if you did not feel that you were serving the best interests of the Nation's farmers. I, sir, am just as firmly convinced that the direction taken by the Administration's farm program is the best for the long-range interests of our farm people."[45]

While some Republicans called for his head, the Democrats made plans to beat him at his own game, introducing legislation to freeze all price supports at 1957 levels, regardless of supply and demand, and increase corn acreage allotments. They hoped the "freeze bill" would either force an unpopular Eisenhower veto during an election year or result in a compromise.

Secretary Benson wasted no time blasting the proposed legislation. Senator Edward J. Thye scolded him for not putting aside personal considerations and cooperating with the "Administration in solving current economic problems." In reply, Ezra reaffirmed he would never support a program unless he believed it to be in the best interest of farmers. While he and Eisenhower agreed to stand against the freeze bill, the Senate confirmed it, 50 to 43.

Subsequently, Ezra sent the president a detailed letter outlining seven reasons for opposing the bill. It was two days before Ike responded, and in doing so he gave his outspoken Secretary a mild reprimand and another lesson in strategy: "Sometimes in the workings of a democratic society, it is not sufficient merely to be completely right. We recall that Aristides lost the most important election of his life because the Athenian people were tired of hearing him called 'The Just.' " In the future, Eisenhower concluded, Ezra should avoid positions of inflexibility and leave some room to maneuver.[46]

Nevertheless, when the House passed the freeze bill, the president vetoed it—and the veto held. Amid it all Ezra traveled to Salt Lake City to perform Reed's temple marriage in

April 1958 to May Hinckley—appropriately, a farmer's daughter from Utah and a granddaughter of the apostle Alonzo A. Hinckley.

Politics are a fickle taskmaster. During the second quarter of 1958, farm prices rose 10 percent over the previous year, and Secretary Benson's popularity enjoyed a similar resurgence. On May 1, in a hearing before the House Congressional Committee, he didn't receive one critical comment. Some congressmen even commended him for his performance. Having gone prepared for the worst, he was totally surprised by the reception.

Suddenly Ezra found himself fielding questions that would have seemed absurd just months, even weeks, before. In one news conference Claude Mahoney of the Mutual Broadcasting System startled him by asking if he had thought of running for the presidency. Others had approached him privately about the same, and some members of the press were referring to him as a possible leader of the conservative wing of the Republican Party. A nationwide poll revealed that "top Republican leaders" favored keeping Ezra Benson as Secretary of Agriculture by a six-to-one margin. And twenty-five to one, they believed farmers were better off than ever. "What a difference a couple of dollars in the prices of hogs and cattle make," Ezra told himself.[47]

When Congress passed the Agricultural Act of 1958 with large sections of Ezra's program intact, the *New York Herald Tribune* called him "something of a political miracle worker. . . . Now talk is heard about him being a party asset," with some even suggesting that "Secretary Benson would be a good Vice-Presidential choice in 1960."

Columnist Roscoe Drummond wrote that because Ezra stood by his convictions, he had "emerged as the most influential member of the Eisenhower Cabinet," explaining, "Mr. Benson did not shrink from crossing wills and matching strategy with the powerful Speaker of the House, Sam Rayburn. When the House was about to do what Mr. Rayburn did not want it to do, namely, vote down a bad farm bill, Mr. Rayburn angrily warned that it must be either this bill or nothing. Mr. Benson riskfully stood his ground and said, let it be nothing. Mr. Rayburn had to back down." Drummond concluded that Ezra held "a large reservoir of the moral and intellectual integrity of the Eisenhower administration."[48]

Charles Bailey, Washington correspondent for several Midwestern papers, said no member of the Cabinet had given the "shirt-sleeves backroom operators of the GOP more nightmares. . . . But there he sits, 5½ years later, not only still in office but possessed of the legislative scalps of some of the toughest warriors in congress." Hubert Humphrey allegedly called Ezra "the toughest two-fisted political operator in Washington."[49]

Even outside of the United States, Ezra's efforts were being hailed. A writer for the *Calgary Herald* in Alberta, Canada, stated on September 3, 1958, "It seems quite probable [Ezra Taft Benson] will be looked upon as one of the greatest, if not the greatest, secretaries of agriculture the U.S. has ever had. Certainly Mr. Benson is making it clear that he is a great man for these days."

The sudden popularity brought a respite from six years of political warfare, but Secretary Benson was skeptical about its duration. He said only, "In the hour of a man's success is his greatest danger."[50]

Nevertheless, speculation about Ezra's political career persisted. A Washington television personality cornered him after church for a comment on the "ground swell" of support underway to nominate him for the vice presidency. The attention was flattering, Ezra admitted, but he "didn't know how to handle it."

The subject came up during a conversation with President McKay on Columbus Day when the prophet asked his associate about the rumors. Ezra repeated that he had no political aspirations. As he remembers it, President McKay smiled gently and said, "No answer could be better than that. Just keep on as you are and we'll wait for the Lord to tell us what the future holds."[51]

Again, as elections neared, Secretary Benson barnstormed the country, crusading for sound principles that touched not only agriculture but also the nation. He pleaded for integrity in government, fiscal responsibility, and peace. And again and again he preached that Americans were "a prosperous people because of a free enterprise system founded on spiritual, not just material, values. Let us tell that to the world. Let us show the world that our system is based on freedom of choice—free agency—an eternal God-given principle."[52]

Though the pace was frenzied, toward the campaign's end he took time for an unusual and serene interlude. He had suggested that the Tabernacle Choir perform for President Eisenhower in the White House, and on the evening of October 26, the choir gave an hour performance at a black-tie affair. Ezra and Flora, with their daughters, joined the Eisenhowers and selected guests. Repeatedly during the program, the president turned to Ezra and expressed his pleasure, particularly after the choir sang "The Battle Hymn of the Republic." At the hour's end, he asked the choir to sing on, which they did for another fifteen minutes. Afterwards the President and Mrs. Eisenhower mingled with the choir and other guests for about an hour.

The Republicans weren't singing nearly so sweet a tune after the 1958 election, when the Democrats picked up fourteen seats in the Senate and fifty-one in the House. The GOP was shell-shocked. At a fund-raising dinner in New Jersey, Ezra philosophically reminded fellow Republicans, "It takes adversity sometimes to bring into focus the principles for which we stand."[53] Despite his optimism, he realized that the implications for agriculture were frightening. The hope of pushing the Eisenhower farm program through to completion had suffered a heavy blow. The Democratic Congress was unlikely to support any of the administration's measures.

On Christmas Eve, with the Marriotts, the Benson family went ice skating at the Marriott Motor Hotel. For the first time in years Ezra donned skates, and about an hour later he took a bad fall, dislocating his shoulder. The injury required a cast that circled his abdomen and extended from his shoulder down to his elbow.

By New Year's Eve, still suffering from pain, he left a Church party early to go home and rest. But that evening he did contemplate the year just passed. Certainly 1958 had been a strange mixture of criticism and adulation. Perhaps it was providential, however, that the past six months had treated him kindly and given him his first extended breather while in office. The coming year didn't look to be nearly as tranquil.

"The supreme test of any government policy,
agricultural or otherwise, should be:
'How will it affect the character, morale,
and well-being of our people?'"

Chapter 17

Spiritual Statesman

With Eisenhower's lame-duck term came a political restlessness. Richard Nixon and Nelson Rockefeller jockeyed for power in the Republican Party; Democratic candidates, bolstered by their party's convincing showing in 1958, engaged in their own power struggle.

Secretary Benson faced a dilemma. Should he take on stiff opposition in the Democratic Congress and try to push through more of his farm program, or be satisfied with what he had accomplished and rest on his laurels? Some Republicans claimed that for their party to resurge, they must compile a liberal record during 1959 to have any hope of giving the Democrats a good run in 1960. To Ezra's dismay, his party began indulging such philosophies.

The cabinet spent four hours one day in January debating federal participation in school construction. When no one else opposed the concept, Ezra delivered a blistering assessment of federal aid. The proposal was eventually blocked, but it disturbed him that his peers seemed to favor increased government involvement. He feared that most Americans didn't understand the fatal flaw in government spending. As he explained, "The federal government has no funds which it does not, in some manner, take from the people. And a dollar cannot make a round

Reprinted from Saturday Evening Post. © 1953 The Curtis Publishing Company

This photo of Secretary Benson was Saturday Evening Post's *picture of the week*

trip from Oklahoma . . . or even Maryland to Washington and back without shrinking in the process." He believed that the power to subsidize was the power to control.[1]

Whenever he spoke, Secretary Benson tied this concept into his farm message. He often wondered who was listening, but decided he couldn't live with himself until he had done everything he could to fight for a sound economy and less government interference for the individual. For that reason, in early 1959 he determined that if he was to push any more of his farm program through Congress, it was now or never, for there would be little hope of enlightened farm legislation passing during a presidential election year.

Yet, the farm situation was still a political hot potato in 1959. To complicate matters, 1958 had seen one of the most prolific spurts in agricultural production in history. With an increase in output of 8 percent, nearly twice the increase recorded during the entire decade of the 1920s, the result was a market

save freedom and the Constitution. . . . Of course this is dangerous reasoning. . . . In the war in heaven, what would have been your reaction if someone had told you just to do what is right—there's no need to get involved in the fight for freedom."[15]

Although there were those who didn't share Elder Benson's concerns or agree with his pleadings, his views were consistent with those of earlier LDS leaders, and he believed that members and nonmembers alike were looking to the Church for counsel on the subject of freedom. The best source for guidance, he felt, was President McKay, and he followed the prophet's direction.

In November 1962, Elder Benson went on a six-week tour of four missions and six stakes in Australia and New Zealand. Because of his international stature and ecclesiastical position, wherever he went, the press followed, with articles in the media on his activities. The headline "Mormon Apostle on Tour of N.Z." from Wellington's *Evening Post* of October 26, 1962, was typical.

One nonmember who heard Elder Benson speak said, "I will never forget it. Tears streamed down Elder Benson's face as he bore testimony of the restored gospel. I left that meeting with an overwhelming conviction that I had at last found the truth. His talk prompted me to study, search and pray. I felt that if such a great man could feel that way about the Church, then there had to be something in it." This man subsequently joined the Church and later served on numerous general Church committees.[16]

Elder Benson's long trip away from home was eased by frequent letters from Flora. After reading of her and Beth's Christmas holiday plans, he replied, "You and Beth are surely the chargers. How do you expect an old man of 63 to keep up with you?" But he had done some planning of his own. Packages were en route from New Zealand, each purposely mismarked. "If you can resist it, don't open till I arrive. Then I'll tell you who they are for," he teased.

In Australia Elder Benson faced a situation that was impeding the spread of the gospel: a low quota had recently been imposed on the number of missionaries allowed in the country.

Just before he arrived, a group of LDS missionaries had played the national basketball team of Australia. While Elder Benson was in the country, Sir Robert Gordon Menzies, the Australian prime minister, and his cabinet hosted a dinner honoring him. Sir Robert commented about the game and commended the Mormon team. Elder Benson joked that had the Church in Australia had more missionaries to choose from, the team would have defeated the Australians more easily, and then asked why the number of elders was limited. The Prime Minister said he knew of no reason that the number of missionaries was limited, and within three days the quota restriction was eased.

In Perth, Elder Bruce R. McConkie, who was serving as mission president, joined Elder Benson as a guest of His Royal Highness Prince Phillip Duke of Edinburgh and Prime Minister Menzies at the Seventh British Empire and Commonwealth Games. Elder McConkie was impressed at the ease with which Elder Benson mingled with world leaders.

When he returned home, Elder Benson found little time to savor the spiritual satisfaction of a fruitful tour. As Christmas approached, he relented and let Flora and Beth open their gifts Christmas Eve rather than wait until the next morning. Then he and Flora left on a hurried trip to Calgary to visit Barbara and her family. Ezra loved Christmases in Canada, where he took a horsedrawn cutter for a spirited ride. The diversion was welcome.

Since he had left Washington, Elder Benson had repeatedly spoken in defense of freedom. He avoided speaking at partisan gatherings of any kind, but in nonpartisan settings he was anxious to teach that the principle of agency was a religious, not a political, issue. He supported the separation of church and state, so far as the establishment and financial support of a state religion was concerned. But where government and/or political issues affected the lives of church members, he said, religious leaders could and should comment. As President J. Reuben Clark had explained: "Today government has touched our lives so intimately in all their relationships and all these governmental teachings have been so tabbed political, that we cannot discuss anything relating to our material welfare and existence without laying ourselves liable to the charge that we are talking politics."[17]

At the April 1956 general conference, Elder Benson's address, "Not Commanded in All Things," listed seven reasons Church members were slow to step forward patriotically—one of which was the controversial nature of the "freedom battle." But he believed there was folly in such logic: "To have been on the wrong side of the freedom issue during the war in heaven meant eternal damnation. How then can Latter-day Saints expect to be on the wrong side in this life and escape the eternal consequences?"[18]

Unfortunately, there were those whose views were not compatible with his words of warning. Some felt that an apostle should refrain from speaking or commenting on what they considered to be political themes. Conversely, many others were attracted to the Church because of his strong stand. For example, after hearing Elder Benson speak on freedom on a televised session of general conference and subsequently reading his book *Title of Liberty*, one family sought out the missionaries and were baptized a week later. Another man was first attracted to the Church after reading one of Elder Benson's patriotic sermons in the *Congressional Record*. And a number of others wrote Elder Benson to say their interest in the Church had been initiated by his patriotic stand.[19]

When Elder Benson delivered a stirring sermon at April 1963 general conference, "Righteousness Exalteth a Nation," in which he called for Americans to return to righteousness as a prerequisite for national peace and prosperity, President McKay requested that the talk be reprinted in its entirety in the *Church News*, an unusual practice, and one rarely extended, at that time, beyond the First Presidency.[20]

As Elder Benson continued to educate himself by reading numerous volumes on international affairs and economics as well as antisocialist materials, he forwarded pertinent information to his colleagues. Since the death of President J. Reuben Clark on October 6, 1961, perhaps none of the Brethren had the practical and political background Elder Benson had in this area. What religious principle, he wondered, was more central to the gospel than agency? And how could the Church, or Church members, afford to be lackadaisical about anything that threatened to deprive man of his freedom?

Additionally, and most importantly, Elder Benson knew he had a mandate from the prophet. On more than one occasion President McKay privately encouraged him to speak out on freedom. On August 30, 1963, for example, Elder Benson indicated in a personal memorandum that he had once again met with President McKay and indicated he would "never say another word on the subject [of freedom] if that was President McKay's wish. [President McKay] said he wanted me to continue to speak out with the assurance I had his support as I have had in the past."[21] Elder Benson's first priority was following the prophet, as a journal entry on October 2, 1963, indicates: "My one desire is to do what the Lord and His mouthpiece, President McKay, would have me do."

On October 18 Elder Benson learned that President McKay did, indeed, have a new assignment for him. "Brother Benson, I have a great surprise," the prophet began. "President McKay," Ezra responded, "this church is full of surprises." Both men laughed and then President McKay announced that Elder Benson had been selected to preside over the European Mission with headquarters in Frankfurt, Germany.

The assignment *was* a surprise, but Elder Benson indicated his great pleasure at the assignment, which was to begin near year's end. That night at dinner he asked his wife and Beth how they would like to live in Germany for a couple of years. "With you two?" Beth asked with delight. "Terrific!"

"The thought of going to Europe with my parents, and having them all to myself, was too good to be true," Beth remembered. Her formative years had fallen during Ezra's cabinet service, and she was delighted at the prospects of two relatively tranquil years in Europe with her parents.

Despite Elder Benson's conviction that his warnings about freedom were critical, he was concerned that, as a result of his critics, his effectiveness as a spiritual leader not be hampered. In mid-December 1963, for example, priesthood leaders in Logan, Utah, became skittish when a group threatened to protest at an upcoming address Elder Benson was to deliver in the Logan

Tabernacle. He assured the local leaders that his remarks would be appropriate for any sacrament meeting, and told them he would hold the meeting in a tent, if need be. "It is amazing to me," he wrote in his journal, "the lack of courage some of our brethren have in this serious controversy involving the future freedom of our people." On December 13, Elder Benson spoke in the Logan Tabernacle as promised and received one of the longest standing ovations of his life.

During the early 1960s several books were published by Elder Benson, containing some of his hardest-hitting addresses on freedom and values essential to protecting the American way of life. These included, among others, *So Shall Ye Reap*, *Title of Liberty*, and *A Nation Asleep*. Further, he was delighted when *Prophets, Principles and National Survival*, a collection of Church leaders' warnings on freedom, was published. More than once he recommended it to the Saints during his general conference addresses. Though some apparently disagreed with his repeated attempts to speak on freedom, Elder Benson explained, "I feel it is always good strategy to stand up for the right, even when it is unpopular. Perhaps I should say, especially when it is unpopular."[22]

Throughout this period he kept a grueling pace—attending stake conferences on weekends; making frequent trips to both coasts for board meetings of Corn Products International, the Boy Scouts, and Olson Brothers, Inc. (the nation's largest independent packer of eggs, to which board he had been named in July 1962, with the approval of President McKay); supervising the MIA programs and all-Church softball tournaments; and making dozens of speeches. And there were many arrangements to make before he could assume his new position in Frankfurt.

Before leaving for Europe, the Bensons were honored at a farewell testimonial in the Parley's Ward. President N. Eldon Tanner, second counselor to President McKay, paid tribute to the Bensons: "I really know of no more courageous and capable proponent of any cause which he thinks is right than Brother Ezra Taft Benson. I know of no more devoted and loving mother and wife than Sister Benson. I know of no more capable, loyal, united children than their children."[23]

By the time Elder Benson left to assume his position, he was anxious to devote himself fully to missionary work. Yet as he left the United States, perhaps some wondered why he hadn't quietly let the subject of freedom drop from his speeches. Though it was sometimes lonely issuing his warnings, Elder Benson's single-minded concerns and convictions motivated him to speak out. He felt that time always vindicated truth. To him, there was but one course. He chose to stand on eternal principles.

When Elder Theodore Burton, the current president of the European Mission, and his wife learned they were to be released and the Bensons had been called to succeed them, Sister Burton wrote Flora, "You both seem so right for this time and can bring so much prestige to the office. . . . The general public opinion of our Church will be greatly helped by your being here."[24] Indeed, improved public relations was one area in which Elder Benson had measurable impact while in Europe.

As president of the European Mission, Elder Benson was responsible for four stakes and twelve missions—six in Germany (Bavarian, Berlin, Central German, North German, South German, and West German), and the Austrian, Danish, Finnish, Swedish, Swiss, and Norwegian missions, with some fifteen hundred missionaries and forty-five thousand Saints. Conditions had long since stabilized throughout Europe in the years since his mission of mercy right after World War II. But while Church membership worldwide was growing rapidly (during the 1950s, 1960s, and 1970s, membership increased more than 50 percent per decade), progress in Europe was modest by comparison. In 1960 fewer than 10 percent of the European Saints resided within stakes. Reemerging prosperity throughout Europe contributed to religious indifference among the people, and lax moral standards counter to the gospel message.

Cultural factors notwithstanding, when the Bensons arrived in Frankfurt on New Year's Day 1964, they hit the ground running. How satisfying Ezra found it to return to the continent he had traversed that bittersweet year of 1946 and find evidence of an economically revived people! But there was little time for reflection. The Burtons were leaving for home in two days, and almost immediately Elder Benson began his briefings with Elder Burton.

Elder Benson was no novice at public relations, and as had been predicted, his presence brought widespread exposure to the Church in Europe. His arrival was duly noted by dozens of leading periodicals. And as he traveled from country to country, he renewed acquaintances with heads of state, ministers of agriculture, and other ranking officials. He selected a director of mission publicity and information whose purpose was to improve the Church's image in Europe. By mid-1964 the European Information Service was operational, and six months later had been responsible for almost 60 percent of 298 articles (5,737 column inches) published in Europe about the Church. The information service also placed Church literature in libraries and hotels and publicized Church events.[25]

In the first six weeks Elder Benson visited all twelve missions, reviewed building programs and local problems, held press conferences, met dignitaries, investigated land prices for new Church buildings, and interviewed dozens of missionaries. Wherever he went, the press followed, curious about the apostle who had been U.S. Secretary of Agriculture. After his initial tour he recorded, "I have been more than pleased with the publicity [for the Church]. . . . Everywhere the press seems to have been favorable. . . . In Berlin we were on a national hookup, and in Switzerland we were on a short-wave program for all of Europe on two different occasions."[26]

After his first tour of the missions under his watchcare, President Benson outlined the state of the missions to the First Presidency and made the following observations and recommendations: Some stakes were weak. Only missionaries in good health should be sent to Europe. Among people of prominence, the Church was virtually unknown. Payment of tithes was weak. Mission presidents and missionaries should use local products as much as possible, such as European automobiles rather than large American cars. The servicemen needed to be more involved in Church activities and missionary work. And the Church needed the image of permanency. "These are but a few hurried observations," he wrote. "The churches of the world have lost hold on their people, and these people need the truth."[27]

President Benson spent most of his time either out among the people or seeking exposure for the Church. In February 1964 a German television station, *Deutsches Fernsehen*, aired a thirty-minute program during prime time in which he delivered a concise summary of the Church. Network officials admitted their invitation had come as a result of what they had seen in the press since the Bensons' arrival in Frankfurt.

Ezra and Flora were often included on the guest lists of prominent Europeans, though socializing had never been important to Sister Benson. She wrote Reed, "We are invited out to so many nonmembers' socials, dinners, etc. I wonder why the Lord selected Dad [and] me to do this social converting—because I know a lot of women would enjoy this type of thing better than I do. But I throw myself into it with all I've got, and the Lord has blessed me."[28] In March 1964, for example, Ezra and Flora attended a dinner at the luxurious home of the Consul General of Chile. Eighteen of the most prominent businessmen in Frankfurt were there, and the Bensons spent nearly three hours in gospel-oriented discussion, including a private hour with the Consul General. The next morning Ezra sent literature about the Church to him and other guests, and he and Flora reciprocated by inviting influential Germans to the European Mission Home.

Ezra was a fearless mission president and missionary. He would talk to anyone about the gospel, regardless of station or position. Under his direction, a colorful brochure about the Church was developed. When it was published, Elder Benson sent copies to Dwight D. Eisenhower, J. Edgar Hoover, *Time's* Henry Luce, columnist William F. Buckley Jr., *Reader's Digest* editor Dewitt Wallace, and others. To associates such as the dean of agriculture of the University of Tehran, he sent Church pamphlets and a copy of *Crossfire*, the autobiographical account of his USDA years, eliciting a warm response: "Your letter . . . once again enlivened our memories to the distant friendly land of Utah, to its people, the disciples of the LDS Church who have not ceased a moment to be pioneers not only in their home country but abroad."[29] President Benson's stature as a former cabinet member gained him entry to key decision-makers who might otherwise have proven inaccessible. As he laid ground-

*Elder and Sister Benson
and daughter Beth
are greeted by children
in Vienna, Austria,
in January 1964
during Elder Benson's
service as president of
the European Mission*

work for a mission in Italy, the Minister of Italian Agriculture, Dr. Mario Ferrari-Aggridi, arranged appointments for him with the four senior officials in the Italian Department of Church Affairs.

During one visit to Italy, President Benson met with the U.S. Ambassador and the Italian Minister of Religion in Rome. The president of the Italian Mission accompanied him. One observer later related, "Much to the surprise of our group President Benson was greeted with open arms. It was evident he had the love and respect of both men and a friendly exchange took place, as well as assurance that our missionaries would be welcome to proselyte in Italy."[30]

Flora and Beth added their own touch. They helped President Benson host guests, spoke at mission and district conferences, and created a warm environment in the mission home. Flora traveled with her husband frequently, and often waited patiently in the car or a foyer for him to conclude his meetings, typically visiting with members, taking an interest in the missionaries, and spending time with the people. Always they were on the go. Beth did her share too. She was called as a missionary, and she proselyted and worked in the office.

Elder Gordon B. Hinckley and his wife, Marjorie, visited the Bensons in Frankfurt during the Christmas season of 1964. Sister Hinckley later wrote Flora her thanks: "After going through the Orient and across Asia, where there was so little evidence of Christmas, and then to suddenly find ourselves in your beautiful home with the Christmas tree and the lights, and music and the red-ribboned staircase, and . . . most of all, the sweet spirit and peace of a Latter-day Saint home, was something that will always remain with us. After weeks in hotels, and strange cities you could not possibly know how we felt when we saw you at the airport. . . . One only has to step inside your home to realize what a wonderful contribution [Beth] is making to the success of the Church in Frankfurt. She adds something that we 'oldsters' cannot give."[31]

Long automobile trips were commonplace for the Bensons. They and their mission president hosts were often traveling either to or from conferences or the airport. On these automobile trips Ezra's love for singing was manifest as he led everyone in his favorite songs—everything from "I Want a Girl Just Like the Girl That Married Dear Old Dad" to "Springtime in the Rockies." The more caught up in the song the group became, the faster the car seemed to roll. Often Sister Benson would start watching the speedometer and say, "I think we'd better stop singing."

Sister Benson enjoyed purchasing mementos for family members, especially items native to the country, though doing so was at times an inconvenience. On one trip to Italy she selected keepsakes for the family and wrapped them in soft articles from her suitcase. She didn't want them damaged.

At the airport she would not allow any of her treasures to be checked through, so she and Ezra carried them on board. The mission president's wife said, "There was President Benson, very dignified, in his black suit, his black Homburg on his head, but being the ever-dutiful, loving husband that he was, lugging these heavy bags loaded with marble and ceramic. As they hurried to the plane, Sister Benson was on a half run beside him, and part of her nightgown was hanging out of one of the bags, flying in the breeze. We wish we'd had a painting of them, but only Norman Rockwell could have done justice to that scene."[32] Sister Benson also carried frozen turkeys and cranberry sauce in a suitcase back to Germany from Utah when she and Elder Benson came home for general conference. She wanted to have a traditional Thanksgiving dinner for the missionaries.

President Benson's lifelong interest in youth persisted in Europe. Because so many young people lived in small branches and were largely isolated from other Latter-day Saint youth, he encouraged youth conferences, and he and Flora attended dozens of them throughout the missions. But more was needed, he felt, to keep the youth active in the Church. First he implemented the Boy Scout program throughout Germany. Then he spearheaded *Freud Echo* (Echo of Happiness), the first conference for all German-speaking youth in Europe.

Beth took charge of the dance festival to be held at the youth conference and devoted months to planning the dances, teaching the routines, and designing costumes. She purchased the fabric, cut out patterns, wrote instructions in German, and sent packets to every MIA-age LDS girl in Germany, Austria, and Switzerland.

From July 29 to August 1, 1965, fifteen hundred youths gathered in Frankfurt for *Freud Echo*. Soccer matches, a huge dance festival, sports festivals, and a cruise down the Rhine made the conference an overwhelming success. A young girl from Czechoslovakia, who was allowed to attend the conference only after emigrating to France, where she received a short-term visa to visit Frankfurt, said, "These have been the happiest, most meaningful moments of my life." A missionary from Germany said, "I never thought I would be willing to stand in line for an hour just for the opportunity of bearing my testimony." The local press wrote glowing reviews of the event.

After attending *Freud Echo*, one newspaper editor in Darmstadt, Germany, subsequently agreed to print frequent articles on the Church in his paper. President Benson learned that the editor had "become convinced that the Church is . . . one of the best hopes the German people have for saving [themselves] from destruction through decadence. . . . He was astonished that a mere church . . . could be running programs for the youth which are designed to meet their real needs."[33]

Elder Benson had the ability to quickly assess areas of weakness and move to strengthen them.

Missionary work had ceased in Italy in 1862, but Latter-day Saint servicemen stationed there since World War II had laid groundwork for the preaching of the gospel. On February 27, 1965, at President Benson's direction, John M. Russon, president of the Swiss Mission, accompanied twenty-two missionaries to northern Italy to begin proselyting.[34] When President Benson returned to Salt Lake City seven months later, the Italian Zone of the Swiss Mission was leading the mission in baptisms. (Eventually Elder Benson would open the Italian Mission and rededicate Italy for the teaching of the gospel.)

President Benson found that proselyting techniques and printed materials in various languages were insufficient throughout Europe, and under his direction new brochures and seven new fellowshipping lessons for postbaptism use were developed. There was a great need for Church buildings throughout Europe, and by the time he left, he had dedicated sixteen chapels, with twenty-five more under construction.

President Benson was also very practical. In several German cities he sold mission homes and consolidated various offices into central locations, saving the Church sizeable sums of money. In one city alone, after selling a large mission home, the savings to the Church was $250,000. Before he left Germany, all Church agencies had been centralized into one location, increasing administrative efficiency and eliminating expense.[35]

President Benson constantly taught fiscal responsibility. At the groundbreaking ceremony of the Dortmund Branch chapel on August 29, 1964, he challenged members to dedicate—and therefore pay for—their building in one year. The branch president responded, "If we complete it in a year's time, will you come and dedicate it?" Elder Benson agreed. He subsequently dedicated the chapel one year to the day later. As far as he knew, it was the first time a building had been completed and paid for so quickly.[36]

The European members heard general conference from Salt Lake City for the first time in April 1965 after President Benson arranged for a station in Frankfurt to broadcast the meetings.

A difficult problem arose when, in early 1965, Elder Benson discovered that the newly released German translation of James E. Talmage's *Jesus the Christ* contained numerous errors with serious doctrinal implications. Two thousand copies were distributed before the inaccuracies were discovered. Before he left Europe, he arranged for a second translation of the book, which he supervised closely.

There was also the spiritual challenge of directing the work in twelve European missions. Beth remembered well those two years. On Thursdays—the day the Twelve met in the Salt Lake Temple—she saw how lonely her father was for his association with the Brethren. But she also saw him magnified in ways she had never imagined. One incident in Switzerland stands out: "Dad was speaking to the priesthood brethren. What I saw there is the closest thing to speaking in tongues I've seen. He didn't actually speak in German, but it was such a flowing experience that you didn't know where the English stopped and the translator began. I could tell the audience understood both languages. There were many experiences like that. Dad had to deal with challenges day after day. The First Presidency wasn't close by. He couldn't do anything but go to the Lord."[37]

One evening a moving experience demonstrated just how close assistance was from the other side. President Benson related: "Soon after retiring I had this impressive dream: Karl G. Maeser stood before me. He was tall, dignified yet pleasing, dressed in a dark suit and white shirt, clean shaven with ruddy face and clear blue eyes. He said to me, 'Brother Benson, what are you doing to promote the sacred work in the temples for my people of Europe? They are a choice people who have played a major role in building up the Kingdom of God in these last days. The sacred ordinances must be performed for them in the temples in order to permit their progress in the spirit world. Will you please do all you can to help bring this about? They are a choice people of our Heavenly Father.' These were his words as nearly as I can recall them. He smiled kindly as he nodded goodbye without further words. The brief message impressed me deeply."[38]

Though they were assigned to Europe, Ezra and Flora made frequent trips to the United States—to New York City for dedicatory services of the Mormon Pavilion at the World's Fair and for board meetings of Corn Products International, which association President McKay asked him to continue, and to Utah to attend general conference.

Elder Benson was surprised to learn the number of visitors to the World's Fair who signed the guest register at the Church's pavilion and said they had been attracted either to the Church or the pavilion because they admired Ezra Taft Benson. One fair-goer, for example, wrote, "Admire your church. Became interested because of Ezra Taft Benson, a wonderful patriot."

Though separated by an ocean, the Benson family stayed close. The children wrote to their parents frequently; and during their hurried trips to the United States, Ezra and Flora made time for short visits with Beverly and Jim, and Bonnie and Lowell, who were living in the East, and to other family members in Utah. They were ever conscious of the goings-on within the family. Ezra would later counsel his children in a family letter, "Stay close as a family. Write to us and each other as often as you can. Pray for each other and be specific in those prayers. We must be bound close together in this life. Be true to your good name and be true and loyal as a family."[39] He often told his children that nothing would bring him more sorrow than if his family were disloyal to the Church or each other.

In the summer of 1965 President Benson learned he was being called back to Salt Lake City, and he returned in time for October general conference. He was encouraged about the Church's future in Europe. Translation work had increased, missionaries were proselyting in Italy for the first time, thousands of Europeans had viewed the film *Man's Search for Happiness*, administrative procedures in the missions had been consolidated, and the media were treating the Church more favorably. His twenty-one months in Europe had been fruitful.[40]

*"No nation which has kept the commandments of God
has ever perished, but I say to you
that once freedom is lost,
only blood will win it back."*

Chapter 19

Sounding a Warning

E lder and Sister Benson were delighted to be home
again—closer to their children and grandchildren, and
involved again in the day-to-day matters of the Church
at headquarters. In some ways, things hadn't changed.
Elder Benson was to supervise seven German missions and four
stakes, so he would visit Europe frequently and maintain associations he had made in Germany; and he was as committed to
the cause of freedom as ever. There was, however, at least one
surprise coming.

It was in October 1965 that he first learned of an organization called the "1976 Committee"—a committee that was to
organize in 1966 and function for ten years. Its purpose was to
inspire, promote, and guide political action to help restore, maintain, and strengthen the Republic. Among other things, it would
promote candidates for U.S. presidential nomination.[1] A spokesman for the committee informed Elder Benson that after three
months of research, the committee had determined there were
two men best suited to provide the United States with the strong
leadership it needed: Ezra Taft Benson and Senator Strom
Thurmond of South Carolina. Elder Benson was asked if he
would be willing to run for president of the United States, with
the senator as his running mate.

Elder Benson declined to respond until he had spoken with President McKay. On October 21, he outlined the situation for the prophet. President McKay indicated that Elder Benson had his permission to allow the committee to proceed, but that he should do nothing to either promote or hinder the campaign.

For the first time since he left Washington, Elder Benson now faced the possibility of renewed political involvement. In addition, he continued to promote the principles of agency and freedom, and even encouraged a course of study on the subject for priesthood quorums—which President McKay approved but which ultimately did not come to fruition.

President McKay continued to speak on freedom. In the October 1966 general conference, answering the question "What shall we preach," he outlined topics of primary concern to Church leaders: "Preach the gospel plan of salvation. . . . It is a great imposition, if indeed not a crime, for any government . . . to deny a man the right to speak, to worship, and to work. . . . Declare the truth that man has the inherent power to do right or to do wrong. . . . Preach that the plan of salvation involves the belief that governments were instituted of God for the benefit of man. Man was not born for the benefit of the state. . . . Preach that honesty in government is essential. . . . Proclaim that God lives, and that his Beloved Son is the Redeemer and Savior of mankind."[2]

Elder Benson explained his willingness to continue to speak out on a subject that was not always received with favor: "Brigham Young said it would never be good for the Church to become popular with the world, or all Hell would want to join it. I feel no compunction to make the Church popular. . . . I do feel responsible to tell the truth."[3]

In fact, he felt responsible for all of the assignments he received. He was pleased to be assigned to the board of directors of Bonneville International, the Church's broadcast communications corporation. Always anxious to familiarize himself with his responsibilities, he immediately arranged for a tour of the broadcasting facilities. Corporation president Arch Madsen told him he was the first of the Twelve to make that request.[4] Elder Benson also sat on the Church's Expenditures Committee, for which he felt more qualified after his experiences in Frankfurt.

Perhaps most of all, he thoroughly enjoyed stake conference assignments, though not all passed without some stress or difficulty. While in the San Luis Obispo Stake in California, his vehicle was involved in an accident. He protected himself from going through the windshield by thrusting out his hand, and later learned he had broken a bone. When he was returning from meetings in North Carolina, his plane was detained in Denver by dense fog in Salt Lake City. After a day in the airport he finally boarded a plane to Ogden, but on the forty-mile drive from Ogden to Salt Lake City the fog was so dense that at times he had to get out of the car to see where he was going.

Whether he was speaking to LDS congregations or secular audiences, there were apparently many individuals interested in what Elder Benson had to say. He spoke frequently across the country to standing-room-only crowds. The Assembly Hall on Temple Square, for example, was filled beyond its capacity of two thousand, and seats were brought in to accommodate the overflow, on February 11, 1966, when he addressed the Utah Forum for the American Idea on the topic "Stand Up for Freedom." President McKay had the address wired into his Hotel Utah apartment so he could hear it.

Elder Benson continued to meet frequently with President McKay. "If you feel at any time I am getting off the right track, please do as you promised and 'tap me on the shoulder,' " he told the prophet.[5] On repeated occasions, he asked President McKay if he wished him to refrain from speaking on freedom, and in each case, Elder Benson was encouraged to continue. (On September 4, 1965, he was named to the American Patriots Hall of Fame.)

A significant number of individuals would continue to be attracted to the Church because of Elder Benson's strong patriotic stand. Nonmembers who wrote him about freedom-related issues got an introduction to the Church as well. To one inquirer he sent a typical response: "May I urge you to take time for fasting and prayer and meditation and reading in the Book of

Mormon. . . . Mormonism is true. I know it as I know that I live."[6]

Then, in the priesthood session of April 1966 general conference, President McKay made an unexpected statement. In part, he said: "We are continually being asked to give our opinion concerning various patriotic groups or individuals who are fighting Communism and speaking up for freedom. Our immediate concern, however, is not with parties, groups, or persons, but with principles. We therefore commend and encourage every person and every group who is sincerely seeking to study Constitutional principles and awaken a sleeping and apathetic people to the alarming conditions that are rapidly advancing about us. We wish all of our citizens throughout the land were participating in some type of organized self-education in order that they could better appreciate what is happening and know what they can do about it. Supporting the FBI, the police, the congressional committees investigating Communism, and various organizations that are attempting to awaken the people through educational means is a policy we warmly endorse for all our people."[7]

President McKay's message pleased Elder Benson, as he, too, continued to feel strongly about anything that threatened freedom.

In early April 1966 Elder Benson enjoyed a lengthy session with President McKay, this one centering around the progress of the 1976 Committee. The prophet advised him to continue to do nothing to either promote or discourage his proposed candidacy, to be cautious and wise, and to keep him (President McKay) informed of developments and seek his counsel. Later on, President McKay provided the following written statement: "I have been informed of the interest of many prominent Americans in a movement to draft Ezra Taft Benson for the Presidency. It appears that this is gaining momentum and is definitely crystalizing into a formal draft movement. Elder Benson has discussed this with me and to whatever extent he may wish to become receptive to this movement, his doing so has my full approval."[8]

As the efforts of the 1976 Committee gained strength, the response was positive enough that it frightened Ezra. With President McKay's consent, he continued to accept many speaking assignments around the nation. He was almost always enthusiastically received—often with capacity crowds, standing ovations, and thousands of subsequent requests for copies of his talks. At a convention in Oregon, for example, his address, "It Can Happen Here," received a prolonged standing ovation. Afterwards, during a question/answer session, he was asked if he would be willing to serve as president. He replied that every American has an obligation to serve his country, and he would do anything to help save the freedom of the United States. The crowd rose for a second ovation. At another convention in Oregon, this one for members of the National Credit Congress, his address, "Stand Up for Freedom," was greeted with a standing ovation that lasted "almost to the point of embarrassment," as he described it.

Elder Benson was the concluding speaker at a three-day "God, Family, and Country" rally in Boston on July 4, 1966, where the overflow audience in the Hilton Hotel's main ballroom responded energetically to his spirited message. And when he addressed the BYU devotional assembly in the Smith Fieldhouse on "Our Immediate Responsibility," overflow accommodations had to be provided in three additional buildings to accommodate the crowds. For weeks he received hundreds of requests for copies of his remarks, and many purchased tape recordings of the address.

Regardless of the setting, Elder Benson's message was consistent. He quoted Church leaders and drew examples from the Book of Mormon to establish scriptural and doctrinal precedents and guidelines on the subjects of freedom and agency. Then he delivered somber warnings about the threats to freedom in the United States.

In his address "It Can Happen Here," he cautioned: "Our complacency as a nation is shocking—yes, almost unbelievable! We are a prosperous nation. . . . We live in the soft present and feel the future is secure. . . . We are blind to the hard fact that nations usually sow the seeds of their own destruction while enjoying unprecedented prosperity. . . . Today as never before, America has need for men and women who possess the moral strength and courage of our forefathers—modern-day patriots,

*Elder Benson
has never
hesitated to
speak out on
the subject
of freedom*

with pride in our country and faith in freedom. . . . This is a worldwide battle . . . between light and darkness; between freedom and slavery; between the spirit of Christianity and the spirit of anti-Christ for the souls and bodies of men."[9]

In "Stand Up for Freedom," he outlined his motivation for addressing patriotic subjects: "From the time I was a small boy I was taught . . . that we should study the Constitution, preserve its principles, and defend it against any who would destroy it. To the best of my ability I have always tried to do this. . . . Some two years ago, however, a critic from Washington claimed that a person who serves in a church capacity should not comment on such matters. He charged that the separation of church and state requires that church officials restrict their attention to the affairs of the church. I, of course, also believe that the institutions of church and state should be separated, but I do not agree that spiritual leaders cannot comment on basic issues which involve the very foundation of American liberty. In fact, if this were true, we would have to throw away a substantial part of the Bible. Speaking out against immoral or unjust actions of political leaders has been the burden of prophets and disciples of God from time immemorial."[10]

After his address at the October 1966 general conference, on "Protecting Freedom—An Immediate Responsibility," he had a difficult time getting out of the Tabernacle, so many crowded around him to comment. His message was direct and forthright. Some of the Brethren called it courageous. In it, he warned the Saints against being indifferent about and detached from the principle and issue of freedom. "Should we counsel people, 'Just live your religion. There's no need to get involved in the fight for freedom'?" he asked. "No, we should not, because our stand for freedom is a most basic part of our religion; . . . our reaction to freedom in this life will have eternal consequences. Man has many duties, but he has no excuse that can compensate for his loss of liberty."[11]

While the principle of freedom was ever on his mind, Elder Benson was constantly alert to other dangers that threatened the Saints, and hence the Church. Often he raised a voice of warning. In the October 1964 general conference he had elaborated on "three threatening dangers" that President Joseph F. Smith had identified years earlier—the flattery of prominent men, false educational ideas, and sexual impurity. Elder Benson implored the Saints to anchor themselves to eternal verities rather than seek the praise and acclaim of men. He illustrated how far the philosophies of man had strayed from morality and correct economic, social, and educational principles. And he warned that promiscuity retarded growth, darkened spiritual power, and made an individual susceptible to additional sin.

Throughout the last half of 1966, frequent telephone calls and letters responding to the news that Elder Benson was a potential presidential candidate indicated that at least a segment of the population had warmed up to the pronouncements of this hard-hitting leader. "It almost fills me with fear when I hear people express their confidence in my humble abilities," he recorded in his journal on October 3. "I am following the counsel of President David O. McKay . . . regarding this draft effort—doing nothing to promote it or to stop it."

Meanwhile, his schedule of Church responsibilities was demanding. During the summer of 1966 he made a presentation at the seminar for new mission presidents on working with public officials. Elder Gordon B. Hinckley wrote him in a memo, "You can render a great service in suggesting to the Brethren how they may meet U.S. Ambassadors, consular officials, governors, mayors, and other public officials. . . . We feel that no one among the Brethren is as well equipped as you for this facet of our work."[12]

The Church was beginning to see substantial growth outside the United States, particularly in Mexico and South America, and diplomatic contacts were increasingly important. For Elder Benson, trips south coupled with supervisory responsibility for six missions in Europe kept him extremely busy.

In late July 1966, he spent two weeks in Europe, where he attended the second *Freud Echo* youth conference. Young people came by bus, train, car, and plane. One young man rode 200 kilometers on his bicycle to attend.

In November 1966 he and Sister Benson returned to Europe. He had long championed the interests of Latter-day Saint servicemen, and, finding that many had not received patriarchal blessings, he arranged for the Patriarch to the Church to visit Europe and confer the blessings.[13] On this trip, he and Elder Paul H. Dunn of the First Council of the Seventy conducted a servicemen's conference at Berchtesgaden, Germany. More than nine hundred servicemen and their families from Germany, France, Italy, and as far away as Lebanon and the Azores, gathered. A conference highlight was the baptism of several servicemen in an icy stream in a small Bavarian village.

Elder Benson had a continuing interest in the work in Italy, and on November 10 he and Sister Benson, with President and Sister John Duns, Jr., of the Italian Mission, and some thirty-five missionaries, drove to the small village of Torre Pellice to rededicate the land of Italy. This was where President Lorenzo Snow had first dedicated Italy 116 years earlier. Sister Duns remembered the events: "As we traveled [to Torre Pellice] President Benson sat with his lap full of papers, scanning the territory and reading from a historical description of the first dedication. He was anxious to rededicate in as close a proximity to where President Snow had stood as was possible to determine. Since the mountain peak where Lorenzo Snow's dedication took place was named Mt. Brigham [by the early Saints], we were scanning the roadside for a sign that would indicate such a mountain, but to no avail. Suddenly President Benson said, 'Stop here!' He got out of the car, pointed his finger up the mountain, and said, 'I think we'll climb right here.'

"About three-fourths of the distance to the top President Benson stopped and waited for the rest of us to catch up. Then he announced, 'This is it, this is the spot!' We all stood in silent, reverent gratitude to be sharing in this wonderful spiritual experience, as President Benson pronounced the dedicatory prayer."[14]

Missionary work was taking hold. The Italian Mission had been created on August 2, 1966, and already two Italian branches and seven combined servicemen/Italian branches were operating.

Upon return to Salt Lake City, Elder Benson gave his recommendations to the First Presidency regarding missionary work in Italy, in Lebanon, and in other areas throughout Europe. As a Church leader, his responsibilities included temporal as well as spiritual concerns, administration as well as teaching. He often made immediate decisions on such concerns as buildings, land, government contacts, and personnel. His decisions had financial and diplomatic, as well as ecclesiastical, ramifications. He was adept at handling these assignments.

Ezra and Flora were always relieved to return home, though. Their children were growing older, and the Bensons were increasingly pleased with them, both in their church and their civic activities. Mark was serving as a counselor in the Texas Mission presidency; Reed had run for Congress, served in two bishoprics, and continued to be involved in the fight for freedom, which his father supported; Barbara, Bonnie, and Beverly and their husbands were active in the Church and busy with their families; sons-in-law were serving as bishops and would serve in stake presidencies; and there were by 1966 sixteen grandchildren being reared under the gospel umbrella.

On June 8, 1966, Elder Benson performed the marriage of his youngest daughter, Beth, to David A. Burton in the Salt Lake Temple. It was an occasion that brought great satisfaction and joy to Ezra and Flora. At that time he recorded in his journal, "We have now reached the one great goal we set for ourselves when the children were very small, that all six of them would be married to choice [companions] in the temple of our Lord. I think I have never seen so many tears of gratitude shed as we experienced in the sealing room."

And Elder Benson continued to be mentioned as a candidate for president of the United States. Following President McKay's advice, he had neither encouraged nor discouraged the 1976 Committee, nor had he discussed it with the Brethren. One journal entry explained the reason: "This, too, is in line with President McKay's counsel . . . that if I made an explanation to the General Authorities as a body, it might be interpreted that I was soliciting their support. . . . Only the good Lord knows what the future holds. I would be willing to do anything in my power to help to promote the work of the Lord or to help safeguard our great country." In the same journal entry, made the last day of 1966, Ezra revealed his overriding perspective: "It is my hope and prayer that the Lord will sustain us and direct us and magnify us in our work that I will be ready to meet any challenge which comes. . . . I am grateful beyond expression for the holy apostleship, for the Church and Kingdom of God restored, for my wonderful companion, and for our six children with their companions."

Momentum of the 1976 Committee picked up in January 1967. Thousands of packets, with information promoting Ezra Taft Benson for president and Strom Thurmond for vice-president, were mailed to households nationwide; bumper stickers appeared on cars; petitions for his nomination arrived at his home and office; and support from the grass roots came by way of financial donations, letters to the First Presidency and the 1976 Committee, and letters to newspaper editors.

In the early stages, however, the press didn't give the movement much publicity, even in Salt Lake City. And while there appeared to be substantial grass-roots approval, on a wider basis the campaign, such as it was with a candidate who did not promote himself, took off slowly.

Ezra's work load was increased by the publicity he received, however. In addition to heavy Church assignments, his volume of correspondence increased noticeably. Some Latter-day Saints were curious about his involvement and about the 1976 Committee itself. Finally the *Deseret News* quoted him as saying it was only a draft movement that he wasn't promoting, and that this was not an attempt to create a third-party movement. Rather, the 1976 Committee hoped to appeal to voters in both the Republican and Democratic parties.[15]

Ezra put principle above political party. Historically, he had affiliated with the Republican Party. During his adult life its platform was typically closer to his own philosophy than that of the Democratic Party. However, he upheld each individual's right to choose for himself. Some years later, in 1974, he drafted a statement outlining his views: "I am in full accord with the official position of the Church of refraining from the endorsement of political parties or candidates. I recognize there are faithful members of the Church affiliated with both political parties. I have personal friends in these parties and they realize that I would not offend them by suggesting they were not faithful members of the Church."

As he explained in a letter to a granddaughter on another occasion, "I have close friends and people whom I greatly admire in both political parties. Many of them are great Americans with ideals closely related to my own."[16]

In reality, Elder Benson lived by his own political and economic creed, which he outlined as follows:

"I am for freedom and against slavery.

"I am for social progress and against socialism.

"I am for a dynamic economy and against waste.

"I am for the private competitive market and against unnecessary government intervention.

"I am for national security and against appeasement and capitulation to an obvious enemy."

There wasn't much time for rest. At times Elder Benson got only four or five hours sleep a night as he shuttled in between conference and other assignments. He especially loved stake conferences in rural areas. In Soda Springs, Idaho, for example, he noted relishing time with the stake presidency, all three of whom were farmers and ranchers. "This is largely a rural stake," he wrote. "It was a real joy to be with these wonderful people."

Apparently it was the rural population who were particularly enthusiastic about a Benson/Thurmond ticket. He was speaking to standing-room-only crowds in large and small cities. For example, in Pasco, Washington, on April 16, 1967, a large delegation met him at the airport. That evening he addressed twelve hundred in the high school auditorium, where he received two standing ovations after a rousing address on freedom.

Eventually, as it became apparent Richard Nixon was the Republican Party's frontrunner, the 1976 Committee's promotion of Ezra Taft Benson and Strom Thurmond dwindled and finally ceased. Later in 1967 a second draft-Benson movement arose, this one by the American Independent Party. It was launched without Elder Benson's knowledge and was short-lived.

Amid his Church assignments and secular activities, Elder Benson made unusual effort to spend time with his children, who were by now scattered around the country. Bonnie and Beverly were both living in Denver, Mark in Dallas, Barbara in Calgary, Reed in Virginia, and Beth in New York City, where her husband was attending medical school. Many of Ezra's travels took him through or near these cities, and when possible he routed his schedule to include layovers for a few hours or perhaps overnight.

As the grandchildren grew older, he tried to make more time for them. After Bonnie and Lowell's family returned home from a visit with Ezra and Flora, Bonnie's son Mark, then age three, told her, "I am just going to dream about what I did at Grandpa and Grandma Benson's home." In May Ezra and Flora took their granddaughter Flora Walker, at their own expense, on an assignment to Europe and made sure she saw some of the famous zoos, castles, and other landmarks. They took her to the opera and loaded her up with posters and brochures to take home to classmates. But after a month in Europe, which had proved "fruitful in every respect," Ezra nevertheless had to admit,

"I think I have never been more tired anytime during the last six years."

At least partly with their posterity in mind, Ezra and Flora purchased four acres in scenic Midway, Utah, and spent what hours they could spare improving the property. Ezra tore down fences, burned an old chicken coop, and arranged for major remodeling on the frame house. They hoped it would be a gathering place for their family and a convenient location for family reunions.

Elder Benson's love for his grandchildren was an obvious extension of deep feelings he had had since young manhood for youth. Youth were the hope for the future, he repeatedly taught, and he took every opportunity to visit youth conferences and to support the Boy Scout program. (In addition to his national BSA assignment, he served several years as chairman of the BSA's Region 12. When the national BSA wanted to raise funds to build a headquarters building in Salt Lake City, they asked him to chair the drive. Elder Benson had received the Silver Buffalo, Scouting's highest honor, in 1954, and the Silver Beaver in 1961.) Though 80 percent of eligible LDS youth were participating in Scouting, Elder Benson felt that wasn't good enough. "We need to have the other 20 percent of our boys in Scouting," he noted in his journal. He felt strongly about this and, in fact, all facets of the Church's program, which was seeing unprecedented growth throughout the world. At times he wondered if the Church was prepared to effectively administrate the burgeoning organization. He believed that while the broad organizational outline was divinely revealed, it was left to man with God's inspiration to work out the details. Good management meant delegating authority.[17]

Late in 1967 Elder Benson presented a seminar to the General Authorities on delegation. The Brethren agreed that he was a master at administering a large organization. After his presentation, Harold B. Lee remarked, "I think I speak for all of us when I say to Brother Benson that he has given us a perfect model in his presentation."[18] Elder Benson therefore enthusiastically supported the call that year of sixty-nine men to serve as Regional Representatives of the Twelve. He had the privilege of setting apart six of the first group, and in due time his son

Mark and son-in-law Robert Walker would be called to this position.

An array of concerns demanded his attention, and he was alert to societal trends that could potentially threaten Latter-day Saints. He called the growing threat of drugs "frightening, weird [and] destructive," and was anxious that every high school and college-age young person be warned. Habit-forming, mind-altering drugs, in addition to being physically dangerous, had the grave potential of robbing people of their freedom. In a general conference address in 1969, he would warn the Saints about the onslaught of evils that threatened the moral fiber of the Church and America: "Today we face insidious, devastating evils that are widespread. Aimed especially at the destruction of America—the last great bastion of freedom—with emphasis on our youth, the evils are everywhere. . . . These evils are prominent in the promotion of drugs. . . . These devilish forces . . . seem to be everywhere. They are spreading into every segment of our social, economic, and religious life—all aimed at the destruction of one whole generation of our choice youth."[19]

Some topics of discussion and activities involved more pleasant topics. In November 1967 the Council of the Twelve enjoyed a memorable meeting in the temple. The Church had recently acquired from the Metropolitan Museum in New York City papyrus fragments related to the Book of Abraham. "It was overwhelming to us as we viewed these writings," Elder Benson noted. "We couldn't help but feel that the Lord has His way of bringing about His purposes. He uses human beings to achieve those purposes. This work is directed by the God of heaven and not by man."

The last two weeks of December 1967 were peaceful. Flora returned home after spending two weeks with Beverly upon the birth of her second child. Ezra and Flora enjoyed several days of relaxation during the holidays at their renovated Midway cottage. Many visitors from the alpine farm community stopped in to pay their respects, and the Bensons appreciated the warm welcome.

Thereafter, Ezra and Flora would slip up to Midway on a rare weekend when he wasn't traveling, or even overnight when possible. It cleared his mind to drive through the beautiful Heber Valley and smell the oak smoke from fireplaces in nearby homes. He and Flora loved to dance to player-piano music. And he loved taking family there. When a granddaughter came to visit, they spent an evening in Midway just for her. Ezra arose early to take her on a snowmobile before the one-hour drive back to Salt Lake City in time to be at the office by eight o'clock.

During the first month of 1968 several groups interested in his running for political office continued to contact and encourage Elder Benson. He paid them scant attention. But in February, a situation arose that he could not ignore. Governor George Wallace of Alabama announced his candidacy for the presidency, and shortly thereafter he phoned Elder Benson to ask if he would be his running mate on the American Independent Party ticket. While he didn't agree with all of Wallace's positions, Elder Benson was impressed with the governor's aversion to big government and his strong emphasis on states' rights.

On February 12, 1968, with the permission of President McKay, Elder Benson and his son Reed met Governor Wallace at the governor's mansion in Montgomery, Alabama. For three hours they discussed dozens of questions in a closed-door session. Ezra found Wallace frank and open, and the governor indicated he was anxious to have Elder Benson join his ticket. He then sent President McKay a letter officially requesting the prophet's permission for Ezra to be his running mate.[20] When he returned home, Elder Benson told the prophet about his visit to Montgomery and his impressions of Governor Wallace. That evening he recorded in his journal: "The President again emphasized that this was going to be a very lively and controversial campaign, and he felt that my being on the ticket would cause me to be criticized and possibly the Church also. He also said that he felt I had served for eight years with distinction. . . . I made it clear to him that . . . I wanted to do what the Lord wanted me to do. . . . Then President McKay said, 'I think the answer should be no. . . . Now is not the time.' "

At President McKay's direction, during the regular Thursday meeting of the Twelve, on February 15, 1968, Elder Benson outlined in detail the various movements and attempts to have him nominated to run for high office. He explained that President McKay had asked him not to discuss these matters earlier, and that he had not encouraged any of these overtures.

The matter did not end there, however. Wallace's popularity increased during 1968, and he invited Elder Benson to reconsider the invitation to run as his vice-presidential candidate. Eventually the question was taken to President McKay a second time. But again, the president felt that his original counsel was wise. On September 12, 1968, Ezra noted in his journal, "I only want to do what the Lord would want me to do, as revealed through His Mouthpiece."

Though from February 1968 on, Elder Benson felt certain he would not run for political office, he still worried about the dangers facing America, and often his remarks attracted national attention. In 1967 Senator Thurmond entered in the *Congressional Record* Elder Benson's address "Trade and Treason," first delivered on February 17, 1967, at the Portland Forum for Americanism.[21]

In the April 1968 general conference, Elder Benson again delivered a strong address on the divine nature of the Constitution. Entitled "Americans Are Destroying America," his hard-hitting remarks, in which he decried the prevalence of such things as juvenile delinquency and moral disintegration, were stimulating: "I do not believe the greatest threat to our future is from bombs or guided missiles. I do not think our civilization will die that way. I think it will die when we no longer care— when the spiritual forces that make us wish to be right and noble die in the hearts of men. . . . If America is destroyed, it may be by Americans who salute the flag, sing the National Anthem, march in patriotic parades, cheer Fourth of July speakers—normally good Americans, but Americans who fail to comprehend what is required to keep our country strong and free. . . . Great nations are never conquered from outside unless they are rotten inside. Our greatest national problem today is erosion, not the erosion of the soil but erosion of the national morality."[22]

Response to the address was overwhelming. Hundreds of letters from all over the country, from members and nonmembers alike, came to the apostle's office. Some respondents ordered thousands of copies of the address. The letters came from clergymen, executives, housewives, educators, diplomats—nearly every sector of U. S. society. Senator John McClellan had the conference address entered in the *Congressional Record* on April 22, 1968, giving it a laudatory introduction on the Senate floor: "Mr. Benson's speech . . . should be read by every American citizen, and I hope the central truth it conveys that Americans, by their lack of self-discipline, by their apathy and indifference, and by their lack of will and resolve, can succeed in destroying America."[23]

A few letters are illustrative of many more. From the U.S. Army Chief of Chaplains: "Only on one other occasion have I felt it my duty to distribute a memorable, thought-provoking, challenging and uplifting address. That was General Douglas MacArthur's famous 'Duty, Honor, Country' speech he gave at West Point."[24] And from the Central States Mission: "We have had many requests for a copy of your conference talk. Most of these requests are from nonmembers who were very much impressed with what was said. Several of them have also expressed a desire to learn more about the Church."[25]

Response to the address was still pouring in several months later, prompting Elder Benson to note that he had never had such widespread and enthusiastic response to any talk given in or out of the cabinet.

In October of that year Elder Benson delivered another powerful discourse, "The Proper Role of Government," in which he defined the appropriate relationship between government and the governed: "Since God created man with certain unalienable rights, and man, in turn, created government to help secure and safeguard those rights, it follows that man is superior to the creature which he created."[26]

Many respondents to these and other Ezra Taft Benson talks commented on how pleased they were to hear honest remarks. Elder Benson rarely toned down his message to entertain audiences. Often he began speeches with the comment, "I come with a solemn message. I am not here to tickle your ears."

Elder Benson remained concerned about the world situation, and he kept abreast of current events. His files, divided into hundreds of subject areas, contained information on everything from foreign policy to inflation—anything that potentially affected the quality of life. Periodically he distributed pertinent materials to the Brethren. In a detailed letter to the First Presidency and Council of the Twelve in April 1968, he outlined the dangers he foresaw the United States facing in coming years—increased racial unrest and violence, a prolonged recession or depression, a monetary and credit squeeze, and the possibility of another world war. He also recommended steps the Church might take to prepare its people: inform the priesthood; implore members to have a year's supply on hand and pay their debts; and encourage priesthood holders to attend to family prayers, hold home evenings, and teach the gospel in the home.[27]

A week later Ezra and Flora left for a month of meetings in Europe. At one baptismal service there he had the pleasure of confirming a prominent attorney who indicated Elder Benson's testimony had led him to a confirming witness of the gospel's truthfulness.

As was his practice, Elder Benson went on these assignments with no preconceived message in mind, but in each stake or mission he determined what the people's needs were and suited his remarks accordingly. He fasted frequently with the missionaries and mission presidents. In Beirut, to the missionaries' delight, a newspaper interview resulted in three positive articles in the *Beirut Daily Star*.[28]

Elder Benson enjoyed immensely having Flora travel with him. On one trip when she had stayed home he lamented in his journal, "I missed having her at the conference. She is always such an influence for good with me and her suggestions are invaluable. She has the unusual ability to win the confidence of audiences wherever she speaks." One man wrote after the Bensons had visited his area, "I don't think the authorities should travel without their wives. We will forever be grateful for having Sister Benson with us. My wife has not been so impressed with anyone."[29]

After nearly a month's absence, the Bensons returned to the United States to find everything well at home. "Before we retired tonight," Ezra wrote, "we held each other in our arms and then knelt in prayer in thankfulness to God for His protection and His sustaining power during the almost one month that we have been away." It was to be their last trip to Europe for a while. In

the way for better relations between the Church and the governments in this area."[11]

In Egypt, President Benson was told it would take three weeks to secure the appointments he needed with key government officials. That night he knelt in his hotel room to ask the Lord for direction. He had consummate faith that the way would be opened. Those traveling with him were astonished when he was able to cut through mounds of red tape in a matter of hours and take care of his business. He subsequently met with four officials, including his old friend Sayed Marei, former Secretary of Agriculture and Speaker of the House, and now Anwar Sadat's first assistant.[12]

Staff members who regularly accompanied President Benson came to realize that there was an abiding spiritual power about him. When he determined that something needed to be accomplished, he had complete confidence that the Lord would prepare the way.

It was President Benson to whom the letter came from Hesi Carmel, former Consul General of Israel, indicating that the mayor of Jerusalem, Teddy Kollek, had authorized the placement of a plaque on the Mount of Olives commemorating Orson Hyde's 1841 dedicatory prayer. President Benson later joined the First Presidency and Elders Mark E. Petersen and Gordon B. Hinckley in lengthy meetings with Carmel to work out details. They reached an agreement that the Church could develop five and a half acres on the Mount of Olives as the Orson Hyde Memorial Park. On several occasions over the years President Benson had talked with leaders in Israel about the Church's doctrine regarding the Jews. He had even suggested a commemorative garden. This project lifted his heart. He felt he had had a small hand in it.

From David Ben-Gurion on, President Benson enjoyed a cordial and mutually respectful relationship with key Jewish leaders. In a meeting with Ben-Gurion in March 1969, the Israeli leader told him, "There are no people in the world who understand Jews like the Mormons." To that President Benson responded, "Mr. Ben-Gurion, there are no people in this world who understand the *world* like the Mormons." Ben-Gurion replied, "Oh, I'm not sure I'd go that far, but what I said was true." He then asked President Benson to pray that his life would be extended ten years, as he hoped to complete a history of the Jewish people in that time. He also indicated he would like a copy of Orson Hyde's prayer for inclusion in the history.[13]

President Benson often spoke on the divine destiny of the Jewish race. He addressed Jewish organizations and weaved the Church's doctrine regarding the House of Israel into his message. After delivering a major address in Calgary in 1978, entitled "A Message to Judah from Joseph," he received generous praise from the president of the United Israel World Union, who said, "What a great document! As a son of Judah who, for some 35 years has been proclaiming . . . the existence of Joseph-Ephraim, I rejoiced greatly in what you declared. . . . I have long felt a strong kinship for the Mormons." Highlights of the address were reprinted in the *United Israel Bulletin*.[14] After President Benson delivered the same address in Seattle, two thousand copies were requested. He also gave this message to a large audience in San Diego and to another in Jerusalem.[15]

The First Presidency recognized President Benson's stature in the non-Church world. In October 1975 President Kimball asked him to represent the Church at the White House Forum on Domestic Policy. In President Benson's remarks (later published as a pamphlet, *A Plea for America*) he stated that only the return of Americans to loving God and living morally would rid America of its political, economic, and social ills. He also used the forum to outline the Church's code of ethics and morality.

So much of what President Benson had to say—about staying out of debt, about loving God and neighbor, about holding on to freedom, and a host of other common-sense subjects—appealed to member and nonmember alike. In 1975 President Benson published his book *God, Family, Country*, incorporating messages on these three loyalties. When it was suggested that he might have rearranged the wording to "God, Country, Family," he replied he preferred the first way, as "the family is eternal. Countries may not be."[16]

Indeed, the eternal family unit and hence temples were extremely important to President Benson. Attending the dedication of the temple in Washington, D.C., in November 1974 was a highlight for him and Flora that they described as "never to be forgotten." Reed and May, Mark, Beverly and Jim, and Bonnie joined their parents at the event, which held special meaning for the entire family. The beautiful, imposing structure situated prominently alongside the Capitol Beltway in Maryland was breathtaking—and particularly inspiring to a man who had spent over a dozen years of his life in Washington and who had presided over the first stake in that area. In his remarks at the dedication he admitted, "For me, this is a dream of more than thirty years come true. Not since the founding of this choice nation and the Restoration of the gospel has such an important event transpired in this great area."[17]

Though he was getting older, President Benson liked to spend as much time in the field as possible, and most weekends he either attended stake conferences or toured missions. He created the first stakes in Ireland (1974), Denmark (1974), and Finland (1977), and attended the Stockholm area conference in August 1974.[18] But amidst the press of administrative responsibilities, he still focused on individuals. Over the years those who had depicted him as driving and unrelenting had overlooked the more accurate, more important, softer, compassionate side seen by those who worked with him intimately.

When President Benson learned that a young man who had received authorization to have his church membership and other blessings restored had died suddenly of cancer, he acquired permission to have the blessings restored by proxy, contacted the family, and drove to Logan to take care of it himself.

While visiting Athens in 1979, he learned of a native-born Greek member of the Church who, despite intense pressure to do so, had refused to renounce his membership. As a result, the man's business had been boycotted, his children were not permitted to attend school, and he had subsequently become inactive. President Benson drove across Athens (though he had only four hours in the Greek capital) to visit the man, who was shocked when the General Authority knocked at his door. An assistant traveling with President Benson recalled the scene: "President Benson wanted to hear this man's story from his own lips. The President was very moved by what he heard. Before we left President Benson pulled this man to him and said, 'God bless you, my brother. I want you to know our prayers are with you.' The man had tears in his eyes. As we left, President Benson turned to me and told me to take down his name, his family's name, and the names of his children, and immediately when we returned, to put them on the temple prayer roll. Several months later the district president from Athens visited Salt Lake City and told us something miraculous had happened. The restrictions had been lifted, the children allowed to return to school, and the man was back at church. President Benson gave that brother who'd been discouraged and downtrodden the courage to come back."[19]

While in Brazil to create the Brasilia Stake, President Benson learned that the stake president's daughter had a large growth on her neck, and doctors insisted on surgery. He asked to see the girl. Elder Ted E. Brewerton was there and described what took place: "President Benson placed his hands on her head and spoke with the Lord for a minute or two and then blessed her, saying she would not require an operation and the growth would disappear. It was a very touching scene full of emotion, the Spirit was obviously tangible, and many tears followed." Five days later the growth had disappeared.[20]

President Benson recorded in his journal an experience one missionary in Argentina related to him. This missionary and his companion had been working for some time with a family who, though they accepted many gospel truths, lacked a testimony of modern-day prophets. On February 22, 1979, President Benson spoke at the Cine Opera in Buenos Aires, concluding his remarks with a powerful testimony of the Savior. This investigator family attended, and afterwards the father approached the missionary and said with emotion, "I do not want to wait for baptism any longer. I have just seen and heard a living prophet."

On another occasion after President Benson had concluded an address to youth and missionaries in Mexico, he felt impressed to ask the congregation to sing their national anthem. Elder Richard G. Scott later told President Benson how powerful that had proven to be: "You observed how deeply everyone was touched with the beauty and depth of spirit of the moment. I will ever recall your turning to me and saying, 'I don't want to leave,' nor did the youth. I received many comments that the morning testimony services were entirely dominated by youth bearing witness that they had been in the presence of one of the prophets of the Lord. . . . They will not forget your visit."[21]

When a young man seeking a blessing came to President Benson's office, the apostle inquired why he didn't ask his father to confer the blessing and found that the father was an inactive elder. After talking at length with the young man, President Benson counseled him to return home and at an opportune time request the blessing of his father. Four days later the young man returned to President Benson's office and reported that his father had agreed, and it had created a bond of love in their home he had never known before. In a meeting of all General Authorities, President Benson instructed his colleagues. "May we be extremely careful not to deprive a priesthood father of that opportunity and privilege."[22]

A mission president related the impact President Benson had in another case involving "a most delicate situation regarding a giant of a man in the Church. . . . This man . . . had been caught in a delicate and unfortunate circumstance regarding some doctrinal matters and was misunderstood by certain people. [President Benson] has turned the situation around totally and brought new light and hope to this person, and it has freed him. [He] has saved that person's soul."[23]

President Benson had a gentle, down-to-earth way with people, perhaps best known by those who talked with him one on one. Young couples, returned missionaries, and those burdened with trouble or sin frequented his office, and he gave counsel, pronounced blessings as appropriate, and performed as many sealings as time allowed. He was much more approachable than some might have imagined. At a BYU basketball game he found himself sitting behind a woman whose son was whistled for his final foul. The woman, momentarily losing her composure, shouted several descriptive words—and instantly remembered who was sitting behind her. But before she could apologize, President Benson leaned forward and chuckled, "Sister, you took the words right out of my mouth."[24]

While President Benson's energies were devoted fully to the Council of the Twelve, his interests in national affairs persisted.

President Benson meets with U.S. President Gerald Ford in the Oval Office of the White House, November 25, 1975

Government concerned him, the economy worried him, and what he perceived as apathy among national leaders frustrated him. President Kimball had made clear the urgency to take the gospel throughout the world and President Benson felt that certain forms of government threatened that growth. When events of national political significance occurred, he was typically the first LDS leader contacted for a response. Such was the case with Watergate and Nixon's resignation, at which President Benson issued a statement expressing his sorrow at the unfortunate incident.

After he became president of the Twelve, President Benson spoke frequently on such topics as prayer, the Savior, genealogy, and missionary work. At the October 1979 general conference he reemphasized the message he had delivered so often before by giving a firm warning on the subject of freedom: "I say with all the energy of my soul that unless we as citizens of this nation forsake our sins, political and otherwise, and return to the fundamental principles of Christianity and of constitutional government, we will lose our political liberties, our free institutions, and will stand in jeopardy before God. . . . Once freedom is lost, only blood . . . will win it back."25

President Benson continued to be an astute observer of world affairs and did what he could behind the scenes to alert and persuade Americans to the encroaching danger. When a non-Mormon U.S. senator came to his office seeking a blessing at his hand, he gladly gave it. Congressmen and officials of influence heard from him regularly on issues that related to the advance of freedom and free enterprise. And he wrote to presidents of the United States recommending prayer in cabinet meetings. In 1977 his book *This Nation Shall Endure* was published—a collection of essays that pled with Americans to overcome their complacency regarding America's destiny. Two years later he forwarded a copy of another of his books, *The Red Carpet—Socialism, the Royal Road to Communism*, to each member of Congress.

President Benson felt that the Twelve should be astute about world affairs, and he led them in discussions on economics, social movements—anything that affected the Church as an institution or its members individually. He also distributed pertinent materials to the Brethren. In response, Elder Vaughn J. Featherstone wrote, "I know the Lord has blessed you with a special understanding of the needs of this country. You have helped breed in my heart a love for this great nation, a love for the founding fathers, and a love for the Constitution."26

Ezra was pleased when the First Presidency issued an official statement in June 1979 reaffirming the Church's devotion to the Constitution and encouraging members to become actively involved in the political process.

By 1975 Mark and Lela had returned from their mission. Reed had accepted a position as area director of seminaries and institutes in northern Virginia and subsequently returned to BYU for graduate studies. And Beth and David were living in Salt Lake City. With some of their families close by, Ezra and Flora were the doting grandparents—listening to their grandchildren's book reports, leading in singing around the piano, showing home movies.

Despite the pleasant times with family, President Benson remained deeply concerned about Flora's health. At times she showed improvement and had some energy; at other times she seemed tired and discouraged. Through it all, he tried to deal with his own anxiety as well as see that she had every medical opportunity. She underwent dozens of tests, and he spent a lot of time on his knees. These concerns were complicated by a heavy travel schedule that kept him away from home a great deal. But he spent as much time with her as possible, though she didn't demand it. "She has always insisted that I do not do anything that would interfere with my duty as an Apostle and President of the Twelve," he wrote in his journal. But to him, caring for Flora was anything but an interference. It did affect his life-style, however. He found himself doing the shopping and performing other tasks she had always taken care of.

In September 1975 Brigham Young University honored President Benson by naming its new agricultural institute after him. The Ezra Taft Benson Agriculture and Food Institute was formed to help relieve world food problems and raise the quality of global life through improved nutrition and enlightened agricultural practices. At the ceremony inaugurating the institute, President Benson touched upon a principle that had guided his approach to agriculture as well as life: "Many of the nations of the world look to American agriculture for a pattern as they struggle to feed their teeming populations. Too often we, as benevolent Americans, have given them food instead of teaching them how to produce food."[27]

During the ceremonies Ezra participated in a cow-milking contest with BYU president Dallin Oaks. Ezra not only won the contest but had a hearty laugh when a touchy Holstein kicked President Oaks head over heels when the college administrator lined up on the wrong side of the animal.

In many countries the influence of the Benson Institute spilled beyond agricultural boundaries and gave President Benson an additional calling card. For example, when Anwar Sadat determined to rebuild his childhood rural community, an Egyptian student attending school in the United States suggested that the institute might be able to help. President Benson made trips to

Courtesy of Deseret News

*President Benson
prepares for a
milking contest,
held in connection
with announcement
of the Ezra Taft Benson
Agriculture and Food
Institute*

Egypt, hoping this development would create goodwill for the Church.

The institute had potential impact in Central and South America as well. In Ecuador, for example, the institute contracted with the government to teach farmers how to support themselves on 2.5 acres or less. President Benson's agricultural accomplishments and connections continued to increase the visibility of the Church in many areas of the world.

In August 1975 President Benson traveled to the Orient for area conferences in Japan, Hong Kong, Taiwan, Korea, and the Philippines. In Tokyo scores of Saints laden with banners and flowers were at the airport. One girl approached President Benson with two dozen red roses for Sister Benson, and he was disappointed to tell her Flora had not made the trip. He wrote Flora that night, "How I miss you and find myself wishing you were here."

The first night in Japan, President Benson retired at 7:30 P.M., tired after working during much of the ten-hour flight. But during the next nine days in Asia, there was little time for rest, with general sessions, youth sessions, and meetings with missionaries, diplomatic calls, and press conferences. He and President Kimball called on the president of Taiwan and had breakfast with the Secretary of Natural Resources in the Philippines. President Benson suffered sleepless nights as he worried about major addresses he would give: to the Sino-American Fellowship Prayer Breakfast in Taipei; on the American Forces Network to Protestant servicemen of the U.S. Eighth Army in Korea; and at the Korea area conference. He was present when President Kimball announced to Japanese priesthood leaders plans to build a temple in Tokyo. Tears flowed freely—including his own.

After the exhausting but inspiring round of conferences, President Benson marveled at President Kimball's dynamic leadership. "It was nothing short of a miracle the way President Kimball came through all that was asked of him during the conferences," he noted in his journal.

Missionary work was moving forward at unprecedented speed. During one meeting of the missionary committee in January 1975, approval was given for the creation of three missions and three stakes. A day earlier two other missions had been approved, including one in the state of Utah, something President Benson had favored for some time. At the June 1975 seminar for new mission presidents, he announced that the Church missionary force had passed the 20,000 mark; twenty-two new missions had been organized in the previous twelve months; and proselyting was taking place in fifty-five countries and twenty-three languages. At the end of 1975 Church membership reached 3.5 million. Ezra felt that the religious world had never been weaker, and the Church couldn't afford to be backward or hesitant about carrying its message. "We have an opportunity the like of which we have never had, to get our message before our Father's children worldwide," he wrote in his journal.

Missionary work permeated the Benson family. Reed and May were two of those attending the 1975 mission presidents seminar, having been called to preside over the Kentucky Louisville Mission. And in July two of Ezra's sisters, Margaret and Lera, were called to serve in England. They immediately called him to tell him the news, expecting to have their brother say that he knew all about it. Instead he replied, "What mission calls? I didn't know you were going on missions." He would later delight in telling the story. "They expected the President of the Quorum of the Twelve to know everything. But it just ain't so!" (Only Ezra's sister Sally remained of his ten brothers and sisters to serve a mission, and eventually she and her husband would serve together.)

President Benson was conscientious about his personal missionary efforts. He constantly sent Church-related materials, particularly copies of the Book of Mormon with his testimony enclosed, and detailed letters containing his testimony to national and international dignitaries. Even within the Benson family there was need for fellowshipping. One of Ezra's brothers and his nonmember wife were frequently on Ezra's mind. After visiting them in California, he sent them a copy of *A Marvelous Work and a Wonder* with a letter that bore his testimony: "I do hope and pray that you will see your way clear to become actively associated with the greatest organization in all the world—The Church of Jesus Christ of Latter-day Saints. There is so much at stake. It is the truth. This I know as I know that I live."

Elder Benson often quoted the poem that reads in part:

> We are all here,
> Father, Mother, sister, brother,
> All who hold each other dear.
> Each chair is filled,
> We are all at home.

With each year Ezra and Flora's feelings for their family grew increasingly tender. When President Benson officiated at the temple marriage of Flora Walker, his first grandchild to marry, a milestone was passed and a new generation initiated properly. As time passed he would perform the marriages of many of his grandchildren—most in the Salt Lake Temple. On trips to Provo he regularly stopped to visit grandchildren attending BYU. He was present when the first baby of his granddaughter Heather Walker Sandstrom was blessed. Heather wondered if her grandfather expected to pronounce the blessing, and she finally asked him about it. "Oh, no," he replied, "that honor is reserved for the father. I've just come to be here with you."

President Benson's grandchildren tended to embrace his philosophies, with his loyalties becoming theirs also. In time, several grandchildren would intern on Capitol Hill and work for political organizations based in Washington, D.C. When his grandson Stephen Benson evidenced talent as a political cartoonist, Ezra sent him materials on freedom, the Constitution, and related interests and encouraged him to be informed about the political and economic philosophies of the Founding Fathers. (Stephen would go on to become a nationally syndicated cartoonist in over one hundred papers and would win the National Headliner Award. Once one of his cartoons was carried in all three of the major weekly news magazines. Queen Elizabeth even requested the original of a cartoon to be displayed in Buckingham Palace.)

Flora's granddaughters also followed her example in staying home with their children, making home and family and the rearing of righteous children the highest priority. Flora had never viewed her role as wife and mother as one of duty. She loved children and felt that a mother's preeminent responsibility was to care for her children's spiritual and temporal welfare. Her positive outlook on motherhood and homemaking was firmly entrenched throughout her extended family. In 1950 she had written a chapter entitled "Your Children and You" for a Mutual Improvement Association course of study. There she placed the importance of parenting in perspective: "Yes, parents are responsible for the direction of their children. To Latter-day Saints, what is more important than effective parental guidance—the greatest need of the home, the community and the nation. With our knowledge of the gospel plan, can there be anything more important, more conducive to our exaltation than the bearing, rearing and proper training of an ideal Latter-day Saint family?"[28]

That his family was on Ezra's mind is evidenced by the constant flow of things he sent to children and grandchildren. His letters were filled with encouragement. On a regular basis, his adult posterity received copies of talks, poems, and books he felt were inspirational. It was standard to share news through the family grapevine—awards, promotions, Church callings.

When President Kimball suggested that all LDS families display a picture of a temple in their homes, Ezra sent a full set of temple photographs to the family of each of his children. He and Flora added to each family's food storage and encouraged their children to get out of debt and to pay for their homes. (President Benson participated in the dedication of several of his children's homes.) They constantly encouraged and advised their children on a variety of matters.

Certainly Ezra had tremendous impact over his posterity, in word and in deed. After receiving a priesthood blessing from her grandfather, for example, a granddaughter wrote, "My heart is much too full to say this out loud so I'll write it. Half of the things you said were answers to my prayers that I had not ever thought would be answered in that way. The other half was an almost word for word quote from my patriarchal blessing. Grandpa and Grandma, I only hope I am worthy of you!"[29]

Within his immediate family, Ezra enthusiastically supported Beth and David Burton's activities to conduct extensive genealogical research, and often helped raise funds to finance the projects. Discussing the four-generation program in general conference, he explained, "I have organized my family, as I'm sure scores of you have done—the Ezra Taft Benson Family Organization—as a grandparent family. Our children and married grandchildren are organizing as part of that organization."[30]

Ezra served for a time as chairman of the George T. Benson Family Association, coordinating reunions and getting behind the four-generation program. A reunion of his brothers and sisters in 1976 in Idaho centered around genealogical research, temple work, and strengthening the family organization.

President Benson had no idea he was about to be honored with a surprise "Ezra Taft Benson Day" during Preston's Idaho

Days, an event that coincided with the reunion. Hundreds of people, including Elder Mark E. Petersen and other General Authorities, as well as representatives from the Boy Scouts and U.S. Department of Agriculture, were there to honor him. Ezra rode a Palomino as grand marshal of what was later called the biggest parade ever held in Cache Valley. The generous tributes he received overwhelmed him. The event was beyond anything he had ever imagined.

Throughout 1976 President Benson was deluged with requests for speeches at patriotic meetings commemorating the Bicentennial of the United States. There was a brief attempt by a resurrected 1976 Committee to mention former Governor of Texas John Connally and Ezra Taft Benson as candidates for president and vice-president, respectively. "It is, of course, impractical and impossible," President Benson responded.

His love of America had made one assignment from President Kimball especially sweet. Ezra was to examine documents stored in the St. George Temple vault verifying that temple work had been performed for many of the Founding Fathers, including the fifty-six signers of the Declaration of Independence. He explained: "In so doing, I realized the fulfillment of a dream I had had ever since learning of the visit of the Founding Fathers to this sacred place. I saw with my own eyes the records of the work that was done for the Founding Fathers of this great nation, beginning with George Washington. I was deeply moved on that occasion to realize that these great men returned to this promised land by permission of the Lord and had their ordinance work done for them. If they had not been faithful men, if they had not been God-fearing men, would they have come to the elders of Israel to seek their temple blessings? I think not. The Lord raised them up, sanctioned their work, and proclaimed them 'wise men.' "[31]

President Benson subsequently elaborated, stating that George Washington had been ordained a high priest at the time, adding, "According to Wilford Woodruff's journal, John Wesley, Benjamin Franklin, and Christopher Columbus were ordained high priests. . . . When one casts doubt about the character of these noble sons of God, I believe he or she will have to answer to the God of Heaven for it."[32]

Several significant administrative changes were made in Church organization during President Benson's tenure as president of the Twelve. At the October 1975 general conference, President Kimball announced the organization of the First Quorum of the Seventy. Heretofore only the seven presidents, known as the First Council of the Seventy, had been serving. At this conference three additional men were called to serve as General Authority members of the quorum.

In April 1976 additional brethren were called to the Quorum of the Seventy, and in October 1976 a major reorganization was effected, with the Assistants to the Twelve called into the First Quorum of the Seventy and a new presidency of that quorum organized. President Benson was intimately involved in guiding the working relationship between the Twelve and the First Quorum of the Seventy. This history-making step pleased him greatly, and he felt sure it was in line with the scriptures and would facilitate efficient Church administration and enhance missionary work.

By early 1976 the Twelve had been relieved of conference assignments one Sunday a month. On that Sunday they met for five hours to review major policy matters. This allowed them to use their time in their weekly Thursday meetings more efficiently, and frequently President Benson noted in his journal his delight at their progress. "We broke all records with 28 items on the agenda," he wrote in his journal. "With good management and a little urging we were able to cover them all."

There was purpose in President Benson's managerial style. He, like others of the Brethren, was interested in simplifying the Church administrative structure worldwide so that the leaders could devote more attention to building faith among members and converting souls to the gospel. As he wrote in his journal, he told the Twelve in one meeting that he wanted fewer "dog and pony shows," where a succession of brief reports didn't always examine the heart of the matter. Elder Neal A. Maxwell explained: "By the time I came into the Twelve in 1981, President Benson had long since lost interest in what I call 'tinkering with the machinery,' and realized that wasn't where progress lay. While he was courteous, thoughtful and sweet, I'm sure there were times when some of the rest of us were trying to tinker with the machinery and he might have liked us to get back to whatever the real issue at the moment might have been."

By 1977 the Twelve were overseeing progress and development of major ecclesiastical areas, while the Seventy handled more of the day-to-day administration. President Benson expected the Brethren to come to quorum meetings well prepared. He encouraged more computerization to streamline procedures, and believed the Church should make better use of the media to get the gospel message to the world.

On many fronts the Church was moving forward. Certain General Authorities were invited to study other languages, especially Spanish; two recorded visions, by Presidents Joseph Smith and Joseph F. Smith, were added to the standard works (1976); an LDS edition of the King James Bible was published (1979); and in 1978 Church membership passed four million.

As concerned as he was about efficiency and productivity, few things were more important to President Benson than unity among the Twelve. Francis M. Gibbons, then secretary to the First Presidency, observed the distinctive unity that prevailed among the Brethren. He commented, "Each of the Twelve brings into office his background, political posture, and so forth. But once opinions have been frankly expressed and a decision made, it becomes a decision of the council. You will never hear one of the Brethren outside of those frank but confidential conversations say anything but in support of the decision reached by the presiding authority."

In February 1977 President Benson noted in his journal, "We have a great spirit in the Twelve. Never has there been greater unity and never have I felt the power of the Twelve as I feel it today." In the April 1984 general conference, President Hinckley concurred: "There is unity between the Presidency and the Twelve, perfect unity. There is unity among the members of the First Quorum of the Seventy and the Presiding Bishopric. I am somewhat familiar with the history of this Church, and I do not hesitate to say that there has never been greater unity in its leading councils and the relationships of those councils one to another, than there is today."[33]

Perhaps that unity was fostered, at least in part, by a Quorum president who genuinely loved his brethren. He told the General Authorities in a meeting on January 19, 1977, "I express . . . love, loyalty, and affection for you. . . . Your reciprocating affection shown to me over the years is among the choicest blessings of my life."[34]

President Benson concerned himself with the "fatherly" aspects of his calling. His concern for his brethren extended beyond the Church offices. As he traveled, he took time with them on the challenges they were facing personally. He was very concerned that they have enough time with their families and take care of their health. In one meeting of all General Authorities, he referred to instances when Brethren who were ill had filled conference assignments. "You don't have to go out when you're ill," he counseled. "We'll find a replacement. Please, Brethren, take care of yourselves." After this demonstration of concern, Elder LeGrand Richards cocked his head and said out loud, "You're a good daddy."

President Benson was typically the first to compliment and praise others—for presentations, talks, anything worthy of notice. As one example, when Elder Royden G. Derrick's work in the Genealogical Department was complimented in a meeting of the Twelve, President Benson made sure Elder Derrick heard of it. President Gordon B. Hinckley said that all who worked with President Benson knew the "gentle side of his nature. I know of no man more considerate of his associates or more concerned for their well-being. Graciousness becomes [him]. He has been blessed with a compassionate heart."[35]

Immediately following the general conference session in which Waldo P. Call was sustained a member of the First Quorum of the Seventy, President Benson walked over to him, took him by both hands, and congratulated him. "He said he loved me," Elder Call remembered. "I am sure he was tired after two days of conference and other days of training meetings, but I will never forget his simple expression of love."

President Benson's deep affection for his associates in the Twelve was demonstrated on one memorable occasion. For some years Elder Richards had served as chairman of the important Boundary Change Committee, but as his age crept toward the century mark and his health and mobility declined, he felt his effectiveness was reduced. At one committee meeting he announced he was resigning as chairman. Almost on cue, President Benson unexpectedly entered the room. Elder Richards repeated his intention to resign, and President Benson responded, "As long as you live, LeGrand, you'll be the chairman of this committee." Then President Benson named Elder Marvin J. Ashton vice-chairman of the committee and told Elder Richards to delegate as much responsibility as he desired. Elder Richards boosted himself out of his chair, and he and President Benson took each other in their arms. Both were in tears. President Benson said simply, "LeGrand, I love you." Then he left.

With his astute observation of national and international affairs, President Benson became increasingly anxious in the late 1970s about the increasing frequency of natural disasters worldwide, the deteriorating U.S. economy, and particularly the willingness of some Latter-day Saints to turn to the government for support rather than becoming self-reliant. During general conference in October 1973 he had implored Church members to prepare themselves for eventualities by storing a year's supply of food, citing a graphic scriptural precedent: "The revelation to store food may be as essential to our temporal salvation today as boarding the ark was to the people in the days of Noah." At a later date, in the October 1980 general conference, again he would repeat his warning, again drawing parallels between the days of Noah and the latter days, and then adding: "Those families will be fortunate who, in the last days, have an adequate supply of food because of their foresight and ability to produce their own. . . . We urge you to do this prayerfully and *do it now*. I speak with a feeling of great urgency."[36]

In February 1977 the General Welfare Services Committee, composed of the First Presidency, Council of the Twelve, and Presiding Bishopric, was formed to place increased emphasis on welfare work in the Church. President Benson frequently quoted Doctrine and Covenants 38:30: "If ye are prepared, ye shall not fear," hoping to prepare Saints who would react with stability rather than panic in times of crisis. And his influence went beyond the Church.

In May 1977 he addressed the board of the prestigious Foundation for Economic Education, of which he had previously served on the board of trustees (as had President J. Reuben Clark, Jr.). He warned that while America had become the world's richest nation because of free enterprise, today's citizen was learning to depend on the state, thus jeopardizing personal freedom.

The following day he was invited by the president of the foundation, Leonard E. Read, to attend a trustees meeting. "The first question [they asked me] was on the Church, and they never left that theme," President Benson wrote that night, "so I spent an hour answering questions, telling them about the Church, bearing my testimony to them and telling of Church policies and my experience in the Cabinet." One board member lingered afterwards and told him, "I want what you have. When we go home, I'm going to look up your church." Shortly thereafter President Kimball received a letter from Leonard Read, who wrote, "Last evening we had some 160 freedom friends to hear President Benson's lecture: 'The Productive Base of Society.' Imagine the audiences and lectures I have arranged during . . . more than 31 years as President of FEE. . . . Well, last evening was the best of all. Never have I witnessed such interest, approval, esteem. This forenoon, however, even topped last evening—this being an hour's discussion with 26 of our Trustees and that many guests. All were profoundly moved by Ezra's economic, intellectual, moral and spiritual insights. Among my acquaintances in this and 22 foreign nations, I have never come upon his equal."[37]

President Benson sent an engraved copy of the book *Meet the Mormons* and a copy of the Joseph Smith story to each trustee of the foundation.

The year 1976, when the nation observed the bicentennial of its independence, marked a precious personal milestone for Ezra and Flora Benson. It had been fifty years since they knelt across an altar in the Salt Lake Temple and exchanged eternal promises. Much of the family gathered in Louisville, Kentucky,

On their fiftieth anniversary, Ezra and Flora pose in auto similar to the one they drove on their honeymoon

where Reed was serving as mission president, to celebrate the golden anniversary.

At the Louisville airport, Reed and May, Mark and Lela, Barbara, and Beverly and Jim, with some of their children (all wearing patriotic hats and sporting a huge Happy Anniversary sign) lined the concourse and sang "Love at Home" as Ezra and Flora (who were traveling with Bonnie and Lowell) deplaned. Passers-by stopped to catch a glimpse of them, and the commotion even caught the attention of the airport photographer.

On a major thoroughfare en route to the mission home, Ezra and Flora spotted a huge canvas sign hanging from an oversized billboard reading "Flora and Ezra T.—Happy Anniversary." Across the street from the mission home was a five-story hot-air balloon proclaiming anniversary wishes. Parked in front was a 1915 Model T Ford, similar to the one they drove to Ames, Iowa, with a sign, "Just Married—50 Years."

That evening, the family dinner and program celebrating the event was elaborate, with tributes penned by family and friends. The following are typical:

From Fred Babbel: "During those strenuous years in Europe . . . when the word 'Flora' was uttered, it always seemed to bring with it an outpouring of love and an inward strength that moved mountains."

From Ezra's brother Ross: "I think I appreciate most how, after the death of father and mother, you two took me under your wing and guided me as you would your own son."

From Beverly: "I'm thankful for the loyalty, the laughter and the love that have always been special to our family. . . . Home was always the safest, the happiest, the best place in all the world."

The six children presented their parents with a gold-framed mirror, on the back of which was written, "To Ezra Taft Benson and Flora Amussen Benson as they 'reflect' on 50 years of eternal marriage, from their grateful children." The following was inscribed on the frame of the mirror:

> Look and see, out of ye, posterity
> Rising up to call thee great
> Like the Church and like the state.
> Thou dost have a noble frame.
> Eternal thanks who claim thy name.

The battle for passage of the Equal Rights Amendment heated up in 1976, and Latter-day Saints from Idaho, in particular, sought President Benson's support in fighting the amendment. He believed, as did his brethren, that the amendment was vague and broad and threatened to undermine the distinctive roles of men and women. After the bill was rescinded in Idaho, President Benson wrote the speaker of the Idaho House of Representatives, "I commend you and your associates for your courageous and wise action in voting down proposed legislation which strikes at the very foundation of the home and family. I know that some of you will be under fire. . . . The Founding Fathers were also under fire."[38]

In 1977 President Benson participated in a successful effort to encourage Latter-day Saint women to attend the International Women's Year convention held in Utah, and to voice their opinions about issues affecting the role of women in society. Later the Twelve, in conjunction with the Seventies, drafted a strong statement in opposition to extending the period of ERA ratification. President Benson was involved in adding the words *A Moral Issue* to the title of a booklet, *The Equal Rights Amendment—A Moral Issue*, that was distributed to members of the Church.[39]

Anything that threatened the home was anathema to President Benson. He told a crowd of 14,000 honoring National Family Week in Seattle that the home was America's strength and only hope for the future. His message was direct: "All is not well with this most basic institution, the American home. In fact, it is in grave danger, if not deadly peril. There is convincing evidence that a creeping rot of moral disintegration is eating into the very vitals of this temple of American civilization." To the audience, which was filled with non-Mormons, he taught that the family is meant to be eternal, quoting the lyrics to "I Am a Child of God." This talk was later entered in the *Congressional Record*.[40]

In an address at the nondenominational "Strong Families/ Strong America" program in Tulsa, Oklahoma, on March 24, 1978, President Benson unabashedly called for prayer in the home and for parental instruction on such crucial matters as sex education. Holding up a copy of the Church's current home evening manual, he admonished parents to forsake so much pleasure-seeking and to spend more time with their children. "The home is the rock foundation, the cornerstone of civilization," he said. "The church, the school, and even the nation stand helpless before a weak and degraded home. No nation will rise above its homes."[41]

Also of concern to President Benson were materials being published by some LDS historians, who he feared were incorrectly placing their emphasis on writing Church history from a perspective that downplayed the divine authorship and doctrines. In a BYU fireside in March 1976, he criticized historians whose emphasis was "to underplay revelation and God's intervention in significant events, and to inordinately humanize the prophets of God so that their human frailties become more apparent than their spiritual qualities." No writer, he asserted, "can accurately portray a prophet of God if he or she does not believe in prophecy."[42]

Later in 1976, in an address to instructors in the Church Educational System, he gave this caution: "When a teacher feels he must blend worldly sophistication and erudition to the simple principles of the gospel or to our Church history so that his message will have more appeal and respectability to the academically learned, he has compromised his message. We seldom impress people by this means and almost never convert them to the gospel. . . . Some teachers have felt that they have to expound some new slant on a doctrine, or reveal sensational or intimate and sacred personal experiences from their own lives, or allegedly from the lives of the Brethren in order to be popular with their students. You were not hired to entertain students."

He explained that to teach, for example, that "Joseph Smith received the vision on the three degrees of glory . . . as he grappled for answers that contemporary philosophers were grappling for, is to infer an interpretation contrary to the prophet's own. . . . Avoid expressions and terminology which offend the Brethren and Church members. I refer to such expressions as 'he alleged' when a president of the Church described a revelation or manifestation; or other expressions such as 'experimental systems' and 'communal life' as they describe sacred revelations dealing with the united order. . . . A revelation of God is not an experiment. The Lord has already done his research."[43]

President Benson was worried that an interpretation of the Restoration that focused more on the societal environment of the time than a spiritual account of sacred events could destroy faith.

His concerns about professional historians reached beyond the Church. Frequently during 1976 he counseled those writing the nation's history. "The recurring theme in America's history is that God governs in the affairs of this nation," he declared. He believed that Columbus was inspired by the Holy Ghost, George Washington and Abraham Lincoln recognized the hand of God, Benjamin Franklin petitioned to have prayer in Congress, and the Lord established the Constitution through choice men raised up for this purpose. He decried the fact that one had to turn to eighteenth and nineteenth century literature to find this view, warning, "Those guilty of defamation of these men in writing or teaching will answer to a higher tribunal."[44]

After five full years of service as president of the Twelve, and at an age when most men only read the news rather than make it, President Benson kept a relentless pace. In April 1978 his longtime friend Ernest Wilkinson passed away. They were the same age. But there was no sign that Ezra was letting up.

In May of that year he took an extensive trip to Asia. In Taiwan he met with Premier Chian Ching Kuo, the president-elect, and discussed missionary work in that island nation; and in Tokyo he dedicated the new seven-story Asia Administration Headquarters. The following month he spent eight days in Hawaii for rededication services of the Hawaii Temple.

With each year, it seemed, he was singled out for commendation. In January 1978, for example, he received the Distinguished and Meritorious Service Award from the American Farm Bureau Federation, considered the most prestigious of agriculture's recognitions. Just four months later he accepted another George Washington Medal Award from the Freedom Foundation at Valley Forge.

But all of the awards and recognitions in the world didn't rival the impact of a signal event in June 1978.

On June 1, following the monthly meeting of the General Authorities in a room on the fourth floor of the Salt Lake Temple, President Kimball invited his counselors and the Twelve to remain when the others were excused. The prophet then raised a subject they had discussed repeatedly in previous months—that of conferring the priesthood on worthy men of all races. President Benson knew the prophet had spent many hours alone in the temple, praying for an answer to this question. And he himself had done extensive research on the subject. This day President Kimball directed a lengthy discussion on the issue and then led in prayer.

Elder Bruce R. McConkie described what happened: "It was during the prayer that the revelation came. The Spirit of the Lord rested mightily upon us all; we felt something akin to what happened on the day of Pentecost and at the dedication of the Kirtland Temple. From the midst of eternity, the voice of God, conveyed by the power of the Spirit, spoke to his prophet. . . . And we all heard the same voice, received the same message, and became personal witnesses that the word received was the mind and will and voice of the Lord."[45]

The experience was electrifying, one of the most glorious occasions in President Benson's nearly thirty-five years as a member of the Council of the Twelve. In his journal he wrote: "Following the prayer, we experienced the sweetest spirit of unity and conviction that I have ever experienced. . . . We took each other in our arms, we were so impressed with the sweet spirit that was in evidence. Our bosoms burned with the righteousness of the decision we had made. Thank God for the inspired leadership and the great and enduring principle of revelation. What a blessing it is to be associated with this, the greatest work in all the world. May God grant that I . . . may measure up to the great responsibility which is mine as one of the watchmen on the tower of Zion."

"This work will go forward till every land and people
have had opportunity to accept out message.
Barriers will come down for us to accomplish this mission."

Chapter 22

The Expanding Church

Even as President Benson approached eighty years of age, he was a vigorous man. His face was unlined and his memory sharp. He looked, and felt, ten years younger.

Flora's health was somewhat unpredictable. She fainted during the funeral of LeGrand Richards's wife, Ina, in January 1978. And a few months later, during a theater performance, she suddenly slumped in her chair. Dr. Russell M. Nelson, who was providentially nearby, noticed and hurried over. Unable to find a pulse, he quickly put his arms around her from the back and pulled sharply against her chest several times until a pulse became evident. Dr. Nelson said he was relieved to hear her say suddenly, "Would you mind not doing that?" Subsequent tests showed no sign of irregularity, but apparently she had suffered a cardiac arrest.

Flora joined Ezra at a four-day family reunion in Nauvoo in July, held in conjunction with the dedication of the women's monument statues. The reunion was carefully planned, with testimony meetings, a special dinner honoring Flora's seventy-seventh birthday, and visits to local historical sites, as well as sports and music activities.

When President Benson
broke his hip,
Steve Benson
produced this
get-well card
for his grandfather

Reed and his family had just returned from their mission in Kentucky, and the Parkers were preparing to leave for Helsinki, where James Parker would preside over the Finland Helsinki Mission. So this reunion marked the last time the family would be assembled for at least three years.

The reunion was exhilarating but somewhat tiring. Upon returning home, the Bensons stole away to Midway for a few days' rest. On July 12, 1978, as President Benson prepared to go horseback riding with a neighbor, a horse he was steadying for his friend to mount suddenly reared, knocking him fifteen feet across the yard onto the hard ground. X rays at the hospital nearby in Heber revealed a multiple break in four places between the ball-and-socket joint of the hip and above the right knee. By that afternoon he was in surgery in Salt Lake City.

Word of the accident spread quickly among the General Authorities and family—even to Finland, where Beverly and Jim and their family had just arrived. The message they received from home had a special P.S.: "He wants you to know everything is okay, and he wants you to especially know that the

horse did not *throw him off*." Flower arrangements, cards, and
telephone calls poured in and visitors arrived at President
Benson's hospital room in such numbers that the doctor finally
restricted visitors to family and General Authorities. When they
learned it would be three full months before he could put full
weight on his leg, Ezra and Flora accepted Beth and David's
offer to occupy a small apartment in their home. A hospital
bed and other conveniences—walker, crutches, wheelchair—were
moved into the house, which is situated on a semiprivate lane,
a perfect location to recuperate.

Beth was a solicitous nurse, keeping constant care of her
parents; and as long as her father stayed down, his pain was
minimal. He could move very little at first, but despite his weakened condition, he asked staff members to visit him three times
a week to review items of importance and keep the work moving back at the office.

David Burton was also recovering from back surgery, and
as he and his father-in-law began to regain strength, they took
walks down the lane, clad in pajamas and bathrobes, leaning
heavily on walkers.

President Benson had been relatively unencumbered by health
problems throughout his life, so he was frustrated at the long
period of recuperation. The feeling that he wasn't carrying his
load gnawed at him and he was an impatient patient. Nevertheless, he took a philosophical approach to the unexpected injury.
"I have no doubt but what blessings will come from this
experience," he wrote in his journal. "Certainly I have been
given time to ponder, to count my blessings, to rest, to enjoy
the blessings of home and family, and to be comforted and
strengthened by the prayers and the unity and love of my noble
family." The experience made him even more tolerant of those
who had poor health.

A month after the accident President Benson attended his
first meeting with the Twelve, but he stayed only briefly, as it
was painful to sit. But it was a relief to be back at work—even
for a short time. His strength gradually returned, and by early
September he was attending several meetings a week, spending
a few hours at the office, and getting around fairly well with
the use of a walker. He had hoped to be mobile enough to

travel to South America after general conference in October for five area conferences and dedication of the Sao Paolo Temple. But his doctor felt the risk for reinjury was too great and requested that he stay home. Ezra was extremely disappointed.

The doctor was not opposed, however, to President Benson's filling a speaking assignment in Idaho Falls on September 17. A battery-operated chair lifted him up the steps of the airliner, and he was carried up the steps to the platform in the Idaho Falls Civic Auditorium. He delivered his first address since the injury, and it felt wonderful. Two weeks later he spoke at general conference. Arrangements had been made for him to sit on a high stool to speak, but when the time came, he stood and leaned against the podium, placing most of the weight on his left leg. That same week he and Flora moved back to their apartment.

President Benson's condition improved substantially before year's end. By January 1979, he felt up to an extended trip to South America, where he created the first Bolivian stake; spoke in Ecuador to crowds that filled aisles and doorways; contended with a national strike in Peru that kept citizens off the street; and met hundreds of faithful Latter-day Saints whose lives were testaments to the power of the gospel. The press in Colombia, Ecuador, and Peru gave him generous and favorable coverage, and in Quito, over five hundred Ecuadorian members sang "I Am a Child of God" as he deplaned at the airport.

The Church was moving forward rapidly. Just two months later he returned to South America to organize the first stake in Paraguay. And on February 18, 1979, commenting that "the eyes of the Church are on us today," he organized the Church's 1,000th stake—in, appropriately, Nauvoo, Illinois.[1]

In May 1979 he enjoyed one of his most satisfying trips as a member of the Twelve—this one to the Middle East, where he conferred with government officials in Egypt, Greece, and Israel. Prime Minister Menachem Begin of Israel adjusted his schedule to accommodate President Benson's and told the church leader, "We respect your people very much. Your people have suffered much, and you have stood by your faith."

In Israel President Benson also conferred in an hour-long meeting with Shimon Peres (then the opposition leader in the

Knesset) and Abba Eban, whom he had met while serving as Secretary of Agriculture. Ezra was received warmly by these men as a former cabinet officer, but now they were to experience even more the impact of his role as an apostle of the Lord whose mission is to witness of the Savior. President Benson related to them his experience in the Baptist Church in Moscow and then bore strong testimony of the Savior. As President Benson prepared to leave, Shimon Peres said to Abba Eban in Hebrew, "Isn't he a great man?" Abba Eban replied, "One of the greatest I have met in my time."[2]

In Greece, President Benson met with Mr. Kontogiorgis, acting minister of agriculture and minister of European Affairs, who effusively embraced him as he entered, commenting, "You don't remember me, do you?" When President Benson confessed that he didn't remember him, Mr. Kontogiorgis explained that he had visited the United States to learn about agriculture by working at the U.S. Department of Agriculture during Ezra's term there. He expressed the indebtedness he and the Greek nation owed Secretary Benson and the United States. "If there is anything I can ever do for you, let me know," he offered. President Benson explained there was an area where he could provide assistance—in helping the Church obtain recognition in Greece. In a matter of months, limited recognition was granted. An assistant traveling with President Benson observed, "I had the strong impression at that moment that there were many reasons Ezra Taft Benson had been placed in the Cabinet. It established his name throughout the world, and literally opened this door."[3]

Reflecting on the trip, President Benson told the Twelve, "I hope much good came from this visit to three nations. . . . I trust that the legal recognition will soon come to the Church in Greece and later in Egypt. The Lord will bless us. I give you my assurance that He will prepare the way for us."[4]

In a very short time President Benson resumed the kind of schedule he had kept prior to his accident. He was home from the Mideast scarcely a week before he left for South America again—his fourth major international trip in five months—to rededicate Venezuela for the preaching of the gospel and work out problems relating to restrictions on missionary visas. Before

President Benson speaks at the dedication of the Orson Hyde Park in Jerusalem, October 24, 1979

year's end he would travel to New Zealand and Australia for area conferences, to Mexico City for meetings with executive administrators on the rapid growth of the Church there and throughout Central America (in four years the number of stakes in Mexico had grown from fifteen to nearly sixty), to Kirtland, Ohio, for groundbreaking ceremonies of the Kirtland Ward chapel (CBS and NBC sent reporters), and to Israel for the dedication of the Orson Hyde Memorial Garden.

The ceremony on the Mount of Olives on October 24, 1979, was deeply moving and satisfying for President Benson, symbolizing fruition in years of friendship with Jewish leaders. As Jerusalem Mayor Teddy Kollek and President Spencer W. Kimball led a procession to a temporary platform at the garden, the crowd spontaneously began singing "We Thank Thee, O God, for a Prophet." In his brief remarks, President Benson recalled the visit of Orson Hyde to Jerusalem in 1841, enumerated the prophecies of Elder Hyde that had been fulfilled, and

then concluded: "Jerusalem, O Jerusalem—a designation signi-
fying city of peace! Today the habitation of Jews, Moslems and
Christians—all children of God, descendants of Father Abraham.
My prayerful desire is that all who reside here and in surrounding nations will have the equanimity of soul to truly make this
the city of peace, a symbol of the brotherhood of man."[5]

Under the stress of near continuous travel, the Bensons were
holding up fairly well. Flora traveled with her husband as often
as possible. In August 1979 at a meeting in the Los Angeles
Temple Visitor's Center, she gave her first talk since the stroke
six years earlier, and Ezra was overjoyed. Others were similarly
affected by her presence and presentation. Elder S. Dilworth
Young, then director of the visitor's center, described the effect
of her talk in a letter dated August 29, 1979: "Sister Benson,
you were indeed eloquent! As you shared choice counsel and
bits from your personal life, we felt the sacredness of that
moment; and then when you moved into your delightful recital
of 'It Takes a Heap o' Livin',' you had that entire audience in
the very palm of your hand. It was a memorable occasion, and
your beautiful example of womanhood will long be cherished
by all."

As for President Benson, he had rarely felt better. On his
eightieth birthday on August 4, 1979, he recorded that he felt
like a young man. "It seems that I feel almost as strong and
active as I did when I was sixty," he wrote in his journal. His
only problem was that the injured hip bothered him some, especially if he remained seated too long. Otherwise he felt strong.

President Kimball's health, on the other hand, was not so
predictable. In September 1979, President Benson pronounced
a blessing upon the prophet's head prior to his undergoing eye
surgery. There was a sweet spirit present, and Ezra felt all would
go well. Two months later, however, the outlook was not as
hopeful. After President Kimball had surgery to relieve pressure from an accumulation of blood on the brain—the second
operation for this problem—President Benson was deeply concerned. At least twice a day alone, and usually twice with his
wife, he prayed that President Kimball's life would be length-
ened.

President Benson traveled with President Kimball to Japan in October 1980 for dedication of the Tokyo Temple and was thrilled that the prophet's voice and health grew stronger as the services went on. But by the end of 1980, the president's condition was not good, and it was beginning to look as though he might never completely recover. In May 1981, when President Kimball entered the hospital for implantation of a pacemaker, President Benson cancelled trips out of the country so he could stay close by. In March 1982 he was called to President Kimball's apartment when the prophet sank into a coma, and joined with Mark E. Petersen in administering to their leader. In tears, he offered comfort to Sister Kimball. His feelings were tender, his heart somber as he left. "I have been on my knees in the apartment since arriving home," he wrote in his journal. "I am praying that the Lord will do whatever is best for President Kimball. . . . We'd be very grateful if he could be blessed and recover to spend many more days, months, and years upon the earth in his inspiring leadership."

On several occasions President Benson was informed that the prophet's health was critical. Each time he visibly evidenced worry and even fear. He would immediately cancel his agenda for the day, go home, and, with Flora, begin to fast and pray that the Lord would preserve and sustain the prophet. The prospects of the weight of the Church wore heavy.

From 1981 on, President Kimball's health declined, and the imminent possibility of his passing was something the General Authorities lived with. As President Marion G. Romney's health also deteriorated, the weight of directing the affairs of the First Presidency fell principally upon President Gordon B. Hinckley. President Benson was eleven years older than President Hinckley and seventeen years his senior in the quorum. Said Francis M. Gibbons, secretary to the First Presidency, "I never once heard anything from President Benson other than complete subordination to President Gordon B. Hinckley. There was no attempt to supersede him in any way. President Benson's only apparent objective was to completely sustain the First Presidency of the Church." Elder Boyd K. Packer commented, "No one sustained President Hinckley more vocally and fully than did President

President Benson visits with LDS Boy Scouts at the national Scout Jamboree in Moraine Park, Pennsylvania, in 1977

Benson. When matters came to the Twelve from the First Presidency, he would say, 'Brethren, we must be about this *now.*' "

In the meantime, and despite a hip that caused him increasing pain, President Benson maintained a fast pace. He and Sister Benson traveled to Europe in the spring of 1980 to form the first stake in Austria, tour four missions in Italy, and visit Finland, where James Parker, Beverly's husband, was presiding over the Finland Helsinki Mission. The Bensons were proud of their family in Finland. Especially were they pleased with the way the Parker children spoke Finnish and were involved in missionary work.

But back in Salt Lake City, after two exhausting weeks of travel, President Benson nearly blacked out one morning while reading the Book of Mormon, and he had to be hospitalized for tests. He disliked the fuss, but he did admit to pushing himself "beyond the point of wisdom," though he made few adjustments in his routine.

Rarely, despite advanced age, did President Benson let a year pass without attending an encampment of Boy Scouts. In the summer of 1980 he visited some 2,800 LDS Scouts at the

Florida ranch, donning his olive drab, 1920-vintage Scout uniform, which he refused to exchange for a modern one. Sacrament meeting on Sunday was held in the ranch's rodeo grounds, with one hundred young men administering the sacrament. President Benson noted that he had never seen so many young men so reverent for so long.

In each visit with the Scouts, he stood for hours while the boys filed by to shake his hand. Elder Robert L. Backman frequently accompanied him on those trips. "You can't imagine," he said, "what it does to the boys to have a man of President Benson's stature show such interest in them. I've seen four thousand Boy Scouts sit spellbound as President Benson tells them his Scouting experiences, praises them and tells them how he loves them. They can feel that he does." As always, President Benson was anxious that young people have every advantage the Church could provide.

President Benson was frequently among the first of the Brethren to speak out on timely issues and trends, especially as they related to youth. He was observant of the times, and alert to challenges posed by society's humanistic trends.

Into the 1980s President Benson was concerned about some of Brigham Young University's curricula, particularly in the social sciences and other departments where various economic and political philosophies were taught. In meetings of the university's board of trustees, he offered suggestions and aired concerns about instructors, courses of study, and guest lecturers invited to campus. For example, after the leader of Utah's Communist Party was invited to lecture in several political science classes, he publicly renounced any "BYU instructor [who] grants a forum to an avowed Communist for the purpose of teaching communism on this campus. It may be done on other campuses in the United States, but it will not be done here."[6]

President Benson's interest in BYU was motivated solely by his abiding interest in youth and his desire that they receive the finest educational opportunities possible. Dallin Oaks described the kind of support President Benson gave him during his tenure as university president: "President Benson was willing to be very outspoken in the crunch, and always *for* the university. When we were in a budget crunch, he would speak for more money. When I wanted more administrative latitude, he supported me. It was not just because he loved BYU, but because he understood the issues. In my judgment, President Benson is one of the best executives we've had in the Church. As I went about clearing the appointment of deans, approving budgets, making policy on admissions, etc., it became obvious that President Benson was preeminent in his understanding of the management of a large organization.

"I remember specifically when I requested authority to carry over unexpended items at the end of the budget year. President Benson understood that quickly, but the proposition was sinking because it hadn't been done before. He took a position and argued for it all by himself and singlehandedly persuaded the board. He played the same kind of role many times. I've always felt that he was the greatest friend BYU had during that period."

There were also other ways that President Benson influenced the BYU studentbody. On Tuesday, February 26, 1980, he delivered what President Oaks called a "landmark address" and what others described as "a classic" at a BYU devotional assembly. In a message on "Fourteen Fundamentals in Following the Prophet," he talked about the calling of a living prophet. He prefaced his remarks by explaining, "To help you pass the crucial tests which lie ahead I am going to give you today several facets of a grand key which, if you will honor, will crown you with God's glory and bring you out victorious in spite of Satan's fury. Soon we will be honoring our Prophet on his eighty-fifth birthday. As a church we sing the song, 'We Thank Thee, O God, for a Prophet.' Here then is the grand key—Follow the Prophet."

President Benson taught that the prophet is the only man who speaks for the Lord, and that his words are more important than those of a deceased prophet. Further, he asserted, while it might not always be popular, a prophet is qualified to speak out on civic affairs. "The world prefers that prophets either be dead or mind their own business," he said. "Some so-called experts of political science want the prophet to be still on politics . . . [but] those who would remove prophets from politics would take God out of government."[8] He also encouraged the students to enroll in the BYU religion class "Teachings of the Living Prophets."

Some of the local media took President Benson to task for his remarks, speculating that he was setting the stage for the day when he might become president of the Church and giving the impression that he had breached the sacrosanct barrier between church and state.[8] But years earlier he had explained his view of the proper interface of religion and government: "I support the doctrine of separation of church and state as traditionally interpreted to prohibit the establishment of an official national religion. But this does not mean that we should divorce government from any formal recognition of God. To do so strikes a potentially fatal blow at the concept of the divine origin of our rights and unlocks the door for an easy entry of future tyranny."[9]

In just two weeks, over six hundred requests for copies of his BYU address came to President Benson's office, as well as hundreds of letters from Saints hailing his message as an inspiring tribute to the role of a prophet. While the talk generated a great deal of publicity, for his part President Benson had intended it to simply underscore President Kimball's prophetic call.

During the April 1980 monthly meeting of the General Authorities, President Benson explained that he had meant only to reaffirm the divine nature of the prophetic call. It was a faith-building, emotional experience. His family were aware of his concerns and had been praying for him. When he returned to his office that day, he found a phone message from Reed and a brief letter from Mark: "All will be well—we're praying for you and *know* all will be well. The Lord knows your heart." There was also a brief message from Elder Packer: "How I admire, respect and love you. How could anyone hesitate to follow a leader, an example such as you? What a privilege!"

President Benson watched the Ronald Reagan–Jimmy Carter presidential campaign with interest. As early as 1974 he had encouraged Reagan to step forward as a spokesman for the nation's conservatives.[10] In fact, Ezra had corresponded with Reagan for several years. They had shared views on a variety of issues. Immediately after Reagan's election, President Benson wrote him that he rejoiced at the election results and added, "We sense that you are a man of deep spirituality and could wish there might be regular prayer in the White House."[11] Reagan responded warmly.

Over time President Benson continued to share his views with President Reagan. In particular, he urged the president to reaffirm America's support of the Monroe Doctrine, insisting it should be central to any foreign policy on Central and South America. (In 1823 President James Monroe set forth this policy asserting that any attempt by a European power to create or maintain a colony in the Western Hemisphere would be opposed by the United States as "dangerous to our peace and safety." Joseph Fielding Smith called the Monroe Doctrine the greatest fortification in America and the "inspiration of the Almighty which rested upon . . . Thomas Jefferson and other statesmen, and which finally found authoritative expression in James Monroe."[12])

On another occasion President Benson sent Ronald Reagan lengthy passages from the Book of Mormon about America's divine destiny and concluded with his testimony: "This nation is the Lord's base of operations in these latter days. Here the gospel of Jesus Christ was restored. Here God the Father and His Son, Jesus Christ, appeared to the young man Joseph Smith, which to me is the greatest event that has transpired in this world since the resurrection of the Master." Reagan agreed America was a "specially favored land," adding, that "as long as Americans have respected spiritual leaders such as yourself, our nation will . . . do wonders in the world."[13]

President Benson continued to maintain contact with the USDA. When he was in Washington for Reagan's inaugural, he met with Reagan's Secretary of Agriculture, John R. Block. There was a fraternity, of sorts, among USDA veterans borne of shared experiences and frustrations, and Ezra Taft Benson was perhaps more highly regarded subsequent to his term as Secretary. The August 1983 issue of *Washingtonian* magazine featured him as the best Secretary of Agriculture ever. And in an article he wrote for the *Washington Post*, Secretary Block quoted from Ezra's book *Farmers at the Crossroads* and called the former

Secretary's views on surpluses sound advice. "We didn't listen then, but we must listen and act now," he warned.[14]

When Ezra and Flora came down with a violent case of twenty-four-hour flu, Reed, Mark, and Beth converged on their apartment bearing soup and an azalea plant. Unfortunately, however, the recurring and increasing pain Ezra was suffering with his hip was not as easily remedied. Almost more worrisome than the physical discomfort was his fear that he would have to stop traveling. In March 1981 Elder Mark E. Petersen administered to him. "I believe the Lord expects us to continue to do what we can on our own," Ezra wrote in a journal entry on March 29, 1981, "but I have faith that this administration will prove to be most strengthening."

In July he started a vigorous physical therapy program to strengthen his right hip and leg. But the pain persisted. It had become next to impossible for him to sit through meetings or walk distances. President Benson traveled, with pain, to Europe to organize the first stake in Italy in June 1981. At the cornerstone-laying of the Jordan River Temple on August 15, 1981, he toured the edifice by wheelchair but stood to deliver his remarks.

With a weak hip but strong convictions, he spoke forcefully on a topic of grave concern at the general women's meeting held September 26, 1981. His message contained a strong warning that mothers belonged in the home. Reaction to his message was mixed—favorable from women who applauded his defense of motherhood, and distress from others who felt his stay-at-home-mother remarks were unreasonable and out of touch with the times.

From his perspective, President Benson felt that he was only echoing the admonitions of President Kimball. At a general women's meeting on October 2, 1975, the prophet had stated, "We have often said, 'This divine service of motherhood can be rendered only by mothers.' It may not be passed to others. Nurses cannot do it; public nurseries cannot do it. Hired help cannot do it; kind relatives cannot do it. Only by mother, aided as much as may be by a loving father, brothers and sisters . . . can the full needed measure of watchful care be given."[15]

President Benson had always been an outspoken advocate of mothers staying home, but as society at large, and Latter-day Saint families in particular, increasingly joined the influx of women in the marketplace, he became alarmed. He often said there had never been a finer "crop" of children than those coming to LDS homes today—children who need their mother's undivided attention.

Again, at the dedicatory services of the monuments to women in Nauvoo in June 1978, he warned: "We hear much talk—even among some of our own sisters—about so-called 'alternative life-styles' for women. . . . Some have even been so bold as to suggest that the Church move away from the 'Mormon woman stereotype' of homemaking and rearing children. God grant that that dangerous philosophy will never take root among our Latter-day Saint women! . . . The conventional wisdom of the day would have [women] be equal with men. We say, we should not have you descend to that level. . . . *Equality* should not be confused with *equivalence*."[16]

This was a volatile topic that often attracted attention when President Benson broached it. At the October 1982 general conference, he again stated that many social ills could be traced to parents who abdicated their responsibilities at home. He did not want to alienate women, but simply to reinforce the critical message that the rearing of righteous children should be the principal aim of all parents and should take precedence over worldly desires and ambitions.[17]

Immediately following October conference in 1981, President Benson announced that a second operation, this one to implant an artificial hip, was necessary. Again with Elder Mark E. Petersen acting as voice, the Twelve administered to him—"the most impressive blessing I have ever received under the hands of my Brethren," he noted in his journal. "There have been many times, in meetings of the Twelve, when the windows of heaven almost seemed to be open. This was one of those special occasions."

The three-hour hip athroplasty was successful, and once again Ezra began a long, painful recovery. When he left the hospital, he and Flora once again moved in with Beth and David, so Beth could give her father full-time care and David could keep a physician's eye on him. After six weeks he felt up to moving home, and he and Flora went back to their condominium. But soon thereafter he took a fall in his office, resulting in a hairline fracture to the pelvis that sent him back to the hospital for two weeks.

At that point Ezra and Flora accepted David and Beth's invitation to move in with their family indefinitely. Ezra and Flora had previously determined to divide their furniture and other belongings among the six children. Most of the furniture went to the girls, and Reed and Mark divided the voluminous library. Over the years Ezra had watched his children defer to each other as possessions were distributed. With most of their material possessions disposed of, and with Ezra and Flora requiring frequent assistance, Beth and David's offer was providential and practical. By February 1982 Ezra was almost entirely free of pain, and a few months later he resumed the schedule he had abandoned while recovering from surgery.

While President Benson's calling took him throughout the Church, there were certain areas that seemed to draw his special attention. Kirtland, Ohio, was one of them. In October 1982 he traveled there to dedicate the Kirtland Ward meetinghouse. He also toured the Kirtland Temple, where the president of the Kirtland stake of the Reorganized Church of Jesus Christ of Latter Day Saints, Sebe Morgan, invited him to offer a prayer. President Benson turned to the man responsible for overseeing the temple to ask if that was his wish also. Finding that it was, he offered a prayer in which he prayed for good relations between the two churches, paid tribute to those who had sacrificed to build the temple, and thanked the Lord for his witness that the Savior of the world had appeared there. Later Sebe Morgan said he was "impressed by the sweetness, dignity, and appropriateness of what President Benson said," and also called attention to the fact that President Benson had been solicitous of the man who oversaw the temple.[18]

The next day President Benson dedicated the Kirtland Ward meetinghouse. In October 1979 when he had presided at the groundbreaking of this building, he had referred to a prophecy in the Doctrine and Covenants (124:83) that stated Kirtland would be scourged after the Saints left, but would be rebuilt later. "I think that this prophecy is being fulfilled today," he had said then. "We have a great day ahead of us. I'm sure of it. . . . The Lord is looking in on the people of this community."[19] (Since then, the Kirtland Stake has been created, a new mission has been formed in the area, nonmember descendants of early Latter-day Saints have been baptized, and new wards have been organized.)

In the spring of 1983 President and Sister Benson took a quick trip to Europe and the Middle East, stopping in Jerusalem long enough to confer with local government officials, who promised to alleviate bureaucratic delays with BYU's plans to build an educational center near the Mount of Olives. They also visited Reed and his family, who were spending six months in Israel while Reed was an instructor in BYU's study-abroad program.

That year President Benson enjoyed a diverse array of activities. He spoke in five sessions of the Atlanta Temple dedication and offered the dedicatory prayer in five others during June. On July 4, he served as grand marshal of the Freedom Festival in Provo and led the parade along a route lined with some 150,000 people. And in November, he was deeply moved when the Utah Farm Bureau and Salt Lake Area Chamber of Commerce honored him for "distinguished service to the people of the world through American agriculture." Representing the Church, President Gordon B. Hinckley saluted his colleague and summarized his contribution to the Church and the nation. "It is a long and interesting odyssey from Whitney, Idaho, to the Oval Room of the White House," he began. "His is a fascinating chronicle of a little boy on an Idaho farm who became Secretary of Agriculture. . . . His is a remarkable epic of faith and faithfulness. . . . Loyalty to leadership is of the very essence of his character. Loyalty to principle is of the very fiber of his being. . . . All of us who have worked with him have known the gentle side of his nature. . . . Unsparing in the use of his own strength, he has sought to lift burdens from the backs of others of us. I know of no man more considerate of his associates or more concerned for their well-being. He does not ask others to do that which he is unwilling to do himself, but rather sets an example of service for others of us to follow." President Benson was so overwhelmed by President Hinckley's tribute that he struggled to hold back the tears.[20]

The centennial celebration of the Logan Temple in May 1984 produced more tender moments as he recalled childhood experiences. He still remembered his Grandfather Benson telling about the first load of rock that was hauled in for the temple. Ezra's heritage was priceless to him, as President Hinckley had noted in his tribute at the Utah Farm Bureau banquet: "President Benson's forebears were of the highest quality. His grandparents were among those who gave their hearts with deep conviction to an unpopular cause. . . . They were winnowed as grain on the threshing floor. . . . When others fell away, they remained true. . . . I see in President Benson the qualities of his remarkable pioneer forebears."

And there were other kinds of happy reflections. In July 1984 President Benson joined other former Secretaries of Agriculture at the White House to commemorate the thirtieth anniversary of the International Food for Peace program. President Reagan paid special tribute to him for having the foresight to launch the program. The trip to Washington also allowed Ezra and Flora time with Beverly and Jim and their children. They reminisced and sang songs around the grand piano in the elegant presidential suite provided for them in the J. W. Marriott Hotel—accommodations "too nice for a farm boy," Ezra told Bill Marriott on the phone that day.

August 4, 1984, marked President Benson's eighty-fifth birthday and a family reunion celebrated the occasion. In many ways, it didn't seem possible to Ezra that he had lived that long. His mobility wasn't quite what it had been ten years earlier, but he was still strong and alert. In fact, he and Flora had moved out of Beth's home a year earlier and were enjoying a condominium in Canyon Road Towers just a block from the Church Office Building.

Of course, there were also concerns and difficulties. President Benson continued to closely monitor world events, and what he saw worried him. Nevertheless, the time for speaking out on political and economic ideologies was not right. The expansive growth of the Church throughout the world, especially with so many various forms of government in operation, made it inappropriate at the time. But within his own family he minced no words. In one family letter he counseled, "Certain bloodlines seem to have the spirit of freedom in their veins. Mother and I are grateful that each of our children has that spirit of freedom . . . and have a love for this country and understand its divine destiny. Make your contribution where you will, but make it."[21] Many family members followed suit in various ways. Some distributed campaign literature and worked at the polls on election day. Other took leadership roles in local party organizations, attended constitutional study groups, or participated in mass meetings and state party conventions.

When it came to challenging his family to serve, Ezra Taft Benson knew whereof he spoke. For nearly eight decades he had been making contributions within the Church, in the privacy of his own family, and throughout the world. With all that he had seen, accomplished, and experienced, nothing was more precious to him than his deep conviction and witness of the divinity of the Savior's mission. He bore testimony of this knowledge again and again, as he did in one general conference address: "With all my soul, I love Him. I humbly testify that he is the same loving, compassionate Lord today as when He walked the dusty roads of Palestine. He is close to His servants on this earth. He cares about and loves each of us today. Of that you can be assured. He lives today as our Lord, our Master, our Savior, our Redeemer, and our God. God bless us all to believe in Him, to accept Him, to worship Him, and to fully trust in Him, and to follow Him."[22]

With each year, it seemed, President Benson was vividly reminded of his age and mortality as dear friends and lifelong associates passed away. On November 27, 1982, President N. Eldon Tanner, his "dear friend and colleague," as he wrote in his journal, died. President Benson represented the Twelve in delivering a tribute at the funeral.

Less than two months later, on January 11, 1983, Elder LeGrand Richards died, and a year to the day later, the man whom he had sat next to in the quorum for forty years, Mark

E. Petersen, passed on. At the funeral service, as well as in his journal, President Benson revealed his deep emotion. "I feel close to each member of the Twelve," he said, "but there has been something special in the relationship I have had with Elder Mark E. Petersen. . . . I love this man as I have loved few men in this world."

Little more than a year later, Elder Bruce R. McConkie succumbed to cancer. Elder Russell M. Nelson was with President Benson in New England when they received word, and he observed how President Benson took the news. "It was as though he'd lost his own brother," Elder Nelson said. "For him it was a very deep personal loss. I calculated then that he had seen over twenty of his brothers in the Quorum of the Twelve pass on while he remained, and I thought that if he'd gone through that kind of mourning for each one, it was a heavy load for him to bear."

At Elder McConkie's funeral President Benson said, "I love Bruce R. McConkie with all my soul. I loved to hear him preach the gospel. We shall miss him. Oh, how he will be missed!"

Then in August 1985 President Benson lost another dear friend when J. Willard Marriott died. At the funeral, he joined Gordon B. Hinckley, Richard M. Nixon, Boyd K. Packer, and Billy Graham in eulogizing the founder of the Marriott empire. President Benson called him "a giant of a man." Then just three months later his brother Ross died. The graveside service in Whitney, Idaho, was a sobering experience.

With President Kimball's health now very tenuous and Marion G. Romney also afflicted with the disabilities of old age, President Benson often felt very alone. In June 1985, during a time when President Gordon B. Hinckley and Elder Thomas S. Monson were in Europe dedicating temples in Freiberg, the German Democratic Republic, and in Stockholm, and breaking ground for a new temple in Frankfurt, he revealed his feelings in his journal: "I feel very deeply how I miss President Hinckley and the Brethren who have scattered somewhat. . . . I hope they will have the protecting hand of the Lord over them. . . . I constantly pray for them."

He had hoped to travel to Ireland to dedicate that country for the preaching of the gospel, but cancelled plans when it was

President Benson greets President Spencer W. Kimball at the prophet's last general conference, October 1985

Courtesy of Daily Universe, Brigham Young University

determined the trip might be too dangerous. "It appears that I am so well known," he wrote, "and would be one of the first to be attacked if there was any danger of a serious nature. . . . I am content to be close at home and will attend various functions in the United States and Canada as time permits."

Since 1983 President Kimball's health had been very unpredictable, and on more than one occasion President Benson had feared the prophet would not live through the night. But always he had rebounded, and had even attended meetings in the temple with the Twelve and some sessions of general conference.

President Benson also wondered if he wouldn't precede President Kimball in death. But this was not to be. On the evening of November 5, 1985, he received word. The prophet, beloved by Saints throughout the world, the man he had loved and respected through forty-two years of service, was gone.

Though this possibility had been imminent for so long, it seemed inconceivable even to consider the implications. He and Flora immediately dropped to their knees. The day they had dared not think about, the day they had even dreaded, had arrived.

*"I bless you with increased understanding of the
Book of Mormon. I promise you that . . . . if we will
daily sup from its pages and abide by its precepts,
God will pour out . . . . a blessing hither to unknown."*

Chapter 23

The Prophet of the Lord

F ew would argue that, over the years, Ezra Taft Benson
had been through a refining process—one unique in its
intensity and scope to the select few who become president of the Church. His life had been a rigorous, intense
schooling process. He had been in the Church's governing council for forty-two years. The difficulty and demands of some of
his assignments had transcended the norm—particularly his
eleven-month emergency mission to war-torn Europe in 1946
and his eight years as Eisenhower's Secretary of Agriculture.
Perhaps no General Authority in the Church's history had
achieved such depth and breadth of international prominence
and respect.

Through it all, Ezra Taft Benson had become known as a
man of integrity, a man who stood firm for principle—at all
costs.

For several days prior to November 5, 1985, President
Kimball's health had deteriorated substantially. Daily President
Benson was apprised of the prophet's condition. He was emotional when he called one son to tell him it looked as though
the prophet would not live long.

The evening of November 5, shortly after 10:00 P.M., the phone call announcing President Kimball's passing came. President Benson was overcome with emotion. He felt physically weak as the realization of the mantle, the burden that now fell on his shoulders, washed over him. In his journal he recorded, "I have never felt weaker and never before have I felt the influence of the Spirit in such great strength. . . . May the good Lord sustain me as I go forward humbly. I think it can be truthfully said, I will never acknowledge the Lord's hand as I have the last few hours."

How he loved Spencer W. Kimball! How often he and Flora had pleaded with the Lord to preserve the prophet's life! How he had marveled at the masterful spiritual leadership President Kimball had given, and at the Church's dramatic growth at his hand! And while it had been impossible to ignore the fact that he was next in the line of succession, in his heart President Benson had not expected the call to come.

But there was little time for reflection. Automatically the attention turned to him as responsibility for carrying the Church forward fell on his shoulders.

Shortly thereafter Mark talked with his father. The tone in President Benson's voice was different than Mark had ever heard—as though a tangible load had been placed on his shoulders.

Announcement of President Kimball's death made the late-evening news in the Salt Lake City area and within hours had traveled worldwide. That first night President Benson's telephone rang most of the night. "I got about two hours of sleep—[everyone] wanting to speak kind words on the matter. All of the children called and assured me they would be fasting and praying for me," he recorded.

The Brethren sought also to assure him of their support and love. And family members called and wrote letters filled with encouragement and love.

Newspapers around the world carried news of President Kimball's death and the imminent appointment of Ezra Taft Benson as the Church's new spiritual leader. The coverage wasn't necessarily more extensive for President Benson than his predecessors, but much of it was distinctive in tone and approach.

Some journalists focused on his political career and ideologies, nearly ignoring his forty-two years of spiritual leadership as a member of the Twelve and reporting as though it were a political appointment, when the opposite was true.

There was no question but that the Lord, in calling President Kimball home, had spoken, and that if President Benson, as the senior apostle, was named president of the Church, it would be because the Lord had selected him as His mouthpiece.

Several years earlier President Kimball had explained: "It is reassuring to know that [a new president is] . . . not elected through committees and conventions with all their conflicts, criticisms, and by the vote of men, but [is] called of God and then sustained by the people. . . . The pattern divine allows for no errors, no conflicts, no ambitions, no ulterior motives. The Lord has reserved for himself the calling of his leaders over his Church."[1]

On Saturday, November 9, President Benson conducted impressive and touching funeral services for President Kimball. He called President Kimball a "star of the first magnitude," and eulogized the late prophet as a "noble and great one," a "prophet of God to the nations of the world." President Benson then put his predecessor's service in perspective: "When the history of this dispensation is recorded, the administration of President Spencer Woolley Kimball will be seen as one of the most progressive in the history of the Church." He concluded, "May we all learn from the life of President Kimball what it means to fight the good fight, to finish one's course, and to keep the faith, that a crown of righteousness may be laid up for all of us."

Now it was time for the Kingdom to move on.

The next afternoon, Sunday, thirteen of the fourteen men sustained as prophets, seers, and revelators convened at 3:00 P.M. in an upper room in the Salt Lake Temple to effect reorganization of the First Presidency. (Elder Marion G. Romney's poor health prohibited him from attending.) President Benson went early to the temple to pray. His demeanor was solemn; he seemed preoccupied. As the meeting convened, he told the Brethren in a voice trembling with emotion that he had never antic-

Courtesy of Daily Universe, Brigham Young University

President Ezra Taft Benson, center, with his counselors in the First Presidency: Gordon B. Hinckley, left, and Thomas S. Monson

ipated this day—that he had felt Harold B. Lee would be the last prophet he would know and serve under on earth.

President Benson was subsequently set apart as president of the Church. He then indicated his desire that Elders Gordon B. Hinckley and Thomas S. Monson serve as his first and second counselors, respectively. Marion G. Romney was named president of the Twelve, with Howard W. Hunter acting president. President Hunter was the mouthpiece as members of the quorum laid their hands on President Benson's head and ordained him the thirteenth president of The Church of Jesus Christ of Latter-day Saints.

Seven of the Twelve were participating in their first reorganization. Elder M. Russell Ballard had been a member of the quorum for only one month. He later said, "The most impressive and spiritual confirmation that came to me is when I was invited to lay my hands on President Benson's head with the other members of the Twelve as President Hunter ordained him. That was a special, spiritual experience, one that confirmed to me without reservation or question that the Lord's will was being accomplished by President Benson being set apart as president of the Church." Later referring to the experience of sustaining a prophet, President Gordon B. Hinckley said, "It is miraculous in its simplicity. It is beautiful in its execution. It is divine in its method." And Elder Neal A. Maxwell relayed to President Benson his conviction that "the hands we placed upon you in the temple were simply a reenactment of other hands placed upon your head a long, long time ago."[2]

Elder David B. Haight described the reorganization: "After much fasting and prayer, and the seeking of personal revelation to know the mind and will of God, it was confirmed to our souls who should be called—even Ezra Taft Benson. This I know!"[3]

That evening, when President and Sister Benson attended the Churchwide Young Women Fireside and joined enthusiastically in singing "Carry On" with the audience, President Benson did so as president of the Church, though that announcement had not yet been made. The capacity audience in the Salt Lake Tabernacle, however, stood in respect for the senior apostle as he entered. He almost seemed surprised at the display, and quickly motioned everyone to be seated.

The Benson children attended the satellite broadcast of the fireside at their respective stake centers. Beth recalled, "As I watched the large video screen and saw Dad enter the meeting, I felt such a sweet and reassuring witness flow through my body that here was the prophet of the Lord. I knew he had the power of a true prophet of God in him. I could not stop the tears from flowing."

The following morning, members of the media gathered at the Church Administration Building to learn details of the reorganization at a press conference. Reading a prepared statement, and in a voice brimming with emotion, President Benson declared that this was a day he had not anticipated. "My wife, Flora, and I have prayed continually that President Kimball's days would be prolonged on this earth, and another miracle performed on his behalf." Then he added, "Now that the Lord has spoken, we will do our best, under his guiding direction, to move the work forward in the earth. We shall miss President Kimball so very much."

Indicating the direction their administration would take, President Benson said, "My heart has been filled with an overwhelming love and compassion for all members of the Church and our Heavenly Father's children everywhere. I love all of our Father's children of every color, creed, and political persuasion." He continued, "Some have expectantly inquired about the direction the Church will take in the future. May we suggest that the Lord, through President Kimball, has sharply focused on the threefold mission of the Church: to preach the gospel, to perfect the Saints, and to redeem the dead. We shall continue every effort to carry out this mission." He also said he would stress the importance of strong homes and family life, and then bore testimony of the Savior: "We should like to reaffirm to all the world that The Church of Jesus Christ of Latter-day Saints is led by our Lord and Savior Jesus Christ."[4]

Response to the announcement that Ezra Taft Benson was now president of the Church was immediate—and global. Letters of praise and commendation flooded his office. They came from General Authorities, stake presidents recalling personal experiences with him, members who had met him as he traveled the Church, mothers and fathers, missionaries in the field, family members, children, politicians, and world and religious leaders he had associated with for decades. Friends from the National Boy Scouts of America, the U.S. Department of Agriculture, the Farm Bureau, Corn Products International, and many other organizations wrote to congratulate him.

The following responses are characteristic:

"Your total dedication to the Lord's work, your deep spirituality throughout your life and your great administrative ability will lead the Church to new heights of achievement."—Elder Joseph B. Wirthlin of the First Quorum of the Seventy.

"May this . . . mark the beginning of the fulfillment of Ezekiel's prophecy regarding the joining together of the 'two sticks.' "—David Horowitz, president, United Israel World Union.

"I know how disappointed [Dad] must be not to have lived to sustain you as our prophet."—J. Willard Marriott, Jr.

"This office is a fitting tribute to your unwavering devotion to your faith and your dedication to the word of God."—President Ronald Reagan.[5]

As pouches of mail were delivered daily those first weeks, it became evident that the Saints viewed Ezra Taft Benson as a man of strength and conviction and welcomed him as their prophet. While Latter-day Saints had universally felt great love for Spencer W. Kimball, there was now a renewed spirit throughout the Church as a new First Presidency presided.

President Benson took the helm of an organization that had experienced rapid growth and prosperity during President Kimball's twelve-year administration. Membership had increased from 3,306,000 to nearly 6 million (5,910,496 as of December 31, 1985) in 1582 stakes and 188 missions. Twenty-one temples were dedicated during that period, with eleven more completed, planned, or under construction.

Over 40 percent of the Church's membership had joined the Church during President Kimball's administration; and while some members had followed Ezra Taft Benson's career closely for years, more had not. Converts were largely unfamiliar with his background. Suddenly throughout the Church many gospel teachers anxious to learn more about the prophet taught lessons on the lives of Ezra Taft and Flora Benson. And that spawned yet another avalanche of mail. Letters from children, in particular, pleased President Benson. One little girl from San Jose, California, even asked if her family couldn't have dinner with him when they visited Utah. Another girl wrote, "I love to sing Primary songs and one of my favorites is 'Latter-day Prophets.' . . . We don't sing it any more in Primary because no one knows how to fit you in. . . . Could you write to the Church publishers and ask them to fit you in?" And a boy asked, "Can a boy become a prophet when he grows up? I respect you very much because you talk with God."

At eighty-six, President Benson was the second oldest man to succeed to the Presidency (Joseph Fielding Smith was ninety-three when he was ordained president in 1970). In recent years, partly due to two hip operations, he had started to slow down. At times his memory had momentarily failed him. Just a month earlier, during October general conference, he had labored while delivering his address and had appeared almost fragile. Friends had asked his children if their father was well. And he had suffered momentary dizzy spells, during which he had struggled to speak for a time. At least twice as president of the Twelve he had been hospitalized briefly for these setbacks. On both occasions his physician had warned him that he was running faster than he had the strength.

But with his call as president, family members and others close to him noticed a change. Staff members were amazed at his physical and mental rejuvenation. Mark Benson told his children that their grandfather's body had literally been renewed.[6] On Sunday afternoon, November 10, just before the Twelve convened in the Salt Lake Temple to reorganize the First Presidency, Beverly telephoned her parents from Virginia. When the voice of a young man answered the phone, she assumed her call had been routed to a Church security officer. "Is this President Benson's apartment?" she asked. "Who is this?" the man responded. "This is his daughter, Beverly. May I speak to my father?" "This *is* your father," President Benson answered. Beverly was taken aback. Her father sounded like a much younger man. "It was a witness to me that the Lord was blessing Dad and giving him the vigor and strength to carry on," she said.

The orthopedic surgeon who had operated on President Benson's hip was summoned to the president's office a few months later. The surgeon related, "I hurried down and as I walked into his office . . . he came out to greet me with a spry step and a big smile. I was absolutely astonished by the change in his appearance—his quick and steady gait."[7]

The Church moved on as members of the new First Presidency familiarized themselves with the weighty matters confronting them on a daily basis. President Thomas S. Monson described the administrative pattern their presidency followed: "President Benson grasps quickly matters which come to his attention. He doesn't need to consider an item at great length before he finds the inspiration of the Lord directing him in a decision. With the expansive nature of the Church today, throughout the world, and with the multitude of matters that come before the First Presidency, this ability to cut through detail and get to the heart of the issue is vital to carrying out the administrative work of the Church."

The matters that came to their attention were varied. Temples were dedicated in Korea, Peru, and Argentina; and ground was broken for temples in Las Vegas and Portland. The missionary force surpassed 30,005 (March 1986); and while he was grateful for those who were serving, President Benson said there weren't nearly enough. President Monson organized the 1600th stake of the Church on June 22, 1986, in Toronto. The translation of the Book of Mormon into the seventieth language was completed. The First Presidency issued a statement opposing gambling, including the legalization and/or government sponsorship of lotteries. And they also announced a policy change authorizing the issuing of temple recommends to worthy members married to an unendowed spouse.

Many Saints from around the world wrote emotional letters thanking President Benson for opening the temple to them. As one woman explained, "I express the gratitude that only those who have been denied something for a long time can understand. . . . I will always remember you as the Prophet who opened the temple doors for me."

At general conference in October 1986, the First Presidency announced that all stake seventies quorums were to be discontinued, and that now all priesthood holders, not just seventies, were responsible for teaching the gospel. This change was prompted by the desire that Church members take a more active role in missionary work.[8]

During the first few weeks of his administration President Benson stayed close to home. He was delighted when a Salt Lake City family presented Flora with a 14-karat gold watch crafted by her father, Carl C. Amussen. On December 1, 1985, he spoke at the annual First Presidency Christmas devotional, and later that month the First Presidency hosted an open house for Salt Lake City area religious leaders. It was the first such reception held.

Almost immediately President Benson and his counselors began to address themes that would become important in their Presidency. In their 1985 Christmas message they proclaimed that peace could be found only in the Savior, and then stretched out a welcoming hand: "To those who are lonely, we extend the hand of friendship and fellowship. We invite you to become one with us in worship and in the service of the Master."⁹ And then, just before Christmas, they issued a special statement, which they called an invitation to come back: "We encourage Church members to forgive those who may have wronged them. To those who have ceased activity and to those who have become critical, we say, 'Come back. Come back and feast at the table of the Lord.' "¹⁰

Repeatedly in his addresses as prophet, President Benson issued challenges or opportunities, and then added, "You can do it, I *know you can*." He believed in the Saints, and he wanted them to know so.

On January 4, 1986, President and Sister Benson traveled to Washington, D. C., to install a new temple presidency and divide the Annandale Virginia Stake (the twenty-seventh stake in the same geographic area he had presided over as president of the first stake in Washington). Though he was, in many ways, returning home, the outpouring of love that met him and Sister Benson took them by surprise. Many Saints came hours early to get a seat in the Annandale Stake Center. Some had driven from as far away as New York to attend. Chairs were set up in every available room, but hundreds had to be turned away.

As President Benson entered the stake center Sunday morning, many of the Saints wept openly. He had a commanding physical presence. He looked like a prophet. When he stood to address the congregation, he said, "My wife just said to me, 'I'll be praying for you.' So under those circumstances I don't know how I can fail." Then he delivered a message that would become a recurring theme of his presidency as he bore testimony of the power of the Book of Mormon to change lives and lead people to Christ. The congregation was visibly moved by his spirited challenge that they study this book of scripture. (A few months later President Benson received a booklet with some five hundred names of members of the stake who had pledged to complete the Book of Mormon by a certain date. And over time he would receive hundreds of similar commitments from wards, stakes, and missions.) Of this stake conference President Benson wrote in his journal, "The spirit of the meeting was electric. The Saints were warm and my feelings tender as I shook hands with the many families and children."

It was President Benson's first experience among people as prophet, and the Saints' eagerness to see him, shake hands with him, hear from him, and be near him humbled him to tears. It was also the first time he was sustained by members in his presence, and that was a tender moment. As the congregation sang "We Thank Thee, O God, for a Prophet," tears welled in his eyes. (Often he would say when that song was sung that it made him think of Joseph Smith and all of the prophets.) The overwhelming expression of support and love was unlike anything he had ever experienced.

His own family noticed the difference. Members of Jim and Beverly Parker's family, whose stake was being divided, were perhaps taken aback as their father and grandfather arrived in Washington. Even during his cabinet days, he had not been accompanied by such an entourage. Surrounded by the press, he moved in a small caravan. TV cameras whirred every time he entered or exited a building. And even as President and Sister Benson enjoyed a family dinner at the Parkers' home afterwards, members of the press requested time with them.

While in Washington, President Benson met with Chief Justice Warren Burger, chairman of the committee to celebrate the bicentennial of the U.S. Constitution; hand-delivered a letter to President Reagan outlining the Church's contribution of some $10 million in 1985 to aid world hunger and presented him with a personalized edition of the new Church hymnbook; and paid courtesy calls on Vice-President George Bush, FBI director William Webster, and Richard Schubert of the American Red Cross. This first trip out among the Saints was exhilarating for President and Sister Benson.[11]

On Saturday following their return from Washington, President Benson fainted. Paramedics rushed him to LDS Hospital, where, after two hours of examination, he was moved to the coronary-care unit. Tests revealed no cardiovascular difficulties, and by that evening he was asking that his glasses and scriptures be brought to him. On Monday he was released.

Official White House Photo

In January 1986 President Benson paid a courtesy call on U.S. President Ronald Reagan in the Oval Office and reported on the Church's contribution of $10 million to aid world hunger

It proved only a minor interruption in what was building into a crusade—President Benson's advocacy of the Book of Mormon. Everywhere he went, he talked about the power of that book: at a regional conference in El Paso, to 8,000; in San Antonio, to 6,000; in Salt Lake City, to 6,000; in Laie, Hawaii, to 6,000; on the slopes of the Hill Cumorah in upstate New York, to 8,000; in Provo, to 16,000; in San Bernardino, California, to 12,000. During his first year as president, he delivered some twenty major addresses on the Book of Mormon. In a temple meeting of the General Authorities in early February 1986, President Hinckley told the Brethren that President Benson would become the Church's greatest proponent of the Book of Mormon.[12]

President Benson's emphasis on the Book of Mormon was nothing new. For years he had quoted the scripture teaching that the Church was under condemnation for taking that book of scripture lightly. (See Doctrine and Covenants 84:54–57.) In 1979 the history and religion librarian at BYU's Harold B. Lee

Library conducted a study of the scriptures that had been quoted in general conferences from April 1950 to April 1978. The research revealed that of the fifty scriptures quoted most often, only three were from the Book of Mormon. President Benson had quoted the Book of Mormon more frequently than the Bible.[13]

In the 1975 April general conference he had delivered what some religious scholars called the finest address ever given on the Book of Mormon. Titled "The Book of Mormon Is the Word of God," the address was considered so powerful by the BYU Department of Religious Instruction that tens of thousands of copies have been distributed to Book of Mormon classes on campus.[14] And it was this theme, in the main, that President Benson repeated from one regional conference to the next. Often, as he did at the conference of the Butler and Sandy East regions held in the Salt Lake Tabernacle in November 1986, he made no apology for the repetition—"because the Saints need it." Repeatedly he counseled the Saints to "make the study of the Book of Mormon a lifetime pursuit."

While perhaps many Latter-day Saints didn't realize how frequent President Benson's admonitions on this subject had been, others did. After the funeral of Elder Bruce R. McConkie, a son of Elder McConkie's wrote President Benson to thank him for the eulogy he had delivered, adding, "From one soldier out in the field who thrills every time I hear you testify of the Book of Mormon, an honest and enduring thank you."[15]

Within the councils of the Church, President Benson had been a persistent advocate of making the Book of Mormon the focal point of proselyting.[16] The Book of Mormon, he taught, was compiled by those who foresaw the latter days and who abridged centuries of records, selecting events, stories, and speeches that would be most helpful to Saints of the latter days. It would bring men to Christ; it would expose the enemies of Christ; it would testify that Joseph Smith was a prophet. And in a troubled world filled with uncertainty, it bore another witness of the Savior and His mission.

President Benson had been equally emphatic with members of his own family. He often wrote exhorting them to study the Book of Mormon daily in their homes. One letter to a grand-

Following the Solemn Assembly in April 1986, the family gathered in President and Sister Benson's apartment

son was typical: "Be sure you read the Book of Mormon each day, if you can. Grandma and I have just started reading it together again. We just finished First Nephi this morning. It is a great book for our time. The Prophets saw our day and they gave us the counsel which they felt we would need."[17] He and Flora set the standard by following their own counsel; in addition, each month they sent dozens of copies of the Book of Mormon, with their photograph and personal testimony, to be used in missionary work.

In a meeting of the General Authorities in March 1986, President Benson explained that he felt moved upon, in the same way President Lorenzo Snow had felt moved upon about tithing, to preach the Book of Mormon. He asked the Brethren to reread the book before April conference.

It was at that April 1986 general conference that President Benson took his Book of Mormon challenge to the entire Church. In his first address to the general membership as president of the Church, he admonished the Saints to cleanse the inner vessel by being morally clean, by conquering pride, and by reading the Book of Mormon. "Watchmen—what of the night? We must respond by saying that all is not well in Zion. As Moroni counseled, we must cleanse the inner vessel, beginning first with ourselves, then with our families, and finally with the Church," he counseled. And he proclaimed that the Book of Mormon is a

493

key in doing so. "We can do it," he reiterated. "I know we can."[18]

In his second address to the general membership, this one during the Solemn Assembly in which he was sustained the thirteenth president of the Church, he emotionally thanked those who had sustained him and then spoke from the heart, declaring, "I have been aware of those who preceded me in this office as president of the Church. I have felt very keenly my own dependence upon the Lord and the absolute necessity of relying upon Him for His direction in the conduct of the affairs of the Church." He then made a personal plea: "If there be any divison among us, let us set aside anything of this kind and join ranks in the great responsibility to move forward the work of the Lord. If there be those who have become disaffected, we reach out to you . . . and stand ready to assist and welcome you back in full fellowship and activity in the Church."

Then he put in context his pleadings about the Book of Mormon: "The Lord inspired His servant Lorenzo Snow to reemphasize the principle of tithing to redeem the Church from financial bondage. . . . Now, in our day, the Lord has revealed the need to reemphasize the Book of Mormon."

And he bore powerful testimony and left an unmistakable blessing on the people: "I want you to know that I know that Christ is at the helm. This is His world. This is His Church. His purposes will be fulfilled. . . . I invoke my blessing upon the Latter-day Saints and upon good people everywhere. I bless you with increased discernment to judge between Christ and anti-Christ. I bless you with increased power to do good and to resist evil. I bless you with increased *understanding* of the Book of Mormon. I promise you that from this moment forward, if we will daily sup from its pages and abide by its precepts, God will pour out upon each child of Zion and the Church a blessing hitherto unknown—and we will plead to the Lord that He will begin to lift the condemnation—the scourge and judgment."[19]

Saints around the world took President Benson's admonition about the Book of Mormon to heart. Seminary and institute classes made reading the Book of Mormon a project; stake organizations emphasized it in training seminars; bishops inau-

President and Sister Benson share a private moment during a visit to Hawaii in May 1986

Church News Photograph

gurated reading programs in their wards. And, judging from hundreds of letters he received from children and adults alike, many families began reading it regularly at home.

Everywhere he went, President Benson talked about the Book of Mormon—at missionary and stake conferences, at regional conferences, in meetings with the Brethren. Imagine the good that would come, he said, if the entire church turned its attention to the Book of Mormon. His message was taken seriously. In the calendar year 1986 over 3 million copies of the Book of Mormon were sold. More copies of the English version (1,693,000) were sold that year than during the years 1982, 1983, and 1984 combined (1,467,000). Nearly 700,000 more English copies of the book were sold in 1986 than the year previous.[20]

A Spanish ward in the Glendale California Stake placed advertisements offering complimentary copies of the Book of

Mormon to those who requested them. Of those who responded to the ad, over 80 percent were baptized. Missionaries in the Florida Tallahassee Mission placed more copies of the book than ever before, and in May 1986 the mission had its best baptizing month in two years. In November 1986 missionaries in the Puerto Rico San Juan Mission placed more copies of the Book of Mormon than were placed before and had more convert baptisms than in any previous November.[21]

Seminaries and institutes throughout southern California launched a "We Have Met the Challenge" program, referring to President Benson's challenge to read the Book of Mormon daily. All who met the challenge—some 5,000 young people—were invited to a special fireside with the prophet on February 8, 1987, in the Anaheim Convention Center.

In October 1986 general conference, President Benson again urged members to launch a lifelong study of the Book of Mormon. He promised, "It is not just that the Book of Mormon teaches us truth, though it indeed does that. It is not just that it bears testimony of Christ, though it indeed does that, too. . . . There is a power in the book which will begin to flow into your lives the moment you begin a serious study of the book."[22]

The Brethren also began to reflect the prophet's counsel in their sermons. In April 1987 general conference, one after another of the General Authorities used the Book of Mormon as their text. When Elder L. Tom Perry stood to speak he began, "President, I'm starting to receive the distinct impression that we've been listening to you. I, too, will take my text from the Book of Mormon."[23]

As he traveled throughout the United States, President Benson visited as many Church historic sites as he could manage.

In March 1986 he and Sister Benson participated in the groundbreaking of the Hiram Branch meetinghouse in Ohio at the site of the historic John Johnson home. While there they visited the Kirtland Temple, where they were hosted by members of the Reorganized Church of Jesus Christ of Latter Day Saints. During brief services in the temple, President Benson was invited to offer a prayer, which he did in a manner that visibly affected the group.

Then they went to the Whitney Store, where President Benson addressed some seventy individuals, many of them seated in the room where the School of the Prophets was held. This meeting commemorated the final steps in the organization of the first First Presidency on March 18, 1833. Here President Benson's extemporaneous remarks centered on missionary work. Stating that only one-third of the young men of missionary age were serving missions, he said, "This is not enough. Here in this sacred room, I know the Lord expects more of us."[24]

Only weeks after his visit, a fire destroyed the Kirtland Stake Center. The mayor of Kirtland wrote President Benson, "While one type of flame consumed your dwelling, please be assured that another flame, one of renewal, burns even brighter in Kirtland." Immediately offers came from members and nonmembers in the community to help rebuild the church.[25]

In August 1986, President Benson visited three sites central to the Restoration. Accompanied by Sister Benson, he toured the Sacred Grove, the Hill Cumorah, and the Peter Whitmer farm.

Two hundred missionaries from the New York Rochester Mission waited quietly in the Sacred Grove for the Bensons to arrive and stood as they walked into the clearing. President Benson's words took on additional meaning as he spoke from that place. "You're here among the trees where, except for the resurrection of the Master, the greatest demonstration of the power of God took place," he said with emotion. As he spoke, others visiting the grove recognized his voice echoing through the trees and were thrilled to find the prophet there. By the time he finished, a large group had gathered, and they sang "We Thank Thee, O God, for a Prophet" as he and Sister Benson left. Parents hoisted their young children on their shoulders for a better view of the prophet.

That evening visitors to the Hill Cumorah Pageant were surprised when the Bensons arrived, and tens of thousands stood, breaking into thunderous applause as they walked past. The next morning, Sunday, he addressed several thousand Saints gathered on the slopes of the Hill Cumorah. People sat on benches, lawn chairs, and blankets to hear him. Standing a short distance from the hill where Joseph Smith received the gold plates from which the Book of Mormon was translated, President Benson concluded his remarks, "I bear my witness that the Book of Mormon is verily true. I know this as I know I live."

As with previous prophets, one of President Benson's primary areas of focus was missionary work. Few subjects affected him more emotionally. For years he had gone to great lengths to attend the farewells and homecomings of family members serving as missionaries or mission presidents. And as president of the Church, he singled out missionaries wherever he went.

President Benson not only preached missionary work and the Book of Mormon to others, but he led the way with his individual effort. On a flight to Honolulu, for example, he asked five flight attendants if they would care to receive a copy of the Book of Mormon. All agreed. This was a frequent practice of his. In fact, he sent dozens of copies of the Book of Mormon monthly—to people he met while traveling, to national and world leaders, to literally anyone who came to mind. When a former president of the national Farm Bureau, a nonmember, spoke at a Church fireside in Illinois about his "good friend" Ezra Taft Benson, he admitted having three copies of the Book of Mormon—each a gift from Ezra Taft Benson.

On one occasion a son-in-law introduced President Benson to two prominent men, one of them a former president of Blue Cross who was now attending divinity school. President Benson recorded afterwards, "I had great opportunity to teach these men the gospel and speak frankly to them. I felt it was time well spent and they left in good spirits with copies of the Book of Mormon and my testimony ringing in their ears." Later the same day he met with other nonmembers, and he concluded his journal entry, "It has been a great missionary day for the Church. The Lord be praised."

After meeting with President Benson two journalists, both nonmembers, remarked that it had been one of the greatest experiences of their lives. One of the men had met President Benson previously, but he remarked that something was different about him. An LDS friend explained that the mantle of the prophet had fallen on President Benson, that he was the Lord's prophet to the entire world, not just the Latter-day Saints. The nonmember replied, "You don't have to convince me of that."[26]

At the seminar for new mission presidents in June 1986, President Benson delivered a powerful address that subdued yet filled the congregation of leaders with the knowledge they were hearing from a prophet of God. He deviated from his prepared text and in a voice full of emotion said, "How I wish I were going with you!" Then he pled with the presidents to let the Spirit guide them, to love their missionaries, and to put the Book of Mormon at the center of missionary work. He promised there would be more and better converts in every mission if missionaries would use the Book of Mormon as the great converter.[27]

President Benson also had a stirring effect on missionaries. While at the Missionary Training Center in Provo for the mission presidents' seminar, he and President Hinckley held an impromptu devotional with the missionaries. One young man wrote his parents about the experience: "President Benson . . . is a glorious man. He spoke to us and everyone was crying. He said it was the most inspiring sight he had seen, 1200 missionaries preparing for the most important work we can do. Three times he said he wished he could go with us. I love him and know that he is truly chosen of God."[28]

One missionary wrote to tell President Benson that he had met a nonmember who had responded warmly when the missionaries told him the name of the Church they were representing. "I'm not a member of your church," the man said, "but I will always have the greatest amount of respect and admiration for The Church of Jesus Christ of Latter-day Saints and its people." Questioned further, the man explained that he had escorted Ezra Taft Benson when, as Secretary of Agriculture, he and Flora visited Hawaii. The missionary told the man that former-Secretary Benson had been an apostle then, but was now president of the Church. The man replied, "I knew there was something special about Mr. Benson the moment I met him." Upon hearing the story, President Benson sent this missionary a personally inscribed Book of Mormon to give the investigator.[29]

After attending a sacrament meeting in Salt Lake City, President Benson paused on his way out to shake hands with the local missionaries. Stopping and holding the hands of one elder (who, unbeknownst to President Benson, had joined the Church and entered the mission field amid persecution from his family), he looked into his eyes and said softly, "Remember, elder, this is the greatest work in all the world. I love this work. If you have the Spirit, you can teach. When you teach, you convert. The Lord will bless you. My wife went on a mission. And see her smiling." Tears streamed down the missionary's face as the prophet blessed him with his personal testimony. The missionary later explained, "As President Benson approached us, my heart burned. His glowing, happy face filled our hearts with peace and love. He was so happy to see us! He took our hands in his and held them tight. . . . Never have I felt such penetrating power from a man. Not since my conversion have I felt so drained by the Spirit. I will never forget it."[30]

Wherever he went, President Benson was overwhelmed by the outpouring of love from the Saints. During Christmas 1986, as thousands of cards streamed in, he took armfuls home each night to share with Flora. Often his eyes filled with tears as the stacks were brought in to him. "What can we do for these wonderful people?" he would ask.

Many of the President's remarks were directed to youth. He loved children, and he would often look out on congregations where there were many children and say, "Zion is growing!" In regional conferences he delighted congregations by singing, a capella, "I Am a Mormon Boy." With all the power he could muster, he proclaimed that this was the rising generation, and while the Lord expected much, He had given much. He promised BYU graduates in April 1986 that they need never feel embarrassed among "people who count, real men and women, because you live according to the . . . ideals of the Church."[31]

On another occasion he summarized his deep feelings about the role of the youth of the Church: "God has saved for the final inning some of His strongest and most valiant children, who will help bear off the kingdom triumphantly. That is where you come in, for you are the generation that must be prepared to meet your God. . . . Make no mistake about it—you are a marked generation. There has never been more expected of the faithful in such a short period of time than there is of us."[32]

At the general priesthood session in April 1986, President Benson directed his remarks to young men and closed with his blessing: "My young men of the Aaronic Priesthood, how I love you, how I respect you, how I pray for you. Remember the counsel I have given you tonight. It is what the Lord would have you hear now—today."

Six months later, at the general women's meeting, held September 27, he spoke to young women and again revealed his deep love for youth: "How I love and respect you! How I pray for you! How my hope abounds in you! . . . Remember who you are and the divine heritage that is yours—you are literally the royal daughters of our Father in Heaven. O 'youth of the noble birthright,' with all my heart I say, 'Carry on, carry on, carry on!' " Both addresses were reprinted in pamphlet form for distribution throughout the Church.[33]

President Benson's health remained fairly good. The pace was strenuous for a man in his late eighties, but some concerns became evident as he occasionally suffered from dizzy spells. One day in his office he lost his balance and fell on the carpet. He was unhurt, but after checking his blood pressure, doctors suggested he go home and rest.

In the weeks following conference in October 1986, he inaugurated a new president at Ricks College; spoke and offered the dedicatory prayer at the first session of the Denver Temple dedication; and addressed a regional conference in Michigan. A storm forced him to miss a connecting flight home from Michigan, so he sat in an uncomfortable airport chair for two hours, his right leg propped on his briefcase, waiting for the next flight to Salt Lake City. He was very disappointed, though, when weakness prevented his attending a regional conference in Boise, Idaho. Elder Marvin J. Ashton presided at the conference and explained that "anxious exhaustion" had prohibited the prophet's attending. Just four days later President Benson entered LDS Hospital for implantation of a pacemaker.

When he finally emerged from the recovery room and was wheeled back to his room, Sister Benson walked over to him and asked if she could kiss him. When the doctor said yes, she leaned over and gave her husband a gentle kiss. "T," she said, "I was so worried about you. I've been praying for you." It was as though they had been separated for weeks.

The Sunday after surgery, President Benson insisted on attending church, though his physician advised against it. It took calls from his children to persuade him otherwise. Only five days after the operation he returned to work, but the first day back he left after a few hours. He was very tired and finally admitted he had better be more prudent in his activities. It was just ten days after surgery, however, that he addressed two regional conferences in the Salt Lake Tabernacle.

That President Benson would speak out on topics related to the family perhaps came as no surprise to those who had followed his addresses over the years. This was the president of a church that was built around the family unit, a church whose previous presidents had preached and popularized such phrases as "no other success in life can compensate for failure in the home." And this was a man whose wife had devoted herself exclusively to creating a gospel-centered home and rearing faithful children. Having a family united for eternity had become the central peg around which the Benson family culture revolved.

It was perhaps fitting that President and Sister Benson celebrated their sixtieth wedding anniversary, on September 10, 1986, during his first year as president of the Church. The event drew churchwide attention to their relationship. The month before, at a family gathering in Washington honoring his eighty-seventh birthday, a representative from Church Public Communications had asked him the secret to his long, happy life. Before he could answer, Sister Benson said, teasingly but with meaning, "He has a good wife." President Benson referred to their wedding day—September 10, 1926—as "the day life began." For thirty years she had worn daily a golden pendant her husband gave her that was inscribed, "To Flora, For constant help, devotion and inspiration. Lovingly, T, 1926–56 Christmas."

Commentator Paul Harvey, on his nationally syndicated radio program, noted the Bensons' anniversary and said, "I never see them together that they're not holding hands."[34]

Church News Photograph

Sister Benson speaks at a regional conference in May 1986

President Benson was so grateful for Flora and so proud of her. He wanted her to travel with him whenever possible, and he was delighted when she could participate. Her very presence provided him with strength and comfort. And she was proud of him. She once turned to him and said, "When I was a little girl, I used to wonder if I would ever meet the prophet." He immediately replied, "Did you ever imagine you would have to *live* with him?"

Occasionally, Sister Benson spoke extemporaneously in meetings and bore her testimony. More often she recited a favorite Edgar A. Guest poem, "Home," which begins,

> It takes a heap o' livin' in a house t' make it home,
> A heap o' sun an' shadder, an' ye sometimes have t' roam
> Afore ye really 'preciate the things ye lef' behind,
> An' hunger fer 'em somehow, with 'em allus on yer mind. . . .
> Ye've got t' sing an' dance fer years, ye've got t' romp an' play,
> An' learn t' love the things ye have by usin' 'em each day.

Then she would blow the audience a kiss. After she had delivered a particularly moving rendition in one regional conference, President Benson began his remarks, "What can a mere man do after that?" Even in advanced age, Sister Benson was still spunky and ever ready with an encouraging word and sometimes a quip. One of her favorite phrases was, "The Lord bless you and the devil miss you."

Those who studied Sister Benson's life found there was much to admire. The University of Utah chapter of Lambda Delta Sigma named her their Woman of the Year in 1986.

President and Sister Benson still took time for family—missionary farewells and homecomings, lunch with family members between sessions at conference time, and family gatherings afterwards. When they were in town, they regularly had Sunday dinner at Mark and Lela's home. He spoke at the missionary homecomings of his grandchildren; attended his grandsons' Eagle Scout Courts of Honor; while in California to install a new presidency of the Los Angeles Temple, visited the California Anaheim Mission where his grandson, David Madsen, was serving; and made a surprise appearance at the August 1986 BYU commencement to honor his graduating grandson, Robert Walker. BYU President Jeffrey Holland abbreviated his own address to give President Benson time to speak, saying, "I feel justified in this shift of speakers because it comes under the heading in your program of President's Greeting—we just didn't tell you which president." The audience was delighted.[35]

One granddaughter lived with her grandparents during much of his first eighteen months as president, and at their request often traveled with them to assist them and attend to their personal needs. And she observed firsthand her grandparents at home—their dates to an ice cream parlor; sitting on the couch and holding hands as they reminisced, sang, and laughed together; the warm visits they had with the home teachers and others who came calling.

President Benson took on almost heroic proportions to his grandchildren, who saw in him the embodiment of everything they had been taught. A grandson, then working in the Canadian Parliament, wrote, "Every day I am faced with having to make decisions on various social programs that have become overrun by fraud. . . . I am fortunate to be able to turn to your books . . . and discover the correct ideology that should be implemented." A granddaughter wrote her thanks after President Benson had counseled her and her husband regarding a difficult decision. "We asked you what you thought and you said, 'Pray about it. I have faith that you will make the right decision.' Your faith in us gave us extra confidence."[36]

It was the family ties, the penetrating links with his heritage, that made the restoration of a four-story gristmill near Tooele, Utah, built by his great-grandfather Ezra T. Benson, all the more meaningful.[37]

President Benson continued to feel strongly that children and youth needed full-time mothers. During an address in July 1986 at the Provo Freedom Festival in which he discussed the Founding Fathers and the Constitution, he commented upon a mother's responsibility to her children. That portion of his address was omitted from press reports. Afterwards he noted in his journal, "I don't know whether it was . . . not wanting to stir up controversy that the statement which I made that mothers should be full-time mothers in the home was not mentioned. I feel very deeply regarding this question, and expect to speak on it later."

That time came on February 22, 1987, when during a churchwide fireside for parents, broadcast via satellite, he delivered a clear message on the role of mothers. Quoting three of his predecessors—Brigham Young, David O. McKay, and Spencer W. Kimball—his statements left little doubt. In a forthright manner, President Benson counseled couples to not postpone having children and to not limit their families for selfish reasons. While acknowledging that some women find themselves in unusual circumstances wherein they are required to work, these "instances are the exception, not the rule." And he placed the responsibility squarely upon fathers to provide adequately for their families so mothers weren't forced to work. "The Lord clearly defined the roles of mothers and fathers in providing for and rearing a righteous posterity," he said. "In the beginning, Adam—not Eve—was instructed to earn the bread by the sweat of his brow. Contrary to conventional wisdom, a mother's calling is in the home, not the marketplace."

Quoting President Kimball, he added: " 'Too many mothers work away from home to furnish sweaters and music lessons and trips and fun for their children. Too many women spend their time in socializing, in politicking, in public services when they should be home to teach and train and receive and love their children into security.' . . . President Kimball spoke the truth. His words are prophetic. Mothers in Zion, your God-given roles are so vital to your own exaltation and to the salvation and exaltation of your family. A child needs a mother more than all the things money can buy. . . . Among the greatest concerns in our society are the millions of latchkey children who come home daily to empty houses unsupervised by working parents." Then he added: "Mothers, this kind of heavenly, motherly teaching takes time—lots of time. It cannot be done effectively part time. It must be done all the time in order to save and exalt your children."

President Benson's final comments were a tribute to his wife, who was a prime example of what he admonished: "I would be remiss if I did not express my love and eternal gratitude for my sweetheart and companion and the mother of our six children. Her devotion to motherhood has blessed me and our family beyond words of expression. She has been a marvelous mother, completely and happily devoting her life and her mission to her family. How grateful I am for Flora!"[38]

The response to the address was as varied as it was volatile. Thousands of women, grateful for the assurance that their role as mothers and homemakers needn't relegate them to a lower social status, were relieved to have the prophet teach that motherhood is the most critical, yet ennobling role a woman can fill. President Benson received hundreds of letters from women expressing their feelings that having mother at home leads to strong, gospel-centered families. One woman wrote, in what was a typical response, "It has seemed to me that there has been some hesitancy among some of our leaders to fervently declare this role, particularly as it relates to the responsibility of women. . . . I am pleased that now we all know that the mission and message of the Church will not be changed." Another mother said she felt as extinct as a dinosaur in today's society, but that the prophet's message had filled her with "love, hope and courage to continue on." She added, "It's so important to know that you're aware of our needs."[39]

There were also those who felt that President Benson was out of touch with their needs—and with the times. Telephone calls came into the Church Office Building from women seeking clarification and from others expressing concern about his message.

But this message was nothing new—from President Benson or his predecessors. He had preached the virtue of full-time motherhood for decades.[40] His motivation was simple. He was convinced that, in the main, children whose parents did not make them their priority were at a great disadvantage in their chance for spiritual and emotional survival. There was no way to say it any clearer, no way to cushion his remarks. His message was not a statement of new policy, but rather a restatement of his predecessors' views. He felt so strongly about the message that it was reprinted in pamphlet form for distribution churchwide through the home teaching program.

President Benson's address received national attention, including mention on Paul Harvey's radio broadcast on April 2, 1987. Mr. Harvey reported the events in his distinctive way: "The President of the Mormon Church, Ezra Taft Benson, says mothers should stay home and care for their children. This administrative guideline from the head of the Church is being resisted because 40 percent of the Church's female members are already in the work force. . . . One of them says it will be easier to deal with the guilt than to live without the income. Nothing they can do about this. President Benson's three predecessors have all said the same thing: that mothers should stay home and care for their children. Benson is just reiterating long-held Church doctrine—long held and increasingly ignored. There's no known connection, but the Great Salt Lake is creeping up higher and higher . . . record high and going higher."

It was providential, and certainly fitting, that President Benson's presidency coincided with the celebration to commemorate the bicentennial of the U.S. Constitution. Certainly a love of country had been a primary focus of his life. He was, in fact, still recognized as a patriot of international stature, and among many of the nation's leaders he was regarded as a patriotic hero, and one of the greatest defenders of the U.S. Constitution. Many of those in U.S. political circles had been schooled on his books and philosophies and considered him one of their formative tutors. A special consultant to President Reagan explained, "I know of no American, or citizen of the world for that matter, who has been more forceful in defense of the Constitution than has President Benson. His record on this, both as a public servant and as a religious leader, is widely known and respected. He has devoted his life to this grand document and its principles." A senior policy adviser to President Reagan declared, "Ezra Taft Benson has always been a great hero of mine. He speaks the truth more purely and courageously than any man I have ever known." Senator Steve Symms of Idaho remarked, "When I first met Ezra Taft Benson, I felt I was talking to one of the Founding Fathers. He has that timbre. It's just too bad he wasn't president of this country. That's what this country needed—a tough guy who understands the Constitution. He gave people who believe in the constitution some credibility when he served in the Cabinet."[41]

President Benson's reputation as a champion of freedom was reemphasized on June 19, 1986, when the Freedoms Foundation at Valley Forge named him the recipient of their Service-to-Freedom Award, the highest honor the foundation bestows. President Benson was only the third person to receive the award (with the other recipients being President Ronald Reagan and Senator Strom Thurmond).[42] (Less than a year earlier he had another high honor as an outgrowth of his distinguished agricultural service. On July 28, 1986, he became only the second recipient of the Service to American Agriculture Award, given by the National Association of County Agricultural Agents in Colorado Springs.)

On September 16, 1986, the largest devotional audience in BYU's history heard President Benson deliver an address highlighting the bicentennial celebration of the U.S. Constitution. In a stirring address entitled "The Constitution: A Heavenly Banner," he outlined his feelings about government, beginning at the beginning—with the war in heaven and the principle of agency: "The central issue in that council, then, was: Shall the children of God have untrammeled agency to choose the course they should follow, whether good or evil, or shall

Photograph by Don Busath

President and Sister Benson with their children and spouses. Left to right, front: Lela Wing Benson, Mark A. Benson, President and Sister Benson, Reed A. Benson, and May Hinckley Benson. Back, David A. Burton, Beth Benson Burton, Beverly Benson Parker, James M. Parker, Robert H. Walker, Barbara Benson Walker, Lowell L. Madsen, and Bonnie Benson Madsen

they be coerced and forced to be obedient? . . . The war that began in heaven is not yet over. The conflict continues on the battlefield of mortality. And one of Lucifer's primary strategies has been to restrict our agency through the power of earthly governments."

The Constitution of the United States, President Benson continued, quoting Wilford Woodruff, was raised up by the best spirits the Lord could find on the face of the earth. "What the framers did, under the inspiration of God, was to draft a document that merited the approval of God Himself." But a liberal interpretation of the Constitution, he explained, had led to an erosion of freedom. Then he quoted Brigham Young: "We are fast approaching that moment prophesied by Joseph Smith when he said: 'Even this nation will be on the very verge of crumbling to pieces and tumbling to the ground, and when the Constitution is upon the brink of ruin, this people will be the staff upon which the nation shall lean, and they shall bear the Constitution away from the very verge of destruction.' "

President Benson outlined four steps of preparation to meet the challenge. First, the Saints must be righteous; second, they must understand the principles of the Constitution and abide by them; third, they should participate in civic affairs; and fourth, they must exercise influence by voting. He then declared: "I have faith that the Constitution will be saved as prophesied by Joseph Smith. . . . It will be saved by the citizens of this nation who love and cherish freedom. It will be saved by enlightened . . . men and women who will subscribe to and abide by the principles of the Constitution. . . . It may cost us our blood before we are through. It is my conviction, however, that when the Lord comes, the Stars and Stripes will be floating on the breeze over this people."[43]

On September 26, 1986, Senator Steve Symms placed the address in the *Congressional Record,* and Senator Orrin Hatch sent a copy to each member of Congress. Deseret Book reprinted the message in pamphlet form, and within just a few days the first printing had sold out. The feedback from many who heard or read the talk was very favorable. For example, Senator Jesse Helms wrote: "Senator Hatch has favored me with a copy of your remarkable book, *The Constitution: A Heavenly Banner.* It is an extraordinary assessment by an extraordinary American. . . . As you know, you are at the top of the list of our nation's leaders whom I have long admired and respected."[44]

In addition, as President Benson spoke on the Book of Mormon throughout the Church, he typically tied its message to the preservation of freedom: "And our nation will continue to degenerate unless we read and heed the words of the God of this land, Jesus Christ, and quit building up and upholding the secret combinations which the Book of Mormon tells us proved the downfall of both previous American civilizations."[45]

In January 1987 the First Presidency restated the Church's view that the Constitution is an inspired document, and encouraged Americans to take advantage of the bicentennial celebration: "We encourage Latter-day Saints throughout the nation to familiarize themselves with the Constitution. They should focus attention on it by reading and studying it. They should ponder the blessings that come through it. They should recommit themselves to its principles and be prepared to defend it and the freedom it provides."[46]

From the time he received the mantle of the prophet, President Benson repeatedly emphasized his intention to carry forth the threefold mission of the Church that the Lord, through President Kimball, had outlined. He did so by making missionary work a high priority and by being alert to his personal missionary opportunities; by pleading with members to read and study the Book of Mormon; and by carrying forth the Church's program of building temples. When they weren't traveling, he and Sister Benson went to the temple nearly every Friday morning. Temple workers related that the effect of having the prophet and his wife participate in a session was electrifying to the patrons and did more to emphasize the importance of temple work than a hundred sermons on the subject.

In his concluding testimony in the April 1987 general conference, President Benson again centered his remarks on the Book of Mormon, this time calling the Doctrine and Covenants the "binding link" between that book and the Restoration. He said that the Book of Mormon was "the keystone of our religion" and the Doctrine and Covenants "the capstone with continuing revelation." He concluded this discourse, which some believed would be hailed as a doctrinal masterpiece, by leaving another powerful blessing upon the Latter-day Saints and by focusing on all three of the Church's objectives: "I bless you with added power to endure in righteousness amidst the growing onslaught of wickedness. I bless you that as you more diligently study modern revelation on gospel subjects, your power to teach and preach will be magnified, and you will so move the cause of Zion that added numbers will enter into the house of the Lord as well as the mission field. I bless you with increased desire to flood the earth with the Book of Mormon, to gather out from the world the elect of God who are yearning for the truth. . . . I promise you that, with increased attendance in the temples of our God, you shall receive increased personal revelation to bless your life."[47]

Like prophets from time immemorial, President Benson frequently bore his personal witness of the Savior, as in the December 1986 First Presidency Christmas fireside: "Men and women who turn their lives over to God will discover that He can make a lot more out of their lives than they can. He can deepen their joys, expand their vision, quicken their minds, strengthen their muscles, lift their spirits, multiply their blessings, increase their opportunities, comfort their souls, raise up friends and pour out peace. Whoever will lose his life in the service of God will find eternal peace."[48]

He spoke as a prophet. But he also spoke as a man who had adhered to that counsel throughout his life.

When Ezra Taft Benson was inducted into the Agricultural Hall of Fame, the man who made the introduction paraphrased a statement by Winston Churchill during a serious stage of World War II—that there were some who must work, and some who must fight, and some who must pray. It was said of President Benson, "We have in him a unique man who does all three."

President Gordon B. Hinckley, in the first general conference held after President Benson's ordination as president of the Church, said of the new prophet: "I give you my testimony that it is the Lord who selected Ezra Taft Benson to become a member of the Council of the Twelve almost forty-three years ago. It is the Lord who over these years has tested and disciplined him, schooled and prepared him. . . . As one who knows him and who stands at his side, I bear witness that he is a man of faith, of tested leadership, of profound love for the Lord and His work, of love for the sons and daughters of God everywhere. He is a man of proven capacity, who has been tempered in the Refiner's fire."[49]

President Thomas S. Monson summarized the singleness of Ezra Taft Benson's heart and the contribution he would make to the kingdom of God: "President Benson has the capacity to bring men and women back to the straight and narrow pathway. He would have made a great wagonmaster in bringing Saints across the plains. He wouldn't have let them wander to the gold fields of California, and he wouldn't have let them stop and plant for two or three seasons in the lush, rich soil of

Iowa. He knows how to say, 'Move on, wagon train.' He would have brought them to the valleys of the mountains successfully.

"Spirituality will be the main contribution and theme of his administration. That spirituality will lead to a greater study of the Book of Mormon. It will lead to more missionary and temple work. It will lead to greater Christian service. And it will lead to an holier people."

It has been said that there is nothing as motivating as to know that yours is a worthy cause. Throughout his life, Ezra Taft Benson has indeed been motivated by worthy causes. His loyalties to God, to his family, and to his country have become legendary. His life has been an exercise in patience and endurance; an example of integrity, conviction, and principle; a model of faith and implicit trust in the Lord. Like those prophets who have preceded him, under his direction the work of the Lord moves forward. And through him, for a season, the Lord communicates with and guides His church.

Ezra Taft Benson's motivations have been, throughout his life, directed by purpose, by a higher power. At the basis of his loyalties and beliefs is devotion to the most worthy of causes—the gospel of Jesus Christ, and all that it contains. Such is the life of a remarkable man—a prophet, patriarch, and patriot. Such is the life of Ezra Taft Benson.

Notes and Sources

Space limitations make it impossible to indicate every source examined in the preparation of this biography. The public papers of, published accounts about, and addresses, articles, and books by Ezra Taft Benson are voluminous, and a complete list of them would require a book-sized presentation. Listed, therefore, are only those materials directly involved in the writing of this biography.

I have drawn heavily from the following: the personal journals of Ezra Taft Benson from 1939 to the present (when an excerpt from his journal is quoted, it is not referenced unless the material illustrates specific facts); speeches and addresses of President Benson; interviews with family members, General Authorities, and numerous colleagues of President Benson through the years; and literally hundreds of published sources (including magazine and newspaper articles), most of which have been preserved in over one hundred scrapbooks, as well as books by and about him.

The following books provided reference information: Richard O. Cowan, *The Church in the Twentieth Century* (Salt Lake City: Bookcraft, 1985); Leonard J. Arrington, ed., *The Presidents of the Church* (Salt Lake City: Deseret Book, 1986): James B. Allen and Glen M. Leonard, *The Story of the Latter-day Saints* (Salt Lake City: Deseret Book, 1976).

The following include biographical overviews of President and Sister Benson's life that were helpful: Merlo J. Pusey, "Ezra Taft Benson: A Living Witness for Christ," *Improvement Era*, April 1956, pp. 234ff.; Lydia Clawson Hoopes, "Ezra T. Benson," *Improvement Era*, October 1943, pp. 592ff.; Mark E. Petersen, "Ezra Taft Benson: A Habit of Integrity," *Ensign*, October 1974, pp. 15-29; Mark E. Petersen, "President Ezra Taft Benson," *Ensign*, January 1986, pp. 2-13; Derin Head Rodriquez, "Flora Amussen Benson: Handmaiden of the Lord," *Ensign*, March 1987, pp. 14-20; "President Benson: Spiritual, Honest and Straightforward," *Church News*, April 21, 1985.

Chapter 1, "A Rich Heritage"

In preparing this chapter, I relied heavily upon genealogical records and family histories prepared by members of Ezra Taft Benson's family (in particular, those histories compiled by David and Beth Benson Burton), as well as the following published sources: John Henry Evans and Minnie Egan Anderson, *Ezra T. Benson* (Deseret News Press, 1947); *Descendants of the George T. Benson, Jr. Family* (1968); Donald Benson Alder and Elsie L. Alder, *The Benson Family* (The Ezra T. Benson Genealogical Society, Inc., 1979). See also "The Kinship of Families," transcript of remarks on the television program "What's Your Name," KDYL-TV, January 31, 1954, BYU Extension Division; Gene Allred Sessions, *Latter-day Patriots* (Salt Lake City: Deseret Book, 1975).

1. Ezra Taft Benson, "Temple Memories," address delivered at Logan Temple, March 13, 1979. President Benson had some interesting ancestral ties. Both George Albert Smith and Joseph Fielding Smith were seventh cousins twice removed. Senator Robert A. Taft was a sixth cousin twice removed, and William Howard Taft, the only man to become both Chief Justice of the U.S. Supreme Court and president of the United States, was a fifth cousin three times removed.

2. "Ezra T. Benson," in Journal History of the Church (hereafter Journal History), July 16, 1846. Church Archives.

3. Evans and Anderson, *Ezra T. Benson*, p. 11.

4. Ibid., p. 14.

5. Journal History, July 16, 1846.

6. Ibid.

7. Ibid.

8. "Oral History, Ezra Taft Benson," *Idaho Heritage* 9 (1977): 15.

9. See *Ezra T. Benson*, p. 114; also "Ezra T. Benson," in Journal History, July 16, 1846.

10. Evans and Anderson, *Ezra T. Benson*, p. 125.

11. Missionary Blessings, in "Docket of the Municipal Court of the City of Nauvoo."

12. See *Descendants of the George T. Benson, Jr. Family*, 1968.

13. Melinda Nelson Benson to Ezra Taft Benson (hereafter ETB in references to correspondence), February 5, 1952.

Chapter 2, "A Boy from Whitney"

Ezra Taft Benson's childhood has been detailed by himself and other family members in numerous talks, addresses, and articles, as well as in various family histories. In addition, interviews were conducted with or written recollections were received from Margaret Benson Keller, George

Benson III, Orval Benson, Lera Benson Whittle, Sarah Benson Eveleth, Florence Peck Packer, Effie Peck Stevenson, and William Poole.

Through the years several detailed oral interviews have been conducted with President Benson. In 1974 Dr. James B. Allen conducted extensive interviews for the James Moyle Oral History Program, a typescript of which is in the Church Archives, Historical Department of The Church of Jesus Christ of Latter-day Saints. Reed Benson interviewed his father at length in 1984, and the author conducted seven additional interviews with President Benson in 1986. All were used heavily in preparing this and subsequent chapters. See also Melvin Leavitt, "A Boy from Whitney," *New Era*, November 1986, pp. 20–31; "Franklin Stake of Zion" in Andrew Jenson, *Encyclopedic History of the Church of Jesus Christ of Latter-day Saints* (Salt Lake City: Corporation of the President, 1941), p. 262; "Man, the Temple of God," an address by Ezra Taft Benson dated June 17, 1978; "Life Sketch of Geo. T. Benson," *Franklin County Citizen*, August 29, 1934; Lera Benson Whittle, "My Life Story" (unpublished manuscript); Mrs. Serge B. Benson to Ezra Taft Benson, February 2, 1952; and the following unpublished manuscripts by Ezra Taft Benson: "Why I Am What I Am" (circa 1925), "Sarah Dunkley Benson," and "Personal Incidents and Observations."

1. Ezra Taft Benson, "The Best Advice I Ever Received," *Reader's Digest*, November 1954, p. 97.

2. Leavitt, "A Boy from Whitney," pp. 24, 26.

Chapter 3, "Man of the House"

Most source materials listed for chapter 2 apply to this chapter also. Additionally, in this and subsequent chapters I refer to handwritten notes of Flora Amussen Benson, all undated.

1. Leavitt, "A Boy from Whitney," p. 28.

2. Sessions, *Latter-day Patriots*, p. 77.

3. Leavitt, "A Boy from Whitney," p. 28.

4. Ezra Taft Benson, "Scouting Builds Men," *New Era*, February 1975, pp. 14–18.

5. Ezra Taft Benson to President Heber J. Grant, June 24, 1921.

Chapter 4, "A Mission to England"

In preparing this account of Ezra Taft Benson's mission, I have referred extensively to his missionary journal, dated August 1921 through December 1923; issues of the *Millennial Star* of the corresponding period; Manuscript History of the British Mission, November 20, 1921, to October 14, 1923; Ezra Taft Benson, "Personal Reminiscences," undated and unpublished; Francis M. Gibbons, *David O. McKay: Apostle to the World, Prophet of God* (Salt Lake City: Deseret Book, 1986); and oral interviews with Ezra Taft Benson.

1. See excerpts from James T. Palmer journal in Roger Toone to author, 1987.

2. David O. McKay to First Presidency, February 27, 1924, David O. McKay Papers, Church Archives. See also Allen and Leonard, *Story of the Latter-day Saints*, p. 505.

3. Sarah Dunkley Benson to ETB, September 4, 1921.

4. Ibid.

5. Excerpts from James T. Palmer journal.

6. Ezra Taft Benson, "A Principle with a Promise," *Ensign*, May 1983, pp. 53–55.

7. *Millennial Star* 84 (1922): 254.

8. *Millennial Star* 84 (1922): 733. See also Gibbons, *David O. McKay*, pp. 123–29.

9. December 15, 1922, David O. McKay Papers, Church Archives.

10. David O. McKay to missionaries of the British Mission, Circular Letter No. 79, May 9, 1923.

11. See Ezra Taft Benson, *God, Family, Country* (Deseret Book, 1974), p. 109; Ezra Taft Benson, "Preparing Yourself for Missionary Service," *Conference Report*, April 1985; Ezra Taft Benson, "The Best Advice I Ever Had," *Reader's Digest*, November 1954.

12. *Millennial Star* 84 (1922): 826; also David O. McKay to Rudger Clawson, February 5, 1923, David O. McKay Papers, Church Archives.

13. ETB to Harriet Andrews, November 3, 1923; also *Millennial Star* 85 (1923): 784; Ralph S. Gray to ETB, August 2, 1943.

Chapter 5, "Her Name Was Flora"

I have referred extensively to family histories (many of them prepared by David and Beth Benson Burton) of Carl Christian Amussen, Barbara McIsaac Smith Amussen, Elizabeth McIsaac Smith, and others. I also quote from Barbara Amussen's personal journal, personal writings (undated) of Flora Amussen Benson, and Ezra Taft Benson's personal journal. See also Noble Warrum, "Carl Christian Amussen," *Utah Since Statehood* 4 (Chicago: S. J. Clarke, 1920): 700–701; "Carl Christian Amussen," *Daughters of Utah Pioneers*, lesson for February 1981, p. 217; "Brief Life Sketch of Barbara Smith Amussen by Herself," December 25, 1932 (unpublished manuscript); Reed A. Benson interview with Flora Amussen Benson, August 12, 1985; Mildred D. Evans, "Remembrances of Barbara S. Amussen" (unpublished manuscript).

1. Brigham Young to Carl Amussen, date unknown.

2. Carl Amussen to Barbara Amussen, June 26, 1900.

3. Blessing by Patriarch Charles Ora Card upon head of Barbara Smith Amussen, February 27, 1903.

4. Barbara Amussen, personal journal, March 24, 1927.

5. See "Barbara S. Amussen," unpublished tribute.

6. Flora Amussen Benson, untitled address, circa 1958.

Chapter 6, "A Wait—Then Marriage"

Most of the information in this chapter is drawn from author's interviews with Ezra Taft Benson, Reed Benson, Mark Benson, and Mark Allen; the Barbara S. Amussen journal; personal writings of Flora Amussen Benson; and an interview of Ezra Taft Benson by Margaret Benson Keller. Also see "My Companion," a tribute by Ezra Taft Benson to Flora A. Benson; Manuscript History of the Hawaiian Mission, 1901–1930, Church Archives.

1. Ezra Taft Benson, "Of One Blood, All Nations," *Improvement Era*, June 1958, p. 433.

2. Confidential Mission Report, June 8, 1926; Benson Family Collection.

3. Letter to Flora Amussen, dated October 2, 1925, signed "Auntie," postmarked Santa Monica, California.

4. See "Hawaiian Mission," *Liahona: The Elder's Journal*, March 9, 1926; "Diamond Anniversary of Missionary Effort in Hawaii," *Improvement Era*, April 1926, p. 613; also Barbara Amussen journal, 1925.

5. Eugene J. Neff to John Q. Adams, June 16, 1926.

6. Orson F. Whitney to ETB, August 3, 1926. Whitney, Idaho, was named after Orson F. Whitney when George T. Benson, Sr., Ezra's grandfather, suggested that the settlement be named after a bright young bishop he had met in Salt Lake City—the same man who would later serve as Ezra's mission president and perform his marriage.

7. Margaret Benson Keller to ETB, October 13, 1926.

8. Sarah Benson to ETB, Thanksgiving Day, 1926; also Sarah Benson to ETB, October 13, 1926.

9. Sarah Benson to ETB, March 27, 1927.

Chapter 7, "Return to the Farm"

In addition to sources cited for chapters 5 and 6, see unpublished biographical sketch, "Ezra Taft Benson"; Ezra Taft Benson, "Franklin County Extension Agent Annual Report for 1929," November 20, 1929; Ezra Taft Benson, "Franklin County Extension Agent Annual Report for 1930," October 31, 1930. Also "Benson Excelled as County Agent," *Deseret News*, December 17, 1952.

1. See Richard B. Morris and William Greenleaf, *The History of a Nation* (Chicago: Rand McNally, 1969), 2:685–89.

2. Orval Benson to ETB, January 7, 1928.

3. See *Deseret News*, December 17, 1952.

Chapter 8, "Agriculture Specialist"

This chapter is based heavily upon author interviews with Ezra Taft Benson (as well as oral interviews with him by Reed Benson and James B. Allen), Reed Benson, Mark Benson, Carol Youngstrom, Eva Labrum, Dr. Maurice Johnson of the University of Idaho, and Joe R. Williams. See also Manuscript History of the Boise Stake (1937–1940); Raymond W. Miller, "Ezra Taft Benson—Agricultural Statesman," unpublished essay; Ezra Taft Benson's "Personal Recollections," unpublished; Barbara S. Amussen journal.

Information on President Benson's activities as extension economist for the University of Idaho Extension Division is detailed through the following bulletins he coauthored: "Planning the Farm Business for the Year Ahead" (December 1936); with Paul A. Eke, "1938 Agricultural Outlook for Idaho" (December 1937); with Karl Hobson, "Annual Report for 1938"; with Paul A. Eke, "The Sources and Uses of State and County Revenue in Idaho." See also Ezra Taft Benson, "Planning for the Year Ahead," *Idaho Farmer*, January 1932.

1. B. Clair Johnson to author, undated, circa May 1986.

2. As quoted in Morris and Greenleaf, *The History of a Nation*, p. 794.

3. *Salt Lake Tribune*, July 1, 1938. See also Benson and Eke, "1938 Agricultural Outlook for Idaho."

4. William E. Hess to ETB, June 27, 1936.

5. See *Idaho Heritage* 9 (1977): 13.

6. Ezra Taft Benson, Tribute to David O. McKay, 1967.

7. Margaret Keller to ETB, July 22, no year given.

8. Ibid.

9. LeGrand Richards to ETB, September 10, 1934. See also "Thousands Attend Funeral Rites of George T. Benson," *Deseret News*, August 18, 1934, p. 14.

10. Ezra Taft Benson, Remarks, Birthday Luncheon for Elder LeGrand Richards, February 6, 1976.

11. Author interview with Thomas S. Monson, April 8, 1986.

12. ETB to Louise Benson Greenwood, August 21, 1934.

13. *Conference Report*, October 1936, pp. 3–4.

14. See Vaughn J. Featherstone, "The Six Priority Needs in Welfare Services," October 5, 1974, LDS Church Library—Archives.

15. Scott B. Brown to David W. Evans, undated.

16. Flora Amussen Benson (hereafter FAB in references to correspondence) to Barbara Smith Amussen, October 5, 1936.

17. FAB to ETB, April 2, 1936.

18. FAB to ETB, October 25, 1936.

Chapter 9, "Rearing an Eternal Family"

Much information cited in this chapter is drawn from author's interviews with Ezra Taft Benson, Flora Amussen Benson, Reed Benson, Mark Benson, Barbara Benson Walker, Beverly Benson Parker, and Alice Marriott. See also Barbara Amussen personal journal; *New Era*, January 1973, p. 4; "Husband, Family and Church Are Mrs. Benson's Whole Life," *Church News*, December 20, 1952, p. 6; Ezra Taft Benson, "My Companion—Memories, Heritage and Tribute," unpublished manuscript.

1. Julia Dalley to FAB, March 4, 1938.
2. Ezra Taft Benson, "To the Elect Women of the Kingdom of God," address at Relief Society Monument Dedicatory Services, Nauvoo, Illinois, June 30, 1978.
3. FAB to Barbara Smith Amussen, June 30, 1935.
4. FAB to ETB, October 10, 1938.

Chapter 10, "Rise to National Prominence"

Ezra Taft Benson's personal journal, which begins in earnest in 1938, provides the framework for this and subsequent chapters. I also have relied on author interviews with President Benson, Reed Benson, Mark Benson, Barbara Benson Walker, Beverly Benson Parker, Bonnie Benson Madsen, Samuel Carpenter, Alice Marriott, Miller F. Shurtleff, Abe Cannon, Louise Bennion, Winston Robinson, Jesse R. Smith, and personal writings of Flora Amussen Benson. See also interview with President Benson by Dr. Maclyn Burg for the Eisenhower Library, May 21, 1975, and the James B. Allen interview of President Benson, Church Archives.

The following sources were also helpful: manuscript histories of the Boise and Washington, D.C., stakes; issues of *Cooperative Digest* (1939–1944); annual reports of the National Council of Farmer Cooperatives (1939–1944); Ezra Taft Brenson, "Are There Any Mormons in Washington," *New Era*, August 1973, p. 7; Ezra Taft Benson, "A Peculiar People," *Instructor*, December 1970, p. 441; "A Year with the Cooperative Council," *National Livestock Producer*, February 1944, p. 3; "Cooperatives Come to Washington," 50th Anniversary Presentation produced by National Council of Farmer Cooperatives, Washington, D.C., 1979.

1. ETB to John D. Miller, January 27, 1939.
2. E. S. Trask to ETB, February 3, 1939.
3. "Benson Accepts Church Post," *Cooperative Digest*, September 1943, pp. 6–8.
4. "A Child's Example," *Children's Friend*, February 1947.
5. See page 51 of the oral history interview with Edgar B. Brossard in the James Moyle Oral History Program, Church Archives.

6. See Ernest L. Wilkinson's introduction of Ezra Taft Benson prior to Elder Benson's address, "LDS Church and Politics," Brigham Young University, December 1, 1952.

7. FAB to Barbara Smith Amussen, July 7, 1940.

8. J. Reuben Clark to ETB, July 23, 1940.

9. ETB to J. Reuben Clark, July 19, 1940.

10. Miller, "Ezra Taft Benson—Agricultural Statesman," p. 4.

11. H. E. (Ed) Babcock to Clyde Edmonds, September 6, 1941.

12. See Manuscript History of Washington Stake, January 5, 1942; letter of stake presidency to members, May 8, 1942.

13. As related in General Authority Training Session, October 3, 1978.

14. H. E. (Ed) Babcock to ETB, October 27, 1942; see also National Council of Farmer Cooperatives Minutes, undated.

15. *Cooperative Digest*, September 1943, pp. 6–8.

16. Ezra Taft Benson, as told to Carlisle Bargeron, *Farmers at the Crossroads* (New York: The Devin-Adair Company, 1956), p. xi.

Chapter 11, "The Call to the Apostleship"

From this chapter on, Ezra Taft Benson's personal journal and the hundreds of addresses he delivered, as well as his personal correspondence files and newspaper and magazine articles about him, are critical to the text. Also important are Flora Benson's handwritten notes, undated, and the James B. Allen oral history interview, 1974.

1. Reed A. Benson to FAB, undated, postmark 1943.

2. See Ezra Taft Benson, personal journal, July 26, 1943.

3. Reported in *Church News*, October 9, 1943; also Report of Washington Stake Conference, September 19, 1943.

4. R. N. Benjamin to ETB, August 19, 1943.

5. Howard A. Cowden to ETB, August 9, 1943, and Louis J. Taber to ETB, August 19, 1943.

6. Miller F. Shurtleff to ETB, November 29, 1943.

7. LeGrand Richards to ETB, August 9, 1943, and John A. Widtsoe to ETB, July 28, 1943.

8. Heber J. Grant, J. Reuben Clark, Jr., and David O. McKay to ETB, August 20, 1943.

9. Ezra Taft Benson, "The Least Among You," *Improvement Era* 46 (November 1943): 679. For information regarding Elder Benson's activities during this conference, see "Two New Apostles Arrive for Church Meet," *Salt Lake Tribune*, September 30, 1943.

10. Frances Elmore to ETB and FAB, October 1, 1943.

11. ETB to Ralph Taylor, October 19, 1943.

12. George Albert Smith to ETB, February 11, 1944.

13. Resolution adopted at Annual Assembly of Delegates of National Council of Farmer Cooperatives, Chicago, Illinois, January 5-7, 1944.

14. Homer L. Brinkley to ETB, August 16, 1943.

15. Ezra Taft Benson, personal journal, February 25, 1944; also "Prime for Progress," BYU Student Leadership Conference, Sun Valley, Idaho, September 1959.

16. ETB to FAB, September 9, 1944.

17. ETB to FAB, September 12, 1944.

18. *Deseret News*, October 14, 1944; also "America, a Choice Land," *Improvement Era* 47 (November 1944): 674.

19. Ezra Taft Benson memo to William O. Nelson, December 22, 1982.

Chapter 12, "Mission of Mercy"

This account of Ezra Taft Benson's emergency mission to postwar Europe is drawn from his and his wife's personal journals as well as correspondence between them; the Manuscript History of the European Mission; Frederick Babbel, *On Wings of Faith* (Bookcraft, 1972); Howard C. Badger, *European Experiences with a Latter-day Prophet* (published privately); Don C. Corbett, "Visit of Elder Ezra Taft Benson to Berlin, Germany, in 1946," unpublished account; Frederick W. Babbel, "Europe's Valiant Saints Forge Ahead," *Improvement Era* 49 (October 1946): 622-23; Ezra Taft Benson, "I'll Go Where You Want Me to Go," *Church News*, November 23, 1946, p. 8; Ezra Taft Benson, "Special Mission to Europe," *Improvement Era* 50 (May 1947): 293; "Elder Benson Reports Europe in Devastation," *Deseret News*, December 14, 1946; Frederick W. Babbel, Oral Interview by Maclyn P. Burg, Dwight D. Eisenhower Library, November 12, 1974, and February 5, 1975.

1. Howard C. Badger to Eleanor Badger, February 21, 1946.

2. Frederick W. Babbel, *On Wings of Faith*, pp. 20-21.

3. Ibid., p. 23.

4. Manuscript History of European Mission, pp. 5, 8.

5. *On Wings of Faith*, pp. 38-40.

6. ETB to First Presidency, March 21, 1946.

7. ETB to George Albert Smith, March 16, 1946. See also Richard O. Cowan, *The Church in the Twentieth Century* (Salt Lake City: Bookcraft, 1985), p. 208.

8. *On Wings of Faith*, p. 69.

9. Ibid., p. 74.

10. Tessy Vojkuvka to FAB, July 17, 1946.

11. Eben R. T. Blomquist to FAB, September 14, 1946.

12. Manuscript History of European Mission, p. 26.

13. *On Wings of Faith*, p. 100.

14. See ETB to First Presidency, June 26, 1946.

15. Ezra Taft Benson, "Ministering to Needs Through the Lord's Storehouse System," *Ensign*, May 1977, pp. 82–84.

16. *On Wings of Faith*, p. 116.

17. Ibid., p. 132.

18. Harold B. Lee to ETB, August 20, 1946.

19. ETB to J. Willard Marriott, October 29, 1946.

20. Cowan, *The Church in the Twentieth Century*, p. 20. See also European Mission History.

21. Ezra Taft Benson, "Spiritual Blessings Overshadow Physical Privations," *Improvement Era* 55 (December 1952): 941.

22. Harold B. Lee to Minnie E. Anderson, August 15, 1947.

Chapter 13, *"Young Apostle"*

This chapter relies on primary source material from Ezra Taft Benson's personal journal, personal correspondence between him and Flora Amussen Benson, and his correspondence files and addresses. See the following of his addresses: "Responsibilities of the Latter-day Saint Home," *Conference Report*, October 1947; "America: Land of the Blessed," *Conference Report*, April 1948; "Responsibilities of the Priesthood," *Conference Report*, October 1948; "Our Homes—Divinely Ordained," CBS "Church of the Air" broadcast, April 3, 1949; "Leadership, and the Needs of Youth," MIA June Conference, June 19, 1948; "Face the Future Unafraid," *Conference Report*, October 1950; "Faith in the Youth of Zion," *Conference Report*, April 1951; "Challenge for Cooperatives Today," American Institute of Cooperation, Utah State Agricultural College, Logan, Utah, August 30, 1951; "America, What of the Future?," *Conference Report*, April 1952.

1. Oktar and Tessy Vojkuvka to ETB, January 1, 1947.

2. See Ezra Taft Benson, personal journal, March 19, 1947.

3. Richard L. Evans to ETB, May 4, 1951.

4. See *Cooperative Digest*, October 1947.

5. ETB to FAB, November 6, 1947.

6. ETB to FAB, November 29, 1947.

7. See Ezra Taft Benson, *Crossfire* (New York: Doubleday, 1962), pp. 6–7.

8. ETB to Dr. C. Arild Olsen, August 9, 1948.

9. John A. Widtsoe to ETB, February 21, 1949.

10. ETB to A. A. McPherson, November 14, 1949.

11. Neal A. Maxwell, personal journal, September 14, 1947, as quoted in Neal A. Maxwell to ETB, March 1, 1985.

12. S. S. Knight to Karl D. Butler, November 1, 1949.

13. As related in Devotional Address, Brigham Young University, December 12, 1950.

14. Joel Richards to ETB, June 8, 1950.

15. Ezra Taft Benson, "Special Mission to Europe," *Conference Report*, April 1947, p. 157.

16. Laura Brossard to FAB, July 9, 1950.

17. See *Conference Report*, April 1951, p. 154.

18. Lester Hoverstein to Richard L. Evans, July 8, 1951.

19. John A. Widtsoe to ETB, February 6, 1952.

20. George F. Richards to ETB, June 2, 1946.

21. Robert D. Hales, in a message delivered in the Finland Helsinki Mission during James and Beverly Benson Parker's service in presiding over the mission, 1978–81.

22. *Church News*, February 20, 1952; also J. Reuben Clark file, Box 193, Church Archives.

23. See "The Challenge for Cooperatives Today," address to American Institute of Cooperation, Logan, Utah, August 30, 1951.

24. Ezra Taft Benson, "A Warning to America," address to BYU Alumnus Regional Council, Washington, D.C., July 3, 1979.

Chapter 14, "Welcome, Mr. Secretary"

Space does not allow for an exhaustive listing of published materials extant on Ezra Taft Benson's term as Secretary of Agriculture. The following books, articles, press conferences, addresses, and clippings are those to which I referred most extensively. In addition, I relied heavily upon Secretary Benson's personal journal, which for this period was particularly detailed; his books *Freedom to Farm* (New York: Doubleday, 1960) and *Crossfire: The Eight Years with Eisenhower* (New York: Doubleday, 1962); extensive correspondence between Secretary Benson and Dwight D. Eisenhower; and talks given by Flora Amussen Benson and Reed A. Benson during this period.

The National Archives in Washington, D.C., house speeches, correspondence, memoranda, and other official papers detailing Secretary Benson's activities, and occupy over three sections of shelves, each eight feet high by forty feet long. I have not examined all of those materials, though I have used extensive sources from the National Archives and Library of Congress, particularly recordings and videotapes of newsreels, speeches, and appearances on "Meet the Press" and the "Longine-Wittnauer Hour." Doug Thurman at the National Archives was most helpful in sorting through Benson-related videotapes. Many pertinent papers relative to Secretary Benson's service in the cabinet are located in the Church Archives and/or the Benson Family Collection.

Interviews were conducted with and/or written recollections received from Miller Shurtleff, Don Paarlberg, D. Arthur Haycock, Lorenzo Hoopes,

Aled Davies, Karl Butler, Wendell Eames, Barry Goldwater, Harvey Dahl, Robert W. Barker, Richard H. Headlee, Byron F. Dickson, George Goold, and Alice Sheets Marriott. See also Oral History Interview, Frederick W. Babbel, Dwight D. Eisenhower Library, Abilene, Kansas, and Ezra Taft Benson Oral Interview, June 23, 1967, Columbia University.

The following resource materials were helpful: Ezra Taft Benson, *Farmers at the Crossroads* (New York: The Devin-Adair Company, 1956); Edward L. Schapsmeier, *Ezra Taft Benson and the Politics of Agriculture* (Danville, Illinois: Interstate Printers & Publishers, 1975); Stephen E. Ambrose, *Eisenhower the President* (New York: Simon & Schuster, 1984); Piers Brendon, *Ike: His Life & Times* (New York: Harper & Row, 1986); Stephen E. Ambrose, *Nixon: The Education of a Politician 1913–1962* (New York: Simon & Schuster, 1987); David W. Evans, "Ezra Taft Benson—Agricultural Statesman," *Improvement Era* 56 (January 1953): 27; Bert Tollefson, Jr., "Indestructible Ezra Taft Benson," unpublished manuscript, Benson Family Collection; David Alma Christensen, "An Analysis of the Speaking Style of Ezra Taft Benson: 1943–68," Master's thesis, Brigham Young University, 1980.

1. Bernard Law Montgomery, *Memoirs* (Cleveland: World Publishing Company, 1958), p. 484. See also Ambrose, *Eisenhower the President*, p. 17.

2. Ezra Taft Benson, *Crossfire*, p. 5.

3. Ibid., p. 12.

4. *Washington Post*, November 26, 1952.

5. As quoted in *Deseret News*, November 27, 1952. See also "Meet the New Secretary and His Family," *Farm Journal*, January 1953.

6. *Cincinnati Post*, November 26, 1952. See also "Agriculture Acclaims the New Secretary," *Cooperative Digest*, December 15, 1952, p. 8; "Ike Picks Ezra T. Benson, Political Unknown, for Agriculture Post," *Wall Street Journal*, November 25, 1952; "Benson's No Stranger to Capital," *Washington Daily News*, November 25, 1952; "Benson for Agriculture," *Washington Post*, November 26, 1952.

7. William Harllee Bordeaux to Robert Tate Allan, September 11, 1953.

8. As quoted in *Improvement Era*, January 1953, p. 28.

9. "Ezra Taft Benson: Agricultural Statesman," unpublished tribute written by Raymond W. Miller at request of David W. Evans. Benson Family Collection.

10. *Deseret News*, November 30, 1952.

11. See J. Willard Marriott to ETB, November 24, 1952; George Romney to ETB, November 26, 1952; Tom Heath to ETB, November 25, 1952.

12. See Paul Friggens, "Meet the New Secretary and His Family," *Farm Journal*, January 1953, p. 28.

13. See Ezra Taft Benson, "Principles of Cooperation," *Improvement Era* 48 (November 1945): 653; Friggens, *Farm Journal*, January 1953; *Salt Lake Tribune*, November 26, 1952. See also Ezra Taft Benson, "Speech Material—Facts Regarding Agriculture," 1956, Item #31, "Free Enterprise Based on Spiritual Qualities."

14. *Time,* March 30, 1953.

15. Maxwell M. Rabb to ETB, July 16, 1982.

16. *Crossfire,* p. 45.

17. Ibid., p. 50.

18. Hearing before the Committee on Agriculture and Forestry, United States Senate, 83rd Congress, January 15, 1953.

19. Angus Deming, "The Revolutionary Farmer," *Wall Street Journal,* January 19, 1953.

20. For some of Secretary Benson's early press coverage see the following: "Elder Benson's Going to Catch It!," *Saturday Evening Post,* March 28, 1953, p. 22; "Benson's Mail Backs Him Overwhelmingly," *Washington Daily News,* February 19, 1953; "Too Much Corn, or Too Much Benson?," *The Nation,* March 21, 1953; "Secretary Benson Tells About Changing the Farm Policy," *U.S. News & World Report,* March 6, 1953, pp. 24–37; "Benson: Prayer, Persuasion and Parity," *New York Times Magazine,* June 14, 1953; "Bravo, Cousin Ezra! He Promises a Sane New Day for Agriculture," *Barron's,* February 16, 1953; "Hold On, Ezra, Help's Coming," *Richmond News Leader,* February 21, 1953.

21. See "Secretary Benson's Faith in the American Farmer," *Farm and Ranch,* September 1956, reprinted in *Reader's Digest,* October 1956, pp. 84–88.

22. See Dwight D. Eisenhower to ETB, February 2, 1953.

23. "Apostle at Work," *Time,* June 13, 1953, pp. 25–28.

24. As quoted in *Communism and the Constitution* (Salt Lake City: Deseret Book, 1964), p. 23.

25. *Crossfire,* p. 59.

26. See "General Statement on Agricultural Policy," quoted in *Crossfire,* pp. 602–5.

27. *Crossfire,* p. 6.

28. *Time,* February 23, 1953.

29. *The Nation,* March 21, 1953; also *Saturday Evening Post,* March 28, 1953.

30. See letter quoted in *Washington Daily News,* February 29, 1953; "Respect Comes the Hard Way," *Life,* February 16, 1953.

31. Madge Ballard to Flora A. Benson, January 28, 1953.

32. *Crossfire,* p. 79.

33. Transcript of remarks by Harold B. Lee, March 1, 1953, Washington, D.C., Stake Conference.

34. Reed A. Benson to ETB, March 18, 1953.

35. Mark A. Benson to ETB, May 22, 1953.

36. *Crossfire,* p. 86.

37. See Elaine S. McKay, "Pray for Dad," *New Era,* January/February 1981, p. 7; also Ezra Taft Benson, "Face the Future Unafraid," *Improvement Era* 53 (December 1950).

38. *Crossfire,* p. 97.

39. See *Crossfire,* p. 102; also Don Paarlberg to author, April 21, 1986.

40. Paarlberg to author, April 21, 1986.

Chapter 15, "Calm in the Crucible"

1. *Crossfire,* p. 143.

2. Untitled talk delivered by Flora A. Benson, May 1962.

3. See, for example, *Newsweek,* November 2, 1953.

4. Josephine Ripley, "Eisenhower Faces Task of Saving Benson," *Christian Science Monitor,* October 15, 1953; also cited in *Crossfire,* p. 149.

5. Barbara Amussen Benson to ETB, November 9, 1953.

6. *Crossfire,* p. 150.

7. *Chicago Sun Times,* as quoted in *Crossfire,* p. 171.

8. "Everybody Picks on Benson," *American,* June 1954, p. 26.

9. *Crossfire,* p. 175.

10. Ibid., p. 184. For additional information, see "Mr. Benson's Flexible Flyer," *Fortune,* March 1954, p. 88; "The Truth About the Farm Business," *U.S. News & World Report,* October 8, 1954, pp. 80–88.

11. *Crossfire,* p. 195.

12. See Don Paarlberg to author; also *Crossfire,* p. 203.

13. "Benson Turns a Tide," *Collier's,* September 17, 1954, p. 96. See also "Victory for Benson," *Washington Post,* July 9, 1954.

14. *Crossfire,* p. 213.

15. Lorenzo Hoopes to author, April 16, 1986; *Crossfire,* p. 218.

16. Dwight D. Eisenhower, *The White House Years: Mandate for Change 1953–1956* (New York: Doubleday & Co., 1963), p. 354.

17. "It Was the Biggest Strength of the G.O.P. and Confounded Benson's Political Foes," *Wall Street Journal,* November 4, 1954. See also *Crossfire,* p. 221.

18. *Crossfire,* p. 221.

19. See ETB to Dwight D. Eisenhower, November 26, 1957; Dwight D. Eisenhower to ETB, December 4, 1957.

20. This and the preceding anecdote are related in Don Paarlberg to author, April 21, 1986.

21. "The Benson Formula for Serenity," *New York Times Magazine,* April 11, 1954.

22. "Everybody Picks on Benson," *American,* June 1954.

23. ETB to Stephen Reed Benson, August 18, 1982.

24. Mark E. Petersen to ETB, November 4, 1953.

25. See William J. Shannon to ETB, September 24, 1954; also J. William Flanders to Milton Eisenhower, September 25, 1954.

26. Mamie Eisenhower to FAB, May 17, 1954.

27. "LDS Home Night Demonstrated to President and Mrs. Eisenhower," *Deseret News*, February 13, 1955.

Chapter 16, *"Respect Comes the Hard Way"*

In addition to sources listed for chapter 14, see "A Homemaker Looks at Farm Policy," address by Flora A. Benson to National Republican Women, September 12, 1956; "Crafty Ezra Benson," *Fortune*, April 1958, pp. 120ff.; "Agriculture: Revolution, Not Revolt," *Time*, May 7, 1956, p. 29; "The Magnificent Decline of U.S. Farming," *Fortune*, June 1955.

1. LeGrand Richards Memo, March 10, 1955.

2. See "Secretary Benson Reports on the Big Blow of 1955," *U.S. News & World Report*, May 6, 1955.

3. Harvey Dahl to author, April 21, 1986.

4. See Ezra Taft Benson, "Respect for Standards," *New Era*, June 1978, p. 11.

5. Edgar B. Brossard to ETB, August 4, 1955.

6. Miller F. Shurtleff to author, tape-recorded reminiscences, June 5, 1986.

7. "Capitol Bride to Marry in Simplicity," *Chicago Daily News*, September 8, 1955.

8. Mamie D. Eisenhower to FAB, March 8, 1955; also *Church News*, July 30, 1955.

9. *Church News*, November 12, 1955.

10. See Ezra Taft Benson personal journal, October 29, 1955.

11. *Crossfire*, p. 273.

12. *Crossfire*, p. 115.

13. See Bert Tollefson, Jr., "Indestructible Ezra Benson," unpublished personal reminiscences, Benson Family Collection.

14. *Crossfire*, p. 294. See also Ezra Taft Benson, "The Official View on How 'Soil Bank' Is Working," *U.S. News & World Report*, May 31, 1957.

15. *Crossfire*, p. 304.

16. Everett M. Dirksen to ETB, January 27, 1956.

17. "Secretary Benson Treated Shabbily in Abusive House Committee Hearing," *Yakima Daily Republic*, March 6, 1956.

18. See, for example, Secretary Benson's 1956 Speech Fact Book, item #5, "Agriculture Not for Sale."

19. Ambrose, *Eisenhower the President*, p. 300.

20. "The Eisenhower Shift," *Fortune*, April 1956, p. 267.

21. Ezra Taft Benson, "Personal Reminiscences," unpublished, pp. 40–41, Benson Family Collection.

22. *Crossfire*, p. 321.

23. Ibid., p. 322.

24. "Secretary Benson's Son Makes Hit with GOP Women's Conference," *Baltimore Evening Sun*, March 9, 1956; also Homer H. Grunether to ETB, March 9, 1956.

25. "Reed Benson's Life Underwent Change After His First Talk Two Months Ago," *Twin Falls Times-News*, May 13, 1956; David O. McKay to ETB, July 2, 1956.

26. See "Cabinet Wives Astir," *Newsweek*, October 15, 1956, p. 43.

27. As quoted in *Deseret News*, June 15, 1956.

28. See *Crossfire*, p. 327.

29. Ezra Taft Benson personal journal, September 27, 1956.

30. "Benson Is Heckled 1st Time in Iowa," *Chicago News*, October 12, 1956.

31. See *Congressional Record* 103, no. 162 (September 19, 1957): A76683; also *Newsweek*, October 15, 1956; "Mrs. Benson Steals Spot in Kabinet," *Salt Lake Tribune*, May 27, 1956.

32. "Tough Talk," *Newsweek*, October 15, 1956, pp. 42–44.

33. *Crossfire*, p. 351.

34. "Are Wives Important," *Newsweek*, February 18, 1957, pp. 32–33.

35. *Crossfire*, pp. 360–61.

36. See "Benson Gets Plaudits after Egg Throwing," *Houston Press*, October 28, 1957; also *Washington Star*, August 17, 1958.

37. Paul Harvey, *Autumn of Liberty* (Garden City, New York: Hanover House, 1954), p. 91. See also "Longines-Wittnauer Chronoscope," August 2, 1954, (NLE) 200–LW–489, National Archives; National Press Club recording, March 23, 1956, Library of Congress; National Press Club recording, February 6, 1958, Library of Congress; National Press Club recording, March 24, 1953, Library of Congress; Ezra Taft Benson address to Seattle Rotary Club, October 1, 1958. Additional items of interest include "Meet the Press," March 28, 1954, Library of Congress; "Longines-Wittnauer Chronoscope," May 20, 1953, (NLE) 200–LW–434, National Archives; Universal Newsreels, January 9, 1953, and November 22, 1955, National Archives.

38. David Ben-Gurion to ETB, January 14, 1958.

39. *Crossfire*, p. 363. For a published account of this trip see Ezra Taft Benson, "We Saw the Church Around the World," *Instructor*, March 1958, pp. 68–70.

40. Karl E. Mundt to Sherman Adams, October 23, 1957.

41. *Crossfire*, p. 373.

42. *Washington Post*, December 4, 1957.

43. *Daily Oklahoman*, March 9, 1958.

44. Public Papers of the President of the United States, Dwight D. Eisenhower, 1958, p. 187.

45. See Arthur L. Miller to ETB, February 22, 1958; Arthur L. Miller to ETB, February 27, 1958; ETB to Arthur L. Miller (undated). As quoted in *Crossfire*, pp. 389–90.

46. See *Crossfire*, pp. 395–96.

47. *Akron Beacon Journal*, May 11, 1958; also *Crossfire*, p. 401.

48. "The Once-Scorned Benson Now Rated Political Asset," *New York Herald Tribune*, August 20, 1958.

49. *Des Moines Register*, exact date unknown.

50. *Life*, June 2, 1958.

51. *Crossfire*, p. 408.

52. See Ezra Taft Benson address to National Federation of Republican Women, Boston, September 25, 1958, p. 8.

53. Ezra Taft Benson address to New Jersey Republican State Committee Fundraising Dinner, February 25, 1959.

Chapter 17, "Spiritual Statesman"

1. See, for example, "Elder Benson's Going to Catch It," *Saturday Evening Post*, March 28, 1953.

2. *Crossfire*, p. 445.

3. Ezra Taft Benson, "He Is Risen," 39th Annual Hollywood Bowl Easter Sunrise Service, Los Angeles, California, March 29, 1959, Church Archives.

4. See Larry P. McDonald to ETB, November 2, 1979; also *Crossfire*, pp. 468–70.

5. As quoted in *Improvement Era* 42 (February 1939): 94.

6. F. Enzio Busche to ETB, April 9, 1981.

7. For a detailed account of the European trip, see *Crossfire*, pp. 472–88, including quotations relating to the experience at the Central Baptist Church in Moscow.

8. Tom Anderson, reprinted in *Straight Talk*, October 2, 1986. See *Crossfire*, pp. 606–8.

9. "An American Visitor Wrings Tears in Crowded Church Near Kremlin," *Washington Star*, October 4, 1959; also "A Church Service in Soviet Russia," *U.S. News & World Report*, October 26, 1959, p. 76.

10. As quoted in *Crossfire*, p. 458.

11. Ibid., p. 508.

12. Ibid., p. 531.

13. Ibid., p. 537.

14. ETB to Joseph Fielding Smith, August 14, 1960.

15. Flora A. Benson, untitled address, delivered May 1962.

16. F. Enzio Busche to ETB, December 2, 1986.

17. A survey of the vote in counties in which over 50 percent of the population was classified as rural-farm in the 1950 census in eight states in the Midwest revealed that the following percentages of the vote went Republican: Iowa, 58.8 percent; Kansas, 65.6 percent; Michigan, 68.1 percent; Minnesota, 52.2 percent; Nebraska, 64.6 percent; North Dakota, 56.1 percent; South Dakota, 60.2 percent; Wisconsin, 56.7 percent. As cited in *Crossfire*, p. 553. See also *Seattle Daily News*, August 29, 1960.

18. "Benson Polls Were Vindicated," undated clipping in vol. 46 of Ezra Taft Benson scrapbooks.

19. Barry Goldwater to author, April 28, 1986. See also Barry Goldwater to Delos Ellsworth, July 20, 1976.

20. See *Deseret News*, November 30, 1960.

21. These included Doctor of Laws degrees from the University of Utah (June 9, 1953), University of Maine (June 10, 1956), University of Hawaii (March 22, 1957), Utah State University (June 7, 1958), and Fairleigh-Dickinson University (February 10, 1959); Doctor of Agriculture degrees from Iowa State College (June 12, 1953) and Michigan State College (February 10, 1955); Doctor of Science degree from Rutgers University (October 6, 1955); and Doctor of Public Services degree from Brigham Young University (June 2, 1955).

22. Dwight D. Eisenhower to ETB, January 4, 1961.

23. Ezra Taft Benson personal journal, January 11, 1961.

24. Ezra Taft Benson, untitled address delivered in Washington Stake conference, Washington, D.C., December 4, 1960, Church Archives.

25. See *Congressional Record*, January 20, 1961, 87th Congress, 1st session.

26. Ibid. See also "Benson Sums Up Agricultural Action," *Christian Science Monitor*, January 14, 1961.

27. *Conference Report*, April 1960.

Chapter 18, "Preaching the Principles of Freedom"

This chapter relies heavily upon Ezra Taft Benson's personal journal and correspondence files, as well as extensive articles published in the press. See also European Mission History, 1964–65; interviews with Reed A. Benson, Beth Benson Burton, Bob Lee, and Scott Stanley; Jerreld L. Newquist, *Prophets, Principles and National Survival* (Salt Lake City: Publishers Press, 1964); Ezra Taft Benson, *The Red Carpet* (Salt Lake City: Bookcraft, 1962); Ezra Taft Benson, *A Nation Asleep* (Salt Lake City: Bookcraft, 1963); Ezra Taft Benson, *Title of Liberty* (Salt Lake City: Deseret Book, 1964).

1. "Home Town Hails Elder Benson at Testimonial Dinner in S.L.," *Deseret News*, April 6, 1961.

2. *Improvement Era* 64 (June 1961): 431.

3. See *New York Times*, July 16, 1959; transcript of Sullivan show as quoted in John A. Stormer, *None Dare Call It Treason* (Florissant, Missouri: Liberty Bell Press), p. 52.

4. *Teachings of the Prophet Joseph Smith* (Salt Lake City: Deseret Book, 1972), pp. 146–47.

5. *Journal of Discourses* 21:8.

6. As quoted in *Improvement Era* 39 (August 1936): 488.

7. *Conference Report*, April 1948, p. 182.

8. David O. McKay, see *Conference Report*, April 1942; *Conference Report*, April 1950; "The Enemy Within," *Instructor* 91 (February 1956): 34; *Improvement Era* 65 (December 1962): 903.

9. "The Book of Mormon Warns America," adapted from address given at Brigham Young University, May 21, 1968.

10. Ezra Taft Benson, "The American Heritage of Freedom—A Plan of God," *Improvement Era* 64 (December 1961): 953.

11. See "We Must Protect U.S.," *U.S. News & World Report*, April 23, 1962.

12. David O. McKay, "Man's Free Agency," *Improvement Era* 68 (December 1965): 1073, 1099.

13. Ezra Taft Benson, "America—A Man and an Event," *Improvement Era* 68 (December 1965): 1150.

14. David O. McKay, *Conference Report*, October 1966, p. 5.

15. Ezra Taft Benson, "Protecting Freedom—An Immediate Responsibility," *Improvement Era* 69 (December 1966): 1144–46.

16. Iain B. McKay memo, 1987.

17. *Church News*, June 16, 1945.

18. Ezra Taft Benson, "Not Commanded in All Things," *Improvement Era* 68 (June 1965): 537.

19. See, for example, Barbara Selka to FAB, February 1, 1972; Hubert L. Hinds to ETB, March 17, 1971.

20. See *Church News*, April 13, 1963; also *Conference Report*, April 1963, pp. 109–14.

21. Memorandum, August 30, 1963, Ezra Taft Benson Personal Files.

22. As cited in Newquist, *Prophets, Principles and National Survival*, pp. 291, 293–94.

23. Excerpts from addresses given at farewell testimonial for the Bensons, December 15, 1963, vol. 80, Ezra Taft Benson scrapbooks. See also "Elder Benson Assigned to European Mission," *Church News*, October 26, 1963; "Benson Named to Head European Mormon Unit," *Los Angeles Times*, October 25, 1963.

24. Minnie P. Burton to FAB, October 27, 1963.

25. See European Mission History, January 30, 1965.

26. Ibid., March 31, 1964.

27. ETB to First Presidency, February 13, 1964.

28. FAB to Reed A. Benson, August 20, 1964.

29. Eng. E. Riahi to ETB, January 9, 1965.

30. Wanda Duns to author, April 30, 1986.

31. Marjorie Hinckley to FAB, January 29, 1965.

32. Wanda Duns to author.

33. Rendell Mabey to ETB, memorandum, September 13, 1965, box 199, file 11, Church Archives.

34. See *Church News*, March 30, 1965.

35. European Mission History, April 22, 1965.

36. Ibid., September 29, 1964; also August 29, 1965.

37. Author interview with Beth Benson Burton, March 12, 1986.

38. Unpublished account, June 8, 1965, Benson Family Collection.

39. ETB to "Our Beloved Children," August 10. 1981.

40. See *Church News*, October 2, 1965; also "44,000 LDS Members Attest to Growth of Church in Europe," *Church News*, October 3, 1964.

Chapter 19, "Sounding a Warning"

Of particular importance in preparing this chapter were James B. Allen interview with Ezra Taft Benson, 1975, Church Archives; references to Elder Benson's personal journal; Jerreld L. Newquist, *Prophets, Principles and National Survival*; Ezra Taft Benson, *An Enemy Hath Done This* (Salt Lake City: Parliament Publishers, 1969); and Ezra Taft Benson, *Title of Liberty*.

1. See Ezra Taft Benson personal journal, October 21, 1965.

2. David O. McKay, *Conference Report*, October 1966, pp. 6–7.

3. As quoted in ETB to Joseph Fielding Smith, March 3, 1966.

4. *Deseret News*, January 15, 1966.

5. ETB personal journal, March 25, 1966.

6. ETB to Michael McGagin, February 10, 1966.

7. David O. McKay, *Conference Report*, April 1966, pp. 109–10.

8. As quoted in Ezra Taft Benson personal journal, June 24, 1966. See also journal entries of May 28, 1966, and June 17, 1966. This letter is referred to in "Benson's Influence Helps Keep Growing Church on Conservative Track," *Wall Street Journal*, August 8, 1966.

9. As quoted in "It Can Happen Here," *An Enemy Hath Done This*, pp. 90, 110, 112.

10. Ezra Taft Benson, "Stand Up for Freedom," first delivered February 11, 1966, at the Utah Forum for the American Idea, Salt Lake City, Utah. Reprinted in *An Enemy Hath Done This*, pp. 37–38.

11. Ezra Taft Benson, "Protecting Freedom—An Immediate Responsibility," *Improvement Era* 69 (December 1966): 1145.

12. Gordon B. Hinckley to ETB, June 21, 1966.

13. See ETB to David O. McKay, July 13, 1966.

14. Wanda Duns account of the event, as retold to author, April 30, 1986.

15. See "Benson's Influence Helps Keep Growing Church on Conservative Track," *Wall Street Journal*, August 8, 1966; "Presidential Draft for Elder Benson?," *Deseret News*, May 3, 1966.

16. See copy of statement in Ezra Taft Benson personal files; also ETB to Flora Parker, June 27, 1983.

17. See Ezra Taft Benson, *Improvement Era*, April 1969, pp. 24–26.

18. See General Priesthood Board Meeting Minutes, November 1, 1967, Church Archives.

19. Ezra Taft Benson, "Godless Forces Threaten Us," *Improvement Era*, December 1969, pp. 69–70.

20. See George C. Wallace to David O. McKay, February 12, 1968.

21. *Congressional Record*, March 14, 1967, pp. S3694-95. See also ETB to Strom Thurmond, March 2, 1967.

22. Ezra Taft Benson, "Americans Are Destroying America," *Improvement Era* 71 (June 1968): 68–71.

23. See *Congressional Record*, April 22, 1968.

24. Francis L. Sampson to ETB, April 9, 1968.

25. Rulon Joel Barlow to ETB, April 17, 1968.

26. Ezra Taft Benson, "The Proper Role of Government," *Improvement Era* 71 (December 1968): 51–53.

27. ETB to First Presidency and the Council of the Twelve, April 10, 1968.

28. See *Beirut Daily Star*, May 3, 1968.

29. Edwin H. White to ETB, May 30, 1969.

30. *Church News*, August 31, 1968.

31. "Family Joys," *New Era*, January 1973, pp. 4–6; also *Church News*, April 26, 1969.

32. Ezra Taft Benson, "Strengthening the American Home," *Improvement Era* 56 (December 1953): 970–72.

33. Ezra Taft Benson, "To the Humble Followers of Christ," *Improvement Era* 72 (June 1969): 43–44.

34. As recorded in Ezra Taft Benson personal journal, March 28, 1969.

35. See "Notes on Ezra Taft Benson's Visit to Vietnam," First Presidency Files, April 12–14, 1969; also "A High Degree of Spirituality," *Church News*, May 10, 1969.

36. LeGrand Richards to ETB, May 8, 1969. See also Ezra Taft Benson, "Vietnam— Victory or Surrender," *Speeches of the Year*, 1968–69 (Provo: BYU Press, 1969), pp. 1–13.

37. Ezra Taft Benson, "Vietnam—Why Not Victory?" in *An Enemy Hath Done This*, p. 188.

38. "Deficit Spending and Inflation," in *An Enemy Hath Done This*, pp. 210–11.

39. Ezra Taft Benson, "A World Message," *Improvement Era* 73 (June 1970): 95–97. See also Spencer J. Palmer to author, January 20, 1987; Ezra Taft Benson, "The Future of the Church in Asia," *Improvement Era* 73 (March 1970): 14–15.

Chapter 20, "Challenges and Rewards"

This chapter relies heavily upon Ezra Taft Benson's personal journals. See also "Press Conference with President Spencer W. Kimball and the First Presidency, and Ezra Taft Benson," December 31, 1973, Church Archives; Ezra Taft Benson, *God, Family, Country* (Salt Lake City: Deseret Book, 1975).

1. "Ezra Taft Benson Tribute to Pres. David O. McKay," September 7, 1967, recorded by Bonneville International.

2. Prayer given by Ezra Taft Benson at David O. McKay funeral.

3. Idaho Falls *Post Register* article in Ezra Taft Benson personal file.

4. W. Stanford Wagstaff to ETB, January 27, 1970.

5. ETB to First Presidency, May 25, 1971.

6. Ezra Taft Benson, "Satan's Thrust—Youth," *Ensign*, December 1971, pp. 53–56.

7. Ibid.

8. Address to BYU ten-stake fireside, May 7, 1972.

9. As recorded in Ezra Taft Benson's personal journals, January 6, 1971.

10. Irene Staples memo to ETB, March 3, 1971.

11. LeGrand Richards to Mark A. Benson, October 28, 1971.

12. Baron Frary von Blumberg to ETB, November 15, 1971.

13. Notes on visit of Archbishop Iakovos, December 3, 1971.

14. See *Boston Globe*, July 5, 1972; also "God, Family, and Country," address delivered at the New England Rally for God, Family, and Country honor banquet, Boston, July 4, 1972, reprinted in *God, Family, Country*, pp. 401–7.

15. Harold B. Lee to ETB, February 22, 1972.

16. H. Burke Peterson to ETB, December 12, 1983.

17. Bonnie Benson Madsen to FAB, July 23, 1973.

Chapter 21, "President of the Twelve"

This chapter and subsequent chapters rely heavily on interviews with many of the General Authorities, including Ezra Taft Benson, Boyd K. Packer, Marvin J. Ashton, Neal A. Maxwell, Russell M. Nelson, Dallin H. Oaks, M. Russell Ballard, Hugh W. Pinnock, Robert L. Backman, Hartman Rector, Jr., Richard G. Scott, and Francis M. Gibbons. Other pertinent interviews include Gary Gillespie, William O. Nelson, Rulon G. Craven, John Hardy, and Betty McDonald. See also Melvin J. Leavitt, "Grandpa's Visit," *New Era*, April 1984, pp. 20–27.

1. Bonnie Benson Madsen to ETB and FAB, January 15, 1974.

2. Mark Amussen Benson to ETB, January 5, 1974.

3. A. Theodore Tuttle to ETB, February 14, 1975.

4. See, for example, Oscar W. McConkie to ETB, October 6, 1977.

5. Mark A. Benson to ETB, January 31, 1977.

6. Remarks at quarterly meeting of the Council of the Twelve, March 31, 1974, Church Archives.

7. William Grant Bangerter, "A Special Moment in Church History," *Ensign*, November 1977, pp. 26–27.

8. Ezra Taft Benson, "President Kimball's View of Missionary Work," concluding message at Mission President's Conference, April 3, 1985, Church Archives.

9. Ted E. Brewerton to ETB, June 19, 1979; also Ted E. Brewerton to ETB, May 28, 1979.

10. Carlos E. Asay to ETB, April 18, 1979; also memo from Kirt M. Olsen to Gene R. Cook, March 8, 1979.

11. Gene R. Cook to ETB, December 17, 1980.

12. See "Report on Trip to the Mideast," May 17, 1979.

13. See Ezra Taft Benson personal journal, March 11, 1969, and October 8, 1972.

14. David Horowitz to ETB, October 9, 1978. See also "Ezra Taft Benson Stresses Close Affinity Between the Mormons and the Jewish People," *United Israel Bulletin*, Winter 1978, pp. 1ff.

15. James M. Paramore to ETB, May 31, 1978.

16. ETB to Robert Welch, January 3, 1975.

17. Ezra Taft Benson, "Temple Blessings," address delivered at Washington D.C. Temple Dedication, November 20, 1974.

18. Among the stakes President Benson organized during his tenure as president of the Twelve were Munich Germany, October 1977; Nagoya Japan, May 1978; Vienna Austria, April 1980; Naha Okinawa Japan, October 1980; San Juan Puerto Rico, December 1980; Bern Switzerland, May 1981; Milan Italy, June 1981; Geneva Switzerland, June 1982; and Barcelona Spain, October 1982.

19. Author interview with William O. Nelson and Rulon G. Craven, June 16, 1986.

20. Ted E. Brewerton to ETB, October 12, 1980.

21. Richard G. Scott to ETB, September 2, 1982.

22. Ezra Taft Benson, "The Image of a General Authority," remarks to General Authorities Priesthood Board Meeting, January 19, 1977, p. 8.

23. Douglas T. Snarr to Mark A. Benson, November 8, 1978.

24. See Roland T. Minson to ETB, October 31, 1983.

25. Ezra Taft Benson, "A Witness and a Warning," *Ensign*, November 1979, p. 33.

26. Vaughn J. Featherstone to ETB, April 12, 1979.

27. Ezra Taft Benson, Response upon Announcement of Ezra Taft Benson Agriculture Institute at BYU, September 23, 1975, Church Archives.

28. *Your Marriage Partnership*, The Church of Jesus Christ of Latter-day Saints, 1950, pp. 15–20.

29. Flora Spackman to ETB and FAB, April 18, 1974.

30. Ezra Taft Benson, "Worthy of All Acceptation," *Ensign*, November 1978, pp. 30–32; also "4 Generations of Genealogy Needed, says Pres. Benson," *Church News*, September 30, 1978.

31. Ezra Taft Benson, "The Faith of Our Founding Fathers," in *Faith* (Salt Lake City: Deseret Book, 1983), pp. 21–22. See also Ezra Taft Benson, "Our Founding Fathers Stood in This Holy Place," St. George Temple Rededication, November 12, 1975, Church Archives.

32. Ezra Taft Benson, "God's Hand in Our Nation's History," BYU twelve-stake fireside, March 28, 1976.

33. Gordon B. Hinckley, "Special Witnesses for Christ," *Ensign*, May 1984, p. 51.

34. Ezra Taft Benson, "The Image of a General Authority," remarks to General Authorities Priesthood Board Meeting, January 19, 1977.

35. Gordon B. Hinckley, Salute to Ezra Taft Benson, November 18, 1983.

36. See Ezra Taft Benson, "Prepare Ye," *Ensign*, January 1974, p. 68; Ezra Taft Benson, "Prepare for the Days of Tribulation," *Ensign*, November 1980, pp. 32–34.

37. Leonard E. Read to Spencer W. Kimball, May 17, 1977, Ezra Taft Benson personal files; also Wendell J. Ashton memorandum to Ezra Taft Benson, May 20, 1977.

38. ETB to Allan F. Larsen, February 22, 1977.

39. Ezra Taft Benson personal journal, May 24, 1978.

40. See "America's Strength, the Family," *Congressional Record*, March 30, 1977, p. S5167; also "Importance of Family Told in Seattle," *Church News*, December 4, 1976, p. 7.

41. Ezra Taft Benson, "America's Strength—the Family," Strong Families/Strong America program, Tulsa, Oklahoma, March 24, 1978, p. 1.

42. Ezra Taft Benson, "God's Place in Our Nation's History," BYU twelve-stake fireside, March 28, 1976. See also "God Shaped Past," *BYU Daily Universe*, March 30, 1976.

43. Ezra Taft Benson, "The Gospel Teacher and His Message," address to Church Education System personnel, September 17, 1976, pp. 8–9, 11. For additional information on this issue see "Apostles vs. Historians," *Newsweek*, February 15, 1982.

44. See "God's Hand in Our Nation's History"; also *Church News*, April 3, 1976; *BYU Daily Universe*, March 30, 1976.

45. Bruce R. McConkie, "The New Revelation," in *Priesthood* (Salt Lake City: Deseret Book, 1981), p. 128.

Chapter 22, "The Expanding Church"

1. See *Church News*, February 24, 1979.

2. See author interview with William O. Nelson and Rulon G. Craven, June 16, 1986. This conversation was confirmed through Flora Parker interview with Joseph Ginat, August 17, 1987. Nelson accompanied President Benson on that trip and recorded the events in his journal. See also "Pres. Benson Visits Leaders in Mideast," *Church News*, June 2, 1979, p. 5.

3. See author interview with William O. Nelson and Rulon G. Craven, April 30, 1987; also "Report on Trip to the Mideast," May 17, 1979; *Church News*, June 2, 1979.

4. "Report on Trip to the Mideast," May 17, 1979, copy of memo in Ezra Taft Benson personal files.

5. Ezra Taft Benson, "Remarks at Orson Hyde Memorial," Jerusalem, October 24, 1979. For additional information on the subject see "Garden to Blossom in Israel," *Church News*, October 29, 1977, p. 3; "The Orson Hyde Memorial Gardens," *Ensign*, January 1978, pp. 76–78; "Plans Move Forward for Park," *Church News*, January 14, 1978, p. 3; "Orson Hyde Garden Grows Outside Jerusalem," *Ensign*, March 1979, p. 78; "President Kimball Dedicates Orson Hyde Memorial Garden in Jerusalem," *Ensign*, December 1979, pp. 67–69.

6. See Ezra Taft Benson, "A Vision and a Hope for the Youth of Zion," April 12, 1977, *BYU Speeches of the Year 1977*, p. 76; *Salt Lake Tribune*, April 13, 1977.

7. See Ezra Taft Benson, "Fourteen Fundamentals in Following the Prophet," BYU Devotional Address, February 26, 1980, *BYU Speeches of the Year 1981*, pp. 26–30.

8. See "Benson Backs Prophets' Politics," *Salt Lake Tribune*, February 27, 1980; "U. Teacher Replies to Benson," *Salt Lake Tribune*, February 28,

1980; "No. 2 Mormon Says Leader's Word Is Law," *Los Angeles Times*, March 1, 1980.

9. Ezra Taft Benson, "Godless Forces Threaten Us," *Improvement Era* 72 (December 1969): 69–73.

10. ETB to Ronald Reagan, November 6, 1974.

11. ETB to Ronald Reagan, January 23, 1981.

12. As quoted in *The Progress of Man* (Salt Lake City: Deseret Book, 1964), pp. 466–67.

13. See ETB to Ronald Reagan, May 29, 1984; Ronald Reagan to ETB, July 17, 1984.

14. See Fred Barnes, "Who's in Charge?," *The Washingtonian*, August 1983, pp. 124–33; also "The Bill the Farmers Want," *Washington Post*, January 24, 1985; and John R. Block to ETB, February 8, 1985.

15. Spencer W. Kimball, "The Blessings and Responsibilities of Motherhood," *Ensign*, March 1976, p. 70.

16. Ezra Taft Benson, "To the Elect Women of the Kingdom of God," dedicatory services of Nauvoo Women's Monuments, June 30, 1978, p. 2, in Ezra Taft Benson personal files.

17. See Ezra Taft Benson, "Fundamentals of Enduring Family Relationships," *Ensign*, November 1982; also William O. Nelson memo to ETB, October 5, 1982.

18. See Karl R. Anderson to ETB, January 17, 1983.

19. See "The Church Comes Alive in Kirtland, Ohio," *Ensign*, December 1979, pp. 69–70; "Kirtland Means Many Things to the Church," *Church News*, October 23, 1982.

20. Gordon B. Hinckley, Salute to Ezra Taft Benson, November 18, 1983, in Ezra Taft Benson files.

21. ETB to "Our Beloved Children," August 10, 1981.

22. Ezra Taft Benson, "Jesus Christ: Our Savior and Redeemer," *Ensign*, November 1983, pp. 6–8.

Chapter 23, "The Prophet of the Lord"

This chapter relies heavily upon interviews with members of the General Authorities, including Ezra Taft Benson, Gordon B. Hinckley, Thomas S. Monson, Boyd K. Packer, Marvin J. Ashton, Neal A. Maxwell, Russell M. Nelson, Dallin H. Oaks, M. Russell Ballard, Robert L. Backman, Hugh W. Pinnock, Hartman Rector, Jr., and Francis M. Gibbons. Interviews with Gary Gillespie were particularly helpful, as well as numerous interviews with members of the Benson family and with Senator Steve Symms, Senator Orrin Hatch, Stephen Studdert, and Ronald Mann.

See also "President Ezra Taft Benson: Ordained Thirteenth President of the Church," *Ensign*, December 1985, pp. 2–7, and "Pres. Benson Called to Lead Church," *Church News*, November 17, 1985, p. 3.

1. Spencer W. Kimball, "We Thank Thee, O God, for a Prophet," *Ensign*, January 1973, p. 33.

2. Neal A. Maxwell to ETB, December 18, 1985.

3. David B. Haight, "A Prophet Chosen of the Lord," *Ensign*, May 1986, p. 9.

4. Statement by President Benson at press conference announcing reorganization of the First Presidency, November 11, 1985. See also "President Ezra Taft Benson Ordained Thirteenth President of the Church," *Ensign*, December 1985, pp. 2–5.

5. See Joseph B. Wirthlin to ETB, November 14, 1985; David Horowitz to ETB, November 12, 1985; J. Willard Marriott, Jr., to ETB, November 14, 1985; Ronald Reagan to ETB, November 13, 1985.

6. Mark A. Benson to his children, November 14, 1985.

7. Dr. W. E. Hess to Gary Gillespie, November 13, 1986.

8. See "Stake Seventies Quorums Discontinued," *Ensign*, November 1986, p. 97; also *Church News*, September 12, 1986, p. 24.

9. *Church News*, December 22, 1985.

10. Ibid.

11. See ETB to Ronald Reagan, January 6, 1986; *Ensign*, March 1986, p. 85.

12. Ezra Taft Benson personal journal, February 6, 1986.

13. See "L.D.S. Scripture Citation Index," comp. Donald H. Howard, Harold B. Lee Library, Brigham Young University.

14. See Ezra Taft Benson, "The Book of Mormon Is the Word of God," *Ensign*, May 1975, pp. 63–65.

15. Mark L. McConkie to ETB, April 26, 1985.

16. See, for example, ETB to Bruce R. McConkie, January 23, 1985.

17. ETB to Stephen Reed Benson, April 21, 1981.

18. Ezra Taft Benson, "Cleansing the Inner Vessel," *Ensign*, May 1986, pp. 4–7.

19. Ezra Taft Benson, "A Sacred Responsibility," *Ensign*, May 1986, pp. 77–78.

20. See "Notes to Printing Advisory Committee," undated, Ezra Taft Benson personal files; also *1987 Church Almanac* (Salt Lake City: Deseret News, 1986), p. 146.

21. See *Church News*, July 13, 1986, p. 3.

22. Ezra Taft Benson, "The Book of Mormon—Keystone of Our Religion," *Ensign*, November 1986, pp. 4–7.

23. L. Tom Perry, "United in Building the Kingdom of God," *Ensign*, May 1987, p. 33.

24. See "Prophet Walks Historic Paths During Ohio Visit," *Church News*, March 30, 1986, pp. 3–4; also *Deseret News*, March 23, 1986.

25. Ezra Taft Benson personal journal, May 21, 1986.

26. Gary Handy to ETB, May 8, 1986.

27. See Ezra Taft Benson, "My Challenges to Mission Presidents," Mission Presidents' Conference, June 25, 1986; also *Church News*, July 6, 1986.

28. Charlene Holmstrom to ETB, June 30, 1986.

29. Darin A. Stubbs to ETB, November 15, 1985.

30. Aaron C. Wilhelm to Lloyd V. Owen, February 23, 1987. Copy in Ezra Taft Benson's files.

31. *Church News*, April 27, 1986.

32. Ezra Taft Benson, "In His Steps," February 8, 1987, address delivered in Anaheim, California.

33. See "To the Youth of the Noble Birthright," *Ensign*, May 1986; also "To the Young Women of the Church," *Ensign*, November 1986, pp. 81–85.

34. As reported in the *Church News*, September 28, 1986.

35. *Church News*, August 24, 1986, pp. 3–4.

36. Robert Benson Walker to ETB, February 10, 1986; Stephanie and David Young to ETB, August 4, 1986.

37. See *Church News*, July 20, 1986.

38. Ezra Taft Benson, "To the Mothers in Zion," address delivered at Churchwide Parents Fireside, February 22, 1987, published in pamphlet form by the Church.

39. Nadine D. Nelson to ETB, February 23, 1987; Christine M. Jeppesen to ETB, February 25, 1987.

40. See, for example, Ezra Taft Benson, "Our Homes Are Divinely Ordained," *Improvement Era* 52 (May 1949): 278.

41. Flora Parker interview with Senator Steve Symms, September 19, 1986; Stephen Studdert memo, June 8, 1987; also David Cannon to Flora Parker, May 4, 1987.

42. "Foundation Commends President Benson," *Church News*, June 22, 1986, p. 6; Freedoms Foundation press release, June 13, 1986; *Salt Lake Tribune*, June 20, 1986, p. 10A.

43. This and subsequent quotations from this address are published in pamphlet form in Ezra Taft Benson, *The Constitution: A Heavenly Banner* (Salt Lake City: Deseret Book, 1986).

44. Jesse Helms to ETB, September 29, 1986.

45. Ezra Taft Benson, "The Book of Mormon Is the Word of God."

46. See First Presidency Statement, January 15, 1987; see also *Church News*, January 31, 1987, p. 11.

47. Ezra Taft Benson, "The Book of Mormon and the Doctrine and Covenants," *Ensign*, May 1987, p. 85.

48. *Church News*, December 14, 1986.

49. Gordon B. Hinckley, "Come and Partake," *Ensign*, May 1986, p. 47.

Index

543

23; on childhood quarrels, 24; caught in storm, 33; throws dustpan, 42; puts farming over college, 45–46; writes to ETB, 53; on mission of mother, 84; suffers from scarlet fever, 113; ETB visits, 195; ETB blesses, 242; receives mission call, 443

Benson, Mark Amussen (son of ETB): birth of, 101; ETB's early impression of, 108; attends campouts, 115; on ETB's call as stake president, 122; suffers from asthma, 128–29; on discipline, 131–32; love of home of, 133–34; plays with ETB, 134–35; travels with ETB, 138, 233; on faith of parents, 139–40; on family loyalty, 142; participates in Scouting, 152; gives opinion to ETB, 152; writes article, 153; ETB worries over effect of move on, 178; goes camping, 179–80, 190, 246; receives Eagle Scout, 187; babysits, 229; prepares for mission, 234; receives mission call, 236; remembers police cars, 237; as counselor, 240; as district president, 243; letter to mother, 249; accomplishments of, 250, 391, 402; fasts for ETB, 254; marriage of, 262; attends graduate school, 263; announces pregnancy of wife, 277; explains missionary program, 298; graduates from Stanford, 321; in Dallas, 394; Regional Representative, 395–96; called as mission president, 413, 418; supports ETB in new calling, 427; hears about ETB at stake conference, 430; attends temple dedication, 435; returns from mission, 439; helps celebrate anniversary, 452; letter from, 469; on tone of voice of ETB, 481; on health of ETB, 487; ETB dines with, 504

Benson, Mathias J., 116, 122, 144

Benson, May Hinckley (daughter-in-law of ETB): marriage to Reed A. Benson, 330–31; greets Soviet visitors, 338; adopts children, 350; travels to South America, 352–53; attends temple dedication, 435; receives mission call, 443; helps celebrate anniversary, 452

Benson, Orval (brother of ETB): begins farming professionally, 80; education of, 81; farming difficulties of, 98; buys ETB's interest in farm, 105; ETB visits, 195

Benson, Pamelia Andrus. *See* Andrus, Pamelia

Benson, Reed Amussen (son of ETB): birth of, 99; remembers criticism of ETB, 112; attends campouts, 115, 179–80; leadership of, 129; on discipline, 131; plays with ETB, 134–35; has chores as youth, 137; on faith of mother, 139; on mother's encouragement, 140–50; boxes with schoolmate, 151–52; participates in Scouting, 152; gives opinion to ETB, 152; remembers beginning of WWII, 162; becomes Eagle Scout, 170; travels with ETB, 171; embraces ETB, 175; ETB worries over effect of move on, 178; counsels with mother, 190; attends BYU, 195; receives counsel from ETB, 195; bids farewell to ETB, 199; babysits sisters, 229; missionary farewell of, 232; in stake mission presidency, 240; returns from mission, 242–43; goes camping with ETB, 246; accomplishments of, 250; fasts for ETB, 254; attends inauguration, 263; attends swearing in, 265; encourages ETB, 277; reports on Congressional proceedings, 289; suggests family home evening for TV program,

Books Written by Ezra Taft Benson

Farmers at the Crossroads (Devin-Adair, 1956)
Freedom to Farm (Doubleday, 1960)
So Shall Ye Reap (Deseret Book, 1960)
Crossfire: The Eight Years with Eisenhower (Doubleday, 1962)
The Red Carpet (Bookcraft, 1962)
Title of Liberty (Deseret Book, 1964)
An Enemy Hath Done This (Parliament, 1969)
God, Family, Country: Our Three Great Loyalties (Deseret Book, 1974)
This Nation Shall Endure (Deseret Book, 1977)
Come unto Christ (Deseret Book, 1983)